Environment and Behavior

Environment and Behavior

edited by

Donald M. Baer
University of Kansas

Elsie M. Pinkston
University of Chicago

with a Foreword by
John Wright

WestviewPress
A Division of HarperCollinsPublishers

Copyright © 1997 by Westview Press, A Division of HarperCollins Publishers, Inc.

Published in 1997 in the United States of America by Westview Press, 5500 Central Avenue, Boulder, Colorado 80301-2877, and in the United Kingdom by Westview Press, 12 Hid's Copse Road, Cumnor Hill, Oxford OX2 9JJ

A CIP catalog record for this book is available from the Library of Congress.
ISBN 0-8133-3158-7.   ISBN 0-8133-3159-5 (pbk.)

The paper used in this publication meets the requirements of the American National Standard for Permanence of Paper for Printed Library Materials Z39.48-1984.

10   9   8   7   6   5   4   3   2   1

We propose this book as a celebration of the outstanding research and teaching career of Professor Barbara Coleman Etzel. The editors and authors are her students and her worldwide colleagues. She directed us toward the issues of antecedent control at a time when we thought altering consequences could solve all problems. She developed a model of how a preschool teaching and research laboratory should be run by creating the very environmental controls evident in her work. This book is testimony to her influence on our professional careers and to our affection for her.

Contents

PART 5
MAKE YOUR OWN ENVIRONMENT! 269

Foreword

An extraordinary thing happened in Kansas, beginning in 1965 and continuing to the present. A group of dedicated behavior analysts, in the tradition of B. F. Skinner, was recruited to the faculty of the Department of Human Development at the University of Kansas in Lawrence. Representing a variety of scientific, academic, and professional disciplines, the group rapidly achieved a critical mass in both size and productivity. "Critical for what?" one might ask. The answer is "critical" for becoming the world center for *applying* the principles and procedures of behavior analysis and modification to real problems of real people in the real world.

The corpus of these principles and procedures constitutes the functional equivalent of a theory for those who subscribe to them. Eschewing conventional psychological, sociological, clinical, and educational theories, these New Applied Behaviorists began to write the new state of the art. The title of the present work, *Environment and Behavior,* is not as presumptuously grandiose as it might at first appear. For it documents some of the most significant and seminal contributions to the practice of solving human problems that have emerged from that world-class critical mass of researchers, under the inspired leadership of Donald M. Baer.

To those already persuaded of the value of applied behavior analysis, there is little that I, a cognitive developmental psychologist and colleague for twenty-eight years, could say that would add to your appreciation and respect for the outstanding investigators whose work graces these pages. But to those readers who find themselves in the mainstreams of developmental, educational, clinical, social, or community psychology, and to those in counseling, education, management, corrections, special education, preventive behavioral medicine, and related fields, I have something I think is truly important to say: The people who do this work the way they were trained to do it at Kansas, and those who train others to do it at Kansas, represent some of the most imaginative, rigorous, careful, precise, and effective human problem solvers there are anywhere. In fact this book was constructed in honor of one of them, Dr. Barbara C. Etzel.

That they are indeed a critical mass is not necessarily a consequence of their shared behavioristic orientation. Rather I consider that it is a consequence of their fundamental commitment to the idea that the environment of a client with a problem or a social system that isn't working well can be rearranged to work better. The varied authors of this book share the conviction that the subject/client/learner is always right, and that it is therefore the fault of the design or execution of an experimental intervention if it fails to solve problems by changing people's behavior in well-specified situations. Moreover they share the view that designs for behavioral problem-solving interventions must ultimately change not only behavior but the ecological supports for that behavior. They are determined to arrange the natural (i.e., no longer manipulated) environment so that it will sustain the progress identified as successful by the results of that intervention. Those who are paradigmatically predisposed to dismiss applied behavior analysis as a small, redundant, and self-absorbed corner of the world of social engineering should open their minds. I call upon them to read this work with the same respect for clients, appreciation of scientific rigor, and genuine affection for the people whose lives are changed for the better that the authors themselves clearly display.

These active interventions are interested in results. They are pragmatic to a fault. Collectively they bring a breath of fresh air to those of us who are tired of the psychobabble of pop psychology, the grand theories of educational practice, where assumptions become requirements of practice, and the rhetorical hyperbole of social engineering. Notice as you read this remarkable collection of original research how they all use the same precise and well-defined language, and the same basic principles and procedures, but with vast imagination and ingenuity, to solve tough, real problems. Note further that they then document the fact that they have done so in ways that make the lives of their research subjects measurably closer to the lives they want to lead.

It is a book about *helping*, for indeed behavioral interventions have been most practical and effective when carried out with those less mature, powerful, knowledgeable, independent, or privileged than the rest of us. Some of them are merely young. Many are living or working or learning in situations where their dependency on others places a strong obligation on the helpers to be sure that what they do is helpful. It would be wonderful if everyone who set out to be a "catcher in the rye" could have the humility and responsibility for their actions as do these folks.

The bottom line is that the dedicated efforts of these authors collectively have been successful (although not so successful as to lead me to become a behavior modifier myself, at least not officially). We are all behavior modifiers, but most of us are not good ones—that is, we don't take evaluative data on our activities in any systematic way. However, it is not the batting average nor the applicability and generalizability of what they have done that matters most. It is their intelligence and humanity.

John C. Wright
Austin, Texas

Preface

Behavior and environment go together, as do bread and butter, law and order, and peaches and cream. Mere pairing does not communicate much, however; as usual, the meaning is in the details. This book is organized around the clusters of details we now know about how behavior is controlled by its environmental antecedents and about how behavior can control its antecedents. There are five clusters of details.

The first cluster, "Part 1: The Basic Principles," reminds us of the basic behavioral science principles and laws that justify the next four sections. It also reminds us that the concept of antecedent control is a fiction, even if a useful one: Antecedents do control subsequent behavior, but the function of that subsequent behavior usually is to alter the environment, including its antecedents. Antecedent control is only a way of slicing the constant interaction between the behavior, its antecedents, and its consequences. Sliced, it is easier to analyze, and the point of this book is that analyzing behavior in terms of its antecedent control has become increasingly urgent. But we also are reminded that once antecedent control has been analyzed, we must put it back in its interaction with behavior and the consequences of behavior.

The second portion, "Part 2: Managing Simple but Crucial Environmental Antecedents to Control Specific Behavior," describes the techniques that can give an event control over a subsequent behavior. It also describes some of the research that attempts sometimes to understand why those techniques work, sometimes simply to make them work better.

The third and largest cluster, "Part 3: Clinical Applications, with Emphasis on Substance Abuse and Autism," exemplifies the application of the principles and techniques discussed to clinically important problems of human behavior. Besides showing examples of the research proving application is possible and valuable, it also displays some of the research asking why these applications are successful and some of the research attempting to make them more successful.

The fourth cluster, "Part 4: Constructing the Whole Environment," expands the focus of the second and third clusters, from the problem of giving a specific antecedent event control of a specific behavior, to the problem of designing whole environments that best support and maintain large classes of behavior, sometimes even lifestyles.

The fifth cluster, "Part 5: Make Your Own Environment," makes the simple but perhaps most important point: If we can serve students and clients by managing their environment, we can serve ourselves by managing our own environment. Environmental control, at its best, is self-control.

Donald M. Baer and Elsie M. Pinkston

Acknowledgments

We thank Ellen P. Reese for her support and guidance in the development of the themes of this book, for recruiting authors, and for her advice regarding its organization.

The authors of these chapters have spent most of their careers making the kinds of analyses they describe here. We feel privileged by their willingness to contribute a piece of their current work to this book.

We are grateful to the following individuals: Betty Bradley, Lynn Campbell, Sidney Colton, and Paul Fatula of the University of Chicago; James Sherman, Wanda Lowe, Rachel Widen, and Irene Grote of the University of Kansas; Francisco and Amalia Lemus of Lawrence, Kansas; Michelle Baxter, Jennifer Chen, and Shena Redmond of Westview Press; Silvia Hines, our copy editor; and all the authors. In different ways, each contributed a great deal to the realization of this book.

D.M.B.
E.M.P.

Environment and Behavior

Part One
The Basic Principles

The first four chapters of this book state the basic principles of behavioral science on which the rest of the book depends. Such definition of terms is a duty of any authors of texts written for readers whose previous education is likely to be diverse. Duty, especially in the form of stating behavioral science principles yet again, is usually a dry exercise, and readers who already know those principles want to see the next level of understanding and application.

Fortunately, these chapters were written differently. Sigrid Glenn has restated the basis principles, not just in terms of how responses relate to the environment, but also in terms of how our behavior relates to the livability and survivability of our world.

Most behavioral science emphasizes the power of the environment; it sees environment as constantly controlling behavior, and it sees behavior as constantly affecting the environment. Indeed, the point of most behavior is to affect the environment. Glenn's account helps us to understand these facts in special terms: to remember that when a vast number of us, individually and as a society, respond lawfully to our environment in ways that alter it in the short run, in our numbers we have the power to endanger it in the longer run. To endanger our environment is to endanger ourselves. Fortunately, the same principles that warn us of dangerous problems also show us solutions.

We should reread the principles of behavior in a new light.

To show readers the next level of understanding and application requires focus, and focus requires restricting our examination to less than everything. In the second chapter of this section, therefore, Donald Baer restates basic principles in terms of antecedent environmental control only. Part of antecedent control involves how to understand and, therefore, design environments in which people automatically behave better and encounter more rewards and fewer misfortunes; almost everything in such an environment would support only good behavior and make rewards more probable and misfortunes less probable.

Part of antecedent control is stimulus control: understanding how behavior comes to depend on the environmental events that evoke it, such that without those events, one can hardly use those behaviors. A practical lesson devolves from that understanding: We should make sure our problem-solving behaviors are responsive to all the relevant parts of all the environments in which we might ever need them. We should make sure our skills are not under the control of too few stimuli, such that when a problem emerges in an environment lacking those stimuli, we are helpless to solve the problem. An understanding of stimulus control shows us that our skills do not automatically emerge whenever we have a problem; that happens only if we have arranged it to happen.

We should reread the principles of stimulus control in a new light.

The third chapter of this section also restates some basic principles but this time to show that one must use enough of those principles in thinking about any problem—not just one principle or a few. Martha Peláez-Nogueras and Jacob Gewirtz use examples from infant behavior to remind us that our principles are contextual. We would like to find scientific principles that are always true, everywhere and every time, but contextualism teaches us (among other things) how unlikely it is that such principles exist. Almost every principle we know is true not everywhere, but only in some places, and not every time, but only sometimes. There are places, and times, when some other principle is true instead. That does not mean an absence of lawfulness; it signals instead the operation of another law, one we should learn as well as the first. Thus, when we overstate a principle, such as, "Behavior comes under the control of stimuli that signal its functional consequences," contextualism teaches us to restate it immediately as, "Behavior comes under the control of stimuli that signal its functional consequences, except when it does not." That restatement recognizes reality; it also tells us to find the conditions "when it does not" and then understand why those conditions alter the principle. That will give us a new, larger, and more inclusive principle. That is the most valuable path science can take.

We should reread the principles of behavioral science in a new light—except when we should not.

Finally, Freddy Paniagua offers four cases of the explanatory principles of one special problem, but an exquisitely important, special problem: the stimulus control that what we say can exert over what we do, and the stimulus control that what we do can exert over what we say. That problem is clearly contextual. It could indeed be problematic if we always did what we said we would and always said exactly what we did. The problem is to understand how to create that control when it would be valuable and how to relax it when that would be valuable.

1

Understanding Human Behavior: A Key to Solving Social Problems

Sigrid S. Glenn

For tens of thousands of years, the facts of everyday human existence remained fairly constant. Our ancestors roamed the earth in small groups—hunting animal foods, gathering plant foods, and gradually learning to build simple tools to aid their efforts. They fashioned coverings for their bodies from animal skins, sought shelter in caves, and eventually depicted some of the important features of their life in drawings on the walls of those caves. They did those things in much the same way from place to place, person to person, and year to year. The particulars of their lives were similar from century to century for thousands of years.[1]

As the second millennium of the current era draws to a close, the facts of daily human existence vary enormously from place to place, and they typically change rapidly. Many people living today remember a world without space travel, air travel, or even auto travel—a world without electricity, telephones, calculators, or typewriters (to say nothing of computers). Today, people must learn to operate new machines, interact with new software, use new documents or systems, take on new assignments in work, listen to new music, abide by new rules, use new products, and even learn new social interactions to keep up with changes in activities, interests, or emotions of family members, friends, colleagues, or neighbors. In short, the world with which people must interact is changing rapidly, and that means that people's behavior must change accordingly.

Curiously enough, all these changes in the world, and countless others, are the direct result of human behavior. Our world is mostly a world that has been constructed by humans, whose coordinated behavior has resulted in our machines, our laws, our libraries and churches, and even the pattern of our interpersonal relations. Most of us like our modern world, perhaps because the variety it provides is so interesting, and we would not want to trade places with one of our ancestors. But there is a downside. Some of the products of human behavior threaten the future of the human race and perhaps the very existence of the biosphere. The behavior of humans is part of every major social problem we face: overpopulation, child abuse, auto accidents, illiteracy, and overconsumption of natural resources, to name a few.

In short, human behavior is the engine behind most of the changes that occurred on earth during the past 10,000 years, and especially during the past 3,000 years, the period of recorded history. During the past few hundred years, humans learned enough about their world to bring about the rapid changes we now see. Our knowledge about the world is lopsided, however; we know a lot about some things and little about others. It is only during the present century that people have turned their attention to behavior itself: how people learn to behave as they do, what causes behavior change, and what can be done when needed behavior is missing or harmful behavior persists.

Behavior Analysis

Many kinds of knowledge are important in order to have a complete understanding of human behavior. We need to know how the body (including the brain) works, because it is the body that behaves. It is the job of the biological sciences to develop that kind of knowledge. We also need to know how cultural systems work, because human behavior is molded by the culture in which a human lives. It is the job of cultural anthropology and sociology to develop that kind of knowledge. We also need knowledge of behavioral systems. *Behavioral systems* are the patterns of relations that exist between activities of human beings and other parts of the world. Behavioral systems are the subject matter studied by behavior analysts, just as central nervous systems are the subject matter of neurophysiologists, cellular systems are the subject matter of cell biologists, and cultural systems are the subject matter of cultural anthropologists. Without scientific knowledge about how behavioral systems become organized and change over time, people are seriously handicapped in solving the many problems that result from human behavior.

At any level of natural phenomena, from atomic through chemical, organic, behavioral, and cultural, explanations may be formulated in one of two ways. One kind of explanation is called *reductionistic,* because phenomena at one level of organization (e.g., chemical reactions) are explained in terms of lawful events occurring at another, "lower" level (e.g., atomic events). The other kind of explanation seeks to identify causes and effects among events occurring at the same level of observation. In behavior analysis, the second kind of explanation is called *functional analysis,* because the point is to determine how events in behavioral systems function with respect to one another to bring about changes in those systems. The causal relations within the system are called *functional relations;* in human behavioral systems, activities of people are functionally related to other events in the world. Although both types of scientific explanation are needed, explaining behavioral systems in terms of functional relations is especially useful if one is interested in taking practical action to solve problems stemming from human behavior. It took scientists hundreds of years to figure out that behavioral systems can be understood at their own level of analysis and did not need to be "reduced" to phenomena at other levels.

Behavior Streams, Principles, and Repertoires

If we observe the behavior of a normal human being going about her everyday business, we see a continuous stream of activity that appears to be integrated almost perfectly with various objects and events of the world. Many of the activities of the person are embedded in the world outside the person. We might see her, for example, arise from bed, walk across the room, push a button on a clock, walk to the kitchen, and make coffee. Other activities are embedded in that part of the world that is circumscribed by the person's body. For example, the person may rub her eyes, stretch her muscles, or push her hair away from her face. Either way, the stream of behavior we observe ordinarily involves a constantly changing flow of activity in which movements of the person are integrated with other parts of the world. Sometimes behavior streams come together temporarily, as when a parent shows a child how to tie his shoe, a group of employees discuss their jobs over lunch, or a team of football players prevents their opponents from gaining yardage on a play. Sometimes behavior streams of two different people come together off and on over a period of years or even decades, as in the case of married people.

Every behavior stream is unique. Each stream is individualized in terms of the particular events and activities that make it up. The uniqueness of a behavior stream is in its content. Record the behavior streams of 100 different people on a Monday morning, and you will see that each person does and says somewhat different things and does similar things in a different order. We can observe a behavior stream for whatever period of time we wish, for example, from birth to death, or from 9:00 a.m. until noon on a particular day, or every morning during breakfast for 3 months.

The behavior stream is the only aspect of behavior that scientists can observe directly. These streams provide the raw data from which behavioral principles are derived. They are also what people in the everyday world are interested in. Will fighting erupt in Bosnia? Will the plumber get the drain unclogged? Will I finish this section of this chapter today? Despite the practical and scientific importance of behavior streams, however, observing them as they occur in the natural environment never leads to a good understanding of behavioral systems. Behavior streams are the surface of behavioral systems. They are the windows through which we peer in order to obtain deeper knowledge.

The deeper knowledge is of two kinds. The first kind is knowledge about lawful relations that exist between human activities and other worldly events. This kind of knowledge is formulated in scientific principles and laws. In formulating principles and laws, scientists begin by observing particular events in their domain of interest: Chemists observe particular chemical events, neurophysiologists observe particular neural events, and behavior analysts observe particular behavioral events. If a scientist's goal is to formulate general principles, however, her attention cannot be focused on the uniqueness of the events she observes; rather, she must look beyond the infinite variety that appears on the surface and find commonalities in the ways the particulars relate to one another. Once such commonalities are discovered and described in scientific laws and principles, other scientists (and the rest of us, as well) can make use of those principles to understand how particular systems in that domain become organized.[2]

The important thing about scientific principles and laws is that they are content free. For example, laws of gravity describe causal relations between mass and distance. Any object having mass moves in relation to other objects having mass according to their relative mass and the distance they are apart. The principles of gravity remain constant whether they pertain to the relation between an apple and planet earth, between Mars and the sun, or between Jupiter and its moons. Similarly, principles of organic evolution describe causal relations between changes in the frequency of genetic characteristics of organisms in a particular lineage and the survival and reproductive requirements of the world in which those organisms live. The same organic evolutionary principles explain the increasing size of brains in a hominid lineage in a world of predators and the increasing intensity of color in a lineage of flowers that depends on bees for pollination.[3]

The scientific principles that describe causal relations between human activity and other worldly events (sometimes including other human activity) are also content free. The principles are constant whether the activity involved is the pressing of keys on a keyboard, the head banging of a child with autism, or the swearing of a teenager at a party. The principles are the same, and they pertain to all the activities occurring in behavior streams.

Because the principles that describe behavioral relations are the same from activity to activity and person to person, they provide a framework within which one can understand how behavioral systems can be organized in individual behavior repertoires. A *behavior repertoire* is everything that a particular person can do, say, think, or feel at any particular time during her life. For example, driving a car, doing a library search, and describing how you feel may be things that you know how to do. You are not doing any of those things just now, however; you are reading this chapter. Reading, then, is also in your repertoire. If we were to observe your behavior stream right now, we would see you reading. If the only thing we knew about you was what we observed right now, we could say little about your behavior repertoire, but we could accurately describe your behavior stream. Perhaps it is obvious that the longer we observe a behavior stream, the more we can say about the particular repertoire that makes such a stream possible.[4]

In summary, the concepts *behavioral system, behavioral principles, behavior stream,* and *behavior repertoire* relate to one another in the following ways: Behavior *streams* and *repertoires* pertain to particular humans. They are particularized in terms of their unique and specific content. The repertoire of a newborn human is made up of a relatively small number of systematic relations between the particular activities of the newborn and other particular worldly events. As a behavior stream flows through time, more and more complex and systematic relations develop between the human's activity and other worldly events. That is, the number of things a child can do, say, think, and feel usually increases rapidly, and there is a concomitant rapid increase in how much of the world enters into the child's activities. Behavioral *principles* describe the ways these relations come into existence and explain why particular activities (and not others) occur in behavior streams at particular times (and not others). Behavioral *system is* a generic term for patterns of relations that characterize any and all behavior repertoires and streams. Behavioral principles describe the generalized relations that characterize behavioral systems. In the following section, I discuss a few of those principles.

Principles of Behavioral Selection: Reinforcement and Extinction

Human activities generally result in fairly immediate changes in the world. Pressing the button on the water fountain usually produces a stream of water; flipping a light switch usually results in increased illumination; and pressing keys on a keyboard results in letters and words appearing on a monitor. These relations between acts and consequences are called *operant contingencies,* because the act operates on, or changes, the world.

Principles of selection describe (a) the functional relations between acts and consequences (operant) and (b) the subsequent frequency of the act. Relations of that kind have the name *contingencies.* As it turns out, some act-consequence relations result in increased or sustained frequency of the act that is part of that contingency, and other act-consequence relations result in decreased frequency of the act that is part of that contingency. Some act-consequence contingencies have no effect on future frequency of the act. When the contingency accounts for increased frequency of an act, the *reinforcement principle* is being described. When the contingency accounts for decreased frequency of an act, *the punishment principle* is being described. I focus here on the reinforcement principle, because it is most relevant to an understanding of how human activities become so highly coordinated with other worldly events (Bijou, 1993; Malott, Whaley, & Malott, 1991; Miller, 1996).

I begin by describing what might be seen in a laboratory where scientists study how behavioral systems evolve. Imagine that you are observing a 5-year-old girl sitting in a small room in front of a computer keyboard with a mouse to the right of the board. The monitor screen is red for a few seconds, then blue, then red, and so on; the intervals between changes vary in length by a few seconds. Marianne has never seen a computer keyboard, monitor, or mouse, and she has been given no instructions other than that she can do whatever she wants to. As you watch, Marianne looks at the changing colors for a short while, then tentatively presses a few keys. Nothing appears on the monitor; it continues changing colors in a random fashion. After about 2 minutes, Marianne has pressed most of the keys once and several of them several times each, and there are longer pauses between her presses. Now, as she reaches over and picks up the mouse, you hear a soft tone, rather like middle C on a piano. Marianne explores the mouse with both hands and eventually presses the left button, producing a different tone, more like E-flat. Marianne presses a few more times, producing tones each time, and then she presses the right mouse button. Maybe she just noticed it, or maybe her thumb was getting tired. Whatever the reason for the press on the right mouse button, the tone sounds. During the next 2 minutes, Marianne presses a mouse button 130 times, sometimes the left button, sometimes the right; a tone follows every press.

While you observed the behavior stream of Marianne, she acquired the act of pressing mouse buttons. (I am calling pressing the left button and the right button the same act because they are interchangeable with respect to the occurrence of the tone.) Although it is possible that the press-tone relation is not the cause of the increase in frequency of pressing that you observed, *you might guess that there is such a causal relation.* Your reasoning might go like this: During the first 2-minute period, Marianne mostly pressed alphanumeric keys, and the frequency of pressing mouse buttons was 0. Remember, she had never seen a mouse. During the next 2-minute period, the frequency of button pressing was 130. The only difference you noticed in the two periods was that the tone followed the button presses only during the second 2-minute period. Your guess that the tone somehow caused the change in behavior would, in fact, be supported by the results of thousands of experiments that have demonstrated behavior change resulting from contingencies between acts and consequences. This kind of functional relationship is seen so often that it has been elevated to the status of a scientific principle: the *principle of reinforcement.* When a guess about any kind of causal relation seems consistent with a known scientific principle, it is usually the best guess to make.

If you wanted to be more cautious in accepting the validity of your guess, you could do your own experiment to test it. You could arrange things so that the tone no longer followed pressing the mouse buttons and observe to see if the frequency of such pressing decreased; if it did decrease, you could arrange for the tone again to follow pressing a mouse button and observe to see if such pressing again increased. You could alternate these two procedures (holding constant as many other things as possible) until you were convinced that a relation between pressing the mouse button and the subsequent tone increased the frequency of the pressing.

Act-consequence relations are called *contingencies* in behavior analysis. Some contingencies increase or maintain the frequency of the acts in operant relations. They sometimes even account for the fact that the act exists at all. In Marianne's case, they turned a somewhat random activity into a well-defined, specific act. Those same reinforcement contingencies also account for changes in the form (or other characteristics, such as intensity) of acts. For example, if pressing the button faster or slower, or harder or softer, were more likely to produce the tone, the button presses would become faster or slower, or harder or softer—whatever worked best. The reinforcement principle accounts not only for the existence and frequency of acts in a behavioral repertoire, but also for the characteristic dimensions of those acts.

In describing how you might go about demonstrating that the relation between pressing mouse buttons and the tone accounted for the increase in pressing those keys, I suggested that you could arrange things so that the tone no longer followed such pressing. By making sure that the tone never followed pressing the mouse button, you would be discontinuing the contingency that accounted for the high frequency of pressing the mouse button. Researchers have repeatedly found that discontinuing a reinforcement contingency results in a gradual reduction in rate (and sometimes disappearance) of an act from a repertoire. This relation between the discontinuation of a reinforcement contingency and a subsequent decrease in frequency of the act in the operant relation is called the *principle of extinction*. If reinforcement contingencies remain in effect, we continue to do and say what we have learned. If the reinforcement contingencies discontinue, our performance deteriorates; we may even become unable to perform without renewed training.

Reinforcement and extinction principles are considered scientific principles because the functional relations they describe do not pertain only to single occurrences: not just to Marianne's behavior, or to button pressing, or to tones as consequences. They pertain to *any and all relations where the frequency of an act can be shown to increase and decrease as a function of the presence or absence of an operant contingency.*

As a result of the process described by the principle of reinforcement, we humans learn to do and say thousands of different things. We do not often learn to do those things in a concentrated 4-minute learning period, as Marianne did in the laboratory. Learning opportunities in the everyday world are distributed in the behavior stream. It is only when what we are learning is considered of great importance, or we want to learn a lot fast, or we are having trouble learning something that we pack a lot of learning into a short time. That is what education is about. If we could learn what we needed to learn simply by going about our business and allowing reinforcement contingencies to take care of themselves, we would not need to take skiing lessons, have basketball coaches and practice, go to drama rehearsals, or do spelling and arithmetic drills.

I have discussed the principles of reinforcement and extinction, using an example in which pressing a left mouse button is the act and a tone is its consequence. The relation between pressing mouse buttons and the tone is an operant contingency. When such a contingency results in new forms of behavior or when it increases or maintains the frequency of particular acts, the functional relation is described as *reinforcement*. Thus, reinforcement accounts for the existence of acts in a behavioral repertoire and the frequency with which they appear in a behavior stream.

Principle of Stimulus Control

The attentive reader might ask what all of the preceding has to do with the fabulously complicated ways that the behavior stream ebbs and flows in the everyday world. After all, one rarely sees people doing the same thing over and over in rapid succession in the way Marianne pressed the mouse buttons. Instead, we see constant change. One act flows into the next in the behavior stream of any person we happen to observe. What accounts for the order in which the acts occur? For example, we turn off the alarm first and then get a cup of coffee. What accounts for an act occurring at the same time every day and at no time in between? For example, Bob switches on the television at 9:00 A.M. and at 10:00 P.M. Why does Matt tease classmates in the classroom but not on the playground? Why does Tina go to bed when directed by her mom but not by her dad? Why does Joe one day grab a gun and shoot his brother, when every other time they have argued, Joe threw a punch?

Sometimes people jump to the conclusion that the incessant variety seen in behavior streams means behavior is not open to scientific investigation. They are not looking deeply enough. The laboratory has revealed more about behavioral selection than I have yet discussed. In addition to affecting the form and frequency of acts, operant contingencies account for some of the power that events in the world have over the occurrence of particular acts in a behavior stream. One of the principles that account for the specifics of a behavior stream is the *principle of stimulus control*. I return to the laboratory to explain how that principle works.

Marianne is still pressing the mouse button, but the tones do not always occur. The experimenter has arranged things so that pressing the left button is followed by a tone only when the monitor screen is red. If pressing the left button occurs while the screen is blue, no tone follows. However, a tone does follow pressing the right button while the screen is blue; pressing the left while the screen is blue does not produce a tone. For a while, Marianne continues to press right or left buttons irrespective of screen color. That is what the previous reinforcement contingencies taught her to do. But her pressing adapts to the new contingencies quickly. Before long, Marianne is pressing the left button when the screen is red, and when it turns blue, she switches to the right button. As soon as it turns red again, she switches back. The reinforcement contingencies have produced more complex behavior. The simple behavior of "pressing mouse button" has become the more complex behavior of "pressing the left mouse button if the screen is red and the right button if the screen is blue."

After a while, the time between color changes decreases. Within a few minutes, one color stays on only for 0.5–1.5 seconds. Marianne must watch closely and move quickly if her pressing is to produce tones. Marianne appears alert and focused fully on the monitor, occasionally checking the position of her hand on the mouse. Her presses are highly coordinated with screen color. This is beginning to look more like the behavior we see in the everyday world.

Readers might wonder why tones have such power over Marianne's behavior. There are many possible reasons. Perhaps the tones are ordered so that a melody is produced by Marianne's pressing. Perhaps she has been told that each musical note she produces will earn a penny for her to take home. The question of why a particular consequence of some particular act has the power to increase the frequency of that act is an important question about individual repertoires. The more general question of why operant relations bring about new acts in a repertoire, change the form and properties of acts already in a repertoire, and change or maintain the frequency of acts is also important. Whatever the answers to these questions, they do not alter the reinforcement principle.

One could arrange Marianne's reinforcement contingencies so that her behavior stream looked even more typical of everyday life. One could, for example, arrange for pictures of animals to appear on the monitor instead of colored screens. One could teach Marianne to press "d" on the keyboard while the picture of a dog is on the screen, to press "c" on the keyboard while the picture of a cat is on the screen, and to press "p" on the keyboard when a parrot is on the screen. If the pictures changed from one to another as soon as Marianne pressed a key once, we would see something like this: The cat would appear; Marianne would press "c"; and the tone would sound at the same time that another picture appeared, perhaps the parrot. Marianne would immediately press "p," and the tone would occur along with a new picture, and so forth. At this point, Marianne's actions would be tracking frequent changes going on in the world around her. Eventually, Marianne's behavior stream would look much like that of a child engaged in a simple computer game.

The causal relations between the various pictures and the different keys that Marianne pressed are *stimulus-control relations.* The *stimulus-control principle* (*stimulus control,* for short) describes causal relations between changes in the world and immediately subsequent changes in behavior streams. As described in the previous paragraphs, reinforcement accounts for the existence of at least some of the stimulus-control relations we see in the everyday world. The origins of other stimulus-control relations that we observe in behavior streams may include additional processes, such as stimulus generalization and stimulus equivalence. Although I do not discuss those processes in this chapter, I do not want to leave readers with the impression that reinforcement by itself explains why one act follows another in the behavior stream of any person observed.

Practical Examples

As I suggested at the start of this chapter, many of the problems humans face today somehow involve human behavior. Some solutions require changes at the cultural level, for example, in organizational policies, laws, educational practices, and other areas that require coordinated efforts by many different people. Even so, any large-scale changes that occur must *begin* with the behavior of individual humans. Knowledge of behavioral principles can lead directly to solutions at the individual level and can contribute to solutions involving coordinated behavior by many people. I conclude this chapter with some examples of how behavioral principles help people to think of practical solutions to social problems that have an impact on many different people.

Scott Geller and Bruce Thyer have done research to determine whether behavioral principles can be used to increase safety-belt use among auto passengers, making use of the principle of stimulus control to bring about such a change in behavior. For 2 weeks, 24 graduate students kept records on whether passengers in the front seat of their cars used the safety belt. Of the 476 passengers who rode in the students' cars, only 162 buckled up (34%). Then the students attached a sticker (1.5 x 2.5 inches) to the dashboard of their car, directly facing the passenger seat, and they continued keeping a record of whether or not passengers in their front seat used the safety belt. The sticker read, "Safety-belt Use Required in this Vehicle." During that 2-week period, 314 of the 448 passengers buckled their seat belts (70%). The students then removed the stickers and continued keeping their records of seat-belt use. They found that 166 of 406 passengers used the seat belt (41%). Finally, once again they affixed the sticker to their dashboards, and once again the number of people using seat belts increased (78% of 392 passengers).[5]

Geller and Thyer found that it was possible to improve safety by taking advantage of a stimulus-control relation that was in the repertoire of the passengers riding in the students' cars. The passengers did not have to be taught to buckle up when they saw a sticker saying that safety-belt use was required. They already knew how to buckle up; they were capable of reading; and they no doubt had a history of reinforcement for following instructions. Furthermore, they would probably say that they were safer when they rode with their safety belts buckled. But without the sticker right in front of them, most of them did not use their safety belts. When the sticker was there, it evoked the behavior of buckling the safety belt, but in the absence of the sticker, there was nothing to evoke that behavior; therefore, it did not occur.

The function of the sticker in this study was to enter a "buckle-up" response into the behavior stream of passengers at just the right time. The researchers did not have to teach new behavior or alter the repertoires of the passengers in any way. That no doubt would have taken considerably more time to accomplish. It is often the case that the only reason that behavior already in a repertoire does not appear in the behavior stream of the person is that a stimulus that would evoke that behavior is not present at the appropriate moment.

Sometimes, however, the goal is to change the repertoire of a person. One way to do that is to increase the number of things the person can do. For example, before a person has learned to ski, she cannot put on skis, maneuver the slopes, and so on, even if promised a great deal of money for doing so. Similarly, before a person can read, putting printed words in front of him will not result in his saying those words. Society has established schools and colleges to ensure that its members have acquired the repertoires they need to participate successfully in the workplace and in the home. People also learn to answer questions about how things relate to one another. Jim Partington and Jon Bailey (1993) were interested in whether teaching young children to name things would enable them to use those names to answer certain kinds of questions. Four 4-year-old children were tested to ascertain whether they could name various kinds of fruits, toys, pieces of furniture, and "things you use to clean a house." They were also asked, "What are some fruits [or toys, or other objects]?" After Partington and Bailey found out just how many items each child could name and how many answers each could give to the questions, they taught the children to name all the pictures by telling each child the names of those he did not name, waiting for the child to say the name, and then praising the child's correct naming. The children learned to name all the pictures without being told.

Most people might assume that the children would be able to answer the questions about fruits, toys, and so forth after they had learned to name the pictures. But 7 of the 8 children had to be taught specifically to do that. Furthermore, after being taught to give all the correct answers to one of the questions, they still needed to be taught to answer the other questions, one at a time. The teaching was done as follows: The child was asked one of the questions, and each correct answer was praised ("that's right!" or "right on" or "uh-huh"). If the child did not continue with more answers, he was asked "what else?" until he answered with all the names he had learned by looking at the pictures or until he could not give any more answers. To help him learn to give answers he did not yet know, the researchers showed the child a picture of an item missing from the answer. Looking at the card allowed him to answer the question. Eventually, the children did not need to see the cards anymore to answer the questions. A standardized test of verbal fluency was given to the children before and after the training. The scores of children who had the training described improved by 10 points, whereas 4 other children, who did not receive the training, had little improvement (0.5 point).

The procedures used by the researchers brought about a change in the repertoires of the children they trained. Specifically, each child could name many more objects than before training and could also use those names to answer questions. Furthermore, these changes seemed to have a positive impact on the children's verbal fluency as measured by a standard test (the McCarthy Scales). The way the child's repertoire changed was that new stimulus-control relations could now be observed in the behavior stream of each child. Before the training, there was no causal relation between the presentation of pictures and the child's naming behavior nor between the question and the answers (Partington & Bailey, 1993).

Conclusion

To deal effectively with many of society's problems, people must behave differently. We must begin to make use of what we know about human behavior to help bring about those behavior changes. Sometimes, changes can be made fairly easily by making use of behavioral principles. Simple things, like putting a sign where people are likely to see it, can move behavior streams in a positive direction at the right moment. But making use of behavioral principles requires changes in the behavior repertoires of many people, because most people do not know enough about them to make effective use of them. For example, many people might forget to say "right" or otherwise provide reinforcement when they are trying to teach a child to read. The reinforcement can be as simple as a smile, a nod, or a wink. Many people forget to prompt the correct response, or forget to be sure the child echoes the answer while looking at the object he is learning to name. In short, making use of the principles of reinforcement and stimulus control is not as easy as it might seem, but the power of these principles to bring about behavior change cannot be overestimated. Improved understanding of these principles helps empower humans to meet the challenges of a constantly changing world.

Acknowledgments

I owe a debt of gratitude to Douglas P. Field. The present chapter makes use of some of the points he and I developed in a previous paper. I also thank Richard G. Smith for taking time to give the manuscript a careful reading and providing excellent feedback that has improved the manuscript considerably.

Notes

1. For more information about the early days of human life, Marvin Harris's *Our Kind* is recommended. It was published in 1989 by Harper & Row.
2. Readers interested in delving more deeply into complex concepts such as these can see the book *The Metaphysics of Evolution*, published in 1989 by the State University of New York Press. It is a collection of essays by the philosopher of science David Hull.
3. A highly readable book on the coevolution of species is *Beauty and the Beast* by Susan Grant, published in 1984 by Scribner.
4. For readers interested in an article not intended for beginners in behavior analysis, an extended treatment of these and other concepts can be found in the article "Functions of the Environment in Behavioral Evolution" by Sigrid S. Glenn and Douglas P. Field. It is in the journal *The Behavior Analyst*, 1994, vol. 17, pp. 241–259.
5. The original report is titled "Dashboard stickers: An effective strategy for promoting safety-belt use." It can be found in the journal *Environment and Behavior*, 1987, Vol. 19, pp. 484–494. The research is also reported, along with many other studies, in a monograph titled *Applications of Behavior Analysis to Prevent Injuries from Vehicle Crashes*, by E. Scott Geller. The monograph was published in 1992 by the Cambridge Center for Behavioral Studies.

References

Bijou, S. W. (1993). *Behavior analysis and child development* (Rev. ed.). Reno, NV: Context Press.
Malott, R. W., Whaley, D. L., & Malott, M. E. (1991). *Elementary principles of behavior* (2nd ed.). Englewood Cliffs, NJ: Prentice-Hall.
Miller, L. K. (1996). *Principles of everyday behavior analysis* (2nd ed.). Pacific Grove, CA: Brooks/Cole.
Partington, J., & Bailey, J. (1993). Teaching intraverbal behavior to preschool children. *The Analysis of Verbal Behavior, 11,* 9–18.

2

Some Meanings of Antecedent and Environmental Control

Donald M. Baer

Red lights stop us; green lights let us go. We pick up a ringing telephone; a chime or buzzer sends us to the door. A calendar page determines whether we do our work now or later. Our checkbook balance tells us if we can make a certain purchase. A watch face says whether we go now or stay. One kind of alarm says when to awaken; another tells us to leave a building; a third says to clear a traffic lane. A favor granted calls for some form of "thank you"; a heard "thank you" evokes some form of "you're welcome." Lines of print in a schedule let us plan the next semester's courses. These lines of print in this chapter teach the reader, by example, that a great deal of our behavior is under the control of its environmental antecedents. They also describe antecedents that evoke behavior quite uniformly in us; those are the things almost all of us do.

Consider some very individualized examples as well: (a) A single father is calm and understanding of his son's rebellious behavior until the father is told his job has been eliminated; his son's next act of defiance, even though ordinary by past standards, this time extracts an unprecedented storm of anger from the father. In other words, an antecedent, impertinence, ordinarily evokes mild commentary, but given a change in environment—life without an income—it evokes anger instead. (b) A woman who can afford to drive only a cheap car uniformly admires all the expensive sports cars she sees and remarks often how happy she would be to have any of them. Suddenly, her income increases, and she decides to buy one of them; she now speaks critically of most of them and admires only a few, one of which she eventually buys. In other words, the members of a class of antecedents, sports cars, all evoke the same admiration in an environment in which they all are out of reach; but in an environment in which acquiring any one of them is possible, most of them become targets of criticism. (c) A writer has great difficulty getting anything written; he does other things instead, saying he must wait for inspiration. A specialist in environmental design radically redesigns the writer's workplace: She eliminates from it everything irrelevant to writing and adds to it everything necessary to writing; now nothing can be done there except write. Soon the writer is spending more and more time there, producing more and more pages. In other words, it has become an environment that evokes and supports only writing, nothing else.

Antecedent control of behavior by the environment is one of the oldest facts of behavioral science and a target of all its explanatory models. This book is devoted to explaining, exemplifying, and furthering the current understanding of those various explanations. This chapter establishes some terms and describes some processes or mechanisms of antecedent control, serving to make the rest of the book accessible. The fundamental questions are as follows:

1. Do certain environmental antecedents reliably cause certain responses?
2. How do we detect this kind of control, and how do we prove it is what it seems?
3. How can we create this kind of control when we want to? What are the mechanisms that can give some aspects of our environment control of some parts of our behavior?
4. Why do some antecedents and environments immediately evoke their subsequent responses, whereas others evoke their responses much later?
5. When we understand the facts of antecedent environmental control, we will be able to put our understanding to work for us. Can we choose what parts of our environment will control what parts of our behavior? If we can make those choices, will we become better teachers or therapists?

The Problem of Detecting and Proving Stimulus Control

Do antecedents reliably evoke certain responses? Everyday experience leads us to answer that question with a *yes*. But we still need clear, descriptive terms and clear, definitive tests of when we have antecedent control rather than coincidental occurrence of a stimulus and a subsequent response.

The control of behavior by its antecedents has earned a variety of labels, for example, *evocation, elicitation, stimulus control, antecedent control, ecological control, and contextual control.* Perhaps the least assuming term is stimulus control (cf. Dinsmoor, 1995a, 1995b). It labels the procedures and observations that define evocation or suppression but leaves unanswered the question of how that evocation or suppression came to be or how one can make it what one wants it to be.

Stimulus control requires that one has either (a) shown an experimental relation between a certain stimulus and a certain response or (b) observed enough natural, uncontrolled facts to infer a relation between some naturally occurring stimulus and a naturally occurring response.

The Experimental Technique

The strongest definition of stimulus control results from an experimental analysis. We experimentally present the stimulus at arbitrarily chosen times; the question is whether doing that changes the probability of the response. If the probability increases, we label that kind of stimulus control *evocation;* if the probability decreases, we label that kind of stimulus control *suppression.*

It takes an experiment to know with certainty that an antecedent stimulus changes the probability of a subsequent response. First, we specify an interval of time, usually a matter of seconds or minutes. Second, we take control of the stimulus so that it occurs only when we present it. Then, we present the stimulus at arbitrary times. We examine all of the many time intervals that began with presentation of the stimulus and ask how many of them contain a subsequent response. We also examine all the time intervals in which we did not present the stimulus and ask how many of them contain the response.

If the many intervals that began with our presentation of the stimulus contain convincingly more responses than the many intervals in which we did not present the stimulus, *evocation* is said to have occurred.

If the many intervals that began with the stimulus contain convincingly fewer responses than the many intervals in which we did not present the stimulus, *suppression* has occurred.

If the many intervals that began with the stimulus contain just as many responses as the many intervals in which we did not present the stimulus, the conclusion is that this stimulus does not control this response.

Whatever the result, it is the truth only for intervals of that length. We should next define a different time interval and do the experiment again. We should do enough of these experiments to explore all the lengths of time during which we want to evaluate stimulus control. Sometimes we will find the strongest stimulus control within a narrow range of time: The stimulus promptly evokes or suppresses the response. Telephone rings are an example. Sometimes we will find that the stimulus controls a response only after considerable time has passed since the stimulus occurred. Many drugs act like that. Sometimes we will find control across a wide range of time; for example, teachers sometimes warn us at the beginning of a term to read a certain book before the final examination. Sometimes we will find that no range of time we investigate reveals stimulus control. The best, most useful statement of stimulus control results from knowing the range of time within which evocation or suppression occurs and whether some parts of that range reveal more powerful effects than others.

The Naturalistic Technique

An alternative definition of stimulus control arises when we do not (or cannot or should not) have experimental control of the stimulus—of either its presence or its absence. For example, studying parent-child interaction, we may find an instance of a particularly punitive relationship. We may ask what events, if any, evoke the parent's physical punishment of the child. Suppose we suspect it is the child's fussing that most reliably evokes the parent's punishment. We cannot ethically or legally control the child's fussing; at best, we can observe and try to analyze what we see, hoping that the analysis will enable us to intervene in a useful way, perhaps to teach the parent to respond to those stimuli very differently in the future.

We would observe the parent and child interacting over long periods of time, recording as exactly as possible when in that time the child fusses and when the parent punishes the child. We would then look at those data for the patterns typical of stimulus control: for the timing, if any, between all instances of fussing and punishment. We would define an interval of time, perhaps 1 minute, and would ask regarding every instance of fussing, How often does the following minute contain a punishment? We would also ask, How often does each minute free of fussing contain a punishment? If the minutes beginning with fussing clearly contain more punishments than the minutes free of fussing, we can suspect that fussing evokes punishment. If the minutes beginning with a fuss clearly contain fewer punishments than the minutes free of fussing, we can suspect fussing inhibits punishment. If the minutes beginning with fussing contain about the same number of punishments as the minutes free of fussing, we can suppose fussing has no stimulus control of punishment and look elsewhere for what controls the parent's punishment. Whatever we find, it is important to do the analysis again with various lengths of interval, just as in the experimental case. Naturalistic analysis of this kind enlarges the range of analysis, but at the same time it makes the analysis weaker. Consider some examples we already understand:

Many of us cry in the presence of newly sliced onions. And many of us console people who cry. Therefore, naturalistic observation of onion slicing and of consolation behavior might make it seem that onion slicing evokes consolation behaviors. But we know it does not.

Earlier generations of Pacific Northwest Native Americans noted that almost every time the inland seagull population suddenly increased, an eastbound Pacific storm blew in a day later. They guessed that seagulls possess a magic power that could be pooled to evoke bad weather. Later generations know that the eastbound Pacific storms are not evoked by seagulls, but rather drive the seagulls inland ahead of them; the sea gulls are seeking shelter.

These examples show that naturalistic observations can only suggest stimulus control and can do so incorrectly. The examples are clear because we already know about the relations under study; however, most research is done because we do not know about the relations under study. In those cases, naturalistic observation can more easily mislead us. It is best at confirming what we already suspect and at quantifying what we know only qualitatively to be true.

Another weakness of observational analysis is the possibility that the behavior under study is evoked by a variety of stimuli that occur fairly often. Suppose a parent's punishments are evoked by four different child behaviors: by fussing, crying, saying *no!*, and running away. Suppose the probability of punishment within 1 minute after fussing is .15, within 1 minute after crying is .40, within 1 minute after saying *no!* is .65, and within 1 minute after running away is .75. Suppose that during the time of observation, the child fusses about twice a minute, cries about once every 3 minutes, says *no!* about once every 5 minutes, and runs away about once every 10 minutes. It will be almost impossible to gather enough observational data to establish these facts. If the four child behaviors that evoke parental punishment occur often enough, our attempt to analyze any one of them by naturalistic observation is likely to show that punishments occur as often in the absence of that one as in its presence, and we will incorrectly conclude that this event has no stimulus control over punishment.

The Explanatory Models

Structure

The simplest explanation of stimulus control is structural: Some of our behavior is quite mechanically wrung from us (Catania, 1984, chap. 2). A tap on the patellar tendon evokes a kick of the leg; a bright light closes the pupil of the eye; a tickling of the palate yields a gag. We say informally that we are "wired that way." We tend to see this kind of control as innate. We hope other disciplines will clarify the actual mechanisms of our "wiring" metaphor, and when those disciplines do that, we expect their explanations will look more functional than structural. (Structure is often a metaphor for ignorance.)

The structural model does not describe much of our behavior, but it undeniably describes some of it. Its implication that to some degree we are essentially a biochemical, neurophysiological version of a switchboard, transistor, or computer makes the model unpopular with many explanation seekers; even so, for some of what we do, it is an accurate model. It is also a model of mechanisms about which we can, so far, do little but understand. We are not very far into the science of "rewiring" our biochemistry and neurophysiology; on the other hand, we have begun to learn how (cf. Donohoe, 1996; Reese, 1996).

Classically Conditioned Stimulus Control

Behavior that is not explained by a structural model still needs to have the following question posed: Why do other environmental antecedents reliably evoke certain responses from us? A somewhat more complex explanatory model of antecedent control is the classical conditioning technique most often attributed to Pavlov. A stimulus that does not evoke behavior, if paired properly with a stimulus that does, may acquire the evocative power of the stimulus that does (Catania, 1984, chap. 2). Perhaps the list of initial, unconditioned, automatic stimulus controls over behavior is not long (although we probably do not yet know all of it), but the classical conditioning mechanism enables the list of conditioned controlling stimuli to be made indefinitely long, even if the list of responses controlled by them remains short. The controlling stimuli can be anything the organism can discriminate. Because we can deliberately perform classical conditioning, in ourselves or in our students or clients, this is not only an explanatory model but also a modestly useful model: It shows us how to teach some of the antecedent controls we think desirable for those responses already under known antecedent control. In Chapter 12 of this book, William Redd illustrates how classical conditioning principles explain the steady development of nausea in patients undergoing cancer treatment and how those principles can be used to alleviate that problem.

Operant Conditioning: Discriminative Stimulus Control

A much more complex model of antecedent control is the operant conditioning technique most often attributed to Skinner. That model notes that most behavior is determined by its consequences and is changed by changing its consequences. Any discriminable stimulus that reliably signals those consequences, or signals changes in those consequences, will control the behavior those consequences control (Catania, 1984, chap. 6). The effect of the antecedent reflects the effect of the consequence it signals: The antecedents of reinforcement evoke the behavior reinforced; the antecedents of punishment and extinction suppress the behavior punished or extinguished and often evoke any previously established avoidances, escapes, or countercontrols.

In operant analysis, a stimulus that signals the likely consequences of a response is usually termed a *discriminative* stimulus: Its presence discriminates when the response will have one sort of consequence or another.

The lists of consequence-controlling behaviors, and of their discriminative, consequence-signaling stimuli, are indefinitely long; they can include almost anything, from the very simple to the exceedingly complex. Furthermore, we can make stimuli signal consequences in useful ways; therefore, this model too is both explanatory and a guide to teaching whatever new antecedent control we think desirable. This model cannot be dismissed as descriptive of only a small corner of behavior.

For example, a child is most likely to talk to a parent who answers lovingly and grants requests. If the parent's smile signals times when the parent will be loving and indulgent and the parent's frown signals times when the parent will be angry and rejecting, the child will talk when the parent smiles and not when the parent frowns. The smile discriminates times when the child's talk will have the desirable consequences; the frown discriminates times when the child's talk will have the undesirable consequences. We could teach parents who want their children to talk to them to smile rather than frown, or at least not to frown. Indeed, parents who understand the operant model could teach themselves that simple skill.

The most fundamental relation in the operant model is between the response and its consequences; that is, the antecedent acquires power only by signaling the consequence of the response. Even so, the operant model has always presented the relations among the antecedent, response, and consequence as the fundamental problem for analysis. In the last half century, great emphasis was given to understanding all possible response-consequence relations; it is only in the last 2 decades that it has seemed important to understand all possible antecedent-response-consequence relations equally well. Yet the response-consequence relations, while fundamental, are often difficult to see, because consequences can be scheduled intermittently and still function powerfully. By contrast, the most immediately powerful, and often the most obvious, relation is between the response and the antecedent that signals its consequences. Even so, in Chapter 21 of this book, John Lutzker argues that programs aimed at solving serious lifestyle problems will do best if they incorporate the natural, sometimes subtle events that make up real life.

Instructional Control

In organisms capable of language—which these days include primates in certain sign-language training programs (e.g., Premack, 1971)—one simple instruction can be a stimulus control (e.g., Milgram, 1963) and can create stimulus controls (cf. Catania, 1984, chap. 9, pp. 238–244). For example, a spellchecker might announce on the monitor screen, "All misspelled words are marked with a [." That establishes [as a stimulus control for the places where the writer's already developed skills of finding misspellings and mistypings will be evoked. But that is not the natural or conventional stimulus control exerted by [; this new relation is a perfectly arbitrary one, created in an instant by an instruction, and to be destroyed at a later instant by a contradictory instruction that will leave [with only its usual meaning.

Stimulus Equivalence: Technique or Explanation?

Categorization is often seen as a hallmark of cognitive function and skill. The ability to group different objects into a category because they all possess some common attribute and then deal with the category as one would deal with the objects, but more easily, is distinctively human, linguistic, and smart. The ability to recategorize those objects according to some other attribute is even more distinctively human, linguistic, and smart. If I want to buy a car, I will categorize cars according to price, newness, utility, economy, appearance, size, reputation, cost of insurance, and a few other attributes. I will thereby create many categories, almost as many as there are cars. But if I want to cross the street, I instantly recategorize all cars into only two categories: those too close or moving too fast for me to cross in front of them and those far enough away or moving slow enough for me to cross in front of them.

This kind of categorization is also readily stated in the logic of antecedent stimulus control: To say that a number of events are all in the same category is to say that each of them is a stimulus control for each of the others. Whatever we can do with any one of them, we can do with them all; whatever we learn about any one of them, we have learned about them all.

There are several ways to make an arbitrary collection of stimuli all substitutable for one another; stimulus equivalence is a label for one way that has attracted much attention in recent years, both as a set of procedures and as an explanatory model (Sidman, 1994). The usual journal report of stimulus-equivalence strikes the new reader as extremely complex and too much to remember all at one time. Therefore, a somewhat fanciful version will be offered here, as if it were an intellectual game played between a teacher and a student.

For this game, I am the teacher, and you are the student. Imagine that I teach you four lessons, by showing you successive pages displaying three stimuli per page, one of which is the correct stimulus for you to touch. The first two lessons are these:

When you see * at the top of a page and M and S at the bottom of the page, you should touch M, whether it is on the left or the right. (On some pages, M will be on the left and S on the right; on other pages, M will be on the right and S on the left.) But when you see # at the top of the page and M and S at the bottom, you should touch S, whether it is on the left or the right. In summary, if * at top, then M, not S; if # at top, then S, not M.

Then I teach you two more lessons:

When you see M at the top and + and – at the bottom, you should touch +, whether it is on the left or the right; but when you see S at the top and + and – at the bottom, you should touch –, whether it is on the left or the right. In summary, if M at top, then +, not –; if S at top, then –, not +.

I will teach you those four lessons until you have memorized them perfectly. Then the game starts. I ask you eight questions, the answers to which I did not teach you and will not teach you. I ask you these questions again and again, but I never tell you whether your answer is correct or incorrect:

Question 1. If M appears at the top and * and # appear at the bottom, will you touch * or #?

Question 2. If S appears at the top and * and # appear at the bottom, will you touch * or #?

Question 3. If + appears at the top and M and S appear at the bottom, will you touch M or S?

Question 4. If – appears at the top and M and S appear at the bottom, will you touch M or S?

Question 5. If * appears at the top and + and – appear at the bottom, will you touch + or –?

Question 6. If # appears at the top and + and – appear at the bottom, will you touch + or –?

Question 7. If + appears at the top and * and # appear at the bottom, will you touch * or #?

Question 8. If – appears at the top and * and # appear at the bottom, will you touch * or #?

You are free to do whatever you want with these eight questions; answers to them were never taught in our game, and I will not respond differently no matter what answers to them you give me. It may interest you to know that if I continue asking these questions, over and over, many players will eventually become consistent in touching

* when M is at the top,
# when S is at the top,
M when + is at the top,
S when – is at the top,
+ when * is at the top,
– when # is at the top,
* when + is at the top,
# when – is at the top.

We can summarize that pattern by two statements: One is that *, M, and + have become equivalent to each other: Each of them is a stimulus that controls touching the others. The other is that #, S, and – have become equivalent to each other: Each of them is a stimulus that controls touching the others. The emergence of all those untaught relations is called stimulus equivalence. Notice that most of this equivalence was not taught: Four relations were taught directly, and in consequence, eight new ones emerged without direct teaching.

A better summary is, If the correct 4 relations are taught, repetition of the 8 questions will evoke another 8 relations that were not taught, and the 12 relations in total represent the logical relation of equivalence. A pragmatic summary might be as follows: If you want to make *, M, and + equivalent to each other, and #, S, and – equivalent to each other, you have 12 relations to establish; teaching only the 4 cited above and asking repeatedly about the remaining 8 can be an economical way to get all 12.

Facts like these have emerged in a wealth of studies, most of them considerably more complex than this introductory example. Perhaps the most impressive of these studies are those that show stimulus control of equivalence: the ability to make a set of events equivalent or not equivalent just by presenting a stimulus (Sidman, 1994). In Chapter 9 of this book, Harry Mackay, Barbara Jill Kotlarchyk, and Robert Stromer cite a number of such accomplishments, and they report their extension of the equivalence principle to one more valuable instance. In Chapter 10, however, Svein Eikeseth and Donald Baer report a study suggesting that the equivalence relation is not automatic or inevitable: Their students, given a problem in categorizing alphabet letters that allowed both equivalence and alphabetical order relations to emerge, preferred to show alphabetical order.

Such accomplishments have generated a storm of questions: Are the untaught instances of stimulus control a puzzling form of generalization from learning of the four arbitrary instances? Or should they be seen as a natural outcome, as basic as the reinforcement phenomenon? But are they robust enough for that to be true?

Alternatively, should these phenomena be seen as likely, logical outcomes, but only in organisms who have a preexisting "identity" or "equals" concept? Remember the game you just played. You were taught that if * is at the top, you should touch M, not S. Suppose you also said, "So, * is M." The consistent appearance of that "is" can mediate all eight untaught relations. The fact that it can does not mean that it always does or often does. But it can. If, at the end of my teaching the first four lessons, you have stated the four identities—* is M, # is S, M is +, and S is —then you will soon answer my eight questions according to the logic of identity: If * is M, then M is *; if # is S, then S is #; if M is +, then + is M; if S is −, then − is S. And if * is M and M is +, then * is +. And if # is S and S is −, then # is −. And if * is +, then + is *; and if # is −, then − is #. So, if * is S, it will not matter which is at the top and which is at the bottom; either one of them implies the other, and the other will be touched without direct teaching to do so. "Is" can engender the answers to my eight untaught questions.

If the phenomena that define stimulus equivalence are found only in language users with a concept of "is," will these phenomena themselves prove subject to stimulus control? That is, will the untaught relations emerge only when some other events evoke the "is" concept for this performance? So far, these questions remain largely unanswered and highly debatable.

Probabilistic Control or Conditional Control?

Another fundamental question is why stimulus control so often is probabilistic: It is not ordinarily a phenomenon in which a particular antecedent stimulus makes a particular response either certain to occur or certain not to occur (within a specified time interval). Instead, it is usually a case of a certain antecedent stimulus changing the probability of a certain response within a specified time interval. Perhaps stimulus control is inherently probabilistic, perhaps because environmental control of behavior is not amenable to totally deterministic analysis.

On the other hand, perhaps the nature of stimulus control is often conditional: Perhaps some stimuli control their behaviors only if some other stimuli are also present, within some specified time interval (cf. Catania, 1984, chap. 6, pp. 152–156). A classical example is imitation. Students do not ordinarily imitate every action of their teachers; however, when a student cannot solve a problem and the teacher says, "I know how; do what I do," that statement makes every immediate subsequent teacher action a model for the student to imitate, that is, a stimulus control for imitation. In other words, teacher actions become stimulus controls for student imitation only conditionally: when certain stimuli have preceded them. The combination of a presently insoluble problem and a teacher's statement of "do what I do" is a stimulus that makes subsequent teacher actions reliable stimulus controls for student imitation.

A naive observer, not knowing that student imitation of teachers is conditional, will conclude that teacher actions have only a modest probability of being imitated by students. If our knowledge of stimulus control is typically that inadequate in everything we observe, we will of course suppose that stimulus control is typically, perhaps inherently, probabilistic. In this example, however, if we know to look for conditional control, we will soon find a class of events—insoluble problems, problems being solved only inefficiently, instructions that someone else knows how to solve the problem better, instructions to imitate—that, if present in certain combinations, suddenly make teacher actions almost certain to be imitated by their students.

Thorough knowledge of conditional control may make stimulus control seem typically more digital than probabilistic: If the correct combination of stimuli has occurred, the response will occur; otherwise, it will not. We will see that kind of control only in almost perfectly analyzed cases. But the existence of even a few cases wherein analysis of conditional control yields near-perfect stimulus control will tempt us to ask if all other cases that now seem only probabilistic are actually cases in which we have so far failed to analyze the conditional control that, understood, would make them seem digital.

If we assume stimulus control is inherently digital, the consequences for research strategy are momentous. Whenever we found an antecedent stimulus that exercised only probabilistic control of a subsequent response, we would search constantly for conditional stimulus relations to see if better and better approximations to digital control could be achieved. By contrast, if we assume probabilistic control is typical and perhaps inherent, the only impetus to search for conditional control is the knowledge that it has proved possible in a few past cases.

Failures of Stimulus Control: Attention and Overselectivity

Stimuli can be placed in exactly the positions that the principles of classical conditioning, operant conditioning, and instructional control say should give them control of some behavior, yet they sometimes fail to acquire that control. Apparently, those positions are not always enough. They are sufficient often enough to let us state a principle, and insufficient often enough to make us doubt the principle. Doubting a principle usually means searching for the special conditions under which it is true and the other conditions under which it is not; few if any principles are true under all conditions.

Failures of stimulus control in these three models have attracted some explanatory hypotheses. A prominent example is a hypothetical but readily plausible behavior called "attention." If stimuli should have acquired control of a response but did not, perhaps it is because the student was not attending to them when they accompanied already powerful antecedent stimuli or discriminated response consequences, or perhaps the student was not attending to the instructions given.

The attention hypothesis has seen two distinctive uses: One makes it a hypothetical construct, intended only to explain. The other assumes that "to attend" is a class of behaviors that could be studied directly (cf. Catania, 1984, chap. 13, pp. 333–336). We are all aware of when we attend to something with special care or intensity; we feel our attention is "real" in us; that it must have physical existence; and if it does, that a suitable technology eventually will make it measurable and subject to experimentation. Real, measurable attending or scanning responses are sought in every sensory modality. Alternatively, existing ones are recruited, strengthened, and made probable. The problem of ensuring that the student attends to the stimulus controls being taught, therefore, reduces to finding the stimulus controls of attending. Sometimes, new ones are created: We can teach the student how to use an experimenter-constructed problem-observing response (see Dinsmoor, 1995a, pp. 60–63, for a summary); from then on, that part of the student's attention to the problem is no longer hypothetical but directly measurable, teachable, and subject to experimentation.

An example is seen in the five studies reported by Stephen Schroeder in Chapter 7 of this book; those studies follow from the development of techniques that let us know just where the eyes are looking. With that technology, "attending" sometimes amounts to "visual fixation." A more fundamental approach to the problem is offered in Chapter 5, by Barbara Etzel. Rather than ask if the student is attending, she uses techniques that virtually command the requisite attention and never let it stop or wander; she knows the stimulus controls of attending in her students. The basic method is to begin with a stimulus that virtually always controls the relevant behavior and to transform it into the desired new stimulus so artfully that correct control of the relevant behavior is never lost. In this case, a large part of "art" is always being "criterion-related" during that transformation, a concept best explained by the examples in her chapter.

A current specialized variation of the attention hypothesis is called "overselectivity" (cf. Lovaas, Schreibman, Koegel, & Rehm, 1971). It follows from the discovery that not every part of the stimulus acquires the intended control, despite being put in the usually effective positions of accompanying already effective antecedents, or discriminating response consequences, or instructing stimulus-response relations. But some parts do. The overselectivity hypothesis supposes the student attended to only part of the stimuli put in those ordinarily powerful positions; the part attended to acquired control as it should, but the other parts did not. In other words, the student seems to have been overselective, by our standards, in learning the stimulus. A better statement might be that we, the teachers, were underselective in guaranteeing that all relevant parts of the stimulus acquired the desired control. This second statement makes the issue workable by inviting us to develop more reliable teaching techniques; the first simply makes it the student's fault.

Overselectivity is probably a common feature of everyone's learning; it is not always a disadvantage. If your task at a party is to learn quickly the names of some new people, and only one of them has a beard, you may well go no further than learn that the beard is named Mark. That will solve your problem at the party with the least effort. Disadvantage will emerge only in later situations when you want to name Mark correctly, but he is no longer the only bearded man present. Only then would it be better if you had learned more of Mark's identifying features the first time. (Chapter 18 of this book, by Angela Duarte and Donald Baer, offers an analysis of techniques that alleviate this problem.) Even if overselectivity does not always make trouble for us, many teachers assume their students should learn all the relevant stimuli the teachers present; that assumption makes overselectivity a clinical problem.

Overselectivity is easily enough assessed by presenting parts of the stimuli alone to see if they do or do not control the intended response. Failures of control, once made evident, can then be remedied by repeated, more insistent teaching, for which the techniques Etzel describes later in this book may well be the best choice. Another path is to teach a more generalized lesson: the skill of always inspecting every part of a stimulus until it is clear which parts are relevant or useful and which parts, if any, are not. Laura Schreibman, in Chapter 17 of this book, summarizes much of the research looking into the overselectivity that is so probable in people with autism.

Contextual Control

The study of stimulus control always implies some range of time within which the control can be seen. When that time interval is short, and when the stimuli and responses are simple, easy to define, and easy to measure, we tend to use the term stimulus control. But there are studies showing a dependable relation between complex experiences early in life and subsequent behavior in adulthood; these are the so-called early experience studies (cf. Solomon & Lessac, 1968). In those studies, extensive experimental alterations were made in the environments of very young laboratory animals, and systematic changes were seen in a range of their adult behavior.

It is problematic to label such studies as demonstrating stimulus control. When we understand why and how an early intervention causes later effects, we are likely to use the terms of that understanding. When we do not understand, we can note that the study fits the fundamental definition of stimulus control, in that an early event reliably changed a later behavior, but that the fit is a strained one. Many researchers prefer a different term, for example, *contextual control.* Contextual control is not an explanation of the observed relation; it only marks the fact that this relation is impressive and needs explanation.

Any proven relation between complex early experiences and subsequent adult behavior is impressive in three ways: (a) The early experiences imposed in such studies are typically not single stimuli; they are complex events applied over considerable periods of time. For example, they might involve a period of diverse, tender handling by humans. (b) The adult behaviors changed by those early experiences typically are not single responses; they are complex patterns of various behaviors, perhaps better called lifestyle patterns than responses. For example, the behaviors might involve a pattern of immediate, fearless attachment to humans and ready acceptance of obedience training. (c) The time between the early experience and the adult lifestyle affected by it is long. The longer that time, the greater the probability of other events entering to dilute, diminish, or reverse the effects of the prior experience. A demonstrable relation between infantile experience and subsequent adult lifestyle behaviors implies an intermediate environment remarkably free of events that can influence the subsequent behavior.

Some theorists find it troublesome to explain how an event in infancy can influence adult lifestyle. Because they conceptualize behavior as always responsive to its immediate environment, they need to postulate a chain of causal events connecting the early experience to the adult behavior. They may suppose the early events somehow make the organism insensitive to much that happens subsequently. Perhaps the early experience creates patterns of self-control that amount to self-insulation from much of what happens later or that transform much of what happens later into experiences similar to what has already happened (cf. Baer, 1982; but note that this kind of analysis is not unlike the speculative account found in Skinner's *Verbal Behavior,* 1957). Alternatively, perhaps the early experience creates biochemical, neurophysiological changes that are similarly insensitive to subsequent environmental influences.

Contextual control and stimulus control are labels for reliable prior-subsequent relations that we cannot yet explain yet try to explain. Prior-subsequent relations that we *can* explain are labeled *structural, conditioned-stimulus control, discriminative-stimulus control, conditional control, instructional control,* or *stimulus equivalence;* those we cannot explain are labeled *contextual control* or *stimulus control.*

These are terms that not only index ignorance, but also provide an event of great value to science: Properly used, these terms do nothing but invite analysis of important cases. Analysis is always a value in science. Perhaps the more important underlying fact is that reliable relations between a prior stimulus and a subsequent response are ubiquitous in any study of behavior, even studies driven by reliance on consequence contingencies as the most fundamental level of explanation.

An interesting challenge is to ask any curious audience for examples of behavior that are not subject to stimulus or contextual control: Very few examples are nominated, even by sophisticated audiences, and the few that are suggested often prove specious on more careful examination. A related challenge is to ask that audience for examples of undiscriminated operants: behaviors whose consequences are the same in every possible circumstance and at all possible times. Few or none survive searching examination, even if the requirement is to specify only testable hypotheses. A third challenge is to ask that same audience to name relations between "simple" events, that is, between events that are not themselves interactions. A fourth challenge is to ask how much of applied behavior analysis is only a problem in behavior change and how much is, instead, a problem of changing not the behavior but only when and where it occurs. The ubiquity of the latter circumstance shows why stimulus control, or contextual control, not only is a growing concern in application, but almost surely will quickly become its dominant concern.

References

Baer, D. M. (1982). Applied behavior analysis. In G. T. Wilson and C. M. Franks (Eds.), *Contemporary behavior therapy* (pp. 277–309). New York: Guilford Press.

Catania, A. C. (1984). *Learning* (2nd ed.). Englewood Cliffs, NJ: Prentice-Hall.

Dinsmoor, J. A. (1995a). Stimulus control: Part I. *The Behavior Analyst, 18,* 51–68.

Dinsmoor, J. A. (1995b). Stimulus control: Part II. *The Behavior Analyst, 18,* 253–269.

Donohoe, J. W. (1996). On the relation between behavior analysis and biology. *The Behavior Analyst, 19,* 71–75.

Lovaas, O. I., Schreibman, L., Koegel, R. L., & Rehm, R. (1971). Selective responding by autistic children to multiple sensory input. *Journal of Abnormal Psychology, 77,* 211–222.

Milgram, S. (1963). Behavioral study of obedience. *Journal of Abnormal and Social Psychology, 67,* 371–378.

Premack, D. (1971). A functional analysis of language. *Journal of the Experimental Analysis of Behavior, 14,* 107–125.

Reese, H. W. (1996). How is physiology relevant to behavior analysis? *The Behavior Analyst, 19,* 61–70.

Sidman, M. (1994). *Equivalence relations and behavior: A research story.* Boston: Authors Cooperative.

Skinner, B. F. (1957). *Verbal behavior.* New York: Appleton-Century-Crofts.

Solomon, R. L., & Lessac, M. S. (1968). A control group design for experimental studies of developmental process. *Psychological Bulletin, 70*(3), 139–150.

3

The Context of Stimulus Control in Behavior Analysis

Martha Peláez-Nogueras and Jacob L. Gewirtz

Some behavior researchers are no longer satisfied that the study of simple cause-and-effect relationships between objectively observable dependent and independent variables is sufficient for understanding behavior development. When the putative controlling variables are kept constant, prediction often is very good. But most of the time we do not know the proximate controlling variables, much less have the ability to keep them constant. There has been increasing evidence that the effectiveness and function of a stimulus in controlling an individual's behavior (by evoking or reinforcing it) depend on the contextual interacting variables, including the current and historical, the organismic-biological, and the environmental-ecological.

Linear Causality Versus Interactionism

The typical view of causality in mother-child studies, particularly in controlled laboratory experiments, has been linear. We have been interested in determining whether the behavior of the mother is a proximal cause of the child's behavior (see Gewirtz & Peláez-Nogueras, 1992b, for a review of operant studies in infancy). At other times, we have asked whether the behavior of the child is a proximal cause of the mother's behavior (Gewirtz & Boyd, 1977). Now we analyze the behavior of the mother and the behavior of the child, not only as concurrent influences on each other, but also as functions of the context in which these behaviors are embedded (e.g., Peláez-Nogueras, 1989). Linear causality models (Rapoport, 1968) and traditional research methods have defined causality in terms of a linear relationship between antecedent stimuli, behavior, and consequent events. A more accurate understanding requires an analysis of the interdependence between this three-term contingency and the interrelated contextual variables participating. This type of analysis presents a major challenge because the various contextual variables involved can create multiple patterns of functional relations in the antecedent, discriminative, and reinforcing stimuli operating. The traditional methods in basic and applied research ordinarily do not take these multiple interrelated influences into account.

This is not an argument against laboratory or experimental research. Perhaps the most reliable knowledge resulting from any study is an experimental demonstration of cause and effect. We have conducted a great deal of basic research in the laboratory controlling for the behavior of mothers and their infants in contrived settings, and we know this type of research is fruitful, although it has limitations.

Our argument is against noncontextual accounts of human behavior. When we control for initial or boundary environmental or biological conditions and demonstrate that some variable causes changes in some behavior, our understanding of behavior development remains incomplete. The cause of the behavior change observed depends on the multiple interacting variables involved. Our goal should be to expand behavior-analytic methods by moving into both descriptive and functional analyses of the contextual determinants of behavior.

Stimulus Function Derives from Its Context

Morris (1988) has emphasized that "the function of behavior emerges from an ever-changing context" (p. 309). To understand behavior, its function (i.e., meaning or purpose) must be known. To attain this knowledge, the organization of interrelated stimuli and responses in context must be discovered (Kantor, 1933; Morris, 1992; Skinner, 1931, 1935). In addition to altering the efficacy of discriminative and reinforcing stimuli, therefore, the contextual variables also determine the functionality (and directionality) of stimulus effects (e.g., whether a stimulus would function as a positive reinforcer or punitive event). Hence, contextual variables not only inflect behavior and the various antecedent and concurrent variables affecting it, but also affect the interplay between reciprocal interactions among stimuli and response functions in context. Because they interact reciprocally with behavior, these variables can be seen to alter the functional relations within the three-term contingency. Perhaps this is one reason many behavior scientists are analyzing the three-term contingency in interaction with context. Indeed, the probability of behavior change denoting learning at any given moment, even within a narrow segment of the life span, may vary as a function of diverse contextual conditions. Numerous researchers have dealt with these variables under different headings: "third variables" (Skinner, 1931), "setting factors" (Kantor, 1946), "setting events" (Bijou, 1996; Bijou & Baer, 1978), "state" and "potentiating" variables (Goldiamond & Dyrud, 1967), "contextual determinants" (Gewirtz, 1972; Morris, 1988), and "establishing operations" (Michael, 1982, 1993).

Rather than held constant, the historical and current context should be subjected to experimental analysis (Morris, 1988, 1992). Knowledge of species-typic boundaries and preparedness in biological structure-vulnerability and behavioral function, as well as of individual-typic boundaries and preparedness in biological and behavioral form and function, is fundamental for completely analytic research.

The structure of the current context involves the biological organism (i.e., the child's anatomy and physiology), the environment (physical ecology), and the changes and variability in both. The function of the current context can potentiate or actualize the functions of stimuli and responses. The function of contextual variables for stimuli and responses involves the analysis of variables such as deprivation, illness, fatigue, drug effects, and history of reinforcement, among many others.

Controlling for Initial Boundary Conditions

Behavior analysts, whenever possible, try to ensure that the potential sources of variability are kept constant. For some, initial boundary factors or conditions (e.g., level of deprivation, reinforcement history) are not cited as components of the laws of behavior (e.g., reinforcement); they only provide the context for interpretation of those laws. Marr (1993a) said that "initial and boundary factors define and set the limits under which a given law will apply . . . they provide a frame of reference to assess those laws" (p. 62). This position may overrule the dynamic role of these variables as interacting variables.

Contextual variables are not restricted to static boundary or initial conditions. They are "interactants," to borrow a term from Oyama (1985). We use the term *contextual interactants* to stand generically for all developmentally relevant factors, rather than other terms such as "setting factors," "setting events," "establishing operations," "potentiating variables," and "third variables," because it has not always been clear what these other terms were intended to encompass. Even so, we should be cautious, because all such terms may carry considerable explanatory burden in an interpretive account (Marr, 1993a). For this reason, we restrict the use of the term contextual interactants to the identities of fundamental classes of variables that interact with the behavior of the organism and with the discriminative and reinforcing contingencies that control it.

Our view of context is not limited to conditions that facilitate or constrain the efficacy of reinforcing stimuli or to momentary effects. Contextual interactants produce relatively stable behavioral changes as a result of their reciprocal interaction with the organism and with the contingencies affecting its behavior. These variables are not static; they are continuously interacting with the organism's behavior as well as with other environmental variables.

In the last decade, new behavioral principles have emerged that describe the role of contextual stimuli in emergent behavior: for example, Sidman's (1986) work on stimulus equivalence and emergent verbal classes, and Hayes's (1991) relational-frames theory. It is conceivable that these new principles can be integrated effectively into the system of principles that compose behavior-analytic theory (Shull & Lawrence, 1993, p. 243).

Expanding Behavior-Analytic Methods

We see an overriding problem in traditional behavior-analytic research. In the experimental analysis of animal behavior, the typical procedure has been to consider

the initial contextual conditions (e.g., food deprivation, animal's history of reinforcement) as a potential source of behavior variation and to hold these conditions constant. In doing so, the researcher has assumed the removal of effects of
these boundary conditions from the contingency manipulations, thereby con-
straining behavior variability. Today, however, behavior analysts can consider
chaotic systems (Marr, in press). A *chaotic system* is defined as one that shows sensitivity to initial boundary conditions. That is, any uncertainty in the initial state
of the given system, no matter how small, will lead to rapidly growing errors in
any effort to predict future behavior. Behavior is sensitive to any minimal change
in initial conditions. In human behavior development, it is precisely the multidirectionality of behavior and its variability, within and between individuals, that is
of most interest. Behavior that shows stability may be easy to predict, but behavior without variability often cannot be well understood.

Context in the Study of Dyadic Interactions

If contextual determinants of stimulus function are to be investigated, some departures from the traditional methods may be necessary. Wahler and Fox (1981)
have proposed departures centered on at least three features: (a) the measurement
unit (global entities monitored through molar units of measurement), (b) the
temporal relationships among the unit of study, and (c) modes of analysis other
than experimental. Their research moves toward conceptual and methodological
expansion in the study of contextual variables in applied behavior analysis.

For the behavior-analytic researchers studying human dyads (pairs), it is ax-
iomatic that a response of the first of two actors that routinely follows a recurring
response of the second actor can constitute a reinforcement contingency for the
second actor's response if that response increases systematically in rate. One feature of the dyadic interaction is the potential bidirectionality of reinforcement effects: Each actor's behavior is influenced by the behavior of the other. However, a
problem arises in the study of spontaneous dyadic interactions: In the parent-
infant case, for instance, the identity and topography of response elements of the
set of turn-taking responses (e.g., smiles, touches, vocalizations, turning away) of
each member of the dyad can change at every turn in the series. For this reason,
behavior-analytic researchers studying the effects of reinforcement contingencies
on behavior preferred, until recently, to study the flow of influence in such interaction sequences in experimentally contrived settings, where no manipulation of
the contextual variables was systematically implemented and tested.

In mother-infant dyadic interactions, therefore, the turn-taking response of
one dyad member (typically the mother) was controlled or manipulated, whereas
the infant's response that provides the dependent variable was left free to vary
(e.g., Gewirtz & Peláez-Nogueras, 1991, 1992a; Peláez-Nogueras, 1989; 1992;
Peláez-Nogueras, Field, Hossain, & Pickens, 1996; Peláez-Nogueras, Gewirtz, et
al., 1996; Poulson, 1983). Infant-mother interactions also can be analyzed in

natural interaction settings without resorting to a limiting experimental procedure as in the studies cited. For example, the behavior analyst may record the behavior-unit elements of each of the two interactors in sequence and then search for conditional relations between adult behavior elements at different turn positions (sequential lags) for each infant behavior of interest (e.g., Haupt & Gewirtz, 1968; Patterson & Moore, 1979). By observing the conditional probabilities, the researcher can examine the impact of presumptive reinforcement contingencies for each infant target response under ecologically valid circumstances, while taking contextual variables into consideration.

There are several models for studying multiple interactions. For instance, contingency frequency analysis is a data-analytic model that attempts to analyze patterns of multiple interactions in causal fields (von Eye, 1990). The lag-sequential model analyzes the contingency and cyclicity in behavior interaction (Sackett, 1979). These tools for identifying *functional* relations among large numbers of responses in interaction pose difficult problems, however. These methods are not optimally conducive to translating the contingencies implied into reinforcement effects; this is because at every turn in the interaction sequence, a dyad member can emit different behavior combinations; different numbers of responses can occur concurrently; and a particular dyad member's behavior might occur intermittently or infrequently. The behavior-analytic researcher therefore may have difficulty isolating the functional relations involved. In the past, these complications led many behavior researchers, like ourselves, to study the flow of influence in two-way parent-infant interaction in experimentally contrived settings, in which the responses of one member of the dyad are controlled.

Kantor (1924) originally distinguished between organismic and environmental setting factors and placed "immediacy" as a temporal restriction on the effects of setting factors. Morris (1992), however, emphasized that the distinction between historical and current context is necessary and that *context* should not be defined temporally or structurally. Rather, he suggested a functional distinction between current and historical context based on effects: "The historical context established what behavior may occur, as a disposition, whereas the current context enables what behaviors can occur and, if it can occur . . . whether the functional relations will be actualized" (p. 7).

A taxonomy of current and historical, phylogenetic and ontogenetic, and biological-organismic and environmental-ecological contextual variables, in terms of form and function of context, has been outlined in detail by Morris (1992; Morris & Midgley, 1990). Earlier researchers have provided a classification of contextual qualifiers (Gewirtz, 1972), setting events (Bijou, 1996; Bijou & Baer, 1961), and establishing operations (Michael, 1982). In what follows, we elaborate on these contextual taxonomies and highlight several studies, mainly from the infancy literature, that may illustrate the function of the contextual variables.

Some Research Examples with Infant Learning

In early intervention programs for infants of depressed mothers, the infants' nursery teachers were trained to promote positive interactions between the mothers and their infants (Peláez-Nogueras, Field, Cigales, Gonzalez, & Clasky, 1994). Depressed mothers who were typically unresponsive to their infants' cues were trained, for instance, to use an attention-getting procedure and to elicit (or evoke) and respond contingently to their infants' initiations of particular behaviors. On the other hand, depressed mothers who showed an intrusive overstimulating behavior pattern were trained to decrease the amount and degree of stimulation and the contingencies they provided their infants through imitation (Malphurs et al., in press).

Mothers learned to regulate their own behavior and also detect the behavioral cues that their infant emitted during the interaction. One such cue for the mother was the infant's state on the arousal dimension (Odom & Haring, 1994), ranging from deep sleep at the low end, active alert in the middle, to high arousal at the high end, as assessed by the Carolina Record of Individual Behavior or the Brazelton Neonatal Behavior Assessment (Brazelton, 1973). If a mother were to initiate an action when the infant was at either end of the arousal continuum, it would be unlikely that the infant would respond positively. A mother can readily detect these states following training. Hence, the infant's state of arousal is an intrachild variable denoted by the infant's overt actions that set the context for the next interaction. More important, the infant's state of arousal may change during the interaction; in that case, the mother adjusts the quality, timing, and intensity of the signaling and reinforcing stimulation provided. The interaction is a dynamic, ever-changing process, as it is in real-life settings.

Our main point is that earlier experience is a contextual interactant that determines stimulus efficacy on later operant learning. This point can be illustrated by the work of DeCasper and associates, who demonstrated the impact of systematic prenatal auditory exposure on postnatal operant conditioning (e.g., DeCasper & Prescott, 1984; DeCasper & Sigafoos, 1983; DeCasper & Spence, 1986). Similar work in the area of memory and remembering has been done by Rovee-Collier and associates (e.g., Rovee-Collier, Griesler, & Earley, 1985). In the DeCasper studies, for instance, human newborns exhibited increased nonnutritive sucking to produce the acoustic properties of a speech passage their mothers had recited repeatedly during the last trimester of gestation, compared to a passage their mothers had not recited: they preferred the maternal passage (DeCasper & Spence, 1986). Also, the maternal voice, to which the fetus was exposed during gestation, was found to function as a more effective reinforcer for the newborn (as evidenced by high sucking response rates) than a stranger's voice to which the infant was never exposed (Spence & DeCasper, 1987). These studies indicate that in-utero auditory experience can affect postnatal behavior and learning in human neonates.

In the area of infant socioemotional development, infant social referencing in ambiguous contexts (i.e., infant behaviors being cued by maternal facial expressions) and subsequent behavior can result from operant learning generated by positive and aversive contingencies for differentially cued infant behavior in those ambiguous contexts. We (Gewirtz & Peláez-Nogueras, 1992a) showed that maternal facial response cues need not be limited to those providing affective or emotional information to their infants, such as those of joy and fear, as proposed by Campos (1983). Nine-month-old infants learned to evaluate nonsensical, originally arbitrary, maternal expressions. The results of that study suggested that the extent to which an infant turns to search its mother's face for discriminative expressive cues in contexts of uncertainty depends on success in obtaining such information, its validity, and its usefulness in such a context.

Two experiments conducted in our laboratory to study mother-infant attachment (Gewirtz & Peláez-Nogueras, 1991; Peláez-Nogueras, 1989) demonstrated that infant protests can come under the close control of discriminative stimuli and reinforcement contingencies generated by a mother's behaviors during her departures and brief separations from her child. By changing the cues and contingencies provided by the mother in the two different sequential contexts (departure and separation), we were able to demonstrate learned discriminations by showing that infant protests were conditioned to contextual variables in addition to maternal cues and contingencies.

The infants learned to respond differentially between the contexts of maternal departures and maternal separations. That is, in one condition their protests were conditioned during their mothers' departures, and they learned behavior alternatives to protesting immediately after the separation occurred. In the second condition, the infants learned the inverse relation of protests to context, that is, to play with their toys during maternal departures and not to protest to her "goodbye" cues, but to protest immediately after she left the room (separations). Those two conditions showed that such infant protests can be differentially shaped by patterns of contingent maternal cues and contingencies in two distinct settings, and they provide evidence for the conditioned basis of the separation protests that, in the developmental literature, have served as indices of attachment for Schaffer and Emerson (1964), to denote security or insecurity of "attachment" for Ainsworth and Wittig (1969), and to denote "separation anxiety" for Kagan, Kearsley, and Zelazo (1978).

A behavior-analytic approach to development calls for an analysis of stimulus structure and functions, response structure and functions, their interchange at a particular moment, and the sequences of such interactions across successive moments. Behavior analysts should be interested not only in the principles responsible for the changes observed in behavior, but also in the different directions, speeds, and contingency arrangements that result from the behavior-environment interchanges as well as in determining how the contextual variables alter these interactions. The operant learning paradigm provides a valuable model for the study of infant (indeed, all human) development, if only to determine which behavior change denoting development could, and which could not, be susceptible to learning operations. Learning operations, therefore, can focus those contextual-environmental factors that can inflect the course of human development.

Contextual Interactants Can Change Stimulus Function

There remains an empirical question at successive developmental points: Which of the myriad potential stimuli function as discriminative stimuli for behavior? Over the years, research has proceeded most fruitfully using the definition of *discriminative stimulus* within the frame of the three-term contingency. Problems arise, however, when discriminative stimuli are not identified as stimuli or related to particular responses in specific contexts. This possibility has led to publication of lists of discriminative stimuli in the literature, with the implication that any of the events is likely to function as a discriminative stimulus for any behavior unit (response) in any context. But the operant-learning paradigm has a clear corollary: A stimulus that functions as a discriminative stimulus for a particular response of an individual in a given context need not function as a discriminative stimulus for a different response in the same context, for the same response in a different context, or for the same response of a different individual in the same or a different context. An organism's responses are functionally related to the controlling stimuli, and no comprehensive empirical account of behavior and its development can be attained if the relations among stimuli, responses, and contextual variables are not delineated.

As the infant's repertoire increases and becomes more complex (owing to maturational-organismic processes and changes in socialization practices), some of these potential discriminative and reinforcing stimuli may drop out and be superseded by others, or their relative ability to function as reinforcers may change. The nature of the event patterns constituting the discriminative and reinforcing properties of certain stimuli changes as the infant physically matures and moves from one capacity level to a higher one. For example, the social (and very likely, conditioned) stimulus of attention produced by the parent may be superseded in salience by that of verbal approval provided by parents for successively more complex performances. This change occurs in restricted settings in which the parent's cues (e.g., smiles) signal the delivery of most of the array of important reinforcing stimuli for the child. A developmental analysis of infant behavior, for example, would examine changes in the efficacy of discriminative and reinforcing stimuli for diverse infant behaviors, considering changes in the infant's receptor and effector capacities caused by early neonatal stimulus-response interactions.

A New Stage of Behavior Analysis

We have noted that, in the behavior analysis of development, changes in the dependent variable (e.g., response frequency) may be difficult to understand outside the network of contextual interactants. In the past, several behavior theorists have recognized that the reinforcement relationship is contextually determined (e.g., Bijou & Baer, 1978; Gewirtz, 1972; Kantor, 1933; Michael, 1982; Morris, 1988; Skinner, 1938). Not until recent years have researchers begun to develop explicit programs of research to demonstrate the effectiveness of a contextualistic approach to behavior development (see Morris & Midgley, 1990, for a review of such research programs).

The inherent contextualism of behavior analysis can be identified in various research programs in basic and applied research. Some recent work has improved our principle-based understanding of contextual interactants with behavior, thereby moving behavior analysis beyond the mere analysis of the components of Skinner's three-term contingency. Today, researchers are interested in more than controlling Skinner's "third variables" (or initial-boundary conditions like food deprivation). They are, in addition, investigating the transactional and dynamic nature of those relationships (e.g., Keehn, 1980).

New approaches and research methods have revealed previously unsuspected effects of manipulating context. For instance, Wanchisen and Tatham (1991) exemplified how studies of historical effects can lend insight into human-nonhuman differences and similarities. They noted that after a particular schedule history, the subsequent fixed-interval behavior patterns of nonhumans were strikingly similar to those of humans. If a particular history can be "the great equalizer," these researchers argued, then perhaps a better way to compare human and nonhuman behavior on schedules of reinforcement is through providing similar and different experimental histories before introducing the target contingency. In cases of similar experimental histories, any behavioral discrepancies in performance noted on the targeted contingency could be explored more fully instead of being attributed to humans' extralaboratory histories. The studies by Wanchisen suggest that historical context is an important contextual determinant of behavior and learning.

New principles are emerging that describe the various effects of contextual stimuli as a result of their participation in simple and higher order contingencies. In some cases, the new principles can be integrated effectively into the system of principles that compose behavior-analytic theory, for example, stimulus equivalence (e.g., Sidman, 1986), functional equivalence (e.g., Dougher & Markham, 1994), and relational-frame theory (Hayes, 1991). Increasingly, behavior analysts are interested in constructing a conceptual taxonomy of environmental events that could affect the behavior to be modified (e.g., Schlinger & Blakely, 1994) and the motivational functions of stimuli (Michael, 1991).

In the area of verbal behavior, Dougher (1993) proposed the use of hermeneutic, or interpretive, research methods in the contextualistic analysis of verbal interactions. Unlike hermeneutics advocates, however, he observed the following:

> Contextualism does not and should not avoid experimentation as a method. . . . From a contextualistic perspective, experiments are not qualitatively different from naturalistic investigations; they differ only in terms of their degree of complexity.

The pragmatic approach is to use experiments when they are useful and naturalistic/interpretive approaches when they are useful. . . . If one is interested in verbal behavior as it occurs in interpersonal settings, interpretive methods seem to be the way to go. (p. 218)

To behavior analysts who rely only on experimentation to understand behavior, the results of interpretive methods might seem speculative and subjective. However, knowledge obtained from experimentation is no different from any other knowledge; results from experimental methods require as much interpretation as any other kind of data (Dougher, 1993). Whether interpretive, narrative, or descriptive, new research techniques that focus on understanding the relation between behavior and its contexts seem consistent and could be used within the field of behavior analysis. Descriptive and interpretive methods allow researchers to identify variables that predict behavior.

Conclusion

The main assumption underlying the present chapter has been that behavior change does not depend solely or straightforwardly on the standard behavioral concepts and principles (e.g., reinforcement, stimulus control) and operations (e.g., reinforcing and evoking stimuli). We emphasized that both contingencies and contextual interactants (historical and concurrent) play primary roles in the prediction, control, and understanding of behavior change. Consequently, the probability of an individual's learning at a given developmental point varies not only as a function of reinforcement (or punishment), but also as a function of the historical and contemporaneous contextual variables interacting.

The study of the contextual interactants may help behavior analysts interested in human development to explain the multidirectionality of behavior development, intraindividual variability, and interindividual differences. Moreover, identifying and, when possible, manipulating these variables are indispensable for a proper analysis of the effects of stimulus control on behavior change. By identifying these variables in descriptive analyses, including them in functional analyses (by controlling reinforcing contingencies and manipulating context), or conducting frequency analyses, sequential analyses, or any other method of analysis, researchers may be better able to understand and predict behavior change and to explain behavior variability.

Furthermore, we may work more successfully with existing data and generate new information about human behavior that could lead us to a greater understanding of human behavior development than has been achieved thus far. Perhaps the growth that has taken place in behavior analysis within the last decade suggests that behavior-analytic theory is undergoing a paradigm shift. It may be moving to a new stage, in which adventurous researchers wish to contribute toward solving everyday practical problems and toward a greater understanding of human interactions.

References

Ainsworth, M. D. S., & Wittig, B. A. (1969). Attachment and exploratory behavior of one-year-olds in a strange situation. In B. M. Foss (Ed.), *Determinants of infant behaviour, IV* (pp. 233–253). London: Methuen.

Baer, D. M. (1993). On Morris's mechanisms. *The Behavior Analyst, 16,* 45–46.

Bijou, S. W. (1996). The role of setting factors in the behavior analysis of development. In E. Ribes & S. W. Bijou (Eds.), *Recent approaches to behavioral development.* Reno, NV: Context Press.

Bijou, S. W., & Baer, D. M. (1978). *Behavior analysis of child development.* Englewood Cliffs, NJ: Prentice-Hall.

Brazelton, T. B. (1973). *Clinics in developmental medicine: Neonatal behavioral assessment scale.* Philadelphia: Lippincott.

Campos, J. J. (1983). The importance of affective communication in social referencing: A commentary on Feinman. *Merrill-Palmer Quarterly, 29,* 83–87.

DeCasper, A. J., & Fifer, W. P. (1980). Of human bonding: Newborns prefer their mothers' voices. *Science, 208,* 1174–1176.

DeCasper, A. J., & Prescott, P. A. (1984). Human newborns' perception of male voices: Preference, discrimination, and reinforcing value. *Developmental Psychobiology, 17,* 481–491.

DeCasper, A. J., & Spence, M. J. (1986). Prenatal maternal speech influences newborns' perception of speech sounds. *Infant Behavior and Development, 9,* 133–150.

Dougher, M. J. (1993). Interpretive and hermeneutic research methods in the contextualistic analysis of verbal behavior. In S. Hayes, L. Hayes, H. Reese, & T. Sarbin (Eds.), *Varieties of scientific contextualism* (pp. 211–221). Reno, NV: Context Press.

Etzel, B. C. (1996). The development of conceptual behavior: Hierarchies of elements in learning complex visual-auditory stimuli. In E. Ribes & S. W. Bijou (Eds.), *Recent approaches to behavioral development.* Reno, NV: Context Press.

Gewirtz, J. L. (1972). Some contextual determinants of stimulus potency. In R. D. Parke (Ed.), *Recent trends in social-learning theory* (pp. 7–33). New York: Academic Press.

Gewirtz, J. L., & Boyd, E. F. (1977). Experiments on mother infant interaction underlying mutual attachment acquisition: The infant conditions the mother. In T. Alloway, P. Plines, & L. K. Krames (Eds.), *Advances in the study of communication and affect: Vol. 3. Attachment behavior* (pp. 109–143). New York: Plenum Press.

Gewirtz, J. L., & Peláez-Nogueras, M. (1991). The attachment metaphor and the conditioning of infant separation protests. In J. L. Gewirtz & W. M. Kurtines (Eds.), *Intersections with attachment* (pp. 123–144). Hillsdale, NJ: Erlbaum.

Gewirtz, J. L., & Peláez-Nogueras, M. (1992a). Infant social referencing as a learned process. In S. Feinman (Ed.), *Social referencing and the social construction of reality in infancy* (pp. 151–173). New York: Plenum Press.

Gewirtz J. L. & Peláez-Nogueras, M. (1992b). B. F. Skinner's legacy to human infant behavior and development. *American Psychologist, 47,* 1411–1422.

Goldiamond, I., & Dyrud, J. (1967). Behavioral analysis for psychotherapy. In J. Schlien (Ed.), *Research in psychotherapy* (Vol. 3, pp. 58–89). Washington, DC: American Psychological Association.

Haupt, E. J., & Gewirtz, J. L. (1968). Analysis of interaction sequences between a focal person and other persons by contingency tables for any data coding scheme. *Behavioral Science, 13,* 83–85.

Hayes, S. C. (1991). A relational control theory of stimulus equivalence. In L. J. Hayes & P. N. Chase (Eds.), *Dialogues on verbal behavior* (pp. 19–40). Reno, NV: Context Press.

Hayes, S. C., & Hayes, L. J. (1992). Verbal relations and the evolution of behavior analysis, *American Psychologist, 47,* 1383–1395.

Hinde, R. A. (1970). *Animal behavior: A synthesis of ethology and comparative psychology.* New York: McGraw-Hill.

Kagan, J., Kearsley, R. B., & Zelazo, P. R. (1978). *Infancy: Its resolution in human development.* Cambridge, MA: Harvard University Press.

Kantor, J. R. (1924). *Principles of psychology.* Chicago: Principia Press.

Kantor, J. R. (1933). In defense of stimulus-response psychology. *Psychological Review, 40,* 324–336.

Kantor, J. R. (1946). The aim and progress of psychology. *American Scientist, 34,* 251–263.

Keehn, J. D. (1980). Beyond an interaction model of personality: Transactionalism and the theory of reinforcement schedules. *Behaviorism, 8,* 55–65.

Keller, F. S., & Schoenfeld, W. N. (1950). *Principles of psychology.* New York: Appleton-Century-Crofts.

Koch, J. (1968). The change of conditioned orienting reaction in 5-month-old infants through phase shift of partial biorhythms. *Human Development, 11,* 124–137.

Malphurs, J., Larrain, C., Field, T., Pickens, J., Peláez-Nogueras, M., Yando, R., & Bendell, D. (in press). Altering withdrawn and intrusive interaction behaviors of depressed mothers. *Infant Mental Health Journal.*

Marr, M. J. (1993a). Contextualistic mechanism or mechanistic contextualism? The straw machine as tar baby. *The Behavior Analyst, 16,* 59–65.

Marr, M. J. (1993b). A mote in the mind's eye. *The Behavior Analyst, 16,* 251–253.

Marr, M. J. (in press). The mingled yarn. *The Behavior Analyst.*

Michael, J. (1982). Distinguishing between discriminative functions of stimuli. *Journal of Experimental Analysis of Behavior, 37,* 149–155.

Michael, J. (1991). Historical antecedents of behavior analysis. *The ABA Newsletter, 14*(2), 7–12.

Michael, J. (1993). Establishing operations. *The Behavior Analyst, 16,* 191–206.

Midgley, B. D., & Morris, E. K. (1992). Nature = f(nurture): A review of Oyama's "The ontogeny of information." *Journal of the Experimental Analysis of Behavior, 58,* 229–240.

Morris, E. K. (1988). Contextualism: The world view of behavior analysis. *Journal of Experimental Child Psychology, 46,* 289–323.

Morris, E. K. (1992). The aim, progress, and evolution of behavior analysis. *The Behavior Analyst, 15,* 3–29.

Morris, E. K. (1993a). Behavior analysis and mechanism: One is not the other. *The Behavior Analyst, 16,* 25–43.

Morris, E. K. (1993b). Mechanism and contextualism in behavior analysis: Just some observations. *The Behavior Analyst, 16,* 255–268.

Morris, E. K., & Midgley, B. D. (1990). Some historical and conceptual foundations of ecobehavioral analysis. In S. R. Schroeder (Ed.), *Ecobehavioral analysis and developmental disabilities: The twenty-first century* (pp. 1–32). New York: Springer-Verlag.

Oyama, S. (1985). *The ontogeny of information: Developmental systems and evolution.* Cambridge, England: Cambridge University Press.

Patterson, G. R., & Moore, D. (1979). Interactive patterns as units of behavior. In M. L. Lamb, S. J. Suomi, & G. R. Stephenson (Eds.), *Social interaction analysis: Methodological issues* (pp. 77–96). Madison: University of Wisconsin Press.

Peláez-Nogueras, M. (1989). *Maternal training of infant protests during departures and separations: A discrimination-learning process.* Unpublished master's thesis, Florida International University, Miami, FL.

Peláez-Nogueras, M. (1992). *Infant learning to reference maternal facial expressions of emotion.* Unpublished doctoral dissertation, Florida International University, Miami, FL.

Peláez-Nogueras, M., Field, T., Cigales, M., Gonzalez, A., & Clasky, S. (1994). Infants of depressed mothers show less "depressed" behavior with their nursery teachers. *Infant Mental Health Journal, 15,* 358–367.

Peláez-Nogueras, M., Field, T., Hossain, Z., & Pickens, J. (1996). Depressed mothers' touching increases infant positive affect and attention in still-face interactions. *Child Development, 67,* 1780–1792.

Peláez-Nogueras, M., Gewirtz, J. L., Field, T., Cigales, M., Malphurs, J., Clasky, S., & Sanchez, A. (1996). Infant preference for touch stimulation in face-to-face interactions. *Journal of Applied Developmental Psychology, 17,* 199–213.

Poulson, C. L. (1983). Differential reinforcement of other-than vocalization as a control procedure in the conditioning of infant vocalization rate. *Journal of Experimental Child Psychology, 36,* 471–489.

Rapoport, A. (1968). A philosophical view. In J. H. Milsum (Ed.), *Positive feedback* (pp. 1–8). Oxford, England: Pergamon Press.

Rovee-Collier, C. K., Griesler, P. C., & Earley, L. (1985). Contextual determinants of retrieval in three-month-old infants. *Learning and Motivation, 16,* 139–157.

Sackett, G. P. (1979). The lag sequential analysis of contingency and cyclicity in behavioral interaction research. In J. D. Osofsky (Ed.), *Handbook of infant development* (pp. 623–649). New York: Wiley.

Schaffer, H. R., & Emerson, P. E. (1964). The development of social attachments in infancy. *Monographs of the Society for Research in Child Development, 29*(3, Serial No. 94).

Schlinger, H. D., & Blakely, E. Q. (1994). A descriptive taxonomy of environmental operations and its implications for behavior analysis. *The Behavior Analyst, 17,* 43–57.

Shull, R. L., & Lawrence, S. P. (1993). Is contextualism productive? *The Behavior Analyst, 16,* 241–243.

Sidman, M. (1986). Functional analysis of emergent verbal classes. In T. Thompson & M. D. Zeiler (Eds.), *Analysis and integration of behavioral units* (pp. 213–245). Hillsdale, NJ: Erlbaum.

Skinner, B. F. (1931). The concept of the reflex in the description of behavior. *Journal of General Psychology, 5,* 427–458.

Skinner, B. F. (1935). The generic nature of the concepts of stimulus and response. *Journal of General Psychology, 12,* 40–65.

Skinner, B. F. (1938). *The behavior of organisms.* New York: Appleton-Century-Crofts.

Skinner, B. F. (1945). The operational analysis of psychological terms. *Psychological Review, 52,* 270–277.

Spence, M. J., & DeCasper, A. J. (1987). Prenatal experience with low-frequency maternal-voice sounds influence neonatal perception of maternal voice samples. *Infant Behavior and Development, 10,* 133-142.

Vince, M. A. (1961). Developmental changes in learning capacity. In W. H. Thorpe & O. L. Zangwill (Eds.), *Current problems in animal behaviour* (pp. 225–247). Cambridge, England: Cambridge University Press.

von Eye, A. (1990). *Introduction to configural frequency analysis: The search for type and anti-type in classification.* Cambridge, England: Cambridge University Press.

Wahler, R., & Fox, A. (1981). Setting events in applied behavior analysis: Toward a conceptual and methodological expansion. *Journal of Applied Behavior Analysis, 14,* 327–338.

Wanchisen, B. A. (1990). Forgetting the lessons of history. *The Behavior Analyst, 13,* 31–37.

Wanchisen, B. A., & Tatham, T. A. (1991). Behavioral history: A promising challenge in explaining and controlling human operant behavior. *The Behavior Analyst, 14,* 139–144.

4

Verbal–Nonverbal Correspondence Training as a Case of Environmental Antecedents

Freddy A. Paniagua

Evolution of Correspondence Training

When people make a report about past or future behavior and then behave according to that report, the resulting relationship is termed *verbal–nonverbal correspondence* (Israel, 1978; Paniagua, 1990). In 1968, Risley and Hart provided the first convincing experimental analysis of verbal–nonverbal correspondence training during which children learned that edible reinforcers were available only if they engaged in an experimenter-selected behavior (e.g., playing with blocks) and then reported on this (nonverbal) behavior after a brief observation period during which playing was expected to occur.

Over the years, the original experimental format reported by Risley and Hart received many replications (e.g., Paniagua & Baer, 1982; Rogers-Warren & Baer, 1976). There were also transformations, in which the reinforcer was presented contingent on a promise about future behavior and on the actual behavior (Deacon & Konarski, 1987; Israel, 1973)—showing the reinforcer immediately after a promise and giving it after the promised nonverbal behavior (Israel & O'Leary, 1973; Paniagua & Baer, 1982). Another method was direct reinforcement of intermediate behaviors occurring between a promise and the corresponding behaviors (Paniagua, Stella, Holt, Baer, & Etzel, 1982). Still another was showing the reinforcer immediately after a series of intermediate behaviors and giving it after the actual promised behavior (Paniagua & Baer, 1982). The usefulness of these verbal–nonverbal correspondence training procedures has also been reported in the development of prosocial behaviors (e.g., Guevremont, Osnes, & Stokes, 1986; Paniagua, 1985; Rogers-Warren & Baer, 1976) and the reduction of problematic behaviors (e.g., Paniagua, 1992).

Explanations of Verbal–Nonverbal Correspondence Training

I comment here on four different but not exclusive levels of explanation regarding the function of verbal–nonverbal correspondence training as a case of behavioral antecedents in the reduction of problematic behaviors and the development of prosocial behaviors. These levels are termed *discriminated, generalized-maintained, intermediated, and preceding* verbal-nonverbal correspondence levels of explanations.

Discriminated

In the *discriminated* verbal-nonverbal level of explanation, the verbal component in the verbal-nonverbal chain could function as an antecedent event to which the corresponding nonverbal behavior could be conditioned (Ward & Stare, 1990). For example, in the management of children with attention deficit hyperactivity disorder (Paniagua, 1992), verbalizations about the inhibition of instances of inattention and overactivity (e.g., "I'll sit still in the classroom" in a report-do sequence or "I sat still" in a do-report sequence) may facilitate the emission of the clinician's preselected appropriate behaviors (e.g., absence of overactivity in that setting). In this explanation, the report about a future or past behavior serves as an antecedent event pointing to *both* the topography of the nonverbal behavior (i.e., the form the behavior should take to correspond with that verbalization) and the expected temporal correspondence between the two behaviors (verbal and nonverbal) for the delivery of the reinforcer. In the case of a report-do sequence, the controlling function of the verbal behavior is assessed immediately after the nonverbal behavior has been recorded; in the case of the do-report sequence the *corresponding* report (e.g., "I sat in the classroom") leads to the delivery of the reinforcer, and it serves as the antecedent event for subsequent measures of nonverbal-verbal relationships. In this case, the sequence would be do-report-do-report-do-report, and so on, across sessions or days of observation until the antecedent function of the verbalization is demonstrated (e.g., a baseline followed by several reinforced do-report sequences in a multiple-baseline design across two participants with ADHD; Paniagua, 1987).

Generalized-Maintained

In the *generalized-maintained* correspondence level of explanation (cf. Deacon & Konarski, 1987), a distinction between contingency-governed and rule-governed behavior is often made. During the introduction of verbal-nonverbal correspondence-training techniques (Paniagua, 1990), participants behave consistently with their reports about past or future behaviors to earn a reinforcer. A demonstration of verbal-nonverbal relationships during this intervention phase is a case of "contingency-governed behavior" (Barkley, 1987; Paniagua, 1987; Skinner, 1969). In this phase, participants learn that some rules or instructions given by the clinician are antecedent events for expected verbal-nonverbal relationships, rather than rules already formulated by the participant.

For example, one rule selected by the clinician would be, "You can say and do what you elect to say and do, but if you want the reinforcer you would have to say and do what I expect from you" (e.g., Paniagua, 1990; Risley & Hart, 1968). One rule in which the verbal-nonverbal relationship is selected by the participant would be, "If you say that you want to do X (or not to do X), then you would have to do it (or not to do it) if you want the reinforcer" (Paniagua et al., 1982). During the contingency-governed behavior phase (verbal-nonverbal relationships leading to reinforcement), these rules are affected by the same contingency of reinforcement that controls the verbal-nonverbal correspondence relationships. Eventually, these rules take the form of verbalizations mediating nonverbal behaviors (Stokes & Baer, 1977) during the generalization and maintenance phases, when direct reinforcement of verbal-nonverbal relationships is not programmed. When this occurs, the resulting process is termed *rule-governed behavior*. Rules involving discriminated verbal-nonverbal correspondences are now transformed into generalized and maintained correspondence rules (e.g., Deacon & Konarski, 1987; Paniagua & Black, 1990; Ward & Stare, 1990).

Intermediated

In the *intermediated* level of explanation, behaviors that occur between a report about future behaviors and the fulfillment of this report could function as antecedent events for the occurrence of the nonverbal behavior (see Paniagua, 1990; Paniagua et al., 1982). The role of intermediate behaviors as crucial antecedent events in the development of verbal-nonverbal relationships has been investigated in four studies (Paniagua, 1978; Paniagua & Baer, 1982; Paniagua & Baer, 1985; Paniagua et al., 1982).

For example, in one study, my colleagues and I (Paniagua et al., 1982) asked children about their future behavior (e.g., painting), and each subsequent intermediate behavior leading to that reported behavior was followed by descriptive social reinforcers (e.g., "Very good, you are picking up the brushes!" if the child had chosen painting). In this example, picking up paint pots, assembling paint pots and easel, and picking up brushes and paper made "painting" more probable. The presence of other intermediate behaviors, such as opening the paint pots and placing the paper on the easel, made painting even more probable. The extension of this chain of intermediate behaviors, such as dipping a brush into an open paint pot in front of an easel with paper, made painting virtually inevitable. In this example, each intermediate behavior functioned as an antecedent event for subsequent intermediate behaviors leading to the final behavior in the chain (e.g., actual painting). In this study, the verbal-nonverbal relationship was not directly reinforced; only intermediate behaviors leading to this relationship were reinforced.

In another study, the researchers (Paniagua & Baer, 1982) compared the programming of the reinforcer contingent on a verbal-nonverbal relationship, using a report-do sequence, with the reinforcer shown after each intermediate behavior, and available only after the participant displayed the expected verbal-nonverbal relationship in a report–intermediate behaviors–do sequence. The results indicated that the second procedure led to more consistent nonverbal correspondence changes over time.

Preceding

In the *preceding* level of explanation, behaviors that precede both the verbalization and its corresponding nonverbal behavior may function as antecedent events for subsequent behaviors, in a do-report sequence. For example, in the study by Risley and Hart (1968), children's reports about past play behaviors (e.g., block play) were reinforced. Before their participation in the experimenter-selected play activity, however, participants had to ask for the activity and receive the necessary implements before their engagement in that activity (asking for blocks and receiving blocks). When a behavior is to be managed by contingencies operating only on subsequent reports about that behavior, the essential prior activities can be called *preceding behaviors*. It should be noted that these activities would function as examples of intermediate behaviors when a behavior is to be managed relative to a report about future behavior in a report-do sequence. Labeling a behavior *preceding* versus *intermediate*, therefore, depends on the position of this particular behavior in the verbal-nonverbal chain. In prior studies, comparative analyses involving the function of preceding behaviors and intermediate behaviors as antecedent events in controlling verbal-nonverbal relationships have not been reported.

The function of the described antecedent events in the development of verbal-nonverbal relationships seems to point to a combination of discriminated verbal-nonverbal rules, intermediated rules, generalized and maintained correspondence rules, and preceding rules. A demonstration of the interrelation among these antecedent events in the control of verbal-nonverbal relationships has not been reported in previous studies. In general, the majority of verbal-nonverbal training studies have emphasized the discriminated verbal-nonverbal level of explanation (e.g., Paniagua & Baer, 1982); a small number of studies have emphasized the generalized and maintained level of explanation (e.g., Williams & Stokes, 1982). One study (Risley & Hart, 1968) included all levels of explanation with the exception of those that were based on the intermediate behaviors. The function of intermediate behaviors as antecedent events in controlling that correspondence has been documented in two studies (Paniagua & Baer, 1982; Paniagua et al., 1982).

The format of the experimental design required to study the interrelation among all of the preceding antecedent events in verbal-nonverbal correspondence training would include a condition in which participants (a) display behaviors, (b) make a report about future behaviors that (c) is followed by intermediate behaviors leading to the corresponding (experimenter- or participant-selected) nonverbal behavior, which (d) is followed by another report about a previous nonverbal behavior. In this format, the sequence of behaviors would include preceding behaviors–report–intermediate behaviors–nonverbal targeted behavior–report. This experimental format not only would involve (a) the programming of reinforcers contingent on different points in this chain of behaviors (see Paniagua, 1990; Paniagua & Baer, 1982), but also would require (b) an understanding of the complexity of controlling behavior through the manipulation of antecedent events as well as (c) the creativity and imagination of the experimenter: three important elements.

References

Barkley, R. A. (1987). Attention deficit-hyperactivity disorder. In E. J. Mash & R. A. Barkley (Eds.), *Treatment of childhood disorders* (pp. 39–72). New York: Guilford Press.

Deacon, J. R., & Konarski, E. A. (1987). Correspondence training: An example of rule-governed behavior. *Journal of Applied Behavior Analysis, 20,* 391–400.

Guevremont, D. C., Osnes, P. G., & Stokes, T. F. (1986). Preparation for effective self-regulation: The development of generalized verbal control. *Journal of Applied Behavior Analysis, 19,* 99–104.

Israel, A. C. (1973). Developing correspondence between verbal and nonverbal behavior: Switching sequences. *Psychological Reports, 32,* 1111–1117.

Israel, A. C. (1978). Some thoughts on correspondence between saying and doing. *Journal of Applied Behavior Analysis, 11,* 271–273.

Israel, A. C., & O'Leary, K. D. (1973). Developing correspondence between children's words and deeds. *Child Development, 44,* 575–581.

Paniagua, F. A. (1978). Efectos de las conductas intermedias sobre la correspondencia entre conducta verbal y no verbal. In S. Speller (Ed.), *Analisis de la conducta: Trabajos de investigacion en Latinoamerica* (pp. 303–321). Mexico, D. F.: Editorial Trillas.

Paniagua, F. A. (1985). Development of self-care skills and helping behaviors through correspondence training. *Journal of Behavior Therapy and Experimental Psychiatry, 16,* 237–244.

Paniagua, F. A. (1987). Management of hyperactive children through correspondence-training procedures: A preliminary study. *Behavioral Residential Treatment, 2,* 1–23.

Paniagua, F. A. (1990). A procedural analysis of correspondence training techniques. *The Behavior Analyst, 13,* 107–119.

Paniagua, F. A. (1992). Verbal-nonverbal correspondence training with ADHD children. *Behavior Modification, 16,* 226–252.

Paniagua, F. A., & Baer, D. M. (1982). The analysis of correspondence training as a chain reinforceable at any point. *Child Development, 53,* 786–798.

Paniagua, F. A., & Baer, D. M. (1985). Correspondencia entre conducta verbal y conducta no verbal: Un analisis secuencial y funcional. *Revista de Analisis del Comportamiento, 3,* 3–20.

Paniagua, F. A., & Black, S. A. (1990). Management and prevention of hyperactivity and conduct disorder in 8–10 year old boys through correspondence training procedures. *Child and Family Behavior Therapy, 12,* 23–56.

Paniagua, F. A., Stella, E. M., Holt, W. J., Baer, D. M., & Etzel, B. C. (1982). Training correspondence by reinforcing intermediate and verbal behavior. *Child and Family Behavior Therapy, 4,* 127–139.

Risley, T. R., & Hart, B. (1968). Developing correspondence between the non-verbal and verbal behavior of preschool children. *Journal of Applied Behavior Analysis, 1,* 267–281.

Rogers-Warren, A., & Baer, D. M. (1976). Correspondence between saying and doing: Teaching children to share and praise. *Journal of Applied Behavior Analysis, 9,* 335–354.

Skinner, B. F. (1969). *Contingencies of reinforcement: A theoretical approach.* Englewood Cliffs, NJ: Prentice-Hall.

Stokes, T. F., & Baer, D. M. (1977). An empirical technology of generalization. *Journal of Applied Behavior Analysis, 10,* 349–367.

Ward, W. D., & Stare, S. W. (1990). The role of verbalization in generalized correspondence. *Journal of Applied Behavior Analysis, 23,* 129–136.

Williams, J. A., & Stokes, T. F. (1982). Some parameters of correspondence training and generalized verbal control. *Journal of Applied Behavior Analysis, 4,* 11–32.

Part Two

Managing Simple but Crucial Environmental Antecedents

The six chapters of this section represent a constant interaction among principle, technique, and results. The underlying principle is that science is at its best when it can state the necessary and sufficient conditions for whatever it studies. What are the necessary and sufficient conditions for giving a particular stimulus control over a specific response? The answer is that we do not yet know.

These six chapters show that even though we do not know, we often succeed in giving a particular stimulus control over a specific response, just as we intended. We do that by placing the stimulus in the various relations to the response that our models of classical conditioning, operant conditioning, instructional control, or stimulus equivalence recommend. That does not always work, but it often works.

If it did always work, we could say those four models were sufficient conditions: At least one of them would always accomplish the desired stimulus control. Then we could ask if these four models represented the only ways to create stimulus control. If we tried many other possibilities and not one of them ever created stimulus control, we could begin to suspect that at least one of these four was necessary, as well as sufficient. We could continue suspecting that until some fifth way of achieving stimulus control was found.

The results seen so far in research and application show that these four models are powerful but not quite sufficient or necessary. These models do not always make stimulus control when they are supposed to, although they usually do, and stimulus control sometimes appears without the use of these models, although not often.

The studies presented here can be seen as ways to move our models ever closer to sufficient. Barbara Etzel begins the section by showing that we can do much better than simply place a stimulus in the right relation to a response and its consequences and hope for the desired control: We can start with a stimulus that already has the desired control and steadily transform that stimulus into the desired one, without losing that control. We have created a new stimulus control by transferring an old stimulus control to it, and if we have done that skillfully enough, the process is seamless. At the end, the student knows something he or she did not know at the beginning, and without making errors in the process.

We can say that Etzel's transformation technique *makes* stimulus control, rather than merely creating conditions in which it can happen; it is an active rather than a passive technique, and because of that, it fairly deserves the label "revolutionary." The previous motto of the operant-discrimination model had been, "Put the stimulus in the right place and hope for control"; Etzel's technique changed that to, "Start with control and transform the new stimulus into it." That is much closer to "sufficient."

It is difficult to describe in words the power of Etzel's technique; the reader will do much better to look at her examples to appreciate the near-inevitability of their success. Those looks may also tell the reader that the success of this technique still relies on some degree of art in stimulus design and transformation. There is more to this power than these words alone can convey.

L. L. A. McCartney and J. M. LeBlanc try to clarify whether that stimulus-transformation process works so well because of its technique of seamless transformation or because it typically, often necessarily, begins with stimuli that already have well-established meanings for the student. It turns out that meaning is neither irrelevant nor useless, but stimulus transformation—"stimulus shaping"—still emerges as a crucial factor in this closer approach to "sufficient."

A frequent interpretation of the power of stimulus shaping is that it recruits and holds the student's attention to the relevant stimuli. The concept of attention surfaces often in interpretations of why new-concept teaching sometimes fails. Too often, it is a purely hypothetical event that explains away failure without teaching us how to avoid it. Stephen Schroeder offers five studies that ask whether objectively measured eye fixation is the "attending" behavior crucial to achieving stimulus control. Studies like these make a hypothetical mechanism into a real, experimentable behavior; they raise us above lame explanations of our failures into the active programming of success: another closer approximation of "sufficient."

These kinds of studies will create a more powerful concept-teaching technology. But that will not be of much value if we do not understand what concepts are best to teach and at what times in a child's development, which requires knowing which ones are fundamental to what other ones. Even more important, we need to understand the entirety of skills and their correct stimulus controls that justify using the term *concept*. Claire Poulson, John Brown, and Ann Brown exemplify that kind of analysis. They take the truly fundamental concept of "identity" and show its logical structure by clarifying what stimuli must control what responses before we can fairly conclude that we have taught a *concept* named *identity*.

Two more studies exemplify the model of stimulus equivalence in achieving the range of stimulus control that might justify the claim that a concept of identity-as-equivalence has been taught. Harry Mackay, Barbara Kotlarchyk, and Robert Stromer target the teaching of a generalized concept of sequence across a range of exemplars; they find the teaching procedures characteristic of stimulus equivalence sufficient for that outcome. Thereby, they remind us of the often-debated possibility that the stimulus-equivalence model is not just another way to achieve stimulus control but may underlie and explain many other ways of doing so, especially in the realm of intellectual skills. It is prudent, therefore, to include a study showing a certain lack of robustness to stimulus equivalence: Svein Eikeseth and Donald Baer show that college students can be taught the few alphabet-letter relations necessary for the emergence of the many more untaught relations definitive of equivalence—but still remain more likely to be controlled by an alphabetical-order relation, when it is equally available as an answer to the questions posed, than by the stimulus-equivalence relation.

The power of the stimulus-equivalence model seems beyond doubt; its role as the fundamental model, rather than just another model capable of creating stimulus control, remains controversial. Perhaps studies like these will create some progress in resolving that controversy.

5

Environmental Approaches to the Development of Conceptual Behavior

Barbara C. Etzel

When people speak about "knowledge" and "thought," they usually mean a process in the "mind." These three terms deserve quotation marks, because none of them is real. Terms like *memory, problem solving, attention, and assimilation* (cf. Schlinger, 1995) seem meaningful to us, yet they all are only inferred, internal mental processes. They must be inferred because they cannot be directly observed or measured. They are invented to explain certain behaviors we can observe and measure, behaviors we like to call "cognitive."

The feeling of explanation is usually a good thing, but it hides a problem. That problem emerges when we decide someone is thinking poorly and needs teaching. The inference that students fail to solve problems because they do not remember, attend, or assimilate well does not tell us how to improve their problem solving, because it does not tell us how to change their memory, attention, or assimilation.

Two branches of behavioral science struggle with this problem: behavior analysis and cognitive science. Each branch shows some diversity of theory and practice within it, but each relies on strategies that are different from the strategies of the other. The clash between those strategies is a persistent theme in the following discussion of how to describe knowledge acquisition and what to do about it. There is one commonality, however: Both cognitivists and behavior analysts consider some behavior "cognitive," but they disagree on how to explain that behavior.

Behavior analysts define *cognitive behavior* in observable and measurable terms, then observe and measure it, and then try to relate it to the environment in which it occurs or has occurred in the past. In particular, they look for events in the environment that systematically precede these behaviors and ask whether those preceding events evoke these behaviors. Similarly, they look for events in the environment that systematically follow these behaviors and ask whether those consequent behaviors maintain these behaviors.

Cognitive scientists show more diversity in approaching the same problem: Almost always, they infer what internal, unobservable mental processes and structures might exist in the mind that would explain the cognitive behaviors of interest. Sometimes they suppose that the systematic relationships of cognitive behavior to the present and past environments are unimportant, simply following automatically from the nature of the mind they have invented. Sometimes they see those relationships as important, but not as explanations; instead, they ask *why* cognitive behavior relates systematically to the environment in those ways, and they invent a mind that not only explains the existence of cognitive behavior but also explains its relationships to the environment.

Schlinger (1992, 1995) noted that cognitive science has not yet developed a single, unified explanation for cognition in general but instead has inferred different explanations for different parts of it. That leaves cognitive theory largely unready for application. According to Schlinger, cognitive theory does not proceed in the manner of a natural science; it relies too heavily on inference and correlational research. By contrast, he argued, behavior analysis operates within the natural-science framework, relies heavily on experimental analysis, and relies on a unified, action-oriented theory of behavior change (cf. also Bijou, 1976; Bijou & Baer, 1961, 1965, 1967; Rosales & Baer, 1996).

These differences are most important when we must teach people better cognitive skills than they have at present. For the behavior analysts, the problem of designing a better environment has an obvious starting point: Decide what environmental events should evoke cognitive skills, and teach accordingly; decide what environmental events should maintain cognitive skills, and program them accordingly. Both of those may well be massive prescriptions, but both are immediate possibilities; we know a lot about the evocation and reinforcement of behavior. By contrast, the redesign of internal, unobservable mental processes that are supposed to explain environmental relations rather than be explained by them is intrinsically problematic.

Consider an example. A kindergarten child is not learning the cognitive skills we identify as "prereading skills." Observation shows the child is out of seat more often than in, talks during the prereading-skills lesson to other children about unrelated topics, and ignores the teacher. The teacher, trying to make the prereading-skills lesson work, often reprimands the child for being out of seat or inattentive to the lesson and sometimes explains at length to the child how important these lessons are. Defeated by consistently wrong answers, however, the teacher less and less often asks the child to name letters and letter sounds, and when the child does name them correctly, the teacher's praise is brief.

A cognitive orientation often explains that pattern of child behavior as "cognitively immature" and that pattern of teacher behavior as the natural result of being unable to teach the intended lessons. That approach prescribes waiting for "development" to make the child ready to deal with the symbolic abstractions implicit in prereading skills; when that happens, the child will be easy to teach and the teacher will not be forced into those unproductive tactics. The result may well be a recommendation that the child not enter first grade for another year.

A behavior-analytic approach would not guess about internal unreadiness. It would instead observe that the way the child's behavior relates to the current environment is a prescription for the child's not learning the skills offered. The current environmental contingencies teach the child that lengthy teacher attention is available mainly in the form of reprimands, which are gained by leaving the chair and the lesson, and by talking to other children, especially when the teacher is trying to teach the prereading skills.

Behavior analysis usually does not prescribe waiting a year but changing the environment now. During the prereading-skills lesson, the teacher should find simpler stimuli for this child: pictures the child can label. The teacher should present these often and attend to and praise the typically correct answer. The teacher should watch for moments when the child is seated and attend approvingly to most of those moments. As staying in seat and correct answers become the norm, the teacher should gradually introduce stimuli more and more relevant to prereading skills and should slowly decrease the initially high rate of attention to being in seat. What observers call attention, interest, and skill will increase; lesson time will become productive and enjoyable and remain so.

All that is much easier to sketch than to do, and if it is to succeed, it must be done well. Even so, it is eminently possible to do and do immediately, and many studies have shown that when it is well done, it is quite likely to succeed. None of it requires waiting for an internal change by the child.

This chapter illustrates many different ways to make the environment achieve the kind of behavior change we can call *conceptual development*. In the process, I often contrast the strategies of behavior analysis and cognitive science. The following five differences are especially notable:

1. Cognitive theory is thoroughly fractionated; it has different ways of explaining cognitive, social, motor, and language development, and sometimes it offers different explanations even within each area. It cannot see the acquisition of knowledge as a unitary process. Behavior analysis, by contrast, is one theory, applicable to all kinds of development, offering both explanation and immediate application (Rosales & Baer, 1996).

2. Naming invented mental structures is not pragmatic. Inferred names tend to imply a structural cause of every problem, which can make the problem seem unchangeable and prevent research from being performed that might have solved the problem. Behavior-analytic research into cognition treats any problem as a set of behaviors to be changed. It asks how the behaviors—not the structures supposedly causing those behaviors—relate to the environment or can be made to relate to the environment. That kind of question nominates experimental variations in teaching; those procedures have a chance of succeeding.

3. Correlational research never tells us unambiguously where to look for cause; thus it does not tell us what to change to solve a problem. By contrast, the experimental control of all variables that prove controllable leads directly to clear statements of cause and effect, which in turn lead to better teaching techniques. A science of knowledge acquisition that is based on teaching techniques is better than one based only on the correlations between knowledge and age, gender, class, and other demographics.

4. Research dependent on group designs makes even its age-based and other demographic explanations nothing more than norms. Norms can nominate an individual as special or not but cannot tell us what to do next. Life-insurance companies, relying on norms, can predict life span but cannot extend it. We wish to avoid a similar trap.

5. The central role of maturation in cognitive explanations discourages the study of direct environmental control; it fails to show us how to teach, both in general and for any individual.

These five differences determine (a) what questions will be asked, (b) what methods will be used to answer them, (c) how studies will be designed, and (d) what kinds of conclusions will be possible.

Behavior-Analytic Questions About Conceptual Behavior

In behavior-analytic theory, to know is to discriminate. To know something is to distinguish what it is and is not—to know to what categories it belongs or applies and does not belong or apply. The fundamental model of that process is to respond differently to one stimulus than to another; given that as a beginning, any complexity can be built on it by refining what stimuli will and will not be responded to, or responded to in what degree, or with what kind of response, and so on. The studies that follow begin with some of the simplest of discriminations—two stimuli and one kind of response—and proceed from that to complexity, analytically and experimentally.

Almost 3 decades ago, Terrace (1963), studying pigeons in a Skinner box, showed how environmental control could make their acquisition of a simple color discrimination either fast or slow. The pigeons' problem was to respond to one color and not respond to another. The study was aimed at disproving the Hull-Spence (Spence, 1936, 1937) position, which was that to teach even so simple a discrimination, it was necessary to reinforce responses to the correct color—call it S+—and not reinforce (i.e., extinguish) responses to the other color—call it S-. The necessity of a trial-and-error approach to both S+ and S- responding was the prevailing theory at the time.

But Terrace (1963) noted that there had been very little measurement of the number of responses to S- as discriminations were learned, especially in cases in which the difference between S+ and S- was a simple physical difference, like color. Terrace thought the trial-and-error method made responses to the S- more likely. Earlier studies had shown that we can decrease errors if we begin with an S+ and an S- that are much more different from each other than in the discrimination we want to teach and then, artfully and gradually, make those differences smaller (fade them). Terrace (1973) noted that many earlier researchers had already tried that tactic and succeeded (James, 1890, pp. 505–515; Lawrence, 1952; Pavlov, 1927, p. 117; Schlosberg & Solomon, 1943); somehow, the relevance of their results had been missed.

Terrace (1963) also thought that *when* S- was introduced into teaching would make a difference (as had Skinner, 1938, pp. 203–206). For example, teaching rats to press a bar to one brightness of light but not another, if done in the process of teaching the bar-press itself, yielded a quick discrimination with almost no errors made in the process. By contrast, the usual trial-and-error tactic of introducing the S- only after many responses to the S+ took much longer and produced many errors.

Terrace (1963) found that error responses to S- were not necessary to teach a simple color discrimination if the S- was introduced early in training and was at first very different from the S+ (e.g., much brighter, much longer, much larger, very different in color). That finding showed that hypothesizing "inhibition" and "excitation" was unnecessary. It is the way that time and brightness are faded (increasing the brightness of the S- and lengthening its time of presentation) and when discrimination training begins that determine how quickly a discrimination is acquired. Both are environmental variables that are easy to manage.

The important message for this chapter, however, is less the answer than the underlying question: Can environmental variables be managed to control all the behavior to all the stimuli that define the process under study? Perhaps it was good that Terrace's first subjects were rats and pigeons. Had they been humans, tradition would have attributed their different rates of learning to their intelligence; they would have been diagnosed as bright, average, or retarded, thus blaming them instead of the environmental conditions that had determined the result. The point is that environmental conditions *did* determine the result, and they did so drastically.

The proper question, then, is whether that is always true; we already know that it is often true. Because behavior analysis deals with experimentable environmental variables rather than making intraorganismic inferences to study conceptual behavior, proponents always ask that kind of question.

Behavior-Analytic Methods for Studying Conceptual Behavior

If the question is how to manage the environment to teach conceptual behavior, the student is placed in a task setting where acquisition of the desired knowledge is possible; the current level of the knowledge is measured, to see if it is indeed deficient; and if it is, the environment is varied experimentally in ways that might result in the learning of the missing skills.

Behavior-analytic studies of conceptual behavior usually consider quite specific types of environmental variables (Figure 5.1). Sidman (1978) listed some everyday English labels for presumably conceptual processes and matched them to the standard behavior-analytic functions of the four-term paradigm: S-S-R-S, or, in order, the *contextual stimulus* (the setting and its history), the *evocative and discriminative stimulus* (the problem to be solved, which, if solved, will gain rein-

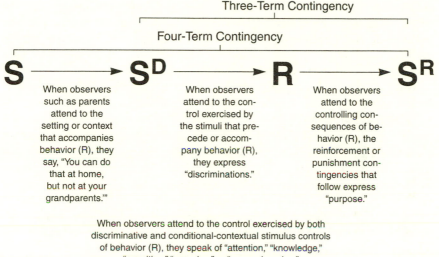

FIGURE 5.1   The Behavior-Analytic Paradigm Illustrating the Three- and Four-Term Contingencies as They Relate to Conceptual Behavior

forcement), the *response* (the solution to the problem), and the *consequent stimulus* (the reinforcer that selects, confirms, or maintains the solution).

When an audience attends to the controlling consequences of the behavior—the reinforcement or punishment contingencies (SR)—they see "purpose." When they consider the control exercised by the stimuli that immediately precede or accompany the behavior—its discriminative stimuli—they see "attention" (to the problem). When they examine the contextual stimuli—the setting—they see background "knowledge," "cognition," "meaning," and "comprehension." Sidman has warned anyone considering the reinforcer to remember that it never creates a problem's control over its solution; it only selects or confirms that this response, not some other one, is the solution to this problem. The four-term contingency is critical. Unless the culture—a parent, teacher, book, or some other agent (including nature)—presents a stimulus while an appropriate response is occurring, and unless that response is reinforced in the presence of that stimulus, the various stimulus controls that audiences call "knowledge" do not exist.

Knowledge is not just a group of responses; it is a group of responses to the stimuli defining the problem that gain the reinforcers programmed only for correct solutions to the problem. A problem's solution is correct if the agency programming reinforcement of its solution presents the reinforcer systematically enough.

How do we prove that a problem controls the response that solves it? Sidman (1978, 1979) argued that we need three conditions: (a) Teaching must already have occurred, because (b) we need to observe a number of consistent instances in which (c) the systematic relation between the problem and its solution can be distinguished from chance. We need to observe enough instances to see that the solution, and only the solution, follows the problem, and only the problem, with such consistency that the sequences cannot be coincidences.

Requiring repeated observation of that kind is a hallmark of behavior-analytic studies of conceptual development. A study by Sidman and Stoddard (1966) illustrated this argument. These researchers meant to develop procedures for low-functioning children and adults that would bring their conceptual behavior above its current levels. The problem was presented as nine keys, arranged in a three x three square matrix: a top, middle, and bottom row of three keys each. Each key was a small projection screen on which a stimulus could be displayed, except for the middle key of the middle row, which was always dark; this setup is shown in Figure 5.2. The problem to be solved was to discriminate an ellipse from a circle. An ellipse would be projected on seven of the keys and a circle on the eighth key. The problem was to touch the circle (S+) wherever it was and not any of the seven ellipses (S-); only touching the circle produced reinforcement.

The first student was an institutionalized 40-year-old microcephalic adult (with an IQ rated as 20 early in life and deteriorated since). That student could not respond differently to circles and ellipses at the beginning of the program, but he could respond to dramatic differences in brightness. Therefore, the first teaching attempt (Figure 5.3) was carried out in three stages, using his ability to discriminate brightness as a beginning.

In the first stage, a dark circle (S+) on a bright background appeared on one key. All other keys were dark. When the participant touched the circle, reinforcers were given. The illuminated circle was projected at random on one key or another as trials progressed, so that the contrast between the bright circle and the

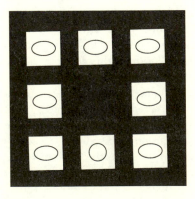

FIGURE 5.2   Sidman and Stoddard's (1966) Nine-Key Matrix. The center key was always dark and not operative. At the final criterion level, seven keys had ovals projected on them, and a circle appeared on one key.

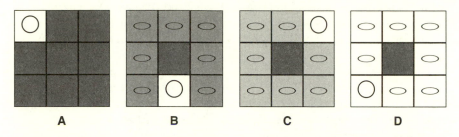

FIGURE 5.3   The First Teaching Program by Sidman and Stoddard (1966). The illustration shows widely spaced steps in fading. S+ was the circle on a bright background during Phase A. Incorrect (S-) keys were dark. As the S- keys became brighter (Phases B and C), the outline of the ellipses also increased. Phase D is at criterion with all backgrounds equally bright.

other dark keys, rather than any key position, would control responding. In the 20 trials of the second stage, the seven dark keys gradually became brighter, and as their brightness increased, initially dim ellipses (S-) began to appear on them. As these trials progressed, the contrast between the ellipses and their background increased, until all eight keys (one circle, seven ellipses) were shown at equal intensities of light, with equal contrast between the light and dark parts of each key. At that point, shape was the only difference to control the correct circle-touching response.

This program failed to teach the final shape (circle vs. ellipse) discrimination. As background brightness increased, errors emerged; what until then had been a consistent touching of the high-contrast circle rather than the low-contrast ellipses now became random touching of all eight illuminated keys. Since shape was now the only difference, the previous consistent responding must have been controlled by more than shape or other than shape. If the control had been by background intensity, that would account for loss of correct responding as the background of the ellipses became more similar to the background of the circle.

Yet that kind of control, although it would explain the loss of the prior discrimination, cannot explain why the new discrimination—control by shape alone—did not occur as background intensity became more and more difficult to use. Some kinds of control preclude our seeing new kinds of control as the first kind becomes problematic; this was not that kind of control.

The answer lies in many earlier studies: The transfer of stimulus control from an initially effective stimulus to a new one, as the initial one becomes less useful, can be made difficult in either or both of two ways: by relying on the initial stimulus too long or by making the initial stimulus too salient. The longer that reliance and the more dramatic that salience, the more difficult it is to transfer control from that stimulus. In the study by Sidman and Stoddard (1966), perhaps too many trials were allowed with background intensity in control or perhaps the initial differences in background intensity were too dramatic (salient) to allow later transfer to shape as background intensity was equalized. (In a different terminology, the background brightness had become a "blocking" stimulus: It blocked transfer of control to a new stimulus because of its longer history or greater ease of observation.)

Sidman and Stoddard (1966) concluded that they had not correctly programmed the transfer of stimulus control from background intensity to shape and revised their teaching program accordingly. The inadequacies were in their technique, not their student. They tried six program revisions for a number of students. They inserted intermediate brightness levels during background fading, reduced program length, and maximized the brightness of the ellipses earlier in the program. These changes were guided by the fact that student errors were not random but emerged at consistent places in each successive program, across a variety of students. In the fifth program, shown in Figure 5.4, brightness fading was done in two stages. The trials with the circle on a bright background (S+) and with all other keys dark were retained. The next fading procedure, however, was to fade in only the background brightness (not the ellipses) on the other seven keys (illustrations B, C, and D). Ultimately, the background brightnesses of the circle key and the seven S- keys were the same; at this point, the successful discrimination could not be controlled by those background intensities and must

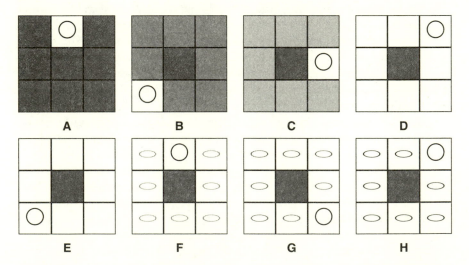

FIGURE 5.4   The Fifth Teaching Program by Sidman and Stoddard (1966). Widely spaced steps are shown. At the entry level (A), the S+ (circle on bright background) was projected on one key, and all other keys were dark. Steps B, C, and D illustrate background intensity fading on the S- keys. At D, all keys had the same intensity of backgrounds. A circle was projected only on the S+ key. Stages F through H were devoted to the simultaneous fading in the intensity of the ellipse (S-) of the remaining keys.

have been attributable to the shape (circle) being on one key versus no shape on the other keys. The second procedure then faded in the seven ellipses (the S-) on the seven previously empty, equally bright, backgrounds (illustrations F, G, and H). The differential intensity of the outline of the shapes (circle intense, ellipses dim) was available as a stimulus control during the second fading phase. But as the outlines became more similar in intensity, control would have to shift to the criterion discrimination of shape: circle from ellipses. Or it would have to disappear.

Whether or not any student used intensity during the first part of this fading program or immediately used shapes (circle vs. ellipse) as the stimulus control is not known, and it need not be known. The crucial fact is that this program revision, unlike its predecessors, showed success with many students. Two other small revisions resulted in an even more consistently successful, virtually errorless teaching program. Its students now could discriminate circles from ellipses. They knew an abstraction they had not previously known.

Consider what these studies by Terrace (1963) and Sidman and Stoddard (1966) have taught us about conceptual learning:

1. Start with S+ and S- stimuli that are different enough physically so that the student can discriminate them, even if the stimuli must be very different from those of the desired final discrimination.

2. Introduce S- immediately.

3. When starting at the student's current competency level means the teaching program will have to fade several initial dimensions to arrive at the desired final discrimination (e.g., beginning with brightness discriminations the student can do to be able eventually to teach shape discriminations the student cannot now do), fade only one dimension at a time so that an ultimately irrelevant dimension will lose its stimulus control when it should.

4. Use each student's errors to diagnose only that student's problems.

5. Consider student errors to be, in fact, teacher errors.

6. One need only analyze and control environmental stimuli, mainly the program materials, to teach conceptual skills.

These are important principles in a science of knowledge acquisition. Note that the methods that produced them (the studies by Terrace and by Sidman and Stoddard) were from typical natural science experiments; they represent the kind of experimental analysis that might have been applied by any natural scientist, even one knowing little about what would eventually be learned about knowledge acquisition. Cumulative, programmatic experimentation can build an effective science even from an initial state of ignorance. It took Sidman and Stoddard seven successive programs to teach the circle-ellipse discrimination effectively to their students, but seven is not a large number. At the end, these researchers could say a great deal more than if they had concluded after the first program that microcephalic persons with IQs under 20 cannot acquire such discriminations. That would have been unfortunate for the students.

The Design of Behavior-Analytic Conceptual Studies

People vary in their skills and knowledge, partly because they vary in how they have been taught, but also partly because they vary in how quickly, how thoroughly, and how well they acquire what they are taught. Researchers in both behavior analysis and cognitive science see the existence of these individual differences as an important problem to understand, but they approach that understanding in different ways. Proponents of cognitive analysis most often describe an individual difference by referring it to the structures that are inferred to characterize minds in general: It is explained as a failure of retrieval from long-term memory, an unreadiness to assimilate, an absence of the conservation schema, and so on. These are not statements of cause, however; they are redescriptions in terms of preexisting classifications. Behavior analysts similarly are likely not to know the past causes of any individual difference; their strategy is to create a present cause for the remediation of this difference, if it needs remediation, or the intensification of this difference, if it needs intensification, or the maintenance of this difference, if it needs maintenance. This is done through the design of an individual-analysis teaching study.

In the usual individual-analysis teaching design, students serve as their own controls: Experimentally created changes in their behavior are validated as real changes by comparing them to the prior and subsequent behavior of the student rather than to the behavior of some comparison group. First, students are assessed for their current skills and knowledge. Then they are taught appropriately and are steadily reassessed to see if the skills and knowledge targeted by that teaching are changing and are changing enough. Sometimes teaching is interrupted to see if the targeted behavior change will be interrupted as well; if so, teaching is resumed to see if the targeted behavior change will resume. When the relation between what is taught and what behavior promptly changes is clearly not coincidence, we know that *this* kind of teaching results in *these* skills and knowledge. In other words, we know at least one way that such individual differences could have been made in the past and one way they can be made, intensified, diminished, or unmade in the future. We know that because we have done that, convincingly, in an individual.

An individual-analysis design often used in my laboratory is the parallel-instruction counterbalanced design (cf. Orth-Lopes, 1992). In this design, shown in Figure 5.5, students are randomly assigned to two groups to create two sets of individual-analysis designs. Each student's case is examined individually to see if the experimental teaching reliably created the new knowledge or skill it targeted. The existence of a group of such students means that each one's case can be compared to every other one's case to evaluate the generality of that reliability. The generality question is, in student after student, How reliably does this kind of teaching create this kind of knowledge or skill?

In this design, each student is taught two different skills, both within the same session; which skill is taught first in any session alternates in successive sessions.

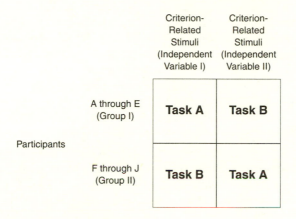

FIGURE 5.5   The Parallel-Instruction Counterbalanced Design. This design encompasses two sets of individual analyses, using two groups of participants to control for (or examine) Task × Variable interaction effects. Each participant receives both independent variables, thus making each participant his or her own control.

One kind of teaching targets one skill; another kind of teaching targets the other skill.

There are always at least two different ways to teach a conceptual skill. For example, my colleague and I (Schilmoeller & Etzel, 1977) noted that consistently successful teaching starts with a discrimination the students can already make and steadily transforms it into the discrimination targeted for teaching. We asked whether the stimuli of that first discrimination can be totally unrelated to the stimuli of the final one, or whether there is an advantage in having at least part of the initial stimuli survive the transformation to be at least part of the final stimuli. When the first stimuli are totally unrelated to the final ones, that is called "noncriterion-related" teaching; when some continuity of stimuli is maintained, that is called "criterion-related" teaching. These two teaching procedures were compared for their effectiveness.

The design in Figure 5.5 shows that each student learned one new skill through criterion-related teaching. One skill was color discrimination, and the other, shape discrimination. Thus, the first stimuli Students A-E saw for the teaching of Skill A were criterion-related; the first stimuli they saw for the teaching of Skill B were noncriterion-related. However, more control is necessary if we want to distinguish the effectiveness of the two teaching methods from some preexisting difference in the difficulty of learning the two skills. Therefore, Students F-J had the opposite skills assigned to the two teaching methods. The question is whether one teaching method will prove better than the other, no matter what skill is being taught. The more consistent the results across students, the more convincing and the more general is our conclusion about the relative effectiveness of the two teaching methods. If the results prove inconsistent, the researcher knows that these two teaching methods have little difference in effectiveness and must look elsewhere for procedures that will prove better than either of them.

When this design is applied to an important question, its results can be powerful enough to speak for themselves when graphed, without statistical analysis. Figure 5.6 shows that power in a graph of the percentage of correct responding by students in the Schilmoeller and Etzel (1977) study. This graph shows that prior to teaching, the 10 students could do no better than chance in the two skills to be taught. Teaching of the two skills (not graphed here) went almost identically well for both procedures (96–100% correct by the end of teaching). After teaching was complete, however, a posttest showed that the skills learned through criterion-related teaching continued to be performed at the 100 percent correct level by all 10 students; in contrast, the skills taught to the same students by non-criterion-related methods were being performed at a level of about 40 percent correct. Retention tests 4 and 7 weeks later showed the same pattern, and each student's graph showed almost exactly this pattern. That is impressive control of memory.

Figure 5.7 shows a parallel pattern with response latencies: the time in each trial between the presentation of the problem and the student's response to it. Attention to the ongoing stimulus transformations is necessary if the final discrimi-

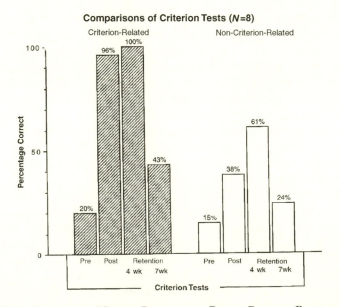

FIGURE 5.6   Percentage of Correct Responses on Pretest, Program, Posttest, and Retention Test, from Schilmoeller and Etzel (1977). The criterion-related instructional programs (hatched bars) and the non-criterion-related programs (open bars) contain the same participants' data.

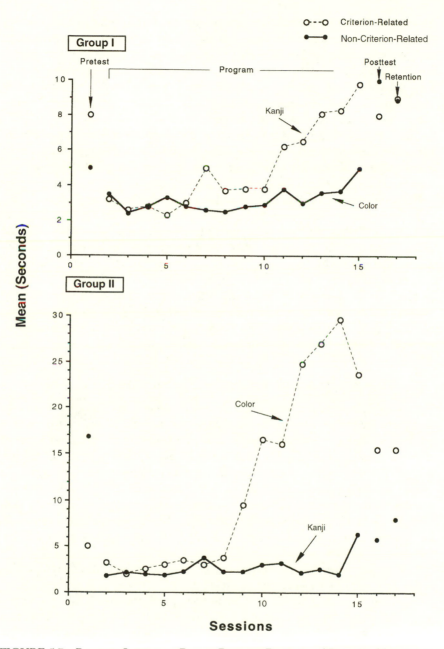

FIGURE 5.7   Response Latency on Pretest, Program, Posttest, and Retention Tests for Groups I and II of the Schilmoeller and Etzel (1977) Study. Latencies are graphed as mean seconds per session. The criterion-related program latencies are illustrated by open circles and dotted lines, and the non-criterion-related latencies by solid dots and solid lines.

nation is to emerge correctly from the always successful initial one. Figure 5.7 shows, for each group of students, that non-criterion-related teaching yielded very short latencies of 2–4 seconds until the final transformation, no matter which skill was taught; by contrast, criterion-related teaching yielded increasingly long latencies as the stimulus transformations proceeded, no matter which skill was taught; the final level was about 30 seconds, which occurred when the stimulus transformations became more thorough.

I cannot argue that the students found the shape discrimination easy relative to the color discrimination, because when teaching conditions changed, the students did the reverse. What skill was taught proved irrelevant here; what method was used to teach it accounted for almost all the variability. Each method was applied for the same number of trials and offered the same number of reinforcers.

In a facetious mode, one might say that each student seemed a thoughtful, attentive genius when what was being tested had been taught by a criterion-related method but seemed, a moment later, learning-disabled and attention-deficit-disordered when what was being tested had been taught by a non-criterion-related method.

The individual-analysis designs eventually prove to be both powerful and meaningful, because they require truly individual analyses that can be compared to all other individual analyses. This design illuminates individual differences by showing both how to achieve them and how to diminish them.

Is the Analysis of Behavior the Explanation of Behavior?

We can explain what people do, first by observing and describing what they do and then inventing the kind of mind that would compel them to do that. Alternatively, we can gain experimental control of a behavior; if we do, we know at least one possible cause of it. We can do that for many different behaviors and ask if any consistent themes emerge. The four-term contingency emerges again and again: Behavior proves repeatedly to be a function of its environmental antecedents, both contextual and discriminative, and its consequences. In each such case, the environment *can* explain that behavior. The question is whether we will rest content with those explanations, and that *kind* of explanation, or seek different ones.

Comparing two studies that investigated the same problem can illuminate this issue. The problem was to evaluate two methods of teaching a conditional discrimination to preschool children. The problem presented the children with a triangle and a circle; their task was to learn when to choose the triangle and when to choose the circle. The answer was signaled by the background behind the triangle and circle: If that background was a single horizontal line, choosing the triangle would be reinforced; if the background was seven horizontal lines, choosing the circle would be reinforced. In summary: If seven lines, circle is S+; if one line, triangle is S+, as shown in Figure 5.8.

Criterion Level Trials

Series I

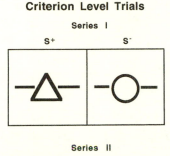

Series II

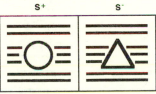

FIGURE 5.8   Stimuli Used in Studies by Gollin and Savoy (1968) and Schilmoeller et al. (1979). The top (Series I) discrimination was trained first, with the triangle and single line as S+. The second discrimination was trained with the circle and multiple lines as S+. These stimuli are shown at the final criterion level. A conditional-discrimination test was then given that randomly intermixed these criterion-level trials from both Series I and Series II.

The first study was done by Gollin and Savoy (1968); the second was performed by Schilmoeller, Schilmoeller, Etzel, and LeBlanc (1979). Gollin and Savoy (1968) meant to show a hidden disadvantage of using the relatively new fading techniques proving so useful at that time in behavior-analytic studies of simple discriminations. Consequently, their study employed two groups of children. One group was taught the conditional discrimination by conventional trial-and-error procedures; the other group was taught the same by fading procedures.

Both groups were taught by the same basic strategy: First, they were taught the simple discrimination that triangle is S+ and circle is S-, using one-line backgrounds, until the discrimination was mastered. Then, the simple discrimination was reversed: They were taught that circle is S+ and triangle is S-, using seven-line backgrounds, until the discrimination was mastered. Finally, they were taught both discriminations simultaneously as a conditional discrimination: Some trials were taught with one-line backgrounds and some with seven-line backgrounds, in a random mix; triangle was reinforced if the background had one line and circle if it had seven lines.

One group was taught all three stages by trial and error. The other group was taught the same three stages, in the same order, by two fading programs, one for the S-, another for the background lines. As seen in Figure 5.9, the S+ stimulus was always presented at the final level, but the S- stimulus started as a blank card.

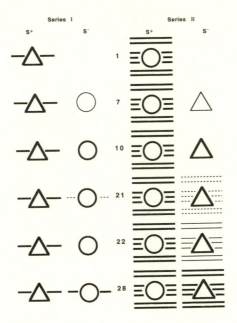

FIGURE 5.9   Sample Fading Steps for Series I and II. The S+ is introduced at criterion level, while the S- is faded in by increasing the intensity of the shape (first) and then the background lines.

Slowly, as trials proceeded, the S- was faded in from dark gray to full brightness. Then the lines were faded in, from being barely discernible to full brightness. Ultimately, S+ and S- were equally bright. The final, conditional discrimination task was taught in the same way as for the trial-and-error group. Notice that the first two stages (the simple discrimination and its reversal) made the background stimuli (one line or seven lines) irrelevant: In the first, both the triangle and the circle had one line as background; in the second, both the triangle and the circle had seven lines as background. In each simple discrimination, therefore, the only basis for making the discrimination was shape: triangle versus circle. The backgrounds did not control either discrimination. Only during the third stage, when the conditional discrimination was taught (if one line, triangle; if seven lines, circle), did the backgrounds have any controlling function.

A minor result in this study was that more children learned the two simple discriminations without error in the fading group than in the trial-and-error group. That result is almost automatic: Trial-and-error teaching necessitates at least a few errors and often many; in contrast, fading is designed to teach without error (and succeeds in that only if done well). This difference was reasonable, therefore. The key result for Gollin and Savoy was that the trial-and-error group learned the final conditional discrimination task (if one line, triangle; if seven lines, circle) with fewer errors than did the fading group, a statistically significant difference (p = 0.02). The authors concluded that fading had implicit disadvantages for at least some kinds of subsequent teachings.

Since 1968, when Gollin and Savoy did this work, the behavior analysis of conceptual behavior increasingly targeted "errorless" teaching procedures. Oddly, the term *errorless* has acquired many definitions. It generally has come to mean, simply, many fewer errors than typical of trial-and-error procedures. Lancioni and Smeets (1986), reviewing many error-reduction applications to the teaching of developmentally disabled people, noted how often conclusions changed when these procedures were used. Error-reduction procedures made it possible to teach low-functioning clients skills that had seemed impossible (and unpleasant to attempt) with previous trial-and-error procedures. In addition, the stimulus-control concept of behavior analysis flourished: the notion that knowledge, fundamentally, means the attachment of all the right responses to all the right stimuli. Antecedent stimuli had become as important as reinforcers.

As that literature grew, however, inconsistencies emerged. Sometimes fading failed to teach difficult discriminations (e.g., Gollin & Savoy, 1968; Schwartz, Firestone, & Terry, 1971), yet other, equally difficult discriminations were taught that way (Bijou, 1968; Sidman & Stoddard, 1966). These inconsistencies led to closer analyses of these procedures, and more of the elements crucial to success were discovered.

One example is the transformation of stimulus fading into stimulus shaping. The strategy begins with stimuli the student can discriminate and goes on to change them into stimuli that define the new skill. Instead of doing that by fading the initial stimulus out as the final stimulus replaces it, the *form* of the initial stimulus is gradually modified to become the final stimulus. This technique is literally transformation.

Sidman and Stoddard's (1966) reversal program (Figure 5.10) is an example. It was designed to reverse a discrimination between circle as S+ and ellipse as S-. As trials proceeded, the S+ circle was gradually squared, while the S- ellipse remained the same. That succeeded; the circle (S+), ellipse (S-) discrimination became a square (S+), ellipse (S-) discrimination. Over trials, the ellipse gradually became a circle, while the square remained unchanged. That too succeeded; the square (S+), circle (S-) discrimination emerged. Then the square was gradually flattened into a rectangle, yielding a rectangle (S+), circle (S-) discrimination. Finally, the corners of the rectangle were steadily rounded to produce an ellipse; the discrimination then was ellipse (S+), circle (S-), the reverse of the original discrimination. That program required 43 trials and involved few errors.

Gradually changing the total configuration of the initial S+ and S- into the final S+ and S- was named "stimulus shaping" by Sidman and Stoddard. Etzel and LeBlanc (1979) pointed out its crucial difference from stimulus fading: Stimulus shaping gradually transforms the total configurations of the original S+ and S- into the total configurations of the final S+ and S- (rather than merely

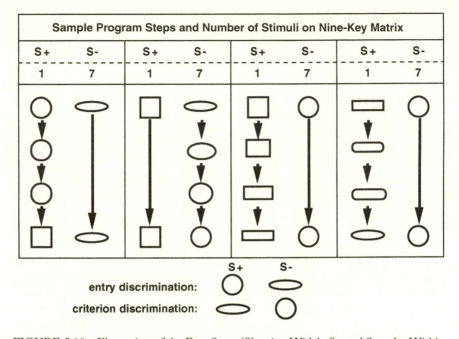

FIGURE 5.10   Illustration of the Four Steps (Showing Widely Spaced Samples Within Each Step) of the Sidman and Stoddard (1966) Reversal Program. In Step 1, the circle (S+) is shaped to a square while the ellipse (S-) remains at entry level. In Step 2, the square (now the S+) remains constant, and the ellipse (S-) shapes to a circle. In Step 3, the square (S+) is shaped to a rectangle, and the circle (S-) remains constant. Finally, in Step 4, the rectangle (S+) is shaped to an ellipse (S+), and the circle remains constant. A complete reversal of the entry discrimination has been accomplished errorlessly.

having the initial ones gradually disappear) along some physical continuum of intensity, color, or size, after the new ones are introduced.

Gollin and Savoy did not change the shape of the triangle, circle, and lines in their study; they faded the intensities of the circle and the lines. Schilmoeller et al. (1979) corrected the conclusion of the Gollin and Savoy study by using stimulus shaping, rather than fading, to teach the same initial simple discriminations to some students and repeated the fading procedures and trial-and-error procedures of Gollin and Savoy with other students.

Figure 5.11 illustrates the stimulus shaping used by Schilmoeller et al. The initial S+ stimulus was a triangle-shaped tree on a hill; the tree gradually became a triangle, and the horizon of the hill gradually became the background line. The initial S- stimulus was an apple with a worm through it; the apple gradually became a circle, and the worm became the background line. Figure 5.12 shows how, in the same way, the triangle with seven lines (S-) and the circle with seven lines (S+) were shaped, respectively, from an initial witch with a witch's hat, straggly

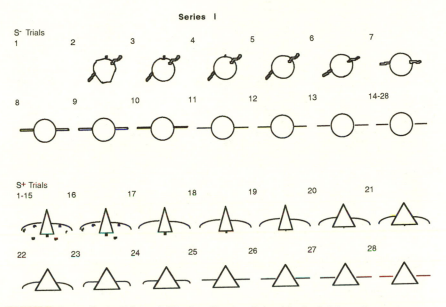

FIGURE 5.11   Series I Stimuli Used in Shaping Procedure by Schilmoeller et al. (1979). The top illustration of the apple and worm (S-) stimulus was shaped to criterion first, starting with Trials 2 through 13, while the tree on a hill (S+) stimulus remained at the entry level. Starting on Trial 15, the tree on the hill (S+) was shaped to criterion level, while the S- remained at criterion level.

hair, and a broomstick and from an initial sun with sunbeams and clouds. These tasks took 28 trials each.

The question was still whether errorless training of the initial discriminations handicaps students in learning a subsequent conditional discrimination based on them. In the 16-student group taught the initial errorless discriminations by stimulus shaping, 12 of the 16 learned the subsequent conditional discrimination with two or fewer errors (Figure 5.13). In the 16-student group taught the initial errorless discriminations by fading, only 3 of the 16 did that well, as did only 2 students of the 8 in the trial-and-error group.

Clearly, it is not errorless discrimination that handicaps certain subsequent learnings; it is how the errorless discriminations are taught. Errorless learning done through stimulus shaping reveals no such handicaps. The problem is in how the experimenter manipulates the stimuli to be discriminated. When that premise is clear, teachers can begin to accept responsibility for the effect of their teaching, rather than attributing failures to deficiencies in their students.

Schilmoeller et al. (1979) imputed no faults to either the students or to fading as such. Instead, they listed the crucial elements of their successful procedure: (a) The initial S+ and S- should be clearly different to the student; (b) some aspects

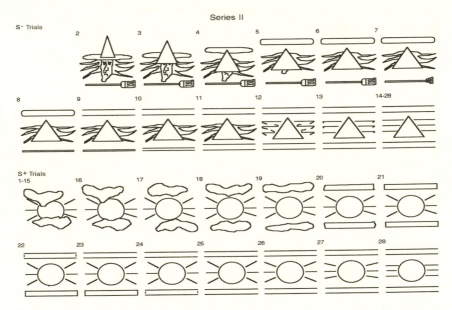

FIGURE 5.12   Series II Stimuli Used in Shaping Procedure by Schilmoeller et al. (1979). The top illustration of the witch and broom (the S-) was introduced at the entry level on Trial 2 and then shaped to the final criterion level of a triangle with multiple lines in the background. The sun, clouds, and rays (S+) remained at the entry level as S- was being shaped. Starting with Trial 16, the sun, clouds, and rays (S+) were shaped to the criterion level of circle with multiple lines in the background, while the S- remained at criterion level.

of the initial shapes should survive in the final shapes, that is, the initial cues should be criterion-related (as mentioned earlier); (c) the S- stimuli should be shaped first; the S+ stimuli should remain in their original form while that is done; (d) the S+ stimuli should be shaped last. We know all organisms look at stimuli when they are changing (being shaped, for example; Stella & Etzel, 1986); therefore, it is better to have the student look at the S+ in the final stages of a training program. As expected, fewer errors result when S+ changes last.

The point is to follow a conceptual model that automatically assumes any desired stimulus control can be achieved (within the organism's sensory limitations). That kind of model tells us to start with stimuli that already perfectly control the desired response and to transform to the desired final stimuli in ways that maintain that perfect control throughout. To do that, some crucial element of the initial stimuli must remain present throughout and be present in the final stimuli; that solves the problem of transfer by avoiding it.

There has been some question about the distinction between fading and shaping (e.g., Deitz & Malone, 1985). The key point is that fading is meant to trans-

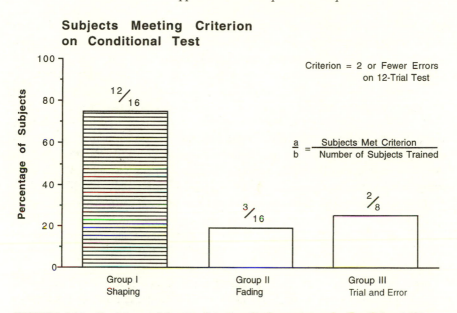

FIGURE 5.13   Participants Meeting Criterion Performance on the Conditional-Discrimination Test by Schilmoeller et al. (1979). The ratio indicates the number of children meeting the criterion of two or fewer errors on a 12-trial test over the total number of children in the group.

fer control from an initial stimulus to the final stimulus; it is a technique derived from the assumption that the problem of working from an existing discrimination to a new one always requires some form of transfer. In fact, shaping, properly done, does not transfer control, because it need not. Properly done, shaping maintains control by a stimulus that is steadily transformed into a new stimulus; control of the response never ends. Furthermore, fading need not always embody a transfer of control.

Consider teaching the concept "larger than" as an example of the *effective* use of fading. A good teaching program would use arbitrary shapes and pictures of people, animals, flowers, toys, and the like. It would begin with pairs of the same kind (e.g., two people, two flowers, two circles) and progress to three or four of the same kind. Reinforcement would always be given for choosing the larger (or largest). In the first pairs, the size difference would be so great that the student would quickly learn with just an instruction and a demonstration. As trials progressed, the instruction and demonstration would be discontinued; the kinds of stimuli used would vary unpredictably; and the size difference would become less and less. By the end of the program, which would not be a long one, the student would be discriminating correctly at threshold levels. That is the same discrimination operative in the first trial, merely refined to its limits. No transfer of stimulus control would be necessary, even though fading of size is involved. It might always be the larger (or largest) stimulus that was faded, or the smaller (or smallest), or both. All these are examples of criterion-related fading; the same stimulus (the larger one) is correct at the beginning and at the criterion level.

The same refinement of the "larger than" concept could be taught by a fading program that *would* require transfer of control: Begin with two stimuli differing only slightly in size from the desired stimulus—the near-threshold level desired. Make the discrimination possible for students not yet skilled at such subtle discriminations by coloring the larger stimulus (S+) red with a black outline and the smaller one white with a black outline. Students who can discriminate red from white will succeed in these initial trials. Then, over trials, fade the red to lighter and lighter shades until all color is gone; now the larger is white with a black outline, as is the smaller. In this program, as color slowly disappears, control must be transferred from red to size before red disappears, if the "larger than" concept is to be taught. This fading is not criterion-related; transfer is necessary. It is also problematic in its results.

Teaching programs that require transfer of stimulus control often fail; that is, transfer often does not occur. Milla (1993) analyzed many published studies of fading and found that criterion-unrelated fading was successful only if the necessary transfer was forced early in the program and no stimulus other than the desired one was available for control. Both Schreibman (1975) and Sidman and Stoddard (1966) have provided examples of this rule.

These examples, and many more like them, suggest forcefully that when children fail to learn what is taught, the first explanation should never be that the child is too young, too immature, or too disabled to learn. Instead, the first hypothesis should be that teaching has not been well designed to produce the stimulus control the new learning requires. The parents of children doing poorly in school should never be offered a diagnosis and be advised to wait a year; they should instead receive proven, descriptive statements such as, "Addition, subtraction, multiplication, and division are done correctly in all number problems but not in word problems involving reading." That kind of description is likely to instigate attempts at error analysis and the design of a special program to remediate the faulty and missing stimulus controls. This approach would always encourage altering the child's teaching environment. The studies reviewed here show the results those alterations could have if education students were taught in college how to identify and remediate problems of stimulus control with the materials they were using.

Vargas (1983) found that problems often occur in the instructional materials given to students for supposedly constructive practice. Many workbook designs let students correctly answer questions about a passage without reading it. Etzel and LeBlanc (1979) suggested procedures appropriate to teaching teachers the essence of instructional control.

Publishers of educational materials rarely guarantee that their materials will teach what they are advertised to teach. It is interesting that the armed forces and some businesses have adopted instructional techniques based on errorless programming and stimulus control. Keller (1982; Keller & Sherman, 1982) and other behaviorists (e.g., Sherman, Ruskin, & Semb, 1982) have pursued such methods at length; they have shown that students at many skill levels can be taught to a given level of competence without failing or being dropped from the course.

In B. F. Skinner's *The Technology of Teaching* (1968), education is viewed as a technology emanating directly from the experimental analysis of behavior. Skinner's contributions to education for over 30 years (1954, 1958, 1965, 1968, 1972a, 1972b, 1972c, 1986, 1989) were primarily teaching machines and programmed instruction. Programmed instruction was found to be quite efficient and, like the Programmed Self-Instruction (PSI) method, which incorporates study guides (Keller & Sherman, 1982), could be used with individuals who had varying backgrounds. By specifying the final complex behavior desired and beginning with the simplest entry-level skill needed, the student moves by small steps through a logical and developmental arrangement of facts, laws, terms, and principles. Holland and Skinner (1961) applied these procedures to an introductory college psychology course on the analysis of behavior and showed that the procedures used in the laboratory could be adapted to educational instruction.

Consider this mere sketch of what we have learned: Error-reduction procedures are more efficient (Terrace, 1963), in part because errors so often beget errors (Sidman & Stoddard, 1966). My colleagues and I have taught many people with developmental delays by carefully arranging the stimulus controls of their educational environments (Dixon, Spradlin, Girardeau, & Etzel, 1974). We have taught the following concepts to students who had failed to learn them by other methods: size (Richmond & Bell, 1983), length (Gold & Barclay, 1973), number (Zawlocki & Walls, 1983), spatial relations (Mosk & Bucher, 1984), letters and words (Wolfe & Cuvo, 1978), shapes and sounds (Schreibman, 1975), mathematics (Smeets, Lancioni, Striefel, & Willemsen, 1984), and manual signs (Smeets & Striefel, 1976), to name but a few of the targets and a few of the studies of each. These studies used procedures derived from research in stimulus control.

Over the years, a variety of effective procedures have been identified: stimulus fading (Sidman & Stoddard, 1966); stimulus shaping (Schilmoeller et al., 1979); superimposition, fading, and shaping (Smeets, Lancioni, & Hoogeveen, 1984); progressively delayed cue programming (Touchette, 1968); within-stimulus prompting (Schreibman, 1975); distinctive-feature analysis (Rincover, 1978); stimulus equalization (Hoko & LeBlanc, 1988); exclusion (Dixon, 1977; Etzel, Milla, & Nicholas, 1996; McIlvane, Bass, O'Brien, Gerovac, & Stoddard, 1984; McIlvane & Stoddard, 1981); S+ and S- manipulation (Cheney & Stein, 1974; Schreibman & Charlop, 1981; Stella & Etzel, 1986; Zawlocki & Walls, 1983); and the use of the student's eye orientation to indicate what elements of the stimuli to change and when (Stella & Etzel, 1986). Each of these techniques merits its own chapter; together, they constitute a powerful technology of teaching. It is a technology that will rarely fail; by the same token, it is a technology formidable to teach and learn.

Johnson and Layng (1992) noted that the continuously accelerating illiteracy in the school systems of the United States parallels the continuous and often-times increasing acceptance of the structuralist (cognitive) models, which empha-size hypothetical constructs of assumed mental processes. This relation has been exemplified in a Mid-continent Regional Education Laboratory report produced by the Presidential Task Force on Psychology in Education (1993) entitled, *Learner-Centered Psychological Principles: Guidelines for School Redesign and Re-form.* The report lists 12 "psychological" principles that "explain" the learner and the learning process. Only the first principle is noted here; the other 11 are simi-lar, in that they describe nothing on which we can act:

> Principle 1. The nature of the learning process. Learning is a natural process of pur-suing personally meaningful goals, and it is active, volitional, and internally medi-ated; it is a process of discovering and constructing meaning from information and experience, filtered through the learner's unique perceptions, thoughts, and feelings.

In summary, the message is rather simple. Regardless of which president's mandate for improvement in education is being considered, or whether increases in funds to help pay for more equipment or more teachers in our schools will occur, we have few options left to carry out the difficult task of education of the children and adults in this country or in this world. This perspective, though widely held by educational leaders, leaves education without specific mandates or even a point of focus for intervention. Many environmentalists talk about our water, our trees, our loss of soil, our air, but most people have completely ignored our conceptual environment. As long as we invent, study, and complain about cognitive processes we place within the student, we will not solve our educational problems. The only option is a natural-science view: that the environment can be made to teach. Only in this paradigm can we do anything to improve the concep-tual environment of humankind.

Acknowledgments

I am grateful to Professors Donald M. Baer and Edward K. Morris for their helpful sug-gestions during the writing of this paper. I presented a shorter version of the paper as the Presidential Address of Division 25, The Experimental Analysis of Behavior, at the annual meeting of The American Psychological Association, in Toronto, Canada, 1993.

References

Bijou, S. W. (1968). Studies in the experimental development of left-right concepts in re-tarded children using fading techniques. In N. R. Ellis (Ed.), *International review of research in mental retardation* (Vol. 3, pp. 65–96). New York: Academic Press.
Bijou, S. W. (1976). *Child development: The basic stage of early childhood.* Englewood Cliffs, NJ: Prentice-Hall.

Bijou, S. W., & Baer, D. M. (1961). *Child development: Vol. I. A systematic and empirical theory.* Englewood Cliffs, NJ: Prentice-Hall.

Bijou, S. W., & Baer, D. M. (1965). *Child development: Vol. II. Universal state of infancy.* Englewood Cliffs, NJ: Prentice-Hall.

Bijou, S. W., & Baer, D. M. (1967). *Child development: Readings in experimental analysis.* Englewood Cliffs, NJ: Prentice-Hall.

Cheney, T., & Stein, N. (1974). Fading procedures and oddity learning in kindergarten children. *Journal of Experimental Child Psychology, 17,* 313–321.

Deitz, S. M., & Malone, L. W. (1985). On terms: Stimulus control terminology. *The Behavior Analyst, 8,* 259–264.

Dixon, L. S. (1977). The nature of control by spoken words over visual stimulus selection. *Journal of the Experimental Analysis of Behavior, 27,* 433–442.

Dixon, L. S., Spradlin, J. E., Girardeau, F. L., & Etzel, B. C. (1974). Development of a programmed stimulus series for training in-front discrimination. *Acta Symbolica, 5,* 1–21.

Etzel, B. C., & LeBlanc, J. M. (1979). The simplest treatment alternative: The law of parsimony applied to choosing appropriate instructional control and errorless-learning procedures for the difficult-to-teach child. *Journal of Autism and Developmental Disorders, 9,* 361–382.

Etzel, B. C., Milla, S. R., & Nicholas, M. D. (1996). Arranging the development of conceptual behavior: A technology for stimulus control. In E. Ribes & S. W. Bijou (Eds.), *New directions in behavior development* (pp. 91–130). Reno, NV: Context Press.

Gold, M. W., & Barclay, C. R. (1973). The learning of difficult visual discriminations by the moderately and severely retarded. *Mental Retardation, 11*(2), 9–11.

Gollin, E. S., & Savoy, P. (1968). Fading procedures and conditional discrimination in children. *Journal of the Experimental Analysis of Behavior, 11,* 443–451.

Hoko, J. A., & LeBlanc, J. M. (1988). Stimulus equalization: Temporary reduction of stimulus complexity to facilitate discrimination learning. *Research in Developmental Disabilities, 9,* 255–275.

Holland, J. G., & Skinner, B. F. (1961). *The analysis of behavior.* New York: McGraw-Hill.

James, W. (1890). *Principles of psychology.* New York: Holt.

Johnson, K. R., & Layng, T. V. J. (1992). Breaking the structuralist barrier: Literacy and numeracy with fluency. *American Psychologist, 47,* 1475–1490.

Keller, F. S. (1982). *Pedagogue's progress.* Lawrence, KS: TRI.

Keller, F. S., & Sherman, J. G. (1982). The PSI handbook: Essays on personalized instruction. Lawrence, KS: TRI.

Lancioni, G. E., & Smeets, P. M. (1986). Procedures and parameters of errorless discrimination training with developmentally impaired individuals. In N. R. Ellis & N. W. Bray (Eds.), *International review of research in mental retardation* (Vol. 14, pp. 135–164). New York: Academic Press.

Lawrence, D. H. (1952). The transfer of a discrimination along a continuum. *Journal of Comparative and Physiological Psychology, 45,* 511–516.

McIlvane, W. J., Bass, R. W., O'Brien, J. M., Gerovac, B. J., & Stoddard, T. (1984). Spoken and signed naming of foods after receptive exclusion training in severe retardation. *Applied Research in Mental Retardation, 5,* 1–27.

McIlvane, W. J., & Stoddard, T. (1981). Acquisition of matching-to-sample performances in severe retardation: Learning by exclusion. *Journal of Mental Deficiency Research, 25,* 33–48.

Milla, S. (1993). *Stimulus fading and the programming elements relevant to discrimination acquisition.* Unpublished manuscript, University of Kansas, Department of Human Development and Family Life, Lawrence.

Mosk, M. D., & Bucher, B. (1984). Prompting and stimulus shaping procedures for teaching visual-motor skills to retarded children. *Journal of Applied Behavior Analysis, 17,* 23–34.

Orth-Lopes, L. (1992). *Individual analysis designs to compare the effects of teaching methods on conceptual learning.* Unpublished manuscript, University of Kansas, Department of Human Development and Family Life, Lawrence.

Pavlov, I. P. (1927). *Conditional reflexes.* London: Oxford University Press.

Presidential Task Force on Psychology in Education. (1993). *Learner-centered psychological principles: Guidelines for school redesign and reform.* Mid-continent Regional Education Laboratory Report. Washington, DC: American Psychological Association.

Richmond, G., & Bell, J. (1983). Comparison of three methods to train a size discrimination with profoundly mentally retarded students. *American Journal of Mental Deficiency, 87,* 574–576.

Rincover, A. (1978). Variables affecting stimulus fading and discriminative responding in psychotic children. *Journal of Abnormal Psychology, 5,* 541–553.

Rosales, J., & Baer, D. M. (1996). A behavior-analytic view of development. In E. Ribes & S. W. Bijou (Eds.), *New directions in behavior development* (pp. 155–180). Reno, NV: Context Press.

Schilmoeller, K. J., & Etzel, B. C. (1977). An experimental analysis of criterion-related and non-criterion related cues in "errorless" stimulus control procedures. In B. C. Etzel, J. M. LeBlanc, & D. M. Baer (Eds.), *New developments in behavioral research* (pp. 317–347). Hillsdale, NJ: Erlbaum.

Schilmoeller, G. L., Schilmoeller, K. J., Etzel, B. C., & LeBlanc, J. M. (1979). Conditional discrimination after errorless and trial-and-error training. *Journal of the Experimental Analysis of Behavior, 31,* 405–420.

Schlinger, H. D. (1992). Theory in behavior analysis: An application to child development. *American Psychologist, 47,* 1396–1410.

Schlinger, H. D. (1995). *A behavior-analytic view of child development.* New York: Plenum Press.

Schlosberg, H., & Solomon, R. L. (1943). Latency of response in a choice discrimination. *Journal of Experimental Psychology, 33,* 22–39.

Schreibman, L. (1975). Effects of within-stimulus and extra-stimulus prompting on discrimination learning in autistic children. *Journal of Applied Behavior Analysis, 8,* 91–112.

Schreibman, L., & Charlop, M. H. (1981). S+ versus S– fading in prompting procedures with autistic children. *Journal of Experimental Child Psychology, 31,* 508–520.

Schwartz, S. H., Firestone, I. J., & Terry, S. (1971). Fading techniques and concept learning in children. *Psychonomic Science, 25,* 83–84.

Sherman, J. G., Ruskin, R. S., & Semb, G. B. (1982). *The personalized system of instruction: Seminar papers.* Lawrence, KS: TRI.

Sidman, M. (1978) Remarks. *Behaviorism, 6,* 265–268.

Sidman, M. (1979) Remarks. *Behaviorism, 7,* 123–126.

Sidman, M., & Stoddard, L. T. (1966). Programming perception and learning for retarded children. In N. R. Ellis (Ed.), *International review of research in mental retardation* (Vol. 2, pp. 151–208). New York: Academic Press.

Skinner, B. F. (1938). *The behavior of organisms: An experimental analysis.* New York: Appleton-Century-Crofts.

Skinner, B. F. (1954). The science of learning and the art of teaching. *Harvard Educational Review, 24,* 86–97.

Skinner, B. F. (1958). Teaching machines. *Science, 128,* 969–977.

Skinner, B. F. (1965). The technology of teaching. *Proceedings of the Royal Society, 8,* 162.

Skinner, B. F. (1968). *The technology of teaching.* New York: Appleton-Century-Crofts.

Skinner, B. F. (1972a). Reflections on a decade of teaching machines. *Cumulative record* (pp. 194–207). New York: Appleton-Century-Crofts.

Skinner, B. F. (1972b). Teaching science in high school: What is wrong? *Cumulative record* (pp. 208–224). New York: Appleton-Century-Crofts.

Skinner, B. F. (1972c). Why we need teaching machines. *Cumulative record* (pp. 171–193). New York: Appleton-Century-Crofts.

Skinner, B. F. (1986, October). Programmed instruction revisited. *Phi Delta Kappan, 68,* 103–110.

Skinner, B. F. (1989). *Recent issues in the analysis of behavior.* Columbus, OH: Charles E. Merrill.

Smeets, P. M., Lancioni, G. E., & Hoogeveen, F. R. (1984). Using stimulus control in normal and retarded children. *Journal of Mental Deficiency Research, 28,* 207–218.

Smeets, P. M., Lancioni, G. E., Striefel, S., & Willemsen, R. I. (1984). Training EMR children to solve missing minuend problems errorlessly: Acquisition, generalization, and maintenance. *Analysis and Intervention in Developmental Disabilities, 4,* 379–402.

Smeets, P. M., & Striefel, S. (1976). Acquisition of sign reading by transfer of stimulus control in a retarded deaf girl. *Journal of Mental Deficiency Research, 20,* 197–205.

Spence, K. W. (1936). The nature of discrimination learning in animals. *Psychological Review, 43,* 427–449.

Spence, K. W. (1937). The differential response in animals to stimuli varying within a single dimension. *Psychological Review, 44,* 430–444.

Stella, M. E., & Etzel, B. C. (1986). Stimulus control of eye orientations: Shaping S+ only versus shaping S– only. Analysis and Intervention in *Developmental Disabilities, 6,* 137–153.

Terrace, H. S. (1963). Discrimination learning with and without "errors." *Journal of the Experimental Analysis of Behavior, 6,* 1–27.

Touchette, P. E. (1968). The effects of graduated stimulus change on the acquisition of a simple discrimination in severely retarded boys. *Journal of the Experimental Analysis of Behavior, 11,* 39–48.

Vargas, J. S. (1983). What are your exercises teaching? An analysis of stimulus control in instructional materials. In W. L. Heward, T. E. Heron, D. S. Hill, & J. Trap-Porter (Eds.), *Focus on behavior analysis in education* (pp. 126–142). Columbus, OH: Charles E. Merrill.

Wolfe, V. F., & Cuvo, A. J. (1978). Effects of within-stimulus and extra-stimulus prompting on letter discrimination by mentally retarded persons. *American Journal of Mental Deficiency, 83,* 297–303.

Zawlocki, R. J., & Walls, R. T. (1983). Fading on the S+, the S–, both, or neither. *American Journal of Mental Deficiency, 87,* 462–464.

6

Errorless Learning in Educational Environments: Using Criterion-Related Cues to Reduce Errors

L. L. A. McCartney and J. M. LeBlanc

In the 1970s, Barbara Etzel and colleagues developed visual stimulus-manipulation procedures (cf. Etzel & LeBlanc, 1979; Etzel, LeBlanc, Schilmoeller, & Stella, 1981; Schilmoeller, Schilmoeller, Etzel, & LeBlanc, 1979; Stella & Etzel, 1979) for better teaching, based on earlier procedures labeled *stimulus shaping* by Sidman and Stoddard (1966). The point was to preclude or greatly reduce errors (cf. Terrace, 1963). The goals of stimulus fading and stimulus shaping are the same, but their stimulus manipulations are very different. Stimulus fading reduces the differences between two or more simple, abstract, and very different initial stimuli. The stimuli usually vary on only one dimension (e.g., a large and a small circle), and their differences are faded (reduced) along that dimension until the learner can discriminate between two that are nearly the same size. Stimulus shaping involves *familiar* initial stimuli composed of many dimensionally different elements (e.g., pictures of a dog and a cowboy) that are therefore easy to discriminate. The shape (topography) of these stimuli is gradually changed across learning trials until they become two very similar (often abstract) and difficult-to-discriminate stimuli. Stimulus shaping always emphasizes an element (criterion-related cue) in each of the stimuli that (a) changes little across learning trials, (b) is emphasized during the shaping process, and (c) forms the basis on which the final, more difficult, discrimination can be made.

Some stimulus-fading research with children conducted after the work of Terrace (1963) and Sidman and Stoddard (1966) did not preclude or greatly reduce errors during discrimination acquisition (cf. Cheney & Stein, 1974; Gollin & Savoy, 1968; Koegel & Rincover, 1976; Schwartz, Firestone, & Terry, 1971). To explain these failures, Etzel and LeBlanc (1979) noted that their fadings occurred on stimulus elements that were not the elements on which the final discrimination was to be based. No wonder that errorless responding was not achieved.

Etzel and colleagues' stimulus shaping was designed to avoid problems of transfer from initial stimulus elements to criterion stimulus elements. Their procedures incorporated the use of familiar picture stimuli (e.g., monkey faces, turtles, cowboys) as the entry-level stimuli, rather than more abstract stimuli (e.g., circles, squares). More important, Etzel and colleagues used *criterion-related* rather than non-criterion-related gradual stimulus changes. That is, an element of the original stimulus becomes the basis for the final discrimination through the stimulus-shaping procedure. When a stimulus element that provides the basis of the initial discrimination is retained throughout the acquisition process and is the criterion cue on which the final discrimination is made, few or no errors are made in the acquisition process.

It is difficult to separate the contributions to learning without errors of (a) stimulus shaping, (b) criterion-related cues, and (c) entry-level stimuli familiar to the children. The typical challenge is that it is the meaningfulness of the initial stimuli, rather than the differences between the stimulus manipulations, that accounts for the better success of some criterion-related stimulus-shaping and stimulus-fading programs.

It is apparent that criterion-related, stimulus-shaping programs can teach complex discriminations to children with few or no errors and that stimulus-shaping procedures without the criterion-related cue component would not be as successful (Etzel & LeBlanc, 1979). What is not known is whether gradually transforming the configurations of stimuli across trials, from originally meaningful (picture) and easy-to-discriminate stimuli to abstract complex stimuli, but using criterion-related cues, differs from discrimination acquisition with a procedure that gradually transforms nonmeaningful (abstract) and easy-to-discriminate stimuli to the same ultimate abstract stimulus complex, also using criterion-related cues. That comparison would provide more information regarding whether initial entry stimuli of criterion-related, stimulus-shaping programs need to be complex (many elements) and meaningful (familiar picture) to initiate and maintain errorless responding. Perhaps it would be easier and equally effective to teach a simple, nonmeaningful stimulus discrimination and subsequently continue reinforcing responding to this element throughout discrimination acquisition, while other elements are gradually brought into the stimulus complex.

To compare the effects of meaningful (picture) versus nonmeaningful (abstract) entry-level stimuli in programs designed to reduce or preclude errors during learning, two procedures were used: (a) a criterion-related, stimulus-shaping procedure that incorporated meaningful entry-level stimuli (designed by Stella & Etzel, 1986, and appearing in their entirety in an article by Etzel & LeBlanc, 1979) and (b) a criterion-related, stimulus-shaping procedure that incorporated nonmeaningful entry-level stimuli (designed by L. L. A. McCartney, Barbara Etzel, and J. M. LeBlanc) that combined equalization procedures similar to those of Hoko and LeBlanc (1988) with stimulus-shaping procedures similar to those used by Stella and Etzel (1986). Both programs used a criterion-related cue, that is, an initial stimulus element that continued to be present during and after the shaping of the initial entry-level stimuli.

Although the two procedures were not expected to differ greatly in the reduction of errors during acquisition, it was thought that they might produce quite different results regarding identification of the separate elements of the final complex stimuli. The final S+ stimulus was tested after participants met criterion on both programs, therefore, to determine if the S+ stimulus elements of one program controlled more correct responding than the other. This information may be important if a discrimination requires control by many rather than only one element of a complex stimulus. The procedures were as follows:

Participants

A group of 33 children who were delayed in conceptual-skill development were selected by their preschool teachers as potential participants. These children received a trial-and-error pretest on the criterion stimuli of the two discrimination tasks of the research. Eight children had 60 percent or lower correct responding on both tasks in the first pretest, 70 percent or lower correct responding on both tasks on a repeated pretest, or made one or more errors on the last five trials of either task. These eight children, whose ages ranged from 2 years, 10 months, to 5 years, 1 month, with a mean of 4 years, 2 months, were the participants.

Setting and General Procedures

The research was conducted in a small room containing a child-sized table and three small chairs: one for the experimenter, one for the child, and one for an observer periodically present in the room. Sessions, conducted once a day for 4 days a week, lasted from 7 to 10 minutes. At the beginning of each session, the child chose a small toy from three alternatives. Tokens were given for correct responding and occasionally for working hard. If a predetermined number of tokens, representing 90 percent correct responding for the combined tasks, were earned in a session, the tokens were exchanged for the toy at the end. If these criteria were not achieved, the toy was saved so the child could work for it again, or select another, at the next session. Toys were always given after pretest and posttest sessions, regardless of the number of tokens earned.

A three-ring binder held the stimuli for each day. For each trial, two stimuli were centered on a sheet of construction paper, 21.75 cm x 28 cm, and covered in plastic. Each trial was separated by a blank, plastic-covered black sheet. The two tasks were separated by a yellow sheet also covered in plastic. The notebook was in front of the child during the session, and trials were presented by turning the plastic-covered sheets.

In each session, 10 trials of one of the two programs were presented to each child followed by 10 trials of the second, with the order reversed daily to balance sequence effects. If 90 percent correct responding was achieved on both programs, the next 10 training trials of both were presented in the next session. If criterion was not met, the same block of trials for both programs was repeated in the following session. This equated the participant's exposure to the two programs. A posttest was presented when each child reached 90 to 100 percent correct responding on the last 10 trials of that program.

Design

To compare meaningful and nonmeaningful programs, the participants were assigned different task and program combinations, controlling potential effects of task difficulty and task preference (Table 6.1). The programs involving meaningful entry-level stimuli had pictures of a duck and an Indian on Task A, and of a cowboy and a dog on Task B. In the nonmeaningful program, Task A had entry stimuli of an angled line "\" and a greater than sign ">" and Task B had a vertical straight line "|" and a vertical curved line "(". Two children were assigned to each of the following combinations of tasks and designations of S+ and S- stimuli: (a) Children 1 and 2, Task A = pictures with S+ = Duck, Task B = abstractions with S+ = "|"; (b) Children 3 and 4, Task A = pictures with S+ = Indian, Task B = abstractions with S+ = "("; (c) Children 5 and 6, Task B = pictures with S+ = dog, Task A = abstractions with S+ = ">" ; and (d) Children 7 and 8, Task B = pictures with S+ = cowboy, Task A = abstractions with S+ = "\".

Stimuli were systematically assigned placement according to a simple set of rules: (a) the S+ or S- could not appear in the left or right position across more than two sequential trials and (b) the S+ and the S- appeared an equal number of times in the left and right positions.

Stimulus-Shaping Programs and Related Pre- and Posttests

The stimuli of the pre- and posttests were the criterion stimuli. On the tests, 10 trials of one program were presented followed by 10 trials of the second program. Tokens were given for correct responding during the pretest to eliminate children

TABLE 6.1   Design and Assignment of Task to Participants

	Meaningful		Nonmeaningful	
	Task A		**Task B**	
	Duck	Indian	"I"	"("
Child 1 and 2	S+	S-	S+	S-
Child 3 and 4	S-	S+	S-	S+

	Task B		**Task A**	
	Dog	Cowboy	">"	"\"
Child 5 and 6	S+	S-	S+	S-
Child 7 and 8	S-	S+	S-	S+

who could learn through trial and error. Tokens were also given for correct responding on all subsequent posttests of the complex stimuli to avoid the participants' shifting from correct to incorrect response patterns because tokens were not given.

On the first trial of the pretests, the experimenter said, "Every time I show you a picture like this, I want you to point to this one" (pointing to the correct stimulus). While pointing to the correct stimulus, the experimenter said, "This is the one that gets the token" and then stopped pointing and said, "Now you point to the one that gets the token." This was done for the first pretest trial of each discrimination task. On the second pretest trial, the experimenter said, "Point to the one that gets the token," and on all subsequent pretest, training, and posttest trials, the experimenter said, "Point."

After the child pointed to one stimulus and was correct, the experimenter turned to the following blank sheet, took a token from a plastic container, and placed it in a plastic container in front of the child, while praising the child for being correct. If the child pointed incorrectly, the experimenter pointed to the "correct" stimulus and said, "This is the one that gets the token" and turned the stimulus sheet to the next blank sheet. If the child pointed to one stimulus and then to the second stimulus on one trial, it was considered an incorrect response. If the child pointed to both stimuli simultaneously, the experimenter started that trial again with the instruction, "Just point to one."

Stimulus-Shaping Program Descriptions

The final stimuli used for the discrimination training programs were the four Kanji symbols shown across the top row in Figure 6.1. Kanji is a system of characters used in Japanese writing. These symbols were chosen because most preschool children in the United States have no exposure to them. The sets of entry-level stimuli for the meaningful shaping programs for both tasks are shown across the center row, and entry-level stimuli for the nonmeaningful programs (also the criterion-related stimulus elements for both types of programs) are shown across the bottom row of Figure 6.1.

One discrimination between two of the Kanji symbols was taught to the children with a program involving meaningful (picture) entry-level stimuli. These stimuli were chosen because they were pictures assumed to have meaning for preschool children: line drawings of a duck and an Indian, or a dog and a cowboy. A second discrimination, between the remaining two Kanji symbols, was taught with a program involving nonmeaningful (abstract) entry-level stimuli; these were also the criterion-related cue that would control responding as the stimuli were changed into Kanji characters in both programs.

On the first 10 trials of both programs, designated as preentry fading trials, the S+ was full intensity and the S- was faded in to decrease the probability of errors on initial trials of the shaping program. Figure 6.2 shows examples for 4 of the 8

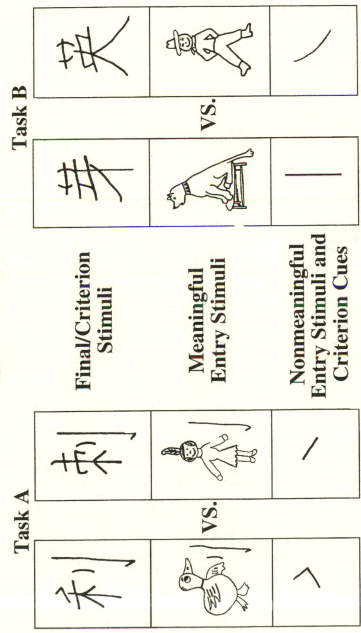

FIGURE 6.1 Entry and Criterion Stimulus Pairs for Tasks A and B. The nonmeaningful entry stimuli were also the criterion-related cues for both the meaningful and nonmeaningful stimulus-shaping programs.

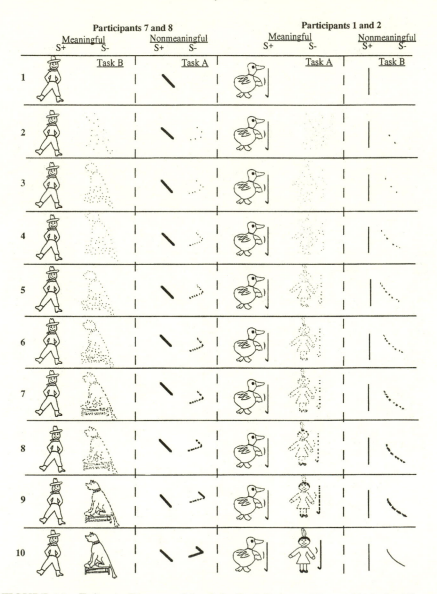

FIGURE 6.2   Fading in Distractor Stimuli for Each Program. First 10 Trials for All Programs. The purpose of these 10 trials was to initiate correct responding to the entry stimuli before beginning stimulus-shaping changes.

participants according to their task assignment in the study. After the 10 preentry fading trials, the entry stimuli were changed into the final Kanji characters, appearing at the end of all programs, across the next 60 program trials.

Selected trials of the meaningful (picture) shaping for Task B are shown in Figure 6.3; the complete programs for Task B were presented in an article by Etzel and LeBlanc (1979).[1] (The left-right placement of the two stimuli shown in Figures 6.3 and 6.4 do not represent their randomly alternated placement when presented to the participants.) After the 10 preentry shaping trials, the rules used to shape the stimuli in the meaningful program were as follows: (a) The elements of the stimulus complex farthest from the criterion-related element (i.e., the upper body of the cowboy and dog) were shaped first; (b) the criterion elements (the dog's tail and the cowboy's legs) were gradually shaped into their final form; and (c) shaping was first applied to the S- and then to the S+ stimuli.

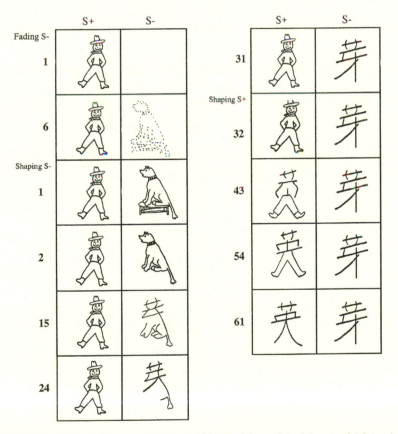

FIGURE 6.3   Task B: Example of Selected Trials of One of the Meaningful Stimulus-Shaping Programs

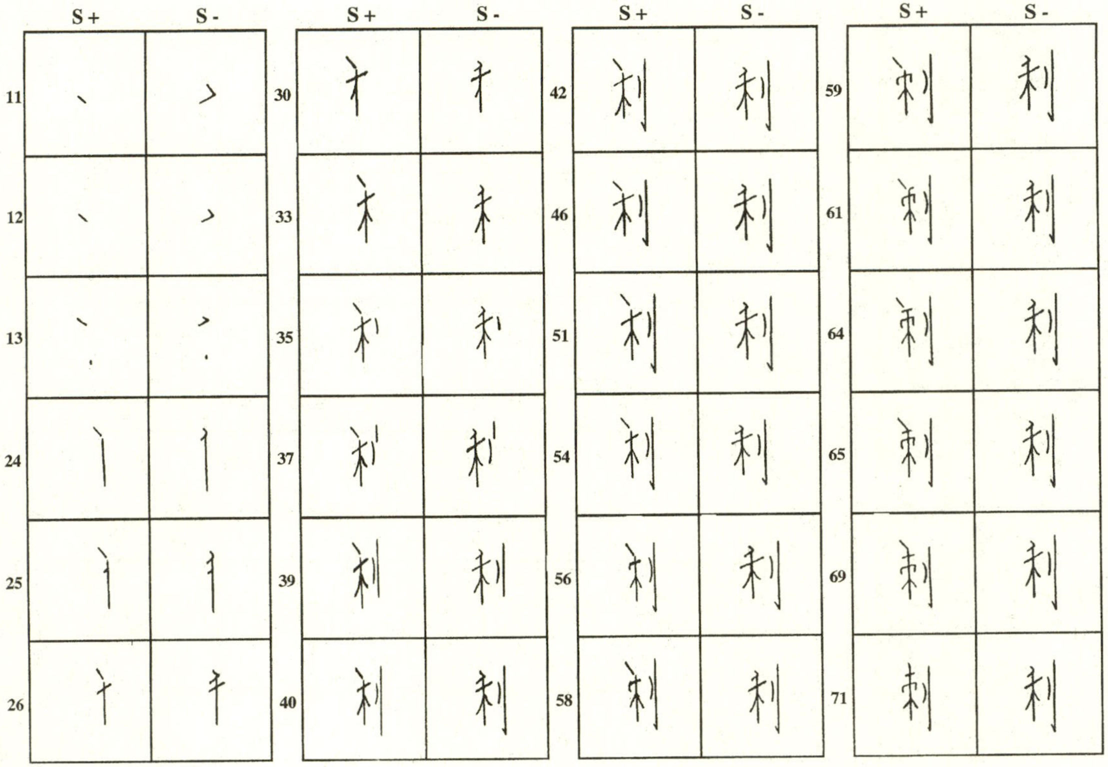

FIGURE 6.4   Task A (Indian and Duck): Examples of Selected Trials of One of the Nonmeaningful Stimulus-Shaping Programs

After the 10 preentry fading trials, the nonmeaningful program for Task A (Figure 6.4) followed two rules: (a) Non-criterion-related elements that were to become parts of the criterion stimuli for both tasks were added to *both* the S+ and the S- stimuli, using stimulus equalization (Hoko & LeBlanc, 1988) until Trial 40, when they were equal except for the criterion-related cues (the diagonal line vs. the greater-than symbol) on the upper part of the figures; this made the S- stimulus (with the greater-than symbol criterion cue) the same as it would be on the final trial of shaping. (b) After Trial 40, the S+ stimulus (with the diagonal line criterion cue) continued to be shaped into the final S+ Kanji character, first by adding more non-criterion-related elements and then by gradually shortening the S+ criterion-related cue.

The differences between meaningful and nonmeaningful programs were (a) the incorporation of meaningful (picture) and nonmeaningful (abstract) stimuli in the initial training trials and (b) that the meaningful program changed complex stimuli into different complex stimuli and the nonmeaningful program changed a simple abstraction into a complex abstraction by adding stimulus elements using stimulus equalization (Hoko & LeBlanc, 1988). Even though the programs differed in the first 30 trials, it was important to ensure learning with few errors during these trials so that the effects of the meaningful and nonmeaningful entry stimuli could be analyzed without the confounding of errors.

Stimulus-Elements Training and Related Pre- and Posttests

After the children learned the meaningful and nonmeaningful discriminations, stimulus-elements pretests were given to determine how the children would respond to separate elements of the criterion stimuli taught with programs using meaningful or nonmeaningful entry-level stimuli. The first two boxes of Figure 6.5 for both tasks contain pairs of criterion-related elements. The last three boxes show pairs of non-criterion-related elements included to see if the participants were responding to elements other than those programmed to be criterion-related. Elements training was conducted following the elements pretest for 6 of the 8 participants, until the students completed two sessions of 100 percent correct for both the meaningful and nonmeaningful elements. Participants 1 and 8 did not complete the training because the school term ended.

Procedures for Stimulus-Elements Pretests, Posttests, and Training

Five trials of elements from each of the two programs were presented on the pre- and posttests of stimulus elements. Tokens were not given for correct responding. Before the pretest, the experimenter said, "Now we are going to do something

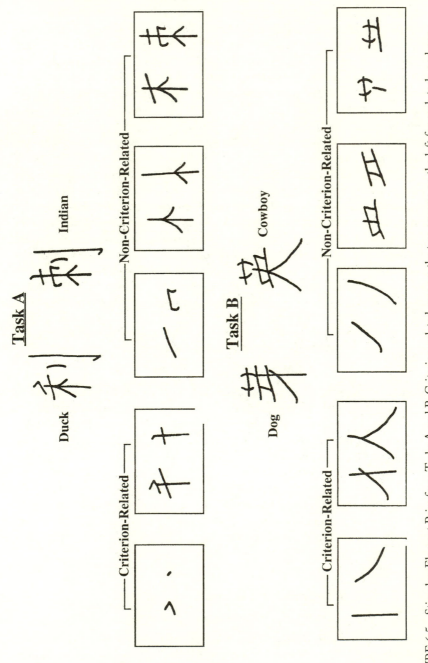

FIGURE 6.5 Stimulus–Element Pairs from Tasks A and B. Criterion-related cues are the two squares on the left for each task, and non–criterion cues are the three on the right for each task.

different, but I can't tell you how well you did until we are finished. Point to the one that gets the token." After the 10 pretest trials, the experimenter said one of the following three statements, depending on the number of correct responses of the child:

"You really did a good job. You almost got them all right!"
"You got them all right!"
"You worked pretty hard!"

Regardless of the statement, it was followed by, "I think you got enough tokens for your toy." If children did not obtain 100 percent correct responding on both elements pretests, they received a program to teach element pairs.

In elements training, the experimenter placed one pair of elements (an S+ and its comparable S- element) on the table in front of the child and said, "Point to the one that gets the token." After the child pointed, the criterion S+ and S- stimuli from which the elements were derived were placed on the table above the elements stimuli. The experimenter then asked, "Which of these [pointing first to the stimulus on the left and then to the one on the right] is this [pointing to the chosen element] a part of?"

If the child chose the correct element and criterion stimuli, the experimenter gave a token and praise. If the child chose the incorrect (S-) element and matched it with the S- criterion stimulus, the experimenter said, "Yes, this one [pointing to the S- element] is a part of this one [pointing to the S- criterion stimulus]. And which one gets the token?" If the child was again incorrect, the experimenter said, "This one [pointing to the S+ stimulus] gets the token." If the child chose the correct element (S+) but matched it to the incorrect (S-) criterion stimulus, the experimenter said, "This one [pointing to the S+ element] is a part of this one [pointing to the S+ criterion stimulus], and which one gets the token?" If the child was incorrect, the experimenter said, "This [pointing to the S+ stimulus] is the one that gets the token." If the child chose the incorrect (S-) element and the S+ criterion stimulus, the experimenter said, "This one [pointing to the element] is a part of this one [pointing to the S- criterion stimulus], and which one gets the token?" If the child was incorrect, the experimenter said, "This [pointing to the S+ criterion stimulus] is the one that gets the token." After a correction procedure, if the child responded correctly, the experimenter said, "Good" and proceeded to the next trial. After the initial correction procedure, if the child again responded incorrectly, the experimenter corrected the incorrect response and proceeded to the next trial.

If the children were not acquiring the discriminations involved in the elements, special elements-training procedures involving slight alterations of stimulus presentations were introduced. The first procedure involved presenting the criterion-level stimuli first, with the instruction to point to each of them. The elements were then presented beneath the criterion-level stimuli, so the children could compare.

If the children continued having difficulty, a second special-elements training procedure was implemented in which the criterion stimuli were initially presented in the same way as they were in the first special-elements training. The elements were placed below, and the children were asked to look at the elements, find the same elements in the criterion stimuli above, and trace them in the criterion stimuli. If the child traced incorrectly, the experimenter modeled and requested the child to imitate. Correction procedures and progressing to the next set of stimuli were the same as in the original elements-training procedure.

Recording and Reliability

The experimenter recorded child responses on a sheet that showed the placement of the S+ and S- stimuli for each trial. The reliability observer recorded "L" if the child responded to the left stimulus and "R" if to the right on a sheet that showed the trials but did not indicate the correct stimulus. Verbal praise and token delivery were also recorded.

Reliability was recorded at least once for each child in each condition; for Children 1, 2, 5, and 6 in 83 of 138 sessions; and for Children 3, 4, 7, and 8 in 24 of 125 sessions. Reliability was calculated for each session by dividing the agreements on trials by the total number of trials in the session. Overall reliability for the three recorded responses ranged from 89 to 100 percent, with a mean of 99 percent.

Results

Table 6.2 provides a summary of the findings for all the children. Individual pretest scores for stimuli of the meaningful and nonmeaningful programs (columns 2 and 3, respectively) show that all scores were between 40 and 60 percent except for Participant 3. The posttest results, shown in columns 6 and 7, indicate that all participants obtained 100 percent correct responding for both programs. The percentage of correct responses during program training, columns 4 and 5, indicates a slightly higher percentage of correct responding during meaningful (average 95%) than nonmeaningful programs (average 88%); this higher percentage of correct responding during meaningful programs was obtained across all participants.

The last two columns on the right of Table 6.2 indicate that a higher percentage of correct responding occurred to elements of stimuli used in the nonmeaningful (75%) than in the meaningful program (65%). These differences are not large, but the direction of differences was the same for 3 of the children (the opposite was true for 1). The other 4 children had the same percentage correct on both program elements. Two of the participants obtained 100 percent correct on

TABLE 6.2 Summary of Percentage Correct for Each Child During Pretest, Program Training, Posttest, and Elements Pretest

Child	Pretests		Program Training		Program Posttest		Elements Pretest	
	Meaningful	Nonmeaningful	Meaningful	Nonmeaningful	Meaningful	Nonmeaningful	Meaningful	Nonmeaningful
1	40	40	97	88	100	100	80	100
2	40	50	94	88	100	100	60	40
3	60	70	100	95	100	100	40	100
4	40	40	93	88	100	100	80	80
5	40	50	95	87	100	100	80	80
6	50	50	99	88	100	100	60	80
7	50	60	97	96	100	100	40	40
8	40	50	87	76	100	100	80	80
Mean	45	51	95	88	100	100	65	75

the nonmeaningful elements, but none of the 8 participants obtained 100 percent correct on both the meaningful and nonmeaningful elements pretests.

Table 6.3, top, shows the number of sessions required for the 6 participants to complete the elements training by obtaining 100 percent correct responding on both meaningful and nonmeaningful elements trials for two sessions in a row. Four of these participants required more sessions to reach criterion during training of meaningful than of nonmeaningful elements. One participant required more sessions to achieve criterion on nonmeaningful than on meaningful elements training, and one achieved criterion in the same number of sessions for both.

Table 6.3, bottom, provides a summary of the percentage of correct responses in element identification during element training. When the elements were criterion-related, the percentage of correct responding was higher (64% and 65%) than when the element was not criterion-related (49% and 48%). These results occurred whether the elements were associated with meaningful or nonmeaningful programs.

Discussion

Comparisons of the effects on discrimination acquisition of the two programs indicated that the percentage correct on meaningful programs was consistently

TABLE 6.3   Elements Training Results

	Sessions to Criterion	
Participant	Meaningful	Nonmeaningful
1	NA	NA
2	22	13
3	22	19
4	12	8
5	15	9
6	25	27
7	16	16
8	NA	NA
Mean	19	15

Percentage Correct: Criterion-Related	
Meaningful	Nonmeaningful
64	65

Percentage Correct: Non-Criterion-Related	
Meaningful	Nonmeaningful
49	48

NA = Not available for this study.

higher than on nonmeaningful programs. In 6 of the 8 children, the larger number of errors on the nonmeaningful program occurred primarily in the first half of the stimulus-shaping steps, indicating that either the stimulus control of the abstract stimulus element was difficult to maintain or the sudden introduction of new stimulus elements on each stimulus-equalization step of the nonmeaningful program distracted the children, or both. Despite the consistency of differences between the programs, the differences were small. It seems, therefore, that either method of stimulus shaping could be used, depending on learner and teacher preferences or the tasks to be taught.

The effects of the two programs were reversed on the elements posttests of the meaningful and nonmeaningful programs: The children made fewer errors on stimulus elements associated with the nonmeaningful program than on those associated with the meaningful program. Perhaps this occurred because the children observed the individual stimulus elements on the initial steps of the non-meaningful program. It is also possible that errors on the nonmeaningful program increased the children's attention to the program after their errors. If making a gross discrimination between two complex stimuli is the goal of teaching, it is probably sufficient to use the stimulus-shaping programs that initially incorporate meaningful stimuli. If the elements of the final stimuli are to serve a future function, however, such as helping to learn other discriminations, it is perhaps better to use shaping programs that incorporate nonmeaningful entry stimuli, programmed on criterion-related cues through an equalization procedure.

It appears errors can be greatly reduced in stimulus-shaping programs incorporating either meaningful or nonmeaningful entry stimuli, as long as the programs use criterion-related cues. The outcomes of the programs were sufficiently similar for us to conclude they were functionally equal for reducing errors in the learning.

The outcome of this and prior research of Etzel, LeBlanc, and colleagues indicates that criterion-related cues (Etzel & LeBlanc, 1979) are essential for increasing correct responding in programs designed to reduce or eliminate errors. *How* stimulus elements are programmed, however, is essential to this reduction. Critical stimulus elements (criterion-related cues) of the final stimuli in the program must be the basis for responding at the outset of discrimination acquisition, as well as during all steps of the stimulus-shaping program, so that these elements can continue to be the basis for discriminations made on the final stimuli of the learning program. Perhaps criterion-related cues should always be used to teach those with learning difficulties so that they do not have to transfer stimulus control; the result will be fewer errors during learning and increased motivation to learn.

Acknowledgments

This research was the M.A. thesis of L. L. A. McCartney, advised by B. C. Etzel and J. M. LeBlanc.

Note

Meaningful and nonmeaningful fading sequences for Tasks A and B can be obtained from Barbara C. Etzel, Department of Human Development, 4001 Dole Building, University of Kansas, Lawrence, KS 66045.

References

Cheney, T., & Stein, N. (1974). Fading procedures and oddity learning in kindergarten children. *Journal of Experimental Child Psychology, 17,* 313–321.

Etzel, B. C., & LeBlanc, J. M. (1979). The simplest treatment alternative: The law of parsimony applied to choosing appropriate instructional control and errorless-learning procedures for the difficult-to-teach child. *Journal of Autism and Developmental Disorders, 9,* 361–382.

Etzel, B. C., LeBlanc, J. M., Schilmoeller, K. J., & Stella, M. E. (1981). Stimulus control procedures in the education of young children. In S. W. Bijou & R. Ruiz (Eds.), *Contributions of Behavior Modification to Education.* Hillsdale, NJ: Erlbaum. (Also published in Spanish by Editorial Trillas, Mexico City, 1985.)

Gollin, E. S., & Savoy, P. (1968) Fading procedures and conditional discrimination in children. *Journal of the Experimental Analysis of Behavior, 11,* 443–445.

Hoko, J. A., & LeBlanc, J. M. (1988). Error analysis and stimulus equalization: Procedures to facilitate visual discriminations of children with learning problems. *Research in Developmental Disabilities, 9,* 255–275.

Koegel, R. L., & Rincover, A. (1976). Some detrimental effects of using extra stimuli to guide learning in normal and autistic children. *Journal of Abnormal Child Psychology, 4,* 59–71.

Schilmoeller, G. L., Schilmoeller, K. J., Etzel, B. C., & LeBlanc, J. M. (1979). Conditional discrimination responding after errorless and trial and error training. *Journal of the Experimental Analysis of Behavior, 31,* 405–420.

Schilmoeller, K. J., & Etzel, B. C. (1977). An experimental analysis of criterion- and non-criterion-related cues in "errorless" stimulus control procedures. In B. C. Etzel, J. M. LeBlanc, & D. M. Baer (Eds.), *New developments in behavioral research: Theory, methods, and applications. In honor of Sidney W. Bijou.* Hillsdale, NJ: Erlbaum.

Schwartz, S. H., Firestone, I. J., & Terry, S. (1971). Fading techniques and concept learning in children. *Psychonomic Science, 25,* 83–84.

Sidman, M., & Stoddard, L. T. (1966). Programming perception and learning for retarded children. In N. R. Ellis (Ed.), *International review of research in mental retardation* (pp. 151–208). New York: Academic Press.

Stella, M. E., & Etzel, B. C. (1979, April). *Application of recent findings in errorless stimulus control technology.* Paper presented at the 12th annual Gatlinberg Conference on Research in Mental Retardation and Developmental Disabilities, Gulf Shores, AL.

Stella, M. E., & Etzel, B. C. (1983). Effects of criterion-level probing on demonstrating newly acquired discriminative behavior. *Journal of Experimental Analysis of Behavior, 39,* 479–498.

Stella, M. E., & Etzel, B. C. (1986). Stimulus control of eye orientations: Shaping S+ only versus shaping S- only. *Analysis and Intervention in Developmental Disabilities, 6,* 137–153.

Terrace, H. S. (1963) Discrimination learning with and without "errors." *Journal of the Experimental Analysis of Behavior, 6,* 1–27.

7

Selective Eye Fixations During Transfer of Discriminative Stimulus Control

Stephen R. Schroeder

The use of fading techniques to transfer a discrimination poses a challenge to traditional methods of teaching and to traditional theories of discrimination learning. As an example, a time-honored concept of teaching normal children is that they learn through trial and error. The assumption that errors are necessary for learning is implicit in this concept. On the other hand, a considerable body of evidence shows that errors are not only unnecessary for but often hinder learning (Skinner, 1958). This is especially true of those who display a long history of learning failures, such as persons with mental retardation.

Over the years, a considerable amount of evidence has accumulated that errorless learning techniques (Terrace, 1966) are successful with animals and with humans who have mental retardation (Sidman & Stoddard, 1967; Stoddard & Sidman, 1963; Touchette, 1968) and with those who do not (Doran & Holland, 1979; Stella & Etzel, 1986). The method involves phases of "fading" a new concept over one already correctly being performed, thereby reducing errors.

The most common paradigm is as follows: A positive stimulus to which the participant is likely to respond is presented alone, initially. The first phase of fading then involves the gradual introduction of the negative stimulus, starting with bare perceptibility, until it is easily perceivable. Once this discrimination is established, new positive and negative stimuli are superimposed on the original stimuli in a second phase. The third phase involves fading out the original stimuli by either reducing their perceptibility or precluding their use as cues for correct choice by making them equal in value.

An interesting question is what determines the exact point when the participant shifts response strategy to the second dimension (Touchette, 1971). As one dimension fades in and the other dimension fades out, are there specifiable psychophysical and perceptual variables that affect the point of shift in attention? Or does it vary within a wide range of trials? As the new dimension fades in, there would be several trials in which a participant might shift dimensions before the old one fades out. What happens during fade-out of the old and fade-in of the new dimension?

Terrace's present technique does not allow one to find this out since the experimenter controls presentation of the stimuli. The observing-response technique

(Wyckoff, 1952) might reveal the point of dimension shift, however, if the compound stimuli could be separated to require an observing response to see each dimension. Observing responses are those that produce stimuli correlated with reinforcement or punishment. The most prevalent view is that they are conditioned reinforced responses. Wyckoff (1952) was the first to show that the proportion of time spent observing is related to the increase and decrease of stimulus control, that is, the correlation between a stimulus and food presentation in experiments with pigeons. Supportive results have now been replicated in a variety of animal-learning paradigms (see Dinsmoor, 1985, for a thorough review) as well as in human discrimination paradigms (Case & Fantino, 1989; Case, Ploog, & Fantino, 1990; Holland, 1958; Schroeder & Holland, 1968).

There are few guidelines for choosing particular sequences of stimuli. Terrace (1963) showed that the amount of training affects the ease of shift from the original to the new dimension in pigeons. The size of the interval between gradations of stimuli on a particular dimension affects the ease with which they can be faded in and out. There has been little formal research on the latter point, however; the gradations are usually chosen for a particular experiment on the basis of pilot work.

Burkholder, Deitchman, Haude, and Sanders (1975) found that stimulus complexity was positively correlated with observing behavior in rats' discrimination. Vlietstra (1978) found that cue salience, verbal instructions, and modeling increased observing behavior in a matching-from-memory task by preschoolers. Stella and Etzel (1986) compared different stimulus-shaping programs involving simultaneously presented stimuli, including stimulus-fading programs, and noted several effects on their preschoolers' eye orientation: greater orientation to the S- when it was shaped than when it was invariant; more orientation to the S- by some children as S+ became more similar to it. Eye orientations were also correlated with pointing responses.

It would seem, therefore, that if the fading technique is to be useful for basic and applied research in the transfer of selective stimulus control in humans, the minimum number of steps required for errorless transfer should be determined, and the variables affecting the response to fading should be delineated.

Four sets of variables seem important and relatively simple to analyze in initial experiments: stimulus characteristics affecting dimensional salience (e.g., relevance, luminance, size, orientation, redundancy); sequential factors in fading (e.g., cue addition or subtraction); practice and training effects (e.g., number of trials); and the reinforcement contingencies (e.g., feedback vs. no feedback).

General Method

Pilot Work

Since the reduction of the eye-movement data was extremely labor-intensive, I developed the stimulus sequences first and selected the ones that showed some difference on the basis of pilot data. I made up 12 fading sequences on index cards and tested 90 college students. Sequences that produced the fewest errors and were most suitable for promoting differential location of fixations were used in the subsequent experiments, in which 450 students participated.

Participants

Undergraduate volunteers with normal vision served as participants for one session each; the sessions were scheduled to last for approximately 5 minutes to avert fatigue and confounding head movements. Half of the students were men and half women.

Apparatus

The main piece of recording apparatus was a Biometrics Eye-Trace Infra-red Eye Movement Monitor, which records horizontal and vertical eye movements by tracking the reflection from the sclera-iris junction. Stimuli were projected through slides in a Kodak Carousel projector onto a rear-view screen with a black template so that two 3.8- × 7.6-cm rectangular areas side by side were visible (see Figure 7.1). The stimuli were white on a dark gray background 2.5 cm high and 0.16 cm wide. In the center of the display was a feedback light, which was lit between trials. An electromechanical apparatus controlled slide presentation and intertrial interval (3 seconds) and recorded choices automatically.

Correct response contingencies were coded on each slide by punched holes around the edges. Light projecting through the holes onto photorelays then set the programming apparatus for each slide. The participant indicated his or her choice of the right side by pressing the button in the right hand and the left side by pressing a button in the left hand.

Procedures

The general procedures were the same for all participants. They entered the dimly lit experimental room and were seated in front of the recorder. The hand and chin rests were adjusted so that the bridge of the student's nose was directly in line with the center of the screen, and the corners of the rectangles were equidistant, subtending a visual angle of 12 degrees. Participants' arms rested on the table, and they held a choice button in each hand. The following taped instructions were then played:

> This is a device for measuring pupil size. Infrared light reflects off your eyes onto photocells and is recorded on the chart in back. Now I am going to present a problem for you to solve, and I want to watch your eyes. Each slide will show some forms on these two areas of the screen. You choose which you think is correct. If you choose

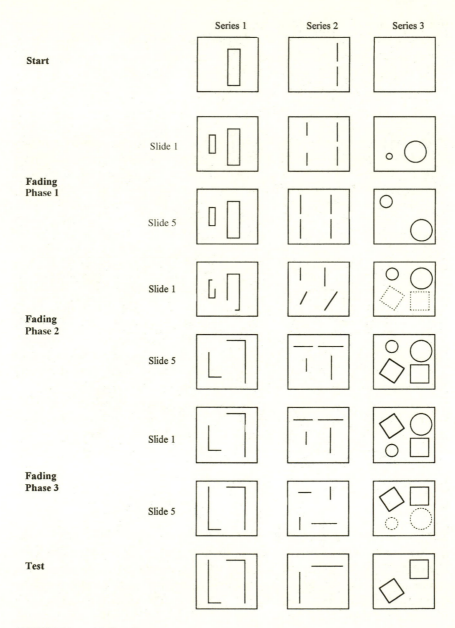

FIGURE 7.1   Fading Sequences

the right side, press the button in your right hand; if you choose the left side, press the button in your left hand. If your choice was correct, a green light will come on here in the middle. If it was wrong, a red light will come on.

First I will show you five slides with nothing on them just to show you how the apparatus works. Okay, press a button and see what happens. [Five blank slide trials ensued.]

Okay, now I am going to calibrate you in the recorder. Look at the X in the center. After you are lined up, make sure you don't move your head. That throws everything off. Also always fixate the light between slides. That will give me a chance to recalibrate if necessary.

The experimenter then adjusted the recorder, flashed on the first slide, and told the student to begin (see Figure 7.1).

The slides all involved transfer of a size discrimination (large vs. small) to one of orientation (e.g., tilted lines). On successive slides, the relative position of the figures followed two rules: The positive or negative stimuli of both dimensions were always presented together on the left or right side of the display, in a Geller-man series, to control for position preferences. The vertical position of the dimensions was also ordered with a Gellerman series. For instance, either of the positive stimuli (large circle and upright square) could be in the upper left and lower left or upper right and lower right but never upper left and lower right positions. Therefore, both of the positive stimuli could change between left and right sides of the display, but always together. The two dimensions of the stimuli could change between the upper and lower positions. This was done to encourage, first, scanning each position, and then, scanning vertically between the two dimensions of the positive or negative stimuli on a particular slide.

Each stimulus, when it occurred, appeared equally often in each of four quadrants on the screen, therefore, but in an irregular sequence. A quadrant analysis of the eye-movement data showed that this procedure was indeed effective in precluding position preferences for looking at a given area, irrespective of the stimulus occurring there.

Experiment 1

In the traditional redundant-relevant-cue (RRC) learning task involving extradimensional concept shift (see Kendler & Kendler, 1962), the participant is presented with a choice between multidimensional stimuli. In the beginning, all dimensions are irrelevant except one. In the next phase, dimensional relevance is shifted: The old dimension is abruptly made irrelevant, and the participant can solve the discrimination only on the basis of the previously irrelevant, but now relevant, cue. Response measures are errors to criterion after shift.

A similar analysis applies to the fading experiment. Since cue relevance and salience are introduced gradually over a series of trials, however, it would be useful to know what methods are best suited for addition or subtraction of relevant and irrelevant cues. The relative frequency of fixation of stimulus components is a useful measure of stimulus control exerted by a cue.

I used three series of fading sequences, exemplified in Figure 7.1, to demonstrate how differential fixation frequency can be used as an index of selective stimulus control. All involved the transfer from size (large vs. small) to orientation, and all involved the same fading sequences, but they differed in the way the relevance and salience of the cue were introduced. In Series 1, the figures became fragmented; in Series 2, similar figures were added to the display; in Series 3, new figures were added to the display. Cue relevance was also changed in the three different phases.

Each phase of each series consisted of five slides. The start phase simply presented the positive stimulus of the old dimension (O+). In Fading Phase 1, the negative stimulus of the old dimension (O-) was added. In Phase 2, the positive (N+) and negative (N-) stimuli of the new dimension were added. In Phase 3, the O+ and O- were subtracted. A test series of five slides with figures in different relative positions followed.

The question of interest was how fixations to O+, O-, N+, and N- were distributed during Phases 2, 3, and Test. In Series 1 and 3, orientation became relevant and redundant in Phase 2 and size became irrelevant in Phase 3, during the test. The salience of orientation could be different for the two, however, since in Series 1 the new dimension was faded by changing O+ to O-. In Series 3, the new dimension of orientation was faded on an irrelevant dimension (brightness).

In Series 2, fading occurred by changing O+ and O-, as in Series 1, but N+ and N- were redundant and irrelevant until the test in which only orientation was relevant.

Method

Participants.   Ninety college undergraduates with normal vision, equally divided by gender, were assigned randomly to each of three groups of 30 each.

Apparatus and Procedure.   The same apparatus and general procedure as discussed previously were used. Each student experienced one session of 25 slides in five phases of five slides each (Start, Fade 1, Fade 2, Fade 3, Test). Thirty students experienced each series of fading sequences. During the Test Phase, they received no feedback for correct or incorrect responses; during all other phases, a green light in the center of the screen signaled a correct response, and a red light signaled an incorrect response.

Results and Discussion

Choice Errors.   Participants made few errors per session, usually only one or two if any. Therefore, only the total errors per session for each subject were used in a

3 × 2 factorial analysis of variance comparing total errors committed for Series 1, 2, and 3 for males and females. No sex difference was observed ($F < 1$), but there was a significant difference in errors produced by the different series ($F = 4.12$; $df = 2$, 84; $p < .025$). In Series 1, fewer errors were made during fading and more during testing than for Series 2 and 3. In all cases, the number of errors was well below chance performance (50%), even though Test Phase performance was not nearly as errorless as was expected. More errors during testing occurred with Series 1 and 2 than Series 3.

Eye Movements.   A 3 × 3 × 4 factorial analysis compared the effects of two within-subjects variables (Phases 2, 3, and Test, and Stimuli, i.e., O+, O-, N+, N-) and one between-subjects variable (Series 1, 2, 3). There was no significant effect of Series on the frequency of fixations ($F = 1.47$; $df = 2$, 87; $p = $ ns). However, all other main effects plus their interactions were significant at $p < .001$. The triple interaction of Stimuli, Phase, and Series was also significant ($F = 2.51$; $df = 12$, 522; $p < .025$). Therefore, there was a significant difference between relative frequency of fixations to the different cues across phases and between series.

Cue Salience.   In Series 1 and 3, where N+ and N- became relevant in Phase 2, the manner in which fading occurred strongly affected the salience (differential fixation frequency) of the new cue. In Series 2, participants looked immediately at the new cue more often and made fewer errors during fading. In Series 3, where fading of line orientation occurred on the brightness dimension, participants persisted in looking for the old cue through Phases 2 and 3 and even into the first two trials of the test phase before switching to N+ and N-. It is interesting that they made more errors during fading but fewer errors during testing than did Series 1 participants.

In Series 2, N+ and N- were introduced in Phase 2, but size was still redundant and relevant on all O+, O-, N+, and N- cues. Participants preferred O+ and O-. In Phase 3, O+ and O- were subtracted; now size was irrelevant on N+ and N-. Participants switched their fixation preferences to N+ and stayed with it during Phase 3 and the Test Phase.

This experiment demonstrates an interaction between cue relevance, salience, and utilization during fading. The manner in which a new cue is faded (i.e., made relevant) affects its salience (differential fixation frequency). If a new redundant but irrelevant cue is added, it probably will not be used until the old cue is made irrelevant.

An interesting question is why participants in Series 1 and 2 made more errors during testing than those in Series 3. A tentative answer is that, since the new cue was added by changing the old stimuli, the relative orientation of the cues was more important for them by the end of fading in Phase 3. This was less true for Series 3, in which a different new stimulus was faded in on an irrelevant dimension. In Series 1 and 2, therefore, errors at the end of Phase 3 and during test trials rarely occurred until the relative location of the stimuli was changed. It may be that participants in Series 1 and 2 had to learn in addition that only the position of the angle or the horizontal line was relevant and not its position relative to the negative stimulus. This was not the case for Series 3, in which the only basis for discriminating the new cues was upright versus tilted orientation of the square.

Finally, it should be noted that there were no differences in total frequency of fixations for the different series. Fixation frequency on this type of problem is related to the ease with which a stimulus is perceived (Schroeder, 1970). It is unlikely, therefore, that the distribution of fixations found in the different series was due only to the difficulty with which the participant could perceive them.

Experiment 2

I showed (Schroeder, 1969a, 1969b, 1970) that, on a discrete-trial, simultaneous-presentation discrimination problem similar to the present design but without fading, reinforced practice decreased fixation frequency of all stimuli but did not alter the pattern of selective fixations. The present experiment examined the effects of familiarization, feedback, and reinforced practice when fading was used.

Method

Participants.   One hundred twenty undergraduate volunteers with normal vision, equally divided by gender, were assigned randomly to 12 groups of 10 each.

Apparatus and Procedure.   The same Series 1, 2, and 3 fading sequence as in Experiment 1 was used for this experiment. There were four conditions in each series: no feedback, feedback, familiarization, and reinforced practice, making a 3 × 4 factorial design. The apparatus and procedure were the same as that of Experiment 1 except for the following:

1. For Group NF (no feedback), the part about feedback was omitted in the instructions, and the students simply made their choice on each trial without the feedback of the red or green light.
2. For Group Fam (familiarization), after instructions, the experimenter told the student to wait until he ran through all of the slides to show what they were like. Slides were exposed automatically for 2 seconds with a 3-second intertrial interval. Then the test session began as usual.
3. Group RP (reinforced practice) received feedback for slides on two sessions, one immediately following the other. Series 1 and 3 participants received Series 2 first; Series 2 participants received Series 3 before the test session.

Results and Discussion

Eye Movements.   The effects of the feedback and practice conditions on eye movements and errors for Phases 2 and 3 and the Test Phase are discussed here.

Separate factorial analyses of variance on eye movements were run for each of the three series, with one between-groups variable (NF, F, Fam, RP) and two within-groups variables: Phase (2, 3, T) and Stimuli (O+, O-, N+, N-). As in Experiment 1, there were significant effects ($p < .001$) of Phase and Stimulus and in the Phase $\times$ Stimulus interaction. There were no differences between Groups NF, F, Fam, or RP in total fixation frequency or its interaction with Phase or Stimulus. There were significant differences ($p < .05$) between Groups NF and F in the Group $\times$ Stimulus and Group $\times$ Phase interactions.

Feedback significantly changed the pattern of fixations, compared to no feedback. The familiarization and reinforced practice conditions differed little in frequency or pattern from the feedback condition. This result differs slightly from previous ones (Schroeder, 1969b, 1970) in which fading was not used. The discrepancy is best explained in terms of reinforcement for looking at a stimulus: Once the information is extracted from a stimulus and it remains the same over many trials, fixation of it extinguishes. In the fading experiment, the relevant stimuli change from trial to trial; so the participant persists in inspecting them.

Errors.   There was a significant reduction of errors ($p < .001$) for each series as a function of familiarization and reinforced practice.

Experiment 3

Since there were four stimulus components (O+, O-, N+, N-) that changed during fading, several options existed in sequencing the fading of the same stimuli that might affect the pattern of fixations and errors. For instance, we tried three methods for adding the new stimulus in Phase 2. In Series 2, N+ and N- were faded in by changing their orientation; in Series 2a, N+ and N- were faded in by changing their size; in Series 2b, only N+ was faded in. In Series 2c, Phase 4, size was made irrelevant by decreasing the size of N+. In Series 2d, N+ remained constant and all the other stimuli were increased in size. In Series 2e, Phase 3, N+ was faded in; in Phase 4, N- was faded in; and in Phase 5, size was made irrelevant by decreasing the size of N+. These are only a few of the combinations.

Method

Participants.   Sixty undergraduate volunteers with normal vision (equally divided by gender) were assigned randomly to each of the six fading series.

Apparatus and Procedure.   These were the same as for Experiment 1.

Results and Discussion

Eye Movements.   Analysis of variance, with series as the between-groups variable and phase and stimulus the within-groups variables, showed no significant difference in total fixation frequency between groups but highly significant differences ($p < .001$) between phase and stimuli and in their interaction. The triple interaction was also significant ($F = 2.75$; $df = 30, 324$; $p < .001$). Therefore, the shift in stimulus fixation patterns across phases differed for the various groups.

The addition of Phase 4 in Series 2c and 2d caused a shift back to less looking at new stimuli. This shift was averted in Series 2e, however, with the addition of the phase in which N- was faded in before size was made irrelevant. As Series 2, 2a, and 2b showed, therefore, it does not matter so much how the new stimulus is added; Series 2c, 2d, and 2e showed, however, that it does matter how the old stimulus is subtracted.

Errors.   A simple analysis of variance comparing total errors made by each group was significant ($F = 3.25$; $df = 5, 54$; $p < .025$). This was likely due to the fact that Series 2c, 2d, and 2e participants had more opportunity than the others to err during fading. Analysis of variance of errors in the test phase showed no significant difference.

Experiment 4

Terrace (1963, 1966) noted that the amount of experience with the old dimension may affect the ease with which attention is switched to the new dimension during fading, and this might affect the number of errors. This notion was tested with the Series 2 fading sequence.

Method

Participants.   Fifty participants with normal vision (equally divided by gender) were assigned randomly to five groups of 10 each.

Apparatus and Procedure.   The apparatus and procedure were the same as those of Experiment 1, Series 2, except for the following:

> Series 2f—the first four slides of the Start Phase were omitted.
> Series 2g—the first four slides of Phases Start and 1 were omitted.
> Series 2b—the first four slides of Phases Start, 1, and 2 were omitted.
> Series 2i—the first four slides of Phases Start, 1, 2, and 3 were omitted.

Results and Discussion

Eye Movements.   There was a shift in preference for the new dimension as the fading slides were progressively eliminated in each of the fading phases. This interaction was significant ($p < .001$), as determined by factorial analysis of variance.

Errors. Errors were reduced by using fewer fading slides in the early phases but were increased when fewer fading slides were used in the later, more critical phases of fading. Therefore, Terrace's contention is supported by the present results. Analysis of variance of errors showed a significant difference between groups ($F = 4, 49$; $df = 2, 82$; $p < .05$).

Experiment 5

Results of errorless-learning experiments using the discrete-trials procedure with both animals (Terrace, 1963, 1966) and people with mental retardation (Sidman & Stoddard, 1967) agree that gradual stimulus change is more effective in reducing errors than abrupt stimulus change. However, little research of this type has been done with humans who do not have mental retardation.

Method

Participants. Sixty undergraduate volunteers with normal vision (equally divided by gender) were assigned randomly to six groups of 10 each.

Apparatus and Procedure. These were the same as in Experiment 1. Slides from Series 2 were used as fading sequences under three different conditions:

1. Series 2 and 2b were used as normal fading sequences for two groups.
2. Series 2j and 2l also used Series 2 and 2b slides, respectively, but all five slides in a given phase had the same stimulus values.
3. Series 2k and 2m also used Series 2 and 2b slides, respectively, but without the first four slides in the Start Phase.

Results and Discussion

Eye Movements. The percentage of fixations of the new stimuli and errors were calculated for each phase of each series. Analysis of variance showed that participants made significantly more fixations during fading than during abrupt stimulus change ($F = 3.02$; $df = 5, 54$; $p < .025$). The main effects across phases and stimuli and their interactions were also significant ($p < .001$). The Group x Stimulus interaction was also significant ($F = 4.79$; $df = 15, 162$; $p < .025$). Therefore, the pattern of selective fixations between abrupt and gradual stimulus change differed. These differences were most evident in the final three phases (adding the new cue, subtracting the old cue, and Test Phase).

Errors. More errors were made during abrupt (Series 2j, 2k, 2l, 2m) than during gradual (Series 2, 2b) stimulus change. Analysis of variance showed, however, that only Series 2k and 2m differed significantly from Series 2 and 2b, respectively

($p < .025$). The discrimination problem was probably too simple for these students to show the large differences usually observed between abrupt and gradual stimulus change (see Sidman & Stoddard, 1967; Terrace, 1963).

General Discussion

The results of the five experiments reported here support previous findings (Schroeder, 1969a, 1969b, 1970) that saccadic fixations of stimulus components are a useful index related to selective stimulus control during discrimination learning and performance. Fixations appear to be operant observing responses, correlated in a complex but systematic fashion with traditional discrimination-learning variables. Furthermore, relative differential fixation frequency and pattern vary systematically with errors and therefore are useful for the design of stimulus presentations to regulate the number of errors produced.

The results of the present experiments suggest that errors in discrimination transfer may be largely a matter of selective observing during the formation of stimulus control. However, choice errors often occur, even in bright college undergraduates. Four sets of variables affected the distribution of their fixations and their errors: (a) stimulus characteristics affecting dimensional salience, (b) sequential factors in the fading sequence, (c) practice and training, and (d) the reinforcement contingencies for choosing correct and incorrect stimuli. These are probably not the only variables affecting stimulus control of fixations and choice during transfer of a discrimination, but they seem to be a logical point to begin the investigation. Our results suggest the following:

Experiment 1 showed that factors affecting cue salience, relevance, and utilization during fading, such as type of figure, arrangement of the dimensional cues, and relative cue position, interacted in a complex manner to affect systematically the distribution of fixations and errors across fading phases. A new redundant relevant cue, if added, was not fixated more frequently until the old cue (S+) was made irrelevant. This was the most likely point in the sequence for an error to occur.

Experiment 2 showed that feedback significantly altered the number of errors and distribution of fixations when compared to no feedback. Familiarization and reinforced practice reduced errors but did not alter fixation frequency or distribution.

Experiment 3 showed that sequential factors, such as adding or subtracting cues in different phases of fading, altered the distribution of fixations but not fixation frequency or errors.

Experiment 4 showed that reducing the number of trials in each phase of fading altered fixation patterns. Errors were reduced with fewer trials in early phases, but they were increased with fewer trials in later phases.

Experiment 5 showed that abrupt stimulus change altered the distribution of fixations to stimulus components, reduced fixation frequency, and increased errors, compared to gradual stimulus change.

These experiments on eye fixations and choice in discrimination transfer yield important information both at the practical and at the theoretical level. At the practical level, they show that under the proper conditions, the oculomotor systems, which control sensory orientation and select the stimuli that come under discriminative control, are a very finely tuned servomechanism in a data-acquisition system. The highly sophisticated, evolutionarily refined coordination of integrated ballistic head and eye movements results in concentration of stimuli from periphery to the fovea of the retina with uncanny speed, accuracy, and efficiency. For these tasks, the fixation sequences average about 250 milliseconds in duration. Under time pressure, they are even faster, much faster and earlier in development than most of the motor responses we ordinarily use in operant research. Information processing is fairly automatic. We tend not to attend to our saccadic eye movements unless instructed to do so; nevertheless they are highly sensitive to behavioral and pharmacological modifications. The main advantage of working with saccadic fixations is the possibility of collecting large amounts of systematic data unobtrusively and in a brief amount of time. These data are often predictive of motor responses related to the formation of attention and stimulus control. A main disadvantage is that data recording is labor-intensive and technically complex. This probably explains why saccadic fixations have not been used more often in human research in applied settings.

At the theoretical level, we might ask, "Is seeing really believing?" It would seem that it is first necessary to ask, "Under what conditions is looking really seeing? And what stimulus conditions control looking?" Seeing, believing, and looking are all related in a complex fashion, but they are usually neither isomorphic nor substitutable for one another.

Perhaps the most elegant behavioral analysis of the role of observing and attention in establishing stimulus control is that of Dinsmoor (1985). His view, most simply and broadly stated, is that "the conformity of behavior to the consequences encountered in the presence of each of two or more alternative stimuli (stimulus control) depends on how much contact the organism has with these stimuli" (p. 365). Contact is established through observing responses, which appear to be conditioned by the consequences of the choice of the discriminative stimuli. These observing responses constitute a discrete functional category and have important effects on other behavior. To the extent that the principles governing observing responses are related to those governing attention, they can serve as a concrete, measurable index of it during the establishment, transfer, and maintenance of stimulus control.

Acknowledgments

This research was supported by National Institute of Mental Health Grant MH 19520 to the author, while he was at the University of North Carolina. Copies of the full report can be obtained from Stephen R. Schroeder, 1052 Dole, University of Kansas, Lawrence, KS 66045.

References

Burkholder, J., Deitchman, R., Haude, R. H., & Sanders, R. E. (1975). Observing behavior in the albino rat: A within-subjects comparison of increasing levels of visual complexity. *Perceptual and Motor Skills, 41,* 523–529.

Case, D. A., & Fantino, E. (1989). Instructions and reinforcement in the observing behavior of adults and children. *Learning and Motivation, 20,* 373–412.

Case, D. A., Ploog, B. D., & Fantino, E. (1990). Observing behavior in a computer game. *Journal of the Experimental Analysis of Behavior, 54,* 185–199.

Dinsmoor, J. A. (1985). The role of observing behavior and attention in establishing stimulus control. *Journal of the Experimental Analysis of Behavior, 43,* 365–381.

Doran, J., & Holland, J. G. (1979). Control of stimulus features during fading. *Journal of the Experimental Analysis of Behavior, 31,* 177–187.

Holland, J. G. (1958). Human vigilance. *Science, 128,* 61–67.

Kendler, H., & Kendler, T. (1962). Vertical and horizontal processes in problem solving. *Psychological Review, 69,* 1–16.

Schroeder, S. (1969a). Effects of cue factors on selective eye-movement patterns during successive discrimination. *Perceptual and Motor Skills, 29,* 991–993.

Schroeder, S. (1969b). Fixation and choice preference during discrimination transfer. *Psychonomic Science, 17,* 324–325.

Schroeder, S. (1970). Effects of luminance on selective eye movements to simultaneously presented stimuli during discrimination. *Perception and Psychophysics, 7,* 121–124.

Schroeder, S. R., & Holland, J. G. (1968). Operant control of eye movements during human vigilance. *Science, 161,* 292–293.

Sidman, M., & Stoddard, L. (1967). The effectiveness of fading in programming a simultaneous form discrimination for retarded children. *Journal of the Experimental Analysis of Behavior, 10,* 3–15.

Skinner, B. (1958). Teaching machines. *Science, 128,* 969–997.

Stella, M. E., & Etzel, B. (1986). Stimulus control of eye orientations: Shaping S+ only versus shaping S- only. *Analysis and Intervention in Developmental Disabilities, 6,* 137–153.

Stoddard, L. T., & McIlvane, W. J. (1986). Stimulus control research with developmentally disabled individuals. *Analysis and Intervention in Developmental Disabilities, 6,* 155–178.

Stoddard, L., & Sidman, M. (1963). The effects of errors on children's performance on a circle ellipse discrimination. *Journal of the Experimental Analysis of Behavior, 6,* 1–27.

Terrace, H. (1963). Discrimination learning with and without "errors." *Journal of the Experimental Analysis of Behavior, 6,* 1–27.

Terrace, H. (1966). Stimulus control. In W. K. Honig (Ed.), *Operant behavior: Areas of research and application.* New York: Meredith.

Touchette, P. (1968). The effects of a graduated stimulus change on the acquisition of a simple discrimination in severely retarded boys. *Journal of the Experimental Analysis of Behavior, 11,* 39–48.

Touchette, P. E. (1971). Transfer of stimulus control: Measuring the moment of transfer. *Journal of the Experimental Analysis of Behavior, 15,* 347–354.

Vlietstra, A. G. (1978). The effect of strategy training and stimulus saliency on attention and recognition in preschoolers. *Journal of Experimental Child Psychology, 25,* 17–32.

Wyckoff, B. (1952). The role of observing responses in discrimination behavior. *Psychological Review, 59,* 437–442.

Zeaman, D., & House, B. (1963). The role of attention in retardate discrimination learning. In N. R. Ellis (Ed.), *Handbook of Mental Deficiency.* New York: McGraw-Hill.

8

Evaluating the Identity Concept Using Matching-to-Sample Procedures

John L. Brown, Ann K. Brown, and Claire L. Poulson

A conceptual understanding of sameness is one specific skill that every child needs to learn early in life (Daehler, Lonardo, & Bukatko, 1979). However, conceptual skills, like identity, can be difficult to teach to young children. Without adequate procedures for testing the extent of a child's conceptual skills, it is impossible to evaluate the effectiveness of specific curricula for each individual child (Etzel & LeBlanc, 1979). Accurately testing conceptual skills is not a simple task.

Researchers and educators have used a procedure called *matching-to-sample* to determine if children have the concept of identity. One of the most significant barriers to the use of matching-to-sample procedures is its wide range of procedural variations, some of which demonstrate the identity concept, whereas others do not. This chapter proposes a conceptual framework to identify procedures that must be in place for the identity concept to be demonstrated.

Matching-to-sample is one of many tasks that can be categorized as a conditional discrimination. There are two major classes of discrimination skills that are important in the education of children. First, simple discrimination is the ability to differentiate stimuli from each other (Reynolds, 1975). For example, differentiating the letter A from the letter B is a simple discrimination. Conditional discrimination, however, is more complex. Lashley (1938) defined it as a simple discrimination task in which the correct response depends on an additional variable. In the preceding example, if a teacher presents two cards, one with the letter A and one with the letter B, and sometimes instructs the child to point to the A and sometimes to the B, the task becomes a conditional discrimination. The teacher's instructions change the simple discrimination into a conditional discrimination. In a conditional-discrimination task, the correct response depends on the value of an additional stimulus, in this case, on whether the teacher said A or B.

A typical matching-to-sample procedure consists of a series of trials, each of which involves the presentation of at least two different stimuli. In the first stage, a participant is presented with a single stimulus known as the sample. When the participant emits a response to the sample, two or more comparison stimuli are added to the stimulus display. One of the comparison stimuli is identical to the sample. If the participant responds to the comparison that is identical to the sample, reinforcement is provided. This stimulus is referred to as the *positive comparison stimulus* (Co+). No reinforcement is provided for responses to any of the other comparisons. These stimuli are referred to as the *negative comparison stimuli* (Co-). For example, Figure 8.1 shows a typical matching-to-sample trial. In the first stage, a circle is presented. When the participant responds to the circle, a square (Co-) and another circle (Co+) are added to the stimulus display. A response to the square is not reinforced, but a response to the second circle is reinforced.

There are two major areas to address. First, stimulus configurations describe how stimuli are repeated and how their behavioral functions change across trials. Second, transfer-testing procedures describe the probe trials necessary to test the generalization of matching-to-sample performances to novel stimuli. These two properties operate independently, such that any matching-to-sample procedure uses at least one type of stimulus configuration and may or may not use a transfer-testing procedure.

FIGURE 8.1   A Typical Matching-to-Sample Trial

Stimulus Configurations

The stimuli in matching-to-sample procedures can be classified in the following ways. A *stimulus pool* consists of all of the stimuli used in a matching-to-sample procedure, regardless of whether they are used as samples, comparisons, or both. Stimulus pools must contain at least two stimuli, with no limit to the maximum number of stimuli. A *stimulus set* consists of all of the stimuli used on a given trial, whether or not the stimuli are used as samples or comparisons. Any specific stimulus can appear in more than one stimulus set. In a matching-to-sample procedure, a stimulus set must consist of the same number of stimuli as the number of comparisons on a given trial. On a given trial, one of the stimuli must appear twice, once as a sample and once as a comparison.

Three major stimulus configurations have been used in matching-to-sample procedures: the constant-comparison-stimulus configuration, the reversal-of-comparison-stimulus configuration, and the unique-stimulus configuration.

Constant-Comparison-Stimulus Configuration

In the constant-comparison-stimulus configuration, the functions of the stimuli in each stimulus set remain constant. Specifically, every time a trial appears that contains a given stimulus set, the same stimulus serves as the sample, and the same stimuli serve as the Co+ and the Co- (Dube, McIlvane, & Green, 1992). Figure 8.2 shows several examples of constant-comparison-stimulus trials. Four

FIGURE 8.2   Examples of Constant-Comparison Matching Trials

matching-to-sample trials are shown in which the comparison functions are constant. In the first trial, the square serves as the sample and the Co+, and the circle is the Co-. In the second trial, the triangle serves as the sample and the Co+, and the diamond is the Co-. The third and fourth trials show the same stimuli with the Co+ and Co- positions reversed.

Each time a constant-comparison-stimulus trial is repeated, the same stimuli serve as the sample, Co+, and Co-, even though the Co+ and Co- positions may vary. Figure 8.3 shows a series of trials that illustrates this feature. On the first presentation of the trial, the participant must perform a conditional discrimination to respond correctly. On the second and subsequent presentations, however, the correct response can be made by simply selecting the stimulus associated with reinforcement during the first trial (the square). To illustrate this concept, the fifth trial does not have a sample stimulus. The fifth trial can be solved simply by discriminating between the circle and square, given the reinforcement history for responses to the square. Constant-comparison-stimulus trials, therefore, can become simple discriminations. Constant-comparison-stimulus trials are not necessarily conditional discrimination trials and therefore cannot be used to test for the identity concept.

Reversal-of-Comparison-Stimulus Configuration

Many researchers have reversed the comparison stimuli to maintain the conditional nature of the discrimination required in matching-to-sample trials. In reversal-of-comparison-stimulus trials, each comparison stimulus serves as the Co+ on some trials and the Co- on other trials (Dube et al., 1992; McIlvane et al., 1987; Sidman, 1980).

Figure 8.4 shows several examples of this reversal of the Co+ and Co- across trials. Two matching-to-sample trials in which the comparison functions are reversed are shown in each column. For example, in the first trial, the square serves as the sample and the Co+, and the circle is the Co-. In the second trial, in the first column, the behavioral functions of the stimuli are reversed, and the circle now serves as the sample and the Co+, and the square is the Co-.

A study done by Carter and Eckerman (1976) serves as an example of reversal-of-comparison-stimulus configuration trials. In this study, pigeons were trained to match to sample, with either a white circle or a cross on a black background. Matching trials began with the sample stimulus on the center key. Five pecks to the sample resulted in the onset of the comparison stimuli. Responses to the comparison that matched the sample were reinforced. On some trials, the cross served as the Co+ and the sample, and the circle served as the Co-. On other trials, the comparison stimulus functions were reversed, with the circle functioning as the Co+ and the sample and the cross as the Co-. This study demonstrates the critical feature of reversal of comparison stimuli.

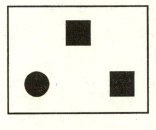

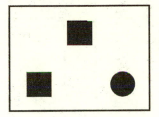

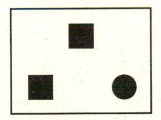

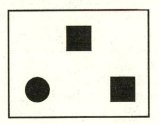

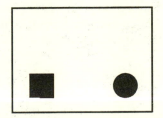

FIGURE 8.3   Series of Constant-Comparison Matching Trials Illustrating How a
Constant-Comparison Trial Can Be Solved as a Simple Discrimination

FIGURE 8.4   Examples of Reversal-of-Comparison Matching Trials

Unique-Stimulus Configuration

The unique-stimulus paradigm variation requires that new stimuli be used on every trial. No stimulus may be presented again once it has been used in a trial. Figure 8.5 shows a series of simultaneous matching trials with unique stimuli. In the first trial, the subject is presented with a triangle as the sample, a triangle as the Co+, and a diamond as the Co-. On each of the remaining three trials, new stimuli are used as samples, Co+s, and Co-s. The fact that each trial is conducted with novel stimuli is the critical aspect of this procedure.

Wright, Cook, Rivera, Sands, & Delius (1988) demonstrated matching-to-sample in pigeons using video-picture stimuli. Their procedure, which they called *trial-unique,* was similar to the unique-stimulus paradigm. In their trial-unique procedure, each stimulus is used only once during each session, but stimuli are repeated in subsequent sessions. Therefore, their training procedure does not meet the critical feature of the unique-stimulus paradigm. In their transfer-testing phase, each unique-stimulus set was used once and only once, thus finally meeting the criteria for the unique-stimulus paradigm.

Testing Matching-to-Sample

The term *matching-to-sample* has been used to refer to the behavior of a participant who chooses the comparison stimulus that is the same as the sample stimu-

FIGURE 8.5 Examples of Unique-Stimuli Matching Trials

lus (Dixon & Dixon, 1978; Wright et al., 1988). In this discussion, the term *matching-to-sample* will be reserved to describe the performances of participants whose behavior is governed by the identity concept. The term *matching perfor-mance* will refer to the performance of a participant who chooses the Co+ during matching-to-sample trials.

Transfer tests are used in a matching-to-sample procedure to test for the pres-ence of the identity concept. Generalization of matching-to-sample to untrained stimuli allows reinforcement history to be ruled out as an explanation for correct responses. There are several procedures that are used to measure transfer, includ-ing repeated-stimulus testing and unique-stimulus testing.

Repeated-stimulus transfer testing is used to test the generality of matching performances to stimuli other than those used in training. One way requires that probe trials be unreinforced and that the stimuli used in probe trials have no prior reinforcement history (Dixon & Dixon, 1978; Sherman, Saunders, & Brigham, 1970).

The study done by Sherman et al. (1970) illustrated this testing procedure. Eight normal preschool-aged children were trained in an identity matching-to-sample task. The children were trained to match lines of varying orientation and geometric forms. They were reinforced for correct responses during training with marbles that later could be traded for a toy or a piece of candy. After training, the children were tested for transfer of matching with a probe stimulus. During transfer testing, the children received no differential consequences. Therefore, their matching performances on test trials were not due to any reinforcement history with the probe stimuli.

Repeated-stimulus transfer testing can also test the generality of matching performances when both correct and incorrect responses are reinforced during testing (Oden, Thompson, & Premack, 1988). During transfer testing, in this procedure, the participants are reinforced regardless of the accuracy of their matching performances. The procedure is sometimes useful because of problems that can occur with testing during extinction. In an extinction procedure, participants may stop responding or display emotional outbursts. Differential feedback is not provided during transfer testing; therefore, transfer performances are not based on reinforcement history in this procedure.

Another repeated-stimulus testing procedure that can be used to assess transfer is random reinforcement. In this procedure, participants are randomly reinforced during transfer testing, whether or not they are matching correctly. The critical feature is that reinforcement is not differential during transfer testing. In this procedure, the transfer of the participant's matching performance is not a function of reinforcement history.

Unique-stimulus transfer testing requires that new stimuli be used on every transfer-testing trial (Brown, Brown, & Poulson, 1995; Wright et al., 1988). Each stimulus can be used on only one probe trial. Because each stimulus is presented in only one trial, unique-stimulus probes can be reinforced. The critical feature of this procedure is that each stimulus used in a probe trial has never been used in another trial.

Figure 8.6 illustrates the conditional discrimination required in a unique-stimulus transfer trial. In the fifth trial, the sample, Lashley's additional stimulus, is missing, so that the conditionality of the trial can be evaluated. If the correct comparison can be identified in the fifth trial, then the trial tests a simple discrimination. If the correct comparison cannot be identified, then it must depend on the value of a sample. In the fifth trial, the correct response cannot be reliably emitted in the absence of a sample; therefore, unique-stimulus testing trials require conditional discrimination.

Brown et al. (1995) conducted a study using the unique-stimulus testing procedure to assess transfer. Three normally developing young children served as participants. The children were trained to match to sample with video picture stimuli. Their correct matching responses were reinforced with a 5-second presentation of a preferred videotape during training and transfer testing. The children were tested for transfer with novel stimulus sets. Each stimulus set was unique and used only once, allowing correct responses to be reinforced. This study meets the criteria for the unique-stimulus testing procedure because unique stimuli were used on every trial. This procedure is especially useful to evaluate the identity concept in young children, because the decrement in performances likely on extinction trials in a repeated-stimulus testing procedure is now less likely, since the child is reinforced for correct responses.

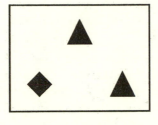

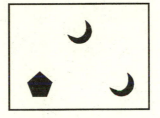

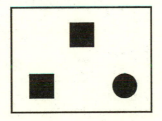

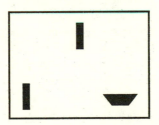

FIGURE 8.6 Series of Unique-Stimuli Matching Trials Illustrating That Unique-Stimuli Trials Are Conditional Discriminations

Matching Responses

The term *matching-to-sample*, or *matching*, suggests that a participant is choosing a comparison in a matching-to-sample trial based on the comparison's perceptual resemblance to the sample. It is possible that a participant can reliably emit correct responses on matching-to-sample trials but not because of the perceptual similarity between the sample and the Co+. In the following discussion, *matching response* will describe a correct performance on a matching-to-sample trial. The term *matching-to-sample*, or *matching*, will describe performances based on the perceptual similarity between the sample and the Co+. Three possible explanations of matching responses are discussed. In only one of these situations can the participant's performance be characterized as matching-to-sample.

A participant can emit a matching response based only on a simple discrimination. The use of constant comparison stimuli, as discussed earlier, results in trials that can be interpreted as simple discrimination trials. If a stimulus set is reused, and one stimulus is always the Co+ and the other stimulus is always the Co-, the trial configuration becomes a simple discrimination (Dube et al., 1992). For example, Figure 8.3 shows a series of matching-to-sample trials in which the Co+ and Co- stimuli remain the same on each trial. On each of the first four trials, the square is the Co+. After the first trial, the participant has a history of reinforcement for responding to the square when it appears as a comparison stimulus with the circle. A correct response can be made on the fifth trial without a sample stimulus by making a simple discrimination between the square and circle.

One-trial learning provides another possible explanation for a matching response. Dube et al. (1992) alluded to one-trial learning as a possible source of control over a matching response. They suggested that one-trial learning may account for the matching responses in matching-to-sample paradigms, if a sample-observing response is required. Observing the sample can be reinforced by the onset of the comparison stimuli. Figure 8.7 shows an example of stimulus control consistent with the one-trial learning hypothesis. In the first stage of Figure 8.7, the sample stimulus is presented. The second stage shows the participant performing an observing response to the circle, which serves as the sample stimulus. In the response chain, the appearance of the comparison stimuli in the third stage may reinforce the response to the circle stimulus. When the comparison stimuli appear, the participant has just been reinforced for responding to the circle. As a result of this immediate reinforcement history, the participant would respond to the circle comparison stimulus in the fourth stage. Therefore, the similarity of the comparison stimulus to the sample stimulus may not govern responding. In this case, responding is conditional on immediate reinforcement history, rather than the perceptual similarity between the sample and the Co+.

McIlvane, Dube, Kledaras, Iennaco, and Stoddard (1990) performed an experiment in which their training procedure demonstrated the plausibility of the one-trial learning hypothesis. In this study, the participant was a mentally retarded

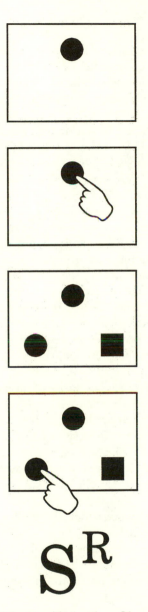

FIGURE 8.7   Example of a Matching Trial with an Observing Response Illustrating the One-Trial Learning Hypothesis

adult who, prior to the study, was unsuccessful in learning matching-to-sample. In the training program, the participant was presented with a single-stimulus teaching trial followed by a simple discrimination trial. For example, in this trial sequence, the participant was presented with a circle that was displayed alone. Selection of the circle stimulus was reinforced. Following this, the participant was presented with a discrimination trial in which the circle was displayed with a square. The participant had to choose the circle to respond correctly on this trial. This procedure does not demonstrate matching, but it serves to illustrate the role that one-trial learning can play in the acquisition of matching performances.

The remaining source of matching-response control is matching-to-sample, or matching (Weinstein, 1941; Wright et al., 1988). In this situation, responses are governed by the perceptual similarity between the sample and the Co+. This type of matching performance was characterized as second-order generalization by Lashley (1938). To conclude that a performance is the result of matching-to-sample, the following four conditions must obtain:

First, a conditional-discrimination procedure must be used. As discussed earlier, some procedures typically used in the matching-to-sample literature do not require conditional discrimination. To draw the conclusion that matching has occurred, there must be clear evidence that the performance was governed by the conditional relationship between the sample and the Co+.

Second, an observing response cannot be required. An observing-response requirement can result in conditioned reinforcement of the responses to the sample. This reinforcement property allows matching-to-sample responses to be governed by immediate reinforcement history, rather than by the perceptual similarity between the sample and the Co+.

Third, only the results of transfer tests can be used to demonstrate matching-to-sample. A conclusion that matching-to-sample has occurred requires that the performances are governed by the perceptual similarity between the sample and the Co+. Training trials cannot be used to demonstrate matching, because matching performances can be based on reinforcement history, rather than perceptual similarity.

Finally, participants must demonstrate above-chance performance on matching-to-sample transfer-test trials.

If these four criteria are met and experimental procedures are otherwise sound, a conclusion that matching-to-sample has been displayed is justified. These are the conditions for the adequate testing of the identity concept.

References

Brown, A. K., Brown, J. L., & Poulson, C. L. (1995). Generalization of children's identity matching-to-sample performances to novel stimuli. *Psychological Record, 45,* 29–43.
Carter, D. E., & Eckerman, D. A. (1976). Pigeons can learn identity or difference, or both. *Science, 191,* 408–409.

Daehler, M. W., Lonardo, R., & Bukatko, D. (1979). Matching and equivalence judgments in very young children. *Child Development, 50,* 170–179.

Dixon, M. H., & Dixon, L. S. (1978). The nature of standard control in children's matching-to-sample. *Journal of the Experimental Analysis of Behavior, 30,* 205–212.

Dube, W. V., McIlvane, W. J., & Green, G. (1992). An analysis of generalized identity matching-to-sample test procedures. *Psychological Record, 42,* 17–28.

Etzel, B. C., & LeBlanc, J. M. (1979). The simplest treatment alternative: The law of parsimony applied to choosing appropriate instructional control and errorless-learning procedures for the difficult to teach child. *Journal of Autism and Developmental Disorders, 9,* 361–382.

Lashley, K. S. (1938). Conditional reactions in the rat. *Journal of Psychology, 6,* 311–324.

McIlvane, W. J., Dube, W. V., Kledaras, J. B., Iennaco, F. M., & Stoddard, L. T. (1990). Teaching relational discrimination to individuals with mental retardation: Some problems and possible solutions. *American Journal on Mental Retardation, 95,* 283–296.

McIlvane, W. J., Kledaras, J. B., Munson, L. C., King, K. A. J., de Rose, J. C., & Stoddard, L. T. (1987). Controlling relations in conditional discrimination and matching by exclusion. *Journal of the Experimental Analysis of Behavior, 48,* 187–208.

Oden, D. L., Thompson, R. K. R., & Premack, D. (1988). Spontaneous transfer of matching by infant chimpanzees (*Pan troglodytes*). *Journal of Experimental Psychology: Animal Behavior Processes, 14,* 140–145.

Reynolds, G. S. (1975). *A primer of operant conditioning.* Glenview, IL: Scott, Foresman.

Sherman, J. A., Saunders, R. R., & Brigham, T. A. (1970). Transfer of matching and mismatching behavior in preschool children. *Journal of Experimental Child Psychology, 2,* 489–498.

Sidman, M. (1980). A note on the measurement of conditional discrimination. *Journal of the Experimental Analysis of Behavior, 33,* 285–289.

Sidman, M. (1987). Two choices are not enough. *Behavior Analysis, 22,* 11–18.

Weinstein, B. (1941). Matching-from-sample by rhesus monkeys and by children. *The Journal of Comparative Psychology, 31,* 195–213.

Wright, A. A., Cook, R. G., Rivera, J. J., Sands, S. F., & Delius, J. D. (1988). Concept learning by pigeons: Matching-to-sample with trial-unique video picture stimuli. *Animal Learning & Behavior, 16,* 436–444.

9

Stimulus Classes, Stimulus Sequences, and Generative Behavior

Harry A. Mackay, Barbara Jill Kotlarchyk, and Robert Stromer

People with mental retardation, autism, and other developmental disabilities pose continuing challenges for their teachers, because direct teaching of the many specific performances that they lack is not feasible in the time available. However, some of these challenges may be met with the use of methods that produce novel, generative performances by arranging environment-behavior interactions in carefully designed instructional sequences. This chapter illustrates the development of such a generative behavior repertoire in a child with mental retardation. Analysis of the instructional sequences that were used advances our understanding of the environmental antecedents of the integrated networks of preacademic performances that involve reading, spelling, and numerical skills. Particularly important are the contingencies that produce stimulus classes, stimulus sequences, and relations among the stimuli in these classes and sequences.

Much attention already has focused on behavior repertoires based on classes of equivalent stimuli (e.g., pictures and their printed and spoken names) that substitute for one another in various matching-to-sample tasks (for reviews, see Mackay, 1991; Remington, 1994; Sidman, 1994; Stromer, 1991). The analyses of generative performances involving relations among the stimuli in sequences have been more recent (for review, see Green, Stromer, & Mackay, 1993). These studies illustrate the analysis of performances, including rudimentary reading and spelling, often viewed in terms of internal cognitive processes. This analysis, however, highlights the environment-behavior interactions that establish such performances. The findings are relevant to issues about generative language performance (cf. Mackay, Stromer, & Serna, in press; Sidman, 1986; Spradlin, 1977), bringing a fresh approach to problems that were not resolved by the verbal-learning research of earlier decades (cf. Jenkins & Palermo, 1964).

Stimulus Equivalence and Emergent Performance: Sidman's Original Study

Sidman (1971) studied the emergence of untrained rudimentary reading performances in a youth with mental retardation, providing the initial data for what is often called the stimulus-equivalence paradigm. In pretests, the youth matched 20 pictures to their dictated names, demonstrating a form of auditory comprehension involving relations between corresponding dictated and visual stimuli. He also named the pictures orally. Next, the youth was taught to match the printed words to their corresponding dictated names, a form of auditory receptive reading that he had failed to do earlier. For example, he earned a token (exchanged later for edibles) when he touched the printed word *car* (rather than other printed words) after hearing "car," the printed word *bed* after hearing "bed," and so on. After this training, tests reassessed other performances he had failed to demonstrate during pretests. The results showed the emergence of three performances that were not trained directly: matching printed words to pictures and vice versa; two forms of visual reading comprehension; and naming printed words, a form of rudimentary oral reading.

These test performances demonstrated that the stimuli were substitutable for one another and justified the inference that the training and testing produced 20 classes of equivalent stimuli. One class consisted of the dictated word "car," pictures of cars, and the printed word *car*. Another class consisted of the dictated word "bed," pictures of beds, and the printed word *bed*.

Sidman's study was important because it used the conditional discrimination procedures called *matching-to-sample* for the teaching and testing. These procedures provided the basis for a behavior-analytic account of emergent performances. The analytic framework has emphasized the relations that typically are established among the stimuli presented (cf. Mackay & Sidman, 1984; Sidman, 1986, 1994). This framework helps to systematize work that clarifies the environment-behavior contingencies on which these simple semantic (meaning) relations may be based and suggests the means for achieving them.

Equivalence Classes and Stimulus Sequences

Research suggests that stimulus equivalences play a part in the acquisition of syntactic (order) relations as well as semantic relations. For example, Lazar (1977) presented pairs of forms (designated A1 and A2, B1 and B2, C1 and C2, D1 and D2) as the stimuli in sequence training with three adults. The task was to touch the stimuli in the sequences A1>A2, B1>B2, and so on. In tests with mixtures of stimuli from different sequences, the participants produced novel sequences (e.g., A1>B2, B1>C2, C1>D2) almost errorlessly. The stimuli from the same position (here only "first" and "second") in different sequences were substitutable for one

another. Next, these same stimuli served as samples in matching-to-sample training with the new stimuli, E1, E2, F1, and F2, serving as comparison stimuli. Selection of E1 was reinforced when A1 was the sample; selection of E2 was reinforced when A2 was the sample; and so on. Finally, sequence tests were given to
assess transfer between the matching-to-sample and sequence contexts. One participant produced the sequences E1>E2, F1>F2, E1>F2, and F1>E2 immediately;
another did so after additional training; and the third failed to show transfer.

Green, Sigurdardottir, and Saunders (1991) replicated Lazar's study with
three-stimulus sequences, also adding formal matching-to-sample tests for equivalences among stimuli. Stromer and Mackay (1993) studied sequence production
in children, but with two five-stimulus sequences, sequences A and B. The length
of these sequences represented a procedural improvement over earlier studies;
with five stimuli, one can test for new sequences that include "embedded" stimuli
that do not have the unique properties conferred by being "first" or "last." The
children produced sequences like A1→B2→A3→B4→A5 without direct training, thus confirming inferences about classes of the stimuli that occupy the same
relative position in different sequences.

Study 1

Sidman's (1971) original study of equivalence classes used pictures and their
printed and spoken names as stimuli, and others have used numbers, quantities,
coins, and other stimuli that are potentially functional in participants' everyday
activities (e.g., Gast, VanBiervliet, & Spradlin, 1979; Green, 1991; Maydak,
Stromer, Mackay, & Stoddard, 1995; McDonagh, McIlvane, & Stoddard, 1984).
However, many studies of stimulus classes and stimulus sequences have used arbitrary nonsense stimuli. This choice of stimuli may mask the general implications of the studies and thus limit the application of the concepts and procedures
on which the research is based. To aid in the translation from lab to life, in this
study we used printed numerals and their printed and spoken names. Furthermore, these stimuli were made from inexpensive materials for tabletop use and
are easily replicated by a teacher or parent (see Stromer, Mackay, & Stoddard,
1992).

Mackay (1985) extended Sidman's study by adding spelling to the network of
matching and naming performances. Figure 9.1 outlines the present systematic
replication of that study (see also Dube, MacDonald, McIlvane, & Mackay,
1991; Mackay & Sidman, 1984). The stimuli were numerals and their names
rather than colors or pictures and their names. A modified version of Mackay's
(1985) anagram-construction procedure was used to teach Jay, a boy with multiple disabilities, to use individual letter tiles to construct the printed words ZERO
through NINE in response to their dictated names (Task AE). All the remaining
performances designated by the arrows in Figure 9.1 were assessed before and
after the training. The posttraining tests thus examined the emergence of classes

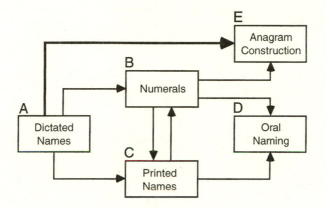

FIGURE 9.1   Schematic Illustration of the Stimulus-Equivalence Paradigm, Including the Anagram-Construction Task Used in This Study. See text for explanation.

of equivalent printed and spoken stimuli and the oral naming of the printed stimuli. The teaching-program modifications (see the following description) were intended to minimize the kinds of errors that occurred previously (Mackay, 1985) when words that had been trained in isolation were mixed with previously learned words to provide a baseline set of increasing size.

Participant

Jay was a 10-year-old boy with cerebral palsy and severe mental retardation; he was confined to a wheelchair. Because of his motor difficulties, he was unable to write. However, he could manipulate the small cardboard tiles with the letters for the anagram-construction task. This task did not require Jay to form the letters in words but still allowed him to produce printed words.

Procedure

Training.   In the terminal performance of anagram training, Jay was presented, for example, with the dictated word "two," and had to pick T, W, and O from the choice pool and place them in that order above a line on a program card. In the first step of training, however, a card with the letters T, W, and O (each underlined) was placed on the table with T, W, and O as a choice pool. The teacher said "two" and Jay had to place the letters T, W, and O on the same letters printed on the card. Eventually, the letters were removed from the cards: Only T and W were on the second card, and only T was on the third. The fourth card had no letters on it, so Jay had to construct the word TWO without these prompts. The fifth card was used for the terminal performance described earlier, and it eliminated the cues that the short lines provided for individual letter placement.

Analogous programs were used for the other nine words. The words taught are shown at the left in Table 9.1 in the order of training. The letters in the choice pool at each stage in training are at the right. The word NINE was trained first (choice pool N, I, N, and E) to a stringent criterion. The word TWO was trained next (choice pool T, W, and O). After that, all the letters for the words TWO and NINE were made available in the choice pool, and Jay had to construct (a) the word TWO and then (b) the word NINE. Finally, these same two words were mixed from trial to trial.

After these initial steps, trials with the words TWO and NINE were mixed in a baseline to which training trials for the word FIVE were added. FIVE then became part of the baseline, and training with ONE began. The program then added one new word at a time to an expanding baseline. The teaching trials in each program were mixed with baseline trials to maintain performance with the words learned previously. In addition, the new letters required to train the next word were introduced into the choice pool during baseline sessions that preceded the training. The acquisition criteria were (a) perfect performance on the last step

TABLE 9.1   Training Sequence and Choice Pools

Sample	Baseline	Choice Pool
NINE		NINE
NINE		NINETWO
TWO		TWO
TWO		NINETWO
NINE TWO		NINETWO
	(NINE TWO)	NINETWOFV
FIVE	(NINE TWO)	NINETWOFV
ONE	(FIVE NINE TWO)	NINETWOFV
	(ONE FIVE NINE TWO)	NINETWOFVSE
SEVEN	(ONE FIVE NINE TWO)	NINETWOFVSE
	(SEVEN ONE FIVE NINE TWO)	NINETWOFVSEX
SIX	(SEVEN ONE FIVE NINE TWO)	NINETWOFVSEX
	(SIX SEVEN ONE FIVE NINE TWO)	NINETWOFVSEXHR
THREE	(SIX SEVEN ONE FIVE NINE TWO)	NINETWOFVSEXHR
	(THREE SIX SEVEN ONE FIVE NINE TWO)	NINETWOFVSEXHRZ
ZERO	(THREE SIX SEVEN ONE FIVE NINE TWO)	NINETWOFVSEXHRZ
	(ZERO THREE SIX SEVEN ONE FIVE NINE TWO)	NINETWOFVSEXHRZU
FOUR	(ZERO THREE SIX SEVEN ONE FIVE NINE TWO)	NINETWOFVSEXHRZU
	(FOUR ZERO THREE SIX SEVEN ONE FIVE NINE TWO)	NINETWOFVSEXHRZUG
EIGHT	(FOUR ZERO THREE SIX SEVEN ONE FIVE NINE TWO)	NINETWOFVSEXRHZUG
	(EIGHT FOUR ZERO THREE SIX SEVEN ONE FIVE NINE TWO)	NINETWOFVSEXRHZUG

Note: Each new word to be trained is italic. Words that were considered learned are in parentheses.

of a given training program and (b) perfect performance on a review (three trials with each previously learned word).

Throughout the training, Jay received praise and a token (poker chip) after a correct trial. The tokens then were traded so that Jay received one edible every seven correct trials, on average. Errors (placement of letters in incorrect order, selection of incorrect letters, rotation of letters) immediately ended trials without a token or praise.

Assessment Procedures. Thirteen tests were used to assess Jay's entering, directly trained, and final performances. Three identity-matching tests (not shown in Figure 9.1) were given before training to determine whether Jay could discriminate among the stimuli used. These tests included (1) matching identical printed numerals (e.g., 5 to 5), (2) matching identical printed letters, and (3) anagram construction of printed number words. Jay was virtually perfect on these tests, confirming that he could discriminate the stimuli and perform the construction task.

Four two-choice matching-to-sample tests, two oral-naming tests, and an oral-sequencing (counting) test were given before and after training. These were (4) matching printed numerals as comparisons to their dictated names (AB), (5) matching printed number words to dictation (AC), (6) matching printed words to numerals (BC), (7) matching numerals to printed words (CB), (8) oral naming of numerals (BD), (9) oral naming of printed words (CD), and (10) oral sequencing of the numbers from "zero" to "nine."

Three tests were given only after training. They were (11) construction of number words to dictation (AE), (12) 10-choice matching of numerals to dictation (AB), and (13) 10-choice matching of numerals to printed words (AC).

No tokens were used during testing. Before each test, the teacher said, "You will not be getting any tokens now, but you will have a chance to get some later." After testing, Jay earned reinforcers by matching identical geometric shapes, a task he did virtually without error.

Matching-to-Sample. For a typical two-choice, visual matching-to-sample display, the numerals or words were printed on white index cards (8 x 13 cm) and mounted in a photograph album under clear plastic covers. A cardboard mask covered the stimuli before a trial began.

Each trial began when the teacher lowered the mask to uncover only the sample. After Jay touched the sample, the teacher removed the mask to reveal the comparison stimuli below the sample. The trial terminated after Jay touched one of the comparisons. On trials with auditory samples (spoken once by the teacher), Jay had to repeat the sample before the comparisons were uncovered. The sample was never the same in more than two consecutive trials, and the position and the order in which comparison stimuli appeared changed unsystematically across trials. The number of trials in a test was 30, each of the 10 samples appearing on three trials.

Ten-choice matching-to-sample tests assessed Jay's performance when all 10 printed numerals or words were available simultaneously in a choice pool. Performance on this form of test is relevant to the procedures used in Study 2.

Oral Naming.   During oral-naming tests, the teacher presented a printed numeral or word and said, "What is it?" Jay then had to name the stimulus orally.

Oral Sequencing.   To assess oral sequencing, Jay was instructed, "Say the numbers out loud in order from smallest to largest" (i.e., from "zero" to "nine"). Each test was considered to involve 10 trials, each consisting of Jay saying a numeral name. If the name was produced in its appropriate serial position, it was considered correct. Names given out of serial order were errors.

Tests that examined whether Jay could order the printed numerals and words were also administered and are described later in conjunction with Study 2.

Results

Test Performances.   Figure 9.2 shows Jay's accuracy on the tests given before and after training. Before training, he matched printed numerals to their dictated names (AB) and named the numerals orally (BD). However, he did not construct words to dictated numeral names (AE) or to printed numerals (BE). He also did not name the printed words (CD). Performances on tests AC (matching printed to dictated numeral names), BC (matching printed number words to printed numerals), and CB (matching printed numerals to printed number words) were at chance level. Analysis of Jay's selections on the AC test showed a clear preference for responding to the right side of the display. The 50 percent score reflects this position preference rather than any ability to match some of the stimuli. Error analyses for the BC and CB tasks revealed no such patterns. Interobserver reliability for these data was always 100 percent.

Jay improved on all reading and anagram-construction tasks after training. He was nearly errorless on matching printed words to dictation (AC), emergent matching of printed words to numerals (BC), and matching of numerals to printed words (CB). He initially constructed number words in response to numerals (BE) with 87 percent accuracy. This was a large increase over the pretest score of 0, but errors occurred on trials with three and eight as the samples. For example, Jay sometimes began to construct the word THREE when EIGHT was the sample and vice versa. After one remedial training session with only the words THREE and EIGHT, posttest performance on the entirely visual BE task was errorless. Jay also matched numerals to printed words, and vice versa, when the 10-choice format was used (data not shown). Finally, he named the printed words orally (CD).

Training.   Jay typically made few or no errors in learning to construct the printed words. He completed five programs errorlessly (NINE, SEVEN, SIX,

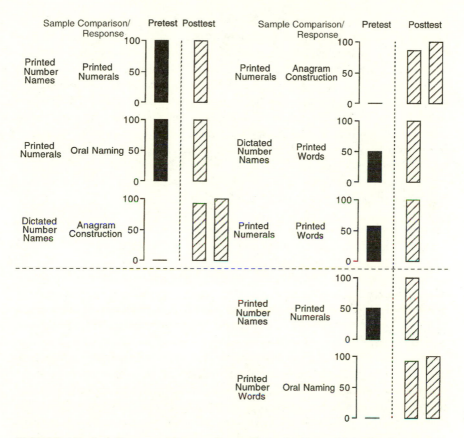

FIGURE 9.2   Jay's Pretest and Posttest Scores. Tasks that Jay could do already or was taught explicitly appear above the broken line. No training was given on tasks shown below the broken line.

FOUR, and EIGHT) and three with only one error (FIVE, ONE, and ZERO). On the programs for THREE and TWO, 3 and 10 errors occurred, respectively. These trained performances were typically perfect on the baseline review trials. Errors occurred only on the review trials with the words FIVE and ONE (1 and 4 errors, respectively).

Discussion

These data systematically replicate other findings (Dube et al., 1991; Mackay, 1985; Mackay & Sidman, 1984). Constructing the printed number words to dictated number names established each dictated and printed name as equivalent members of the same class and enabled matching with these stimuli (AC). The emergence of the untrained performances (BC, CB, and BE) confirmed the formation of 10 classes of equivalent stimuli, each class containing a printed numeral and its dictated and printed names.

The success of the training method is also reflected in the high accuracy of performance on training trials. This resembles what Mackay (1985) found using colors and their printed names as the stimuli. However, the almost errorless performance on the baseline review trials differs from the finding of many errors made by Mackay's students when a newly trained word was added to previously learned words to form a new baseline set. It is likely that the procedure of mixing training trials with baseline trials in the present study virtually eliminated the many errors that occurred in previous research, when each (color) word was trained and then added to an increasing baseline.

The economy of teaching demonstrated by these data mirrors that shown in the earlier studies (cf. Mackay, 1991; Mackay & Sidman, 1984). The educational implications of the study are also enhanced when considered in the light of the work of Gast et al. (1979). These investigators used sets of objects or dots as members of equivalence classes with numerals and their dictated names. The addition of such stimuli to the repertoire displayed by Jay would greatly increase the number of relations (correspondences among stimuli) involved and introduce the stimuli required for performances that display understanding of the relations among quantities.

The durability and stability of the performances established during this study deserve note because of their practical importance. Early in the study, transportation difficulties, vacations, and illnesses resulted in the occurrence of only one training session on some weeks and 2–3 week absences. Some extended breaks also occurred later in training. Jay's typically accurate baseline performances suggest excellent retention that likely was enabled by the virtually errorless training.

Study 2

This extension of Study 1 used tasks that required ordering of the stimuli. Recall that Jay could recite in order the number names "one" through "nine." The training then established equivalences between these oral names and the corresponding printed numerals and words and created the "zero" class. Would Jay now sequence the printed visual stimuli?

Procedure

The materials included the same black printed numerals (anagram numerals) used earlier, small cards with the number words (5 x 3 cm to 9 x 3 cm, depending on word length) printed on them, and anagram program and test cards like those used earlier.

Sequencing Tests.   These tests were like the oral sequencing test described earlier and assessed whether Jay could order the printed numerals and words. They were given prior to the training in Study 1, repeated after the formation of equivalence classes had been confirmed, and repeated before and after the limited sequence training described in the following text.

For the numeral-sequencing task, a line on the test card marked where the numeral tiles were to be placed. The printed numerals 0–9 lay in a choice pool to the right of the test card. Jay had to place the numerals on the card in order from 0 to 9. The same procedure was followed with the printed words as the stimuli and with only the numerals 0–3 (as a pretraining test).

Before each test, the teacher said, "You will not be getting any tokens now, but you will have a chance to get some later. Okay? I want you to put these [pointing to choice pool] in order from smallest [pointing to left side of response line] to largest" [sweeping finger to the right across the response line].

Sequence Training.   Sequence training was given using the printed numerals 0, 1, 2, and 3. The training program resembled the word-construction procedure in Study 1. The first program card had the numerals 0, 1, 2, and 3 printed on it, rather than the letters of a word. These numerals then were removed, one at a time, in the order 3, 2, 1, and 0. After the training, sequencing posttests with all 10 numerals and all 10 printed words were given.

Results

Figure 9.3 (top panel) shows that Jay could not sequence the numerals 0–3 before training but did so after training (striped bars). No errors occurred during the training. On virtually every trial, Jay named the numerals aloud, although he was not required to do so.

The bars at the left in the lower three panels of Figure 9.3 (marked A) show Jay's sequence-pretest performances. He recited the number names "one" to "nine" aloud. He did not place the printed numerals or the printed words in appropriate orders, but he did place these stimuli side by side on the response line. Such performances suggested general comprehension of the spoken and gestural instructions about placing the cards in order.

These performances remained essentially the same in repeated tests (open bars shown in the segments marked B, C, and D) given after the formation of stimulus classes had been confirmed (Study 1). However, after he had learned to sequence the numerals 0, 1, 2, and 3, Jay performed perfectly on the numeral and word-sequencing posttests (solid bars). During these tests, Jay pointed to each card after he had placed it in its serial position and named the numeral or word. He also continued to produce the oral sequences, but he now began with "zero" rather than "one." Interobserver reliability for these data was always 100 percent.

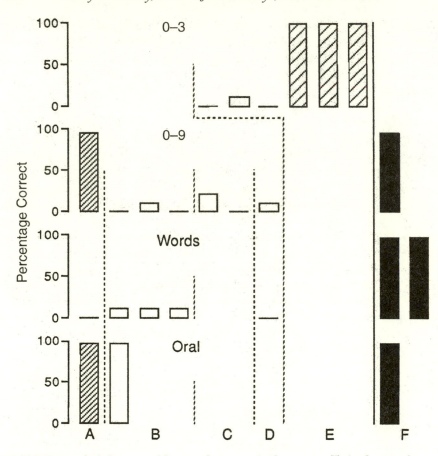

FIGURE 9.3   Jay's Pretest and Posttest Scores on the Sequencing Tasks. See text for explanation.

Discussion

These results are consistent with studies demonstrating that sequence training with stimuli from several classes of equivalent stimuli may result in the other stimuli from each class acquiring the same serial functions (Green et al., 1991; Lazar, 1977; Maydak et al., 1995). Most previous discussion has addressed the relevance of such research to the occurrence of systematic word order, perhaps relevant to syntactic behavior in language. This study shows the relevance of the same phenomena to instruction with and about numbers.

The generative power of the methods is impressive. Limited training with only a subset of the numerals yielded additional untrained performances in which Jay sequenced the remaining numerals and all the printed words. These performances reflected the oral counting from "one" to "nine" that Jay could do before training. In addition, the visual training determined the position of the spoken word "zero" and the printed word ZERO in the respective sequences to which they belonged. These phenomena suggest that relations of equivalence among stimuli may play an important part in the rapid development of complex behavior repertoires and in the integration of new with preexisting knowledge.

General Discussion

This chapter illustrates environment-behavior interactions that result in the emergence of novel performances without direct training. The work pursues some implications of recent research on stimulus classes and stimulus sequences. Such research not only increases our understanding of the instructional sequences that establish specific generative behavior repertoires; it also provides the bases of a technology for teaching integrated networks of preacademic performances that involve rudimentary reading, spelling, and prearithmetic skills (cf. Stromer et al., 1992).

Our findings raise important considerations about the properties of stimuli in classes and possible differences between equivalence classes and functional classes (Goldiamond, 1962; Sidman, 1994). For example, after the anagram training, Jay's emergent performances on matching-to-sample and anagram-construction tests showed that the numerals and their oral and printed names belonged to equivalence classes. However, membership in these classes did not guarantee membership in other potential stimulus classes, for example, classes composed of stimuli that occupied the same position in different sequences (functional classes). Although the oral number names (at least from "one" to "nine") possessed specific serial properties (cf. oral-sequencing test), the corresponding printed numerals and number words in each equivalence class did not. In other words, the oral and visual sequencing performances were independent of each other rather than components of an integrated repertoire. Limited training in sequencing the printed numerals 0, 1, 2, and 3 appeared to provide critical prerequisites for the formation of functional classes. These classes in turn provided the basis for coordinated stimulus control of sequencing that encompassed the remaining numerals and the printed words.

Additional research is needed to clarify these notions about stimulus classes and the properties and functions of these environmental events in the control of behavior. For example, what are the conditions that produce stimulus classes that, as demonstrated by Jay, include stimuli that control independent performances? What are the training variables that promote changes in the relations among stimuli in classes and thus the relationships between performances involving these stimuli (cf. Sidman, Wynne, Maguire, & Barnes, 1989; Stromer & Mackay, 1993)? The rapid development of the integrated repertoire demonstrated by Jay suggests that answers to such questions may yield instructional methods that are simple, efficient, and effective.

Our findings are consistent with those of verbal-learning studies carried out to investigate syntactic behavior in normally capable children and college students. For example, Brown and Berko (1960) exposed their participants to sentences that contained nonsense syllables in particular syntactic positions (noun or verb). These participants then continued to use the syllables in the same position in new sentences. (For related research see Glucksberg & Cohen, 1965.) It should be noted that the nonsense syllables appeared in different serial positions in the sentences used by Brown and Berko. In contrast, the stimuli in the present study always were in the same position. This procedural difference is important; it emphasizes that further study of syntactic equivalence (grammatical class membership) using the present methods will require more than the sharing of serial position by the stimuli in sequences. Syntactic function of a word and its absolute ordinal position in a sequence (or utterance) often differ. Functional analysis of how rudimentary syntactic behavior may be determined by sources of stimulus control in addition to serial position has yet to be undertaken. For example, it will be important to examine how semantic features (e.g., equivalence-class membership) of the words used as stimuli may affect their use in sequences (e.g., phrases or sentences), because the syntactic position of a particular word depends on the context provided by the other words. The challenge is substantial. However, the procedures and concepts outlined here may help to reinvigorate functional analyses of semantic and syntactic aspects of behavior.

References

Brown, R., & Berko, J. (1960). Word association and the acquisition of grammar. *Child Development, 31,* 1–14.

Dube, W. V., MacDonald, S. J., McIlvane, W. J., & Mackay, H. A. (1991). Constructed response matching to sample and spelling instruction. *Journal of Applied Behavior Analysis, 24,* 305–317.

Gast, D. L., VanBiervliet, A., & Spradlin, J. E. (1979). Teaching number-word equivalences: A study of transfer. *American Journal of Mental Deficiency, 83,* 524–527.

Glucksberg, S., & Cohen, J. A. (1965). Acquisition of form-class membership by syntactic position: Paradigmatic associations to nonsense syllables. *Psychonomic Science, 2,* 313–314.

Goldiamond, I. (1962). Perception. In A. J. Bachrach (Ed.), *Experimental foundations of clinical psychology* (pp. 280–340). New York: Basic Books.

Green, G. (1991). Everyday stimulus equivalences for the brain injured. In W. Ishaq (Ed.), *Human behavior in today's world* (pp. 123–132). New York: Praeger.

Green, G., Sigurdardottir, Z. G., & Saunders, R. R. (1991). The role of instructions in the transfer of ordinal functions through equivalence classes. *Journal of the Experimental Analysis of Behavior, 55,* 287–304.

Green, G., Stromer, R., & Mackay, H. A. (1993). Relational learning in stimulus sequences. *Psychological Record, 43,* 599–616.

Jenkins, J. J., & Palermo, D. S. (1964). Mediation processes and the acquisition of linguistic structure. In U. Bellugi & R. Brown (Eds.), *The acquisition of language* (pp. 141–169). *Monographs of Social Research and Child Development, 29*(1).

Lazar, R. M. (1977). Extending sequence-class membership with matching to sample. *Journal of the Experimental Analysis of Behavior, 27,* 381–392.

Mackay, H. A. (1985). Stimulus equivalence in rudimentary reading and spelling. *Analysis and Intervention in Developmental Disabilities, 5,* 373–387.

Mackay, H. A. (1991). Stimulus equivalence. In B. Remington (Ed.), *The challenge of severe mental handicap: An applied behaviour analytic approach* (pp. 235–259). London: Wiley.

Mackay, H. A., & Sidman, M. (1984). Teaching new behavior via equivalence relations. In P. H. Brooks, R. Sperber, & C. MacCauley (Eds.), *Learning and cognition in the mentally retarded* (pp. 493–513). Hillsdale, NJ: Erlbaum.

Mackay, H. A., Stromer, R., & Serna, R. W. (in press). Generalization and transfer of stimulus control. In S. Soraci & W. J. McIlvane (Eds.), *Perspectives on fundamental processes in intellectual functioning.* Norwood, NJ: Ablex.

Maydak, M., Stromer, R., Mackay, H. A., & Stoddard, L. T. (1995). Stimulus classes in sequence production and matching to sample: The emergence of numeric relations. *Research in Developmental Disabilities, 16,* 179–204.

McDonagh, E. C., McIlvane, W. J., & Stoddard, L. T. (1984). Teaching coin equivalences via matching to sample. *Applied Research in Mental Retardation, 5,* 177–197.

Remington, B. (1994). Augmentative and alternative communication and behavior analysis: A productive partnership. *Augmentative and Alternative Communication, 10,* 3–13.

Sidman, M. (1971). Reading and auditory-visual equivalences. *Journal of Speech and Hearing Research, 14,* 5–13.

Sidman, M. (1986). Functional analysis of emergent verbal classes. In T. Thompson & M. D. Zeiler (Eds.), *Analysis and integration of behavioral units* (pp. 213–245). Hillsdale, NJ: Erlbaum.

Sidman, M. (1994). *Equivalence relations and behavior: A research story.* Boston, MA: Authors Cooperative.

Sidman, M., Wynne, C. K., Maguire, R. W., & Barnes, T. (1989). Functional classes and equivalence relations. *Journal of the Experimental Analysis of Behavior, 52,* 261–274.

Spradlin, J. E. (1977). Language and emergent behavior. In P. Mittler (Ed.), *Research to practice in mental retardation: Education and training* (Vol. 2, pp. 253–260). Baltimore: University Park Press.

Stromer, R. (1991). Stimulus equivalence: Implications for teaching. In W. Ishaq (Ed.), *Human behavior in today's world* (pp. 109–122). New York: Praeger.

Stromer, R., & Mackay, H. A. (1993). Human sequential behavior: Relations among stimuli, class formation, and derived sequences. *Psychological Record, 43,* 107–131.

Stromer, R., Mackay, H. A., & Stoddard, L. T. (1992). Classroom applications of stimulus equivalence technology. *Journal of Behavioral Education, 2,* 225–256.

10

Use of a Preexisting Verbal Relation to Prevent the Properties of Stimulus Equivalence from Emerging in New Relations

Svein Eikeseth and Donald M. Baer

Psychologists have long recognized that certain aspects of human behavior, such as language, reasoning, and problem solving, may develop in the absence of direct training. Therefore, psychologists are faced with the challenge of accounting for such untrained verbal and cognitive skills. Recently, a growing behavior-analytic literature has been addressing these issues. Much of this behavioral literature concerns the development of stimulus classes. What has been known as *stimulus equivalence* is a special case of stimulus classes and provides a rigorous means of predicting and assessing untrained cognitive and verbal performances. Perhaps for that reason, the equivalence paradigm has recently attracted increased attention.

Stimulus equivalence is demonstrated when the stimulus elements of at least two interconnected conditional relations display the properties of reflexivity, symmetry, and transitivity (Sidman, 1986; Sidman et al., 1982; Sidman & Tailby, 1982). The property of reflexivity is demonstrated when participants match any stimulus of a prospective class to an identical stimulus without differential reinforcement. For example, if A1 is presented as a sample stimulus in a match-to-sample format where A1 is among the comparison stimuli, the A1 comparison will be selected even without differential reinforcement. The property of symmetry requires that the roles of the sample and comparison stimuli in a match-to-sample discrimination can be reversed and still yield the same function: After participants are taught to match sample stimulus A1 to comparison stimulus B1, a sample B1 will be matched to a comparison A1 without differential reinforcement. Finally, the property of transitivity requires that a participant who, in two interlocked discriminations, is taught to match A1 to B1 and B1 to C1 will match A1 to C1 without differential reinforcement. The symmetry of the transitivity property is a C1-to-A1 match. Symmetric transitivity is often called *equivalence*, on the premise that if it emerges, reflexivity, symmetry, and transitivity must be present; and it is increasingly used as a sufficient and complete test for stimulus equivalence (Sidman, 1990; Sidman et al., 1982; Sidman & Tailby, 1982).

The stimuli employed in most equivalence research are Greek letters or arbitrary geometric forms. The experimenter-provided relations among the stimuli are arbitrary. This procedure reduces interactions between the experimenter-provided stimulus relations and the participant's idiosyncratic learning history. Indeed, most equivalence researchers establish arbitrary relations for exactly that reason—an obvious virtue for initial experimental analysis. However, a more compete analysis of a phenomenon also involves an evaluation of its generality. In the case of stimulus equivalence, an evaluation of its generality should involve an evaluation of how robustly new conditional relations are acquired as equivalence relations in the everyday world of behavior, a world to which the concept is increasingly applied as explanatory or at least descriptive, thus making that evaluation increasingly urgent.

As a step toward that evaluation, the present study asked whether new relations would be acquired as equivalence relations when the stimuli involved were members of a preexisting verbal relation that is not an equivalence relation—in this case, an alphabetical order relation.

Recently, it was demonstrated that a paper-and-pencil format can be used as a quick and effective protocol to study stimulus equivalence (Eikeseth, Rosales, Duarte, & Baer, in press). Because of its cost effectiveness, the paper-and-pencil format was employed in the present study. It incorporated written instructions, training, and subsequent testing.

Method

Participants

A total of 36 undergraduate university students participated in this study. The students were recruited from an introductory course in child development at the University of Kansas. They were not paid and received no compensatory credits for participating in the research; they were asked for 30 minutes of class time as a contribution to the department's research, and none refused.

Materials and Procedure

The materials were matching-to-sample exercises presented in a paper-and-pencil format, incorporating training and subsequent testing. The upper-case Roman letters used as stimuli were arranged so that the participants' knowledge of alphabetical order could operate as a bias: as a stimulus control competitive with the acquisition of the relations as equivalence relations.

Figure 10.1 exhibits the materials as they were seen and marked by the students. The first page of the materials described the experiment and this form of

Page 1

You are about to play a matching game. The format of the game is called match-to-sample. Here is an example of the format:

J

G

G

The sample is the item to the left, in this example a G. Your task is to circle the one of the items to its right that you consider to be its match. In the absence of any other instructions, most people would circle the right-side **G** because it is identical to the sample, like this

J

G

Ⓖ

However, in this game, the relation between the sample and its correct match is determined by some rules. These rules are stated on the next page. You need to learn these rules before you can play this game. Please go on to the next page.

Page 2

Here are some rules. You need to **memorize** them:

Ⓑ F
(1) A and B
E Ⓒ

B Ⓕ
(2) D and E
Ⓔ C

After having learned these relations, please complete the following exercises:

E	E	B	C	F
A	A	A	B	B
B	B	E	F	C

C	E	B	E	F
B	D	D	D	E
F	B	E	B	C

F	C	B	F	B
E	E	A	B	D
C	F	E	C	E

Page 3

C	C	F	E	E
E	B	B	D	A
F	F	C	B	B

B	C	E	F	F
A	E	D	E	E
E	F	B	C	C

E	E	C	C	C
D	A	B	E	B
B	B	F	F	F

B	E	E	F	B
A	D	A	B	D
E	B	B	C	E

F	B	F	B	C
E	A	E	D	B
C	E	C	E	F

Page 4

Now complete the game by doing these matches:

B	B	A	C	E
A	D	B	E	C
E	E	D	F	B

F	C	D	E	C
A	B	C	F	B
C	F	A	B	F

C	E	D	E	A
D	D	C	A	E
F	B	A	B	D

F	D	A	D	C
D	E	C	B	A
C	A	D	A	F

A	C	B	D	F
F	B	C	F	D
D	F	E	A	C

E	D	C	B	A
A	F	A	D	F
B	A	F	E	D

F	F	C	B	A
A	E	D	F	C
C	C	F	E	D

C

E

F

Thank you for your cooperation.

FIGURE 10.1   The Materials as They Were Seen by the Participants

match-to-sample. The second page established by example four baseline relations, in the form of two interlocking discriminations, to serve as rules for the trials of this page and the following pages. These instructions were followed by 40 training trials during which the four original relations were present for visual inspection by the participants; however, the participants were instructed to "memorize" the original relations before completing these 40 trials. An additional page (page 4 on Figure 10.1) then presented 36 probes, 24 for the symmetry, transitivity, and symmetric-transitivity properties of the original relations, interspersed unpredictably with 12 probes for the maintenance of those original relations, now with the original relations no longer present for visual inspection. The students found a next-letter bias in the original relations and in the probes for the equivalence properties of those relations: In the original relations, the correct comparison stimulus was always the next letter in the alphabet after the sample stimulus; in four trials of the eight equivalence probes, the *nonequivalence* comparison stimulus (a novel stimulus) was the next letter in the alphabet after the sample letter, and in the other four trials it was not.

No programmed consequences were ever given to participants for correct or incorrect comparison choices, compliance with the instructions, or completing the task. Both training and testing were completed in one session lasting approximately 30 minutes.

Results and Discussion

Analysis was restricted to students whose probe performances showed that they had memorized the original relations, on the premise that it is futile to probe for the equivalence properties of nonacquired relations. Of the 36 students, 26 (72%) marked correctly at least 11 of the 12 probes for the maintenance of the original relations; these students were considered to have entered the experiment. Of those 26, 16 (62%) marked correctly at least seven of the eight symmetry probes, none of which contained a next-letter-bias comparison competitive with the symmetry comparison; 6 students (23%) marked correctly at least seven of the eight transitivity probes, none of which contained a next-letter-bias comparison competitive with the transitive comparison; but none of the 26 students correctly marked at least seven of the eight symmetric-transitivity probes, 4 of which contained a next-letter-bias comparison competitive with the symmetric-transitivity comparison. Instead, 96 percent of the students responded to the next-letter-in-the-alphabet comparison in *every* probe that offered one. Scoring only symmetric-transitive probes that did not contain a competitive next-letter bias shows that 50 percent of the students chose symmetric-transitivity comparisons in all four of those probes. By contrast, none of the students chose the symmetric-transitivity comparison in all four of the probes containing a competitive next-letter-bias comparison.

These results suggest that the extent to which conditional relations will be responded to as equivalence relations can be thoroughly controlled by the confounded presence in training and probing of a preexisting relation of alphabetical order. Most college adults respond to alphabetical order almost every day, usually under the specific conditions of finding names in a directory, authors and titles in a card catalog, authors in a reference list, the correct queue in which to wait, or the correct container or file in which to look; figuring out where to find a file name on a monitor screen; or anticipating when their name is likely to be called.

Alphabetical order is not characterized by reflexivity or symmetry. A is not followed by A, and it does not precede A; if A is followed by B, then B is not followed by A; and if A precedes B, then B does not precede A. If symmetry is absent, symmetric transitivity should also be absent, and the "equivalence" test commonly used in current stimulus-equivalence studies as the criterion of equivalence relations should not be responded to in the consistent manner that implies equivalence. On the other hand, a form of transitivity will be seen: If A precedes B, and B precedes C, then A precedes C, but it does not immediately precede C (cf. Chapter 9, this volume).

It is possible that the next-letter bias present in the original relations caused these relations to be acquired as simple intraverbal chains rather than conditional match-to-sample relations typical of most equivalence studies. Of course, we have no proof that participants in the usual equivalence studies do not do similarly. The question of the generality of equivalence for everyday relations remains: If the presence of an alphabetical order relation can alter the functional nature of acquisition, a concept of stimulus equivalence dependent on that not happening is correspondingly fragile. These results do not establish that fragility with any generality, only its possibility; they do establish the need to evaluate the generality or robustness of stimulus equivalence in a variety of ways.

Similarly, it should be noted that the paper-and-pencil format used in this study differs from those typically used in equivalence research (Eikeseth et al., in press). Therefore, fragility should also be questioned in the more traditional format. However, if the present format is seen as a reasonable exemplar of a great deal of everyday teaching and relation acquisition, then the results of this study suggest a somewhat restricted generality of the equivalence paradigm. In this study, stimulus equivalence was not robust enough to compete with a familiar preexisting relation that is not an equivalence relation. Apparently, the stimulus control inherent in alphabetical order was sufficient to disallow acquiring the original relations as equivalence relations.

To state the issue about generality somewhat differently: In the initial exploration of a conceptually new process such as stimulus equivalence, participants' idiosyncratic histories should indeed be treated as "noise," because they could conceal or distort an underlying, perhaps more fundamental process such as stimulus equivalence. But it may be imprudent to classify any process as "underlying" or "fundamental" until its generality can be evaluated. In particular, it is important to determine how well a new process can operate within exactly that kind of noise, if it is to be used widely as a descriptive or explanatory concept. Within mathematics, which is the model for Sidman and Tailby's (1982) definition of stimulus equivalence, equivalence is only one of the many relations that can be defined and imposed on abstract terms. In that context, it has no superior, fundamental, or explanatory status. Will that be the analogy that ultimately describes the place of stimulus equivalence in the analysis of behavior? So far, most equivalence studies establish arbitrary (usually match-to-sample) relations between arbitrary stimuli, using a forced-choice format and deliberately limiting experimenter-provided verbal instructions, with the goal of isolating stimulus equivalence from other stimulus-control phenomena. *Within that format*, stimulus equivalence emerges with wide generality. However, a more thorough examination of its generality would involve use of familiar stimuli in a large variety of training and testing formats and procedures to allow its evaluation in the various realistic contexts to which it is increasingly applied as an explanation and for which it may indeed have considerable explanatory function.

The data from the present study suggest that at least in one context of a kind not unusual in everyday life, equivalence effects are not robust. That demonstration, however, is only one of many required for a thorough evaluation of the generality and robustness of stimulus equivalence. Meanwhile, the equivalence paradigm should be added to the often referenced list of generalization-facilitating methods sketched by Stokes and Baer (1977), and at the same time, it should be studied as a possibly analytic basis for, perhaps, that entire list.

Acknowledgments

This study was supported by Grant HD26927 from the National Institute of Child Health and Human Development, USPHS. The manuscript is based on the first author's doctoral dissertation: S. Eikeseth, 1991, The experimental use of a language bias to prevent the properties of stimulus equivalence in new instructed discriminations. *Dissertation Abstracts International, 54,* 9323008B.

References

Eikeseth, S., Rosales, J., Duarte, A., & Baer, D. M. (in press). The quick development of equivalence classes in a paper-and-pencil format through written instructions. *Psychological Record.*

Eikeseth, S., & Smith, T. (1992). The development of functional and equivalence classes in high functioning autistic children: The role of naming. *Journal of the Experimental Analysis of Behavior, 58,* 123–133.

Sidman, M. (1986). Functional analysis of emergent verbal classes. In T. Thompson & M. D. Zeiler (Eds.), *Analysis and integration of behavioral units* (pp. 213–245). Hillsdale, NJ: Erlbaum.

Sidman, M. (1990). Equivalence relations: Where do they come from? In D. E. Blackman & H. Lejeune (Eds.), *Behaviour analysis in theory and practice: Contributions and controversies* (pp. 93–114). Hove, England: Erlbaum.

Sidman, M., Rauzin, R., Lazar, R., Cunningham, S., Tailby, W., & Carrigan, P. (1982). A search for symmetry in the conditional discriminations of rhesus monkeys, baboons, and children. *Journal of the Experimental Analysis of Behavior, 37,* 23–44.

Sidman, M., & Tailby, W. (1982). Conditional discrimination vs. matching to sample: An expansion of the testing paradigm. *Journal of the Experimental Analysis of Behavior, 37,* 5–22.

Stokes, T. F., & Baer, D. M. (1977). An implicit technology of generalization. *Journal of Applied Behavior Analysis, 10,* 349–367.

Part Three

Clinical Applications, with Emphasis on Substance Abuse and Autism

This section of the book presents nine reports of the application of stimulus-control and contextual-control principles to the amelioration of important clinical problems. It is the largest of the book's five sections, as well it should be. Application is the acid test of the goodness of principles. Inapplicable principles are untestable in acid; for all we know, they are closer to fantasy than science.

Trevor Stokes and colleagues show us some probable pernicious stimulus-control traps implicit in dealing with any case of illness. It is exactly when we are trying to be nothing but benevolent that these traps become most probable. The solution is to be even more benevolent, by understanding these traps and programming around them. William Redd reports that cancer treatment often conditions nausea in patients; his five remedial or preventive techniques use stimulus-control processes, sometimes to avoid dysfunctional conditionings and sometimes to weaken the effects of unavoidable conditioning. Steven Wolf and Elsie Pinkston offer a stimulus-control analysis of how sexual abusers of children select and engage their victims—an analysis that emerged in the process of treatment.

Kimberly Kirby, Richard Lamb, and Martin Iguchi discuss drug abuse in both the classical conditioning and operant models. They point out that the crucial stimulus controls are not the drugs (which have seen much study as stimulus controls) but the events that evoke drug use. They indicate the path that analysis now can take. Warren Bickel and Thomas Kelly follow a similar logic for a better understanding of drug abuse, one that could improve treatment. Kenneth Silverman offers the study of caffeine effects as a productive way to develop the measures necessary for the safe experimental research that all substance abuse will require, before we will know whether its treatment can become thoroughly effective.

Laura Schreibman turns our attention to autism and considers an age-old tactic: Is there some fundamental flaw in people with autism that accounts for the malady and that, if understood, would show us its cure? She considers overselectivity because it is seen so frequently in cases of autism, and she discusses the research that has evaluated its importance in those cases. In counterpoint, Angela

Duarte and Donald Baer show that quite normal university students also can display a stubborn overselectivity, especially if the desired stimulus control is established in the wrong way. Kathleen Zanolli uses contextual control—a very brief history of rapid-paced instructions about social interactions—to promote the desirable kind of social interaction children with autism need but usually lack.

11

Nurturance Traps of Aggression, Depression, and Regression Affecting Childhood Illness

Trevor Stokes, Debra Mowery,
Kimberly R. Dean, and Stacey J. Hoffman

Psychological Complications of Childhood Medical Conditions

With experience and biological maturation, a child develops a diversity of abilities that contribute to a happy and productive lifetime. Sometimes, that normative development is affected by trauma or illness. When a child is ill or recovering from illness, it is natural that parents, teachers, physicians, therapists, and other caregivers react by offering therapeutic care, comfort, and attention to the physical, social, and emotional needs of the child. In fact, these are necessary for the child to make progress toward a suitable recovery. Even so, some continuing nurturant reactions can become countertherapeutic traps that inhibit adaptive recovery from illness or trauma.

Despite improvement in physical health, there often remain sequelae of psychological factors not readily treated by biological medicine. For example, there may be apparent regression in performance repertoires, increases in aggression, and the development of depression. These complications are treated frequently with nurturant support of the child, which is not always ameliorative, despite the best efforts of conscientious parents and care providers.

The psychological factors related to children's medical conditions weave a complex pattern, both during and following illness. If handled well, optimal developmental progression can be ensured in the face of serious health challenges. However, the reality is that aggression, depression, and regression are challenging nurturance traps for parents, teachers, physicians, and therapists. Aggression can be toward oneself or others; depression can be that of activity engagement or moods; and regression can be apparent in physical health, in social and emotional behavior, and in cognition.

The natural outcome of an overgeneralized increase in positive interactions and supportive actions as a result of illness is to reinforce performance at a level below that attained in the previous developmental progression. Therefore, the risk is that regression itself is reinforced independent of the trauma, illness, and medical condition of the child. There may be a controlling differential reaction to general regressions in performance. A lower level of displayed ability may become the most efficient way for the child to maximize pleasant and nurturing interactions provided by adult caregivers.

Nurturance Traps

A *nurturance trap* may be described as a psychological variable, secondary to the health disorder, that effectively enables a maladaptive and countertherapeutic reaction from caregivers. For example, when a child displays a level of skill below previous performance, following a disorder such as a seizure, caregivers are likely to show increased friendly interaction and concern. This nurturance is prompt, natural, and advisable in reaction to innocent dependency and medical need. The caregiving repertoire is reminiscent of styles typical of earlier childhood, when the child was less self-sufficient.

Yet, as the medical condition of the child improves, the child may appear to show little physical or psychological improvement because of the controlling effects of secondary gain in positive interaction following illness. It is as if the child's behavior is reporting that there is a preference for the supportive interactions of dependency, rather than for the efforts required for developmental progression. Similarly, when a child shows increased aggression and assertiveness or increased withdrawal and depression, there is often a strong therapeutic concern expressed through additional interactions from caregivers, independent of the child's adaptive functioning.

Although nurturant interactions are advisable during exacerbation of illness, if a child's aggression, depression, and regression strategically enable errors in psychological management, the behavior and emotional problems are enhanced rather than diminished, and developmental progression becomes more elusive as a function of psychological complications rather than direct medical factors. Therefore, the task of a parent, teacher, physician, or therapist is to recognize potential nurturance traps and to react to them in a therapeutic manner, facilitating recovery and optimal developmental progression.

In reaction to illness and trauma, it is to be expected that there will be developmental regression across various physical, cognitive, and social-emotional dimensions. After these health complications, caregivers are more friendly, do more for the child, and excuse the child from performance requirements previously in effect. This increased frequency of friendly interaction is a widely overgeneralized reaction to declining performance. The dramatic adjustment in the experience of the child needs to be managed carefully to prevent actions countertherapeutic for the child. A caregiver's attempt to require improvement in performances is likely to be met with a combination of factors; each of the following scenarios may be considered the child's recruitment of support for regressed behavior and the child's attempt to control the schedule of interactions concerning preferred behavior.

Aggression and coercive activity toward oneself or others can be employed to ensure that people and activities stay or return or that they leave or remain absent. A child's crying, screaming, hitting, or self-abuse may be regarded as a cue to the environment that the child is operating to gain access to certain events (e.g., to play) or to avoid certain events.

Depression and withdrawal can similarly have multiple functions depending on the child's history and current circumstances. A child may present with inactivity and withdrawal, with and without indicators of emotional distress, mood change, and sadness. These reactions may be regarded as strategies to influence the approach and avoidance of environmental consequences mediated by caregivers.

Regression is often part of the health disability, but it may continue in the face of apparent physical recovery, as a psychological variable controlled by its effect of enabling additional interaction or preventing further demand for improved performance. These are complicated traps; a caregiver may be satisfied with a partial recovery ("At least I see that improvement"), even though the child is now capable of demonstrating skill consistent with greater developmental progression. Unfortunately, approach and avoidance reactions to many of these child-produced antecedents of aggression, depression, and regression are likely to be countertherapeutic errors, whether the caregiver understands what is happening or not. For example, the child's negative reaction to renewed requirements often sets up an escape trap, wherein the adult backs off and reduces the pressure for improved performance. It appears to the adult as if the ill child should not be overly stressed. Alternatively, the child who performs at a level below that shown recently, but with some residual ability, will be responded to with relief and acceptance of the lower level of performance. At least some skills are being shown by a child who has recently had a serious setback. Finally, the child who withdraws or is inactive is likely to be responded to with additional nurturance. After all, the child is medically stressed and in need of support.

In these scenarios, there is likely to be an additional downward spiral in performance with accompanying increased nurturance. Maintenance of these reciprocal effects between child and caregiver, over time, results in a change in the course of development, which becomes resistant to recovery. With the passage of time and adequate medical treatment, caregivers start to become concerned about their inability to facilitate recovery to developmental progression. They become trapped with the child at a regressed developmental level. These phenomena are common to children with general medical conditions. In each of the following cases, the behavior of the child and the caregivers is subject to reciprocal control within the environment, best conceptualized as the child's behavior being the antecedent control, discriminant for the caregiver's nurturant reaction, which in turn affects the child's behavior, and so on in reciprocity.

Case Histories

Visual Impairment

Bobby, a 5-year-old boy who was clinically blind, had been diagnosed with septooptic dysplasia, an absence of the septum pellucidum and deformity of the ventricles of the brain. But his presenting behavior problems could not be attributed to the physical abnormalities of the brain.

Initial assessment indicated that Bobby displayed a meager repertoire of adaptive behaviors. Communication was limited to a few words and phrases, and he spent most of his time at school engaged in self-stimulatory behaviors. When there was contact and interaction with other people, especially adults, Bobby reacted with a combination of positive and negative behaviors, for example, greetings, affection, whining, crying, screaming, scratching, hitting, and biting. Caregivers reacted to Bobby's approaches in a predictable manner, first providing pleasant interactions and affectionate touch, followed quickly with requests to stop the aggressive behavior and pushing Bobby away to avoid being hurt. Additionally, in demand situations, many adults would allow Bobby to avoid further effort when he was aggressive. To compound the problem, adults often consoled Bobby with physical affection when attempting to reduce aggressive behavior.

Bobby's rich repertoire of approach and resistance to interaction, in combination with a high frequency of tantrums and self-stimulatory behavior, seriously limited his opportunity to learn and participate in ongoing activities at school. These environmental antecedents of social initiation and interaction effectively trapped nurturant caregivers and therapists. Predictably, people responded to Bobby's initiations with a combination of approach, avoidance, and confusion. It appeared as if Bobby could not predict how a person would respond to him, but he seemed to have learned that socially appropriate approaches worked better with some people, aggression worked better with others, and the combination was best with many. Unfortunately, Bobby had not learned to distinguish between demand situations and nondemand social opportunities. That is, Bobby may have been motivated to avoid teachers' and therapists' requirements, but he did not discriminate those situations from occasions when a person approached, interacted, and showed affection just to be friendly, to chat, or to play.

One aspect of treatment involved differential consequences: more pleasant reactions from therapists when he showed progress in calming. For example, he would be physically restricted to his chair while having a tantrum but allowed to stand and receive a hug when he relaxed. He would receive a slight touch to the back of his hand during a tantrum but have the palm of his hand stroked when he relaxed.

An additional important aspect of our work was to teach Bobby that if he initiated activity in the world about him, to operate on it, he would learn from the reaction of his environment and that many times communication and cooperation would be followed by pleasant experiences. One example of a carefully managed sequence designed for his learning follows. This structure required an interplay of demands and consequences to teach Bobby to tolerate requests from teachers and therapists and to provide an array of experiential consequences designed to allow Bobby to enjoy activities and learning.

A request for imitation of a verbalization or sound ("Say, hi Kim"), a request for the completion of an action ("Stand up, please"), or a request for the answer to a question ("What did you have for breakfast?") was provided once each 20 seconds. If Bobby reacted quickly, he promptly received attention, friendly talk, affectionate touch, and pleasant activities, which lasted the remainder of the 20-second interval. If he was slow but still responded appropriately, he received attention until the end of the interval. If he had not responded within 10 seconds, he was guided to complete the behavior (e.g., clap hands) or the verbalization was repeated once, and then there was a delay of further attention until the beginning of the next 20-second interval.

This timed strategy was developed because Bobby was still attempting to recruit attention through maladaptive behavior. With these procedures, a prompt compliance was efficient in recruiting positive interaction and attention. It made delayed compliance moderately successful in recruiting attention and noncompliance inefficient, followed by few interactions. In essence, Bobby learned that the best way to proceed was to do quickly what was asked by the therapist, because the differential payoff was for cooperation and participation without aberrant behavior. Also, the paced interactions precluded Bobby's control of presentation rate through misbehavior and self-stimulation.

These procedures effectively reduced aggression, increased compliance, increased appropriate verbalizations, and led to a generalized improvement in task engagement and positive social interactions with adults and other children.

Cerebral Hemorrhage

Sienna was born 10 weeks prematurely, with intracerebral hemorrhage, apnea, and a later diagnosed cerebral palsy. Although her development was delayed, it was consistent, and developmental progression was evident in her early years. She was talking, counting, reciting rhymes, and playing physical games by the age of 4. As a result of the spasticity and tightness of the lower limbs, Sienna underwent dorsal rhizotomy surgery. At about the same time, she contracted influenza. The former was an artificial trauma to the body, the latter an illness. Both were rapid-onset assaults that occurred prior to a change in developmental trajectory, evident in motivation decline and withdrawal. Communication skills decreased, and self-abuse and aggression toward others increased. A downward spiral of problems was seen across the next years, stubbornly resistant to attempts to provide ameliorative intervention.

The interfering behavior and emotional complications led to the discontinuation of various therapies, including physical therapy. This had adverse consequences, because physical therapy was necessary to promote independent walking.

In fact, Sienna refused to walk; she used crawling as her primary mode of mobility, even though physical therapists considered her to be capable of walking with the assistance of a walking frame.

Although she was withdrawn and depressed, Sienna demonstrated consistent attempts to recruit interactions, touch, and sensory stimulation, as well as consistent efforts to escape from any demands of caregivers that required effort. Resistance to walking and extreme aggression were naturally powerful nurturance traps. Both were efficient for Sienna because they brought others quickly to her side or kept them close and interacting.

An initial therapeutic goal was to promote the productive use of the walker and the development of more independent mobility. Walking was made an unavoidable requirement. Attention was limited when walking was resisted, whereas additional positive consequences were provided when walking occurred. Parents, teachers, and therapists all assertively followed the same protocol to increase Sienna's motivation to walk, by placing natural and artificial impediments in the way of mobility that did not involve walking. The program was effective, and Sienna returned to physical therapy.

Specific recommendations included the following. Sienna was told what was required, e.g., "We are going to the classroom; please stand up and walk." She was allowed 10 seconds to follow a request, and approval was voiced if she did what was asked. She was physically guided, by making her stand and begin walking, if she did not follow an instruction within 10 seconds. Instructions were not repeated, and no additional attention was provided following noncompliance, because physical assistance without comment was sufficient to ensure walking. No comments followed Sienna's inappropriate behavior, e.g., giggling, aggression, self-abuse, crying, and complaints, because they were escape-motivated communications. If Sienna moved to sit on the floor when she should have been walking, she was promptly picked up; her hands were placed on the handlebars of the walking frame; and she was moved on. Crawling from one place to another was prevented. If necessary, Sienna was taken back to her starting point, so that she could move from one place to another only by walking. Interaction, positive attention, and affection were provided when Sienna was walking, in an effort to make her feel good when she walked more independently. Rests were allowed when Sienna was walking well. Also, whenever possible, walking was made to have a purpose and pleasant outcome, such as going to get a drink or another positive, tangible consequence.

A second major problem for Sienna was aggression toward others. If a caregiver came close by or sat down in front of her, Sienna would frequently hit, scratch, and pull the person's hair, as well as scream and cry. Frequently, the reaction to this serious assault was physical restriction and efforts by caregivers to escape the potential and real harm and pain inflicted.

Analysis of these circumstances revealed that Sienna appeared motivated by the assertive, intrusive touch and strong physical restriction she was able to recruit with her aggressive behavior. Mild nonintrusive affectionate touch did not appear to have much effect. On the basis of this assessment of function, intrusive deep-muscle touch to the hands and arms, similar to that provided by a massage therapist, was provided whenever Sienna refrained from aggression and whenever she approached others in a positive and friendly manner. There was a substitution in the effective repertoire, therefore, in that aggressive approaches were not met with sustained and intrusive touch; only pleasant approaches were reacted to with the assertive touch. Over the course of a few months, pleasant initiations of interactions increased, and aggression declined consistently. Recruitment by affectionate approach became much more prevalent, and withdrawal and depression diminished. Furthermore, independent reports from the school demonstrated evidence of excellent generalization of decreased aggression and improved social interaction.

Stroke

Jillian was a 5-year-old girl who suffered a stroke early in life and developed cerebral palsy. Jillian had shown consistent but delayed developmental progress. Subsequent to experiencing multiple seizures over a weekend, physical changes in performance occurred, for example, there were more physical spasms and the right leg dragged in a more pronounced manner. Cognition, knowledge, and understanding initially appeared unimpaired but later showed signs of decline to a less sophisticated level. There was also a regression in social and emotional behavior to a less adaptive developmental level, for example, more crying, resistance to requests, and inappropriate grabbing of other children.

Of particular interest was that the regression of her abilities varied across domains over a few months. Physical decline occurred first, cognitive regression followed, and problems in social-emotional performance were last, appearing after partial resolution of physical and cognitive concerns.

In the face of this physical assault and developmental regression, how could therapy protect development and facilitate recovery to the prior level of developmental progression? The therapeutic reaction needed to be different from what a nurturing caregiver would normally consider. Instead of providing frequent friendly and supportive interactions independent of Jillian's behavior, it was necessary to provide positive consequences differentially to reinforce development rather than regression. Negative procedures were not recommended, consistent with the wishes of the parents. It was important to provide friendly and nurturing support during the health setback but also to provide more friendly interaction when movement was in the direction of improved skill and recovery to developmental progression. This is a form of therapeutic guidance.

The consistent differential in consequences provides the motivation to guide the child toward adaptive growth and development. For example, affectionate touch and social attention were used as consequences to signal progress, by making

Jillian feel good when she was performing well enough to progress developmentally. Whenever possible, touch was limited to the minimum necessary to challenge her physical balance. Caregivers were also encouraged to delay verbal interaction somewhat to allow more time for information processing and expression of answers and independence. With careful therapeutic management, Jillian recovered to her previous developmental progression.

Conclusion

Increased nurturance, solicitous attention, and support are often the appropriate reaction to acute and chronic health challenges. Unfortunately, nurturance traps can operate within this scenario, potentially compromising the developmental progress sought. Aggression, depression, and regression are characteristics of children's repertoires associated with pain and discomfort. They show complaints, crying, immaturity, dependence, noncommunicativeness, withdrawal, tantrums, unwillingness to share attention, moodiness, pouting, emotional distress, and other behaviors related to behavior and emotional disorders. If these problems are effective in influencing the environments of children with medical conditions, problems secondary to the medical concerns may develop and be maintained. A child may demonstrate strong preference for attention and personal control at a maladaptive regressed level of performance and may be resistant to attempts to facilitate developmental recovery. Children have a significant effect on the way caregivers interact with them. They are not helpless, but they do not have the insight to understand what is happening during the functional reciprocity of interactions with caregivers.

Treatment requires an analysis of medical and psychological factors, which appear to change together but in fact operate independently and are a function of variables concerning health and the environment. Treatment involves a discrimination of different classes of declining performance and a clear communication to the child that developmental progression will result in a more positive outcome. Nurturance continues in relation to the aspects of the repertoire for which it is medically indicated, but one must beware the nurturance traps of aggression, depression, and regression.

12

Behavioral Intervention in Cancer Treatment

William H. Redd

It has now been slightly over 10 years since the first reports appeared on the use of behavioral intervention procedures with cancer patients (Redd & Andrykowski, 1982). That early work was clinical in focus, and it included a series of individual analytic studies of various clinical problems: refusal to eat (Redd, 1980a), excessive crying (Redd, 1982), and somatic symptoms (Redd, 1980b). The response of both medical and university audiences to this approach has been extremely positive. Initially, some clinicians expressed concern that the application of behavioral principles with very sick and terminally ill patients ignored existential and spiritual issues, but today objections are rare, and many hospitals and clinics routinely offer behavioral intervention to their patients. Indeed, results from research on behavioral intervention with cancer patients indicate that behavioral procedures have no negative side effects and are accepted by most patients. Moreover, the cancer-treatment setting provides an unusually good opportunity to carry out clinically meaningful and methodologically rigorous individual analyses of important phenomena.

The purpose of this discussion is to provide a concise summary of the major advances in this area. The discussion describes the role of behavioral intervention in comprehensive cancer treatment, behavioral procedures to control aversive side effects of treatment, and behavioral intervention to control child distress during invasive procedures. The discussion ends with a consideration of new directions for research and practice.

Behavior Analysis with Cancer Patients

Behavioral intervention in cancer therapy is founded in behavior research and theory. It has a relatively short history (slightly over 15 years) compared to behavioral medicine applied to disorders such as heart disease (Thoresen & Powell, 1992), gastrointestinal troubles (Whitehead, 1992), and diabetes (Cox & Gonder-Frederick, 1992).

As in applied behavior analysis, the therapist is a teacher, providing the patient with specific skills. Although psychologists have been the primary champions of behavioral intervention in oncology, the techniques have been effectively used by other health care professions. Behavioral intervention has been used to treat a variety of problems including pain, anxiety, insomnia, and treatment noncompliance. By far the best-known application of behavioral medicine in oncology, however, has been to control nausea and vomiting associated with chemotherapy (Carey & Burish, 1988; Morrow & Dobkin, 1988; Redd & Andrykowski, 1982).

It is important to point out that behavioral intervention is not meant to replace more traditional psychotherapeutic approaches. It is an adjunct. The therapist often integrates behavioral techniques with supportive psychotherapy, as the problem dictates. Moreover, when the therapist has completed the behavioral intervention for which the initial request was made, patients often ask that treatment be continued so that other issues can be addressed. Some writers have suggested that the behavioral intervention often provides the patient with a trusting relationship with the therapist and becomes the basis of subsequent counseling (Redd, 1989). It is probably important to the wide acceptance of behavioral medicine in oncology that those working in the area hold the notion that behavioral intervention is not the entire answer to psychosocial support of the cancer patient.

Reduction of Aversive Side Effects of Treatment

Nausea and Vomiting

There is probably no other advance in behavioral medicine that has generated as much interest among those treating cancer patients as the introduction of behavioral interventions to control the classically conditioned nausea and vomiting that some patients experience in anticipation of chemotherapy (anticipatory nausea and vomiting, ANV). Despite recent advances in antiemetic drugs, ANV continues to be a clinical problem for as many as 50 percent of those receiving chemotherapy (Bovbjerg et al., 1992). On the strength of the research to date, many health insurance companies cover the costs of behavioral intervention in the treatment of ANV. Table 12.1 summarizes the five methods that have been effectively used to treat ANV.

Relaxation with Guided Imagery

A number of relaxation-distraction procedures have been developed to reduce ANV, including hypnosis, passive relaxation, active relaxation, and electromyographic (EMG) biofeedback. These procedures are similar, differing mainly in the way in which relaxation is induced. In passive relaxation, hypnotic-like (i.e., indirect) suggestions of relaxation are used; in active relaxation, the patient tenses and releases different muscle groups to induce relaxation. In biofeedback, patients receive information regarding their own muscle tension, which they use to learn

TABLE 12.1   Behavioral Control of Anticipatory Side Effects (Nausea and Vomiting) of Cancer Chemotherapy

Reference	*Behavioral Method*	*Outcome*
Burish, Shartner, and Lyles (1981)	EMG biofeedback with guided imagery	Reduction in nausea and anxiety
Lyles, Burish, Krozely, and Oldham (1982)	Progressive relaxation with guided imagery	Reduction in nausea and anxiety
Morrow and Morrell (1982)	Systematic desensitization	Reduction in nausea and vomiting
Redd, Andresen, and Minagawa (1982)	Passive relaxation (hypnosis) with guided imagery	Reduction in nausea; elimination of anticipatory vomiting
Redd et al. (1987)	Cognitive and attentional distraction (via video games)	Reduction in nausea and anxiety

how to relax. In all cases, relaxation training is combined with descriptions of quiet scenes.

It should be pointed out that this imagery does not focus on the cancer or in any way resemble the "healing" images that have been used by some therapists. The images are intended solely to distract the patient. The goal of all of these techniques is to relax the patient (presumably reducing physiological arousal) and then to block both perceptions of the stimuli that elicit conditioned nausea and sensations of nausea.

To date no clinical guidelines indicate which methods are most effective or how they might be combined. Choice appears to be a matter of personal preference. Some argue that passive relaxation is better for very sick patients, for whom the tensing and releasing of active relaxation might be difficult. Others argue that active relaxation is easier to learn. Although initial reports on the use of biofeedback were quite positive (Burish, Shartner, & Lyles, 1981), the procedure is often unreliable and generally not practical because of the necessary equipment (Vasterling, Jenkins, Matt Tope, & Burish, 1993).

Systematic Desensitization

Systematic desensitization involves three steps. The patient is instructed in the use of a relaxation technique, usually progressive muscle relaxation training; the patient and therapist devise a hierarchy of anxiety-provoking stimuli related to the feared situation, ranging from the least to the most frightening; and the patient practices relaxation while systematically visualizing the increasingly aversive scenes.

Attentional Distraction

A third strategy, cognitive or attentional distraction, involves blocking the patient's perception of the nausea by active involvement in a task, such as a video game (Kolko & Rickard-Figueroa, 1985; Redd et al., 1987; Vasterling et al., 1993). The strategy is quite simple: Engage patients in activities that capture their attention so that they ignore the aversive stimuli. The task can be introduced whenever the patient is likely to experience the symptom or to begin to worry about it.

In our research, my colleagues and I have found that, for children over the age of 9, video games can successfully block nausea and anxiety, as measured by both self-report and behavioral observation. Vasterling and her colleagues (1993) observed similar benefits in adult patients who were provided video games in the waiting room. It should be noted that video game playing is certainly not the only or necessarily the best method of distraction for all patients. Depending on the patient's own interests and skills, music, reading, and working a puzzle may be more effective. The critical factor is to involve the patient's attention. It is important to remember that the term *attentional distraction* implies a functional definition of *distraction*. If the task does not engage the patient (i.e., if the patient is not "absorbed"), it does not represent attentional distraction, and it is not likely to control symptoms.

Pain and Anxiety

Behavioral relaxation and attentional distraction have also been effective in reducing pain and anxiety associated with invasive procedures. In addition to reducing anxiety, behavioral interventions with chemotherapy reduce procedural pain and anxiety in cancer patients (Manne et al., 1990).

Since behavioral symptom control requires active and focused patient involvement, behavioral interventions are probably more effective with intense transient pain than with chronic pain. The problem is that patients are generally unable to maintain active coping procedures for an extended period of time. For patients suffering with chronic pain, behavioral techniques are generally used as an auxiliary to pharmacological methods. Such patients are taught various distraction techniques for temporary pain relief and as a sleeping aid. They are also helped to develop daily activity schedules that prevent increased disability stemming from inactivity.

Fear and Distress Associated with Invasive Procedures

Although pharmacological interventions to reduce pain and anxiety in pediatric cancer patients are available, many clinicians limit their use; they fear long-term neurological side effects. Increased interest has focused on behavioral methods for reducing distress during invasive procedures. The major effort has been toward developing multifaceted interventions: positive reinforcement, blocking behavior with attentional distraction, hypnosis, and multimodal behavioral programs.

Positive Reinforcement

The most obvious application is in recognizing and praising the child's efforts to cope. Behavior therapists (e.g., Manne et al., 1990; Manne et al., 1993) have devised various incentive systems by which parents and nurses let children earn points toward a prize for using their new intervention skills. The child has only to use the skills to earn the reward; being still or not crying is not required to earn points.

Behavior Blocking

In conjunction with the attentional distraction techniques previously described, various behavior-blocking techniques have been used to control child distress during painful medical procedures. The goal is to engage children in activities that both distract their attention and physically block their actual distress behavior. The task must be both physically and cognitively incompatible with behavioral distress.

In our work at Memorial Sloan-Kettering Cancer Center, my colleagues and I give young children party blowers (a whistlelike toy made of paper that expands like the trunk of an elephant and makes noise when blown into; Manne et al., 1990). Play with the blower makes crying and resistance less likely. We have found this strategy effective with most young children. In fact, some children begin requesting a party blower before all their medical procedures and keep one at home. Needless to say, all involved (the child, the parent, the nurse, and the physician) experience the procedure as less stressful when an effective behavior block is used. As discussed in the review of the use of attentional distraction, the critical factor is the child's interest in and willingness to continue play during the entire procedure. The particular task is not critical, although we have found the party blower to be especially convenient, because it is inexpensive, enjoyed by the child, and easily introduced into the treatment setting.

Hypnosis

Many behaviorists are unfamiliar with hypnotic procedures and may question their use, but hypnosis can be effective. Moreover, it is compatible with behavioral methods (Hendler & Redd, 1986), and some researchers consider it a behavioral technique. The use of hypnosis to relieve acute pain has a long history, although many clinicians and most laypersons do not understand it, and some people fear it. This attitude is unfortunate, since research has demonstrated the effectiveness of hypnosis for children with cancer (Hilgard & LeBaron, 1984). Hypnosis involves a relatively simple process in which patients learn to focus their attention more and more intensely on thoughts or images that are unrelated to the pain. It is thus similar to distraction through storytelling, which is often used with young children as well as adults. Because hypnosis appears to rely on many of the same skills required for attentional distraction, we should expect similar results.

Multimodal Behavioral Intervention

A number of clinical investigators have devised interventions that integrate specific behavioral procedures to reduce distress and increase cooperation (Hilgard & LeBaron, 1984; Jay, Ozolins, Elliot, & Caldwell, 1983; Manne et al., 1990). An important part of multimodal intervention is parent participation. We found that the parent has a significant impact on the child's behavior (Manne et al., 1993), which can be positive or negative depending on the parents' anxiety (more parental anxiety means more child distress) and their behavioral rapport with the child (the less the parent matches the child's arousal, the more child distress). A relatively simple parent-coaching program teaches parents to use behavioral intervention with their child during invasive procedures. When the parent does that, both parent and child experience less anxiety and show less behavioral distress (Manne et al., 1990).

Future Directions

The contributions of behavior researchers to comprehensive treatment have been many; they are used in an increasing number of cancer centers. One of the main thrusts of future work may well be the application of behavior theory and research to *prevent* problems. More and more behavior researchers are becoming interested in how the administration of cancer treatment might be modified to avoid some of its pernicious side effects. For example, how can chemotherapy be given to reduce the development of aversive side effects such as food aversions? How can parents be trained to prepare their child for protracted therapy from the beginning?

Another growing area of behavioral oncology is the study of basic behavioral principles in the context of cancer treatment. In this work, cancer treatment and its side effects are used as models of the development of behavior disorders. The reason is that cancer treatment is carefully controlled, and critical behavioral events for patients are programmed and occur at regular intervals. This precision allows the behavior researcher to carry out controlled experimental analyses and learn how to provide better treatment. A related factor is the keen acceptance of behavior research strategy (including individual-analysis experimental designs) among medical and surgical oncologists.

It is clear that behavior researchers and clinicians have made a significant contribution to the understanding of patients' responses to cancer treatment and to the design of effective methods for reducing patient distress.

Acknowledgments

This research was supported by Grant MH45157 and a Research Scientist Award MH00882 from the National Institute of Mental Health.

References

Bovbjerg, D. H., Redd, W. H., Jacobsen, P. B., Manne, S. L., Taylor, K. L., Surbone, A., Crown, J. P., Norton, L., Gilewski, T. A., Hudis, C. A., Reichman, B. S., Kaufman, R. J., Currie, V. E., & Hakes, T. B. (1992). An experimental analysis of classically conditioned nausea during cancer chemotherapy. *Psychosomatic Medicine, 54*, 623–637.

Burish, T. G., Shartner, D., & Lyles, J. N. (1981). Effectiveness of multiple-site EMG biofeedback and relaxation in reducing the aversiveness of cancer chemotherapy. *Biofeedback Self-Regulation, 6*, 523–535.

Carey, M. P., & Burish, T. G. (1988). Etiology and treatment of the psychological side effects associated with cancer chemotherapy: A critical review and discussion. *Psychological Bulletin, 104*, 307–325.

Cox, D. J., & Gonder-Frederick, L. (1992). Major developments in behavioral diabetes research. *Journal of Consulting and Clinical Psychology, 60*, 628–638.

Hendler, C. S., & Redd, W. H. (1986). Fear of hypnosis: The role of labeling in patients' acceptance of behavioral intervention. *Behavior Therapy, 17*, 2–13.

Hilgard, J. R., & LeBaron, S. (1984). *Hypnotherapy of pain in children with cancer.* Los Altos, CA: William Kaufmann.

Jay, S. M., Ozolins, M., Elliot, C., & Caldwell, S. (1983). Assessment of children's distress during painful medical procedures. *Health Psychology, 2*, 133–147.

Katz, E. R., Kellerman, H., & Siegel, S. E. (1980). Behavioral distress in children with cancer undergoing medical procedures: Developmental considerations. *Journal of Consulting and Clinical Psychology, 43*, 356–365.

Keefe, F. J., Dunsmore, J., & Burnett, R. (1992). Behavioral and cognitive-behavioral approaches to chronic pain: Recent advances and future directions. *Journal of Consulting and Clinical Psychology, 60*, 528–536.

Kolko, D. J., & Rickard-Figueroa, J. L. (1985). Effects of video games on the adverse corollaries of chemotherapy in pediatric oncology patients: A single case analysis. *Journal of Consulting and Clinical Psychology, 53*, 223–228.

Lyles, J. N., Burish, T. G., Krozely, M. G., & Oldham, R. K. (1982). Efficacy of relaxation training and guided imagery in reducing the aversiveness of cancer chemotherapy. *Journal of Consulting and Clinical Psychology, 50*, 509–524.

Manne, S., Redd, W. H., Jacobsen, P., Gorfinkle, K., Schorr, O., & Rapkin, B. (1990). Behavioral intervention to reduce child and parent distress during venipuncture. *Journal of Consulting and Clinical Psychology, 58*, 565–572.

Morrow, G. R., & Dobkin, P. L. (1988). Anticipatory nausea and vomiting in cancer patients undergoing chemotherapy treatment: Prevalence, etiology, and behavior interventions. *Clinical Psychology Review, 8*, 517–556.

Morrow, G. R., & Morrell, B. S. (1982). Behavioral treatment for the anticipatory nausea and vomiting induced by cancer chemotherapy. *New England Journal of Medicine, 307*, 1476–1480.

Redd, W. H. (1980a). In vivo desensitization in the treatment of chronic emesis following gastrointestinal surgery. *Behavior Therapy, 11*, 421–427.

Redd, W. H. (1980b). Stimulus control and extinction of psychosomatic symptoms in cancer patients in protective isolation. *Journal of Consulting and Clinical Psychology, 48*, 447–455.

Redd, W. H. (1982). Treatment of excessive crying in a terminal cancer patient: A time-series analysis. *Journal of Behavioral Medicine, 5*, 225–236.

Redd, W. H. (1989). Behavioral intervention to reduce child distress. In J. Holland & J. Rowland (Eds.), *Handbook of Psychooncology* (pp. 573–581). New York: Oxford University Press.

Redd, W. H., Andresen, G. V., & Minagawa, R. Y. (1982). Hypnotic control of anticipatory nausea in patients undergoing cancer chemotherapy. *Journal of Consulting and Clinical Psychology, 50*, 14–19.

Redd, W. H., & Andrykowski, M. A. (1982). Behavioral intervention in cancer treatment: Controlling aversion reaction to chemotherapy. *Journal of Consulting and Clinical Psychology, 50*, 1018–1029.

Redd, W. H., Jacobsen, P. B., Die-Trill, M., Dermatis, H., McEvoy, M., & Holland, J. C. (1987). Cognitive/attentional distraction in the control of conditioned nausea in pediatric cancer patients receiving chemotherapy. *Journal of Consulting and Clinical Psychology, 55*, 391–395.

Reeves, J. L., Redd, W. H., Minagawa, R. Y., & Storm, C. K. (1983). Hypnosis in the control of pain during hyperthermia treatment of cancer. In J. J. Bonica, U. Lindbland, A. Iggo (Eds.), *Advances in Pain Research* (Vol. 5, pp. 857–861). New York: Raven Press.

Thoresen, C. E., & Powell, L. H. (1992). Type A behavior pattern: New perspectives on theory, assessment, and intervention. *Journal of Consulting and Clinical Psychology, 60*, 595–604.

Vasterling, J., Jenkins, R. A., Matt Tope, D., & Burish, T. G. (1993). Cognitive distraction and relaxation training for the control of side effects due to cancer chemotherapy. *Journal of Behavior Medicine, 16*, 65–80.

Whitehead, W. E. (1992). Behavioral medicine approaches to gastrointestinal disorders. *Journal of Consulting and Clinical Psychology, 60*, 605–612.

13

Structure of Victim Engagement in Sexual Abuse

Steven C. Wolf and Elsie M. Pinkston

This chapter describes an analytic structure for examining how adolescent male sexual offenders target, engage, and control their abuse victims. Operant constructs of stimulus-response and response-response are used to examine the way sexual-abuse patterns may be established and maintained. This structural approach facilitates the design of test hypotheses within the limitations of retrospective data. The behavior-chaining concept provides a basis for studying the environmental interaction between the sexual abuser and the victim.

The patterns of abuse in sexual offenders are chronic rather than spontaneous and isolated (Abel, Becker, Mittelman, Rouleau, & Murphy, 1987). Offenders often report emotional comfort with their assaultive behavior and look forward to the next incident of abuse rather than experience the behavior as an unpleasant or spontaneous event (Conte, Wolf, & Smith, 1989). Not infrequently, patterns of sexual preference for aggression first emerge during the offender's childhood (Becker & Stein, 1988). Adult offenders disclose an emotional attraction to sexual aggression and have long baselines of abuse dating back to their childhood (Becker & Stein, 1988; Conte et al., 1989; Segal & Stermac, 1990). Research data indicate that a preference for sexual aggression produces a variety of positive consequences, both sexual (Laws & Marshall, 1990; Stermac, Segal, & Gillis, 1990) and instrumental (Bandura, 1973). Sexual gratification accompanying aggressive acts reinforces and thus facilitates the construction of robust and complex patterns of sexual preference for aggression. This may, in part, explain why sexually aggressive individuals find it difficult to acknowledge the harmful impact of their actions and are so persistent in their abuse.

From the data, the following propositions emerge: (a) The duration and complexity of aggressive sexual patterns are a result of the reinforcing quality of sexual gratification and other desirable consequences associated with abuse, a plausible explanation for the resistance to amelioration by counseling. (b) The high level of emotional comfort, or congruence, with aggression (Finkelhor, 1984) accompanying this behavior may also be explained by an operant model (Laws & Marshall, 1990). This combination of early onset with the development of emotional congruence with, and sexual arousal to, aggression are likely mechanisms for strengthening abusive behavior. These highly correlated response-consequence relationships, unless we consider them trivial, suggest the undertaking of a structural analysis of sexual abuse. This chapter proposes a structure for investigating these patterns of attraction, expectation, and perpetration of sexual abuse.

To analyze these phenomena, we apply a series of operant structures. We selected this approach because it is a model that generates causal variables to define patterns and structures of behavior that can be investigated. (For a historical ordering of these developments, see Honig, 1966; Honig & Staddon, 1977; Keller & Schoenfeld, 1950; Skinner, 1938, 1953.)

Baer (1982) has described behavioral structures as variations on two forms: stimulus-response dependencies and response-response dependencies. It is response dependencies that are usually cited in the sexual-offender literature. Structures associated with lawful relationships allow at least a systematic approach for studying patterns of behavior in the engagement of victims for sexual abuse.

In the previous explorations of these processes, Wolf (1985) and Conte et al. (1989) found that sexual aggression was described by offenders as a highly patterned and systematic strategy for achieving sexual gratification and other instrumental needs, such as power, control, or humiliation of their victims. The 20 men studied reported abusing 146 children, with one abusing 40 children and the others averaging about 6 victims each. Abel and his colleagues (1987) reported finding similar patterns of multiple paraphilias and victims in their sample of 561 adult offenders.

Retrospective reports of adult offenders show individual sets of well-developed rules of conduct that take on a near-lawful significance. Sexual offenders report great care in selecting individuals they consider controllable and whose physical and behavioral characteristics arouse sexual feelings. Preference in victim characteristics and sexual behavior shape their strategies for selecting, approaching, sexualizing, and controlling their victims during acts of sexual aggression. In the sample studied by Conte et al. (1989), sexually aggressive patterns frequently began during childhood, with 50 percent abusing before age 20, 40 percent before age 14, and 20 percent at or before age 10. Most also reported engaging in multiple paraphilias and abusing multiple victims during their early childhood and adolescent years.

Because sexual aggression frequently begins during the perpetrator's childhood, it is important to include children who sexually abuse others in our study of sexualized aggression patterns. Studying these children could inform early intervention at a time when the strength of the sexual aggression patterns is arguably weaker. In childhood, it is plausible to assume that aggressive behavior has been less frequently reinforced and is therefore less complex, less well integrated, less sexually arousing, and less emotionally congruent.

Such studies, while enhancing our knowledge of the syndrome, would also help in our efforts to develop successful protocols and policies for treating and preventing future sexual aggression; it is hoped that such protocols would forestall the development of full-blown sexual aggressors (Salter, 1988). Research is needed to determine whether the patterns of juvenile offenders differ or duplicate those found in adult offenders. More to the point, such research will address the continuing debate among professionals and laypersons about whether sexually aggressive juveniles should be categorized as sexual offenders. This ambiguity about juvenile sexual offending has hindered the identification of juveniles who have a preference for sexual aggression as well as the development of appropriate interventions.

Recent research on juveniles describes how children act out paraphilias, reports their frequency, and calculates the average number of victims per offender. Presently, Becker and her colleagues (Becker & Abel, 1984; Becker, Kaplan, & Tenke, 1992; Becker & Stein, 1988) are leading in the study of both the nature of juveniles' sexual arousal to aggression and the ethics of such research. They have suggested that juvenile sex offenders are similar to adults in their arousal to aggressive themes.

Six Elements of Engagement

In the early literature on human sexual behavior, beginning with the unpublished work of Watson in the 1920s (Rosen & Beck, 1988), sexual aggression was conceptualized as a special case of learned human response. McGuire, Carlisle, and Young (1965) suggested that "sexual deviation" is conditioned behavior, and Barlow (1974, 1977), Barbaree (1990), and Laws and Marshall (1990) argued that sexual aggression is the result of a long operant chain consisting of shorter, contextually and temporally interdependent chains that collectively motivate the actor toward sexual satiation through an idiosyncratic set of behaviors that are abusive of others.

This conceptualization uses the operant chain model of behavior, in which each node, or link, in the chain consists of three terms ($S^D \to R \to S^R$). S^D, the discriminative stimulus, sets the occasion for a response (R) that is reinforced by the consequent stimulus, S^R. The term *node* is used to refer to a pattern of functional relationships. In this structure, the rate of movement within the chain is controlled by two principal variables, reinforcer strength at each node and the node's temporal distance from the end of the chain: the strength of the actor's attraction to the behavior and the actor's beliefs about the proximity of sexual gratification. The outcome of each node acts as a consequent reinforcer for those behaviors immediately preceding and sets the occasion for the occurrence of the subsequent behaviors (Walker, 1989). When the chain is successful—when some level of sexual gratification without punishment is achieved through abuse—the chain ends in reinforcement and thus establishes the initial discriminative stimulus (D. M. Baer, personal communication, 1992).

In chaining, the consequence produced at each node acts as a conditioned reinforcer of the preceding behavior and as the discriminative stimulus for the next.

The conditioned reinforcer–discriminative stimuli at each node could be said to strengthen an expectation of success at the next step: an operant definition of anticipation.

We must necessarily infer that anticipation will act as either an incentive or a disincentive for continuing the chain, depending on the probability of success signaled by the prevailing conditions. Anticipation, in this sense, acts as a conditional discriminative stimulus setting the occasion for the continuing versus exiting response, depending on the valence of the expectation of success.

The data reported in adult-offender research suggest a sexual-abuse chain of at least the following elements or nodes listed in Figure 13.1: (a) an eliciting stimulus, (b) target-selection behavior, (c) movement to contact, (d) sexualizing the contact and sexual abuse, (e) physical and emotional risk management, and (f) a reconstitution phase consisting of emotional rationalization and physical distancing. These are not necessarily the only components of the chain; they are suggested as its general structure, a structure that will be elaborated by the individual's idiosyncratic patterns of behavior. It is intended that the actual structure of the chain, if it exists, will be articulated, extended, and refined through the collection of further empirical data.

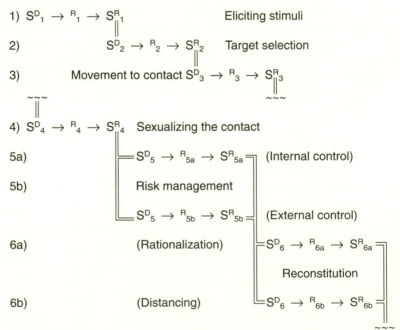

FIGURE 13.1   Behavior Chain of Sexually Aggressive Engagement Pattern, Node by Node

Adult sexual offenders report that they have often used sexual behavior, including sexual aggression, to manage anxiety (Conte et al., 1989; Wolf, 1985). What is not known is whether they are accurately reporting their use of sexuality in this manner or how they acquired this response to anxiety. These reports suggest that the sexualization of aggression might be an example of an escape or avoidance response, but why some individuals select sexuality to manage stress and anxiety is a matter for speculation.

Finkelhor (1984), in his model, supposes four specific preconditions that must be present before an act of sexual aggression can be expressed: (a) The sexually aggressive behavior to be perpetrated is acceptable to the actor and is expected to result in gratification (congruence and motivation). (b) Its consequences represent no immediate threat of emotional discomfort (overcoming internal inhibitions) or (c) of social consequence to the actor (overcoming external inhibitions). (d) The target of the sexual aggression will not be able to prevent the abusive sexual behavior (overcoming victim resistance). Our model incorporates those preconditions in the development of a structural analysis.

Node 1: Eliciting Stimuli

Perhaps no other components of sexual aggression have been as extensively explored as the environmental and psychological conditions that precede aggression. Stress, anxiety, and other unpleasant emotional conditions have frequently been suggested as eliciting stimuli for aggressive acts. Several authors, among them Rosen and Fracher (1983) and Wolf (1985), have argued that many offenders use sexual fantasy and masturbate to it as a strategy for suppressing or supplanting the unpleasant thoughts and emotions elicited by stressful conditions. In operant terms, we propose that stress and anxiety can come to serve as discriminative stimuli for a sexual escape response. Using sexuality in this manner could be highly reinforcing, because it produces an increase in the level of sexual arousal–gratification, suppresses anxiety, and reinforces the response. If this is so, sexuality can come to function as an escape from stress and anxiety.

Describing this node requires that we specify both the structure of the sexual aggression being expressed and the nature of its reinforcement. The latter task would also describe how these behaviors are acquired. Although much has been written about behavior acquisition generally and how sexually aggressive behaviors specifically are acquired, all such explanations are speculative. The justification of including this node in the chain, given its highly speculative nature, is that it provides a focusing function for directing future study and treatment.

Node 2: Target Selection

The sexual response of the first node evokes the second node, by setting the occasion for more intense, more frequent attention-to-target-identification and selection. These target-selection behaviors are reinforced by a consequent increase in the level of arousal to and anticipation of sexual gratification with the selected target or targets.

The shift in attention to a sexual focus engages the powerful psychophysiological mechanisms of sexuality, which in turn inhibit or displace stress and anxiety. The consequent reduction of stress and anxiety through the reciprocal inhibiting effects of this psychophysiological response process reinforces the use of sexuality as an escape strategy and increases the individual's interest in engaging in sexual activity, thereby setting the occasion for the next node of the complete chain.

Node 3: Movement to Contact

Target selection, with its subsequent increases in sexual arousal, also increases the individual's expectation of later contact and sexual success with the selected target. At the same time, it decreases inhibitions against contacting the target. The occasion is then set for planning, fantasy, and beginning contact with the target: initiating conversation, touching, isolating, or some other strategy (Conte et al., 1989). Successful contact with the target at this point is the next reinforcer. Prolonged contact success, paired with fantasy rehearsal of sexual behavior with the target, increases arousal, reinforcing still more contact and evoking the expectation of future sexual success with the target.

Fantasy about sex with the target has several functions: (a) reinforcing the initiating contact, (b) conditioning more forms of contact (reinforcing each new attempt with sexual arousal), and (c) reciprocally inhibiting any anxiety associated with approaching the target—anxiety is supposedly incompatible with, and is suppressed by, a state of sexual arousal. This last function, the reciprocal inhibition of approach anxiety by sexual arousal, sets the occasion for the next node: attempting sexual contact with the target.

Node 4: Sexualizing Contact

This node describes a pattern of manipulating the environment and the target to facilitate the introduction of sexuality. The prolonged contact success and fantasy rehearsal of sex with the target selected in the last node increases the perceived sexual attractiveness of the target and therefore sets the occasion for sexualizing the contacts with that individual. This occasion of increased expectation of sexual gratification evokes perpetrator attempts at managing environmental conditions and circumstances that expedite gaining *isolated* access to the target.

At the same time, the actor may be systematically desensitizing the preferred target to tolerate being approached and touched. Offenders report doing this by initially avoiding any physical contact with the target, by touching the target at first on nonsexual parts of the body, or by arranging isolation and protected access to the victim. Having thus achieved access and control over the target and the setting, the abuser overtly introduces sexual content into the relationship through sexual talk, humor, sexual media, direct sexual assault, or some other means. Sexual gratification is achieved either directly with the target during the sexual abuse or afterward during postabuse behavior such as fantasy of the target paired with masturbation.

This part of the chain represents a complex transition from the anticipation and planning of contact to making sexual contact with the targeted individual. This node clearly can build to facilitate movement toward sexual gratification. It produces the greatest degree of sexual gratification for the offender, resulting finally in sexual satiation and setting the occasion for the next node, risk management.

Node 5: Risk Management

This part of the chain consists of two related nodes: internal and external risk management. The sexual satiation just achieved lowers the abuser's interest in sexuality generally and in sexual aggression specifically. Now, awareness of the risks to self (discovery and shame) associated with sexual aggression is no longer displaced, and fear of being discovered reenters. This fear evokes a set of *internal* self-protective behaviors: rationalizing and minimizing the seriousness and hurtful nature of the aggression, blaming the target for causing the aggression, and many other similar strategies. These behaviors suppress the anxiety associated with feeling or believing oneself to be responsible for the abuse, being discovered, or being punished for the abuse. Their probability increases for future occasions of similar discriminative stimuli.

When awareness of the risk of discovery and punishment is no longer displaced, a belief that discovery and punishment are possible and perhaps even imminent emerges. As in internal risk management, this evokes a conditioned set of overt self-protective behaviors, such as manipulating the target through bribery, threats, or other forms of coercion to reduce the risk of disclosure. The relative success of these behaviors in reducing anxiety reinforces their use and increases the probability of their future expression under similar circumstances. When discovery does occur, these self-protective acts are punished, and the sexual offender denies that these acts will happen in the future.

This is the phase in which clinicians most often have first contact with sexual offenders. In this time of postdiscovery suppression of the aggressive sexual interest, offenders frequently feel afraid of the power of their aggressive sexual preferences and want to believe they will not act this way again. Offenders fail to recognize that postsexual satiation, disgust, and aversion for their recent sexual aggression are temporary. They fail to recognize that the recurrence of similar discriminative stimuli will evoke the chain again.

Node 6: Reconstitution (Rationalization and Distancing)

Like the previous node, Node 6 has both an internal (rationalization) and an external (distancing) function. The feelings of relief and safety resulting from the actions of Node 5 evoke a perception of being physically and emotionally separated from the abuse, in control of the target, and in control of the circumstances. In the absence of sexual arousal, which functioned as a powerful reinforcer of aggression, and of any overt aversive consequences, the internal shift away from holding oneself personally responsible continues. Blame is shifted from the offender to a variety of external targets, especially the victim, by redefining the aggression as nonsexual or by describing the victim as the actual aggressor. Escape to religious conversion or rededication, or promising to "never do it again," are also common. This distancing has the effect of recasting the abuse as a historical event resulting from external factors, rather than a personal, continuing preference for sexual aggression. The excuses and rationalizations reinforce the abuser's dissociation from feeling responsible and accountable for the aggressive actions.

The feelings of relief and safety also evoke behaviors that seek confirmation from the environment that the offender is a good person. Lacking external, overt aversive consequences for his actions, the actor finds or reinterprets experiences that confirm his desired self-image as good and nonabusive. That reinforces the confirmation behaviors and increases the probability of their future use.

Why is it that the negative emotions and fear of discovery and punishment evoked in this node do not punish the sexual aggression? What may happen instead is that the rationalizations and environmental confirmations of the offender's inherent goodness simply reinforce the aggressive behavior through disconfirming the negative expectations associated with this node. Furthermore, acting aggressively produces a variety of gains for the offender: It produces sexual access to the desired target; it produces sexual gratification and perhaps feelings of control and power; and it has not produced punishment. The individual has escaped negative consequences.

The ultimate outcome is an increased probability of the abuser repeating the aggression. Each node of the chain powerfully reinforces the offender's actions, either by providing sexual gratification or by allowing him to get away with the aggression one more time.

This risk of reoffending may be confounded by the attributions that the offender makes in the final links of the chain. Especially at Nodes 5 and 6, risk management and reconstitution, he must convince himself that his actions are not hurtful, that they may in fact be desired by the target, or that they are the fault of someone or something outside of himself. He may come to believe that he is the victim of the abuse (Ptacek, 1988; Wolf, 1985). This may be the precondition for action that Finkelhor (1984) describes as "emotional congruence" for aggression. It is possible that these attributions serve the function of setting the occasion for the next entry into the aggressive chain.

Finally, seeming to confirm Finkelhor's notion that the abuser must overcome his internal inhibitions against aggression, the abuser finds his expectation of negative consequences disconfirmed by his environment; it is incrementally easier to believe that the aggression is acceptable (Wolf, 1985). Eventually, the abuser takes no precautions to prevent a recurrence of the aggression. To do so would require admitting culpability.

Discussion

This structure for sexual aggression contains a method for establishing and shaping a research and treatment agenda. Within the structure of each node, the possibility exists for experimental manipulation of the various discriminative stimuli to measure their actual effects on the individual's responses.

In the broader context of treatment, these structures could be beneficial in the treatment of sexual aggression by focusing efforts on the development of management strategies for aggressive sexual preferences. Knowing the elements of these structures can give both the clinician and the client access points where the chain might be most easily disassembled.

This structure also could facilitate the definition and assessment of sex offenses. At present, treatment consists of the application of multiple techniques without a method to analyze the relationship of specific treatment variables to specific treatment outcomes. Although some aspects of sexual abuse may still evade empirical study, this structural approach increases the variables available for experimental study. It suggests possible measures of client progress and expedites the operation of appropriate and quantifiable outcome measures that can form the basis of testable hypotheses. As sexual offenders are studied and specific patterns emerge, it will be possible to determine the generality of plausible relationships and the nature of their properties and dimension.

References

Abel, G., Becker, J., Mittelman, M., Rouleau, J., & Murphy, W. (1987). Self-reported sex crimes of nonincarcerated paraphiliacs. *Journal of Interpersonal Violence, 2,* 3–25.

Baer, D. M. (1982). The imposition of structure on behavior and the demolition of behavioral structures. In D. J. Bernstein (Ed.), *Nebraska Symposium on Motivation: Vol. 29* (pp. 217–254). Lincoln: University of Nebraska Press.

Bandura, A. (1973). *Aggression: A social learning analysis* Englewood Cliffs, NJ: Prentice-Hall.

Barbaree, H. (1990). Stimulus control of sexual arousal: Its role in sexual assault. In W. L. Marshall, D. R. Laws, & H. E. Barbaree (Eds.), *Handbook of sexual assault: Issues, theories, and treatment of the offender* (pp. 115–142). New York: Plenum Press.

Barlow, D. H. (1974). The treatment of sexual deviation: Toward a comprehensive behavioral approach. In K. S. Calhoun, H. E. Adams, & K. M. Mitchell (Eds.), *Innovative treatment methods in psychopathology.* New York: Wiley.

Barlow, D. H. (1977). Assessment of sexual behavior. In R. A. Ciminero, K. S. Calhoun, & H. E. Adams (Eds.), *Handbook of behavioral assessment* (pp. 461–508). New York: Wiley.

Becker, J. V., & Abel, G. G. (1984). *Methodological and ethical issues in evaluating and treating adolescent sexual offenders* (Monograph). Washington, DC: National Institute of Mental Health.

Becker, J. V., Kaplan, M., & Tenke, C. (1992). The relationship of abuse history, denial, and erectile response profiles of adolescent sexual perpetrators. *Behavior Therapy, 23,* 87–97.

Becker, J. V., & Stein, R. (1988). The assessment of adolescent sexual offenders. In R. J. Prinz (Ed.), *Advances in behavioral assessment of children and families* (Vol. 4, pp. 97–118). Greenwich, CT: JAI Press.

Church, R. (1989). Theories of timing behavior. In S. Klein & R. Mowrer (Eds.), *Contemporary learning theories: Instrumental conditioning theory and the impact of biological constraints on learning* (pp. 41–71). Hillsdale, NJ: Erlbaum.

Conte, J., Wolf, S., & Smith, T. (1989). What sexual offenders tell us about prevention strategies. *Child Abuse and Neglect, 13,* 293–301.

Finkelhor, D. (1984). *Child sexual abuse: New theory and research.* New York: Free Press.

Honig, W. K. (1966). *Operant behavior: Areas of research and application.* Englewood Cliffs, NJ: Prentice-Hall.

Honig, W. K., & Staddon, J. E. R. (Eds.). (1977). *Handbook of operant behavior.* Englewood Cliffs, NJ: Prentice-Hall.

Keller, F. S., & Schoenfeld, W. N. (1950). *Principles of psychology.* New York: Appleton-Century-Crofts.

Knopp, F. H. (1982). *Remedial intervention in adolescent sex offenses: Nine program descriptions.* Syracuse, NY: Safer Society Press.

Laws, D., & Marshall, W. (1990). A conditioning theory of the etiology and maintenance of deviant sexual preference and behavior. In W. L. Marshall, D. R. Laws, & H. E. Barbaree (Eds.), *Handbook of sexual assault: Issues, theories, and treatment of the offender* (pp. 204–229). New York: Plenum Press.

McGuire, R. J., Carlisle, J. M., & Young, B. A. (1965). Sexual deviation as conditioned behavior. *Behavior Research and Therapy, 2,* 185–190.

Ptacek, J. (1988). Why do men batter their wives? In K. Yllo & M. Bograd (Eds.), *Feminist perspective on wife abuse.* New York: Sage.

Rosen, R. C., & Beck, J. G. (1988). *Patterns of sexual arousal: Psychophysiological processes and clinical applications.* New York: Guilford Press.

Rosen, R. C., & Fracher, J. C. (1983). Tension-reduction training in the treatment of compulsive sex offenders. In J. G. Greer & I. R. Stuart (Eds.), *The sexual aggressor: Current perspectives on treatment* (pp. 144–159). New York: Van Nostrand Reinhold.

Salter, A. C. (1988). *Treating child sex offenders and victims: A practical guide.* Newbury Park, CA: Sage.

Segal, Z., & Stermac, L. (1990). The role of cognition in sexual assault. In W. L. Marshall, D. R. Laws, & H. E. Barbaree (Eds.), *Handbook of sexual assault: Issues, theories, and treatment of the offender* (pp. 131–134). New York: Plenum Press.

Skinner, B. F. (1938). *The behavior of organisms: An experimental analysis.* New York: Appleton-Century-Crofts.

Skinner, B. F. (1953). *Science and human behavior.* New York: Macmillan.

Stermac, L., Segal, Z., & Gillis, R. (1990). Social and cultural factors in sexual assault. In W. L. Marshall, D. R. Laws, & H. E. Barbaree (Eds.), *Handbook of sexual assault: Issues, theories, and treatment of the offender* (pp. 143–160). New York: Plenum Press.

Walker, E. L. (1989). Reinforcement: "The one ring." In J. T. Tapp (Ed.), *Reinforcement and behavior* (pp. 47–62). New York: Academic Press.

Wolf, S. C. (1985). A multi-factor model of deviant sexuality. *Victimology: An International Journal, 10,* 359–374.

A previous version of this paper is presented in Mr. Wolf's dissertation proposal, *An Exploration of Victim Engagement Patterns of Male Juvenile Sex Offenders,* October 1992, School of Social Service Administration, The University of Chicago.

14

Stimulus Control of Drug Abuse

Kimberly C. Kirby, Richard J. Lamb,
and Martin Y. Iguchi

Although Skinner proposed a conceptual unit of analysis based on a three-term contingency, the relationship between behavior and its consequences has received the most attention in behavior analysis, whereas the relationship of behavior and consequences to antecedent events has been neglected. Work on the analysis of drug abuse is no exception. Behavioral models of drug abuse often are defined by the examination of consequences maintaining behavior, with emphasis on the pharmacological properties of drugs (e.g., Stitzer, Bigelow, & McCaul, 1983). Although there is no doubt that pharmacological properties are important, they do not provide a complete understanding of drug abuse. Like any other reinforcement process, drug reinforcement is a malleable function of the drug, the past reinforcement history of the organism, establishing operations, and the current behavioral context and stimulus control.

This chapter reviews the behavior-pharmacology literature that has systematically addressed antecedent control, with particular focus on the antecedents to drug self-administration and abuse. We review three areas of research: (a) drugs as discriminative stimuli, (b) classically conditioned antecedents to drug use, and (c) operantly conditioned antecedents to drug use.

Drugs as Discriminative Stimuli

When behavior pharmacologists address antecedents in the three-term contingency, they typically are interested in examining the discriminative functions of drugs (e.g., Glennon, Järbe, & Frankenheim, 1991). Drugs, once ingested, can serve as discriminative stimuli that set the occasion for behavior. For example, as diagrammed in Figure 14.1, a discrimination between two drugs can be trained by reinforcing Response 1 after administering Drug A and Response 2 after administering Drug B. This training is used as a preparation for the next step, which is to administer Drug X and see if it sets the occasion for the response trained under Drug A or the one trained under Drug B.

$$D_A - R_1 - S^R$$

Training:

$$D_B - R_2 - S^R$$

Test: $D_X - R_?$

FIGURE 14.1 Drug Discrimination Training and Testing Procedure

This procedure and its variations have been used in the animal laboratory and recently have been extended to human laboratories (Bickel, Preston, Bigelow, & Liebson, 1986; Chait, Uhlenhuth, & Johanson, 1986; Preston, Bigelow, Bickel, & Liebson, 1987). They are useful procedures for examining drug classifications and for determining abuse liability of new drugs.

One important finding from research examining drugs as discriminative stimuli is that drugs (just like nondrug stimuli) can simultaneously serve discriminative and reinforcing functions for behavior. The implications of these dual functions have been clarified through studies demonstrating that noncontingent administration of a drug that previously maintained responding can reinstate responding, even after relatively lengthy periods of extinction. For example, de Wit and Stewart (1981) trained rats to self-administer cocaine by making cocaine available for each bar press. Once the rats were reliably self-administering, they were exposed to an extinction condition in which no cocaine infusions occurred. After lever pressing was extinguished, the rats were given a noncontingent cocaine injection. This markedly increased lever pressing and maintained it for as long as 30 minutes, despite the extinction schedule. Furthermore, the effect was drug-specific: Only drugs with stimulus properties similar to cocaine reinstated cocaine-reinforced responding. Similar results have been found with nonhuman self-administration of amphetamine (Davis & Smith, 1976), ethanol (Karoly, Winger, Ikomi, & Woods, 1978), heroin (de Wit & Stewart, 1983), and morphine (Davis & Smith, 1976), and with human self-administration of alcohol (Bigelow, Griffiths, & Liebson, 1977). Therefore, both human and nonhuman studies suggest that interoceptive stimulus properties of drugs can set the occasion for drug self-administration and drug seeking.

Classically Conditioned Antecedents

It's this feeling that you get, like when you get money in your hand, and it's a feeling first like you might think about the idea of using cocaine, then you feel it. It comes . . . it's a physical feeling, it's like an adrenaline start building up. You might get butterflies in your stomach, sometimes you might get the shakes, and you have a feeling of knowing you got money and you can get that drug. [From E. G., a client at an addiction research and treatment program]

The role of classically conditioned antecedents in drug administration has been recognized since the 1940s. A variety of Pavlovian, or classical conditioning, models suggest that conditioned drug effects result from pairing drug (or drug-related) effects with environmental stimuli (e.g., Siegel, 1983; Stewart, de Wit, & Eikelboom, 1984; Wikler, 1980). In the example that follows, crack cocaine is the unconditioned stimulus (US), and a physiological effect of drug administration, decreased skin temperature, is the unconditioned response (UR). In this example, by pairing the drug crack with a crack pipe, the pipe itself becomes a conditioned stimulus (CS) that elicits a conditioned physiological response (CR) of decreased skin temperature (Figure 14.2).

This model has been carefully studied by Childress and her colleagues (e.g., Childress, McLellan, Ehrman & O'Brien, 1988; Childress, McLellan, & O'Brien, 1986a, 1986b). Cocaine-experienced participants and nondrug-using controls were shown both cocaine-related and nondrug stimuli in a laboratory setting. The cocaine-related stimuli featured a video of simulated drug buying, selling, and administration of cocaine, followed by a cocaine-related task in which participants underwent a mock drug-preparation ritual. The nondrug stimuli consisted of a nature video, and the nondrug task was a computer game. A variety of physiological responses to the stimuli were measured, including temperature, heart rate, and galvanic skin response (GSR). In addition, participants were asked to rate sensations of drug high, drug withdrawal, and drug craving.

Changes in physiological and self-report measures occurred as a function of the different stimulus presentations. Skin temperature responded particularly dramatically; cocaine-experienced individuals had significant reductions in skin temperature in the presence of the cocaine video and task. Also, their temperature returned to baseline after the offset of the cocaine stimuli. These responses reflected a history of cocaine use rather than nonspecific properties of the stimuli, since nondrug-using controls did not have these responses to cocaine-related stimuli. Also, cocaine users did not demonstrate these physiological changes in response to opiate-related stimuli.

These results and the results of other studies suggest that through classical conditioning, antecedent stimuli can control physiological responses of opiate and cocaine users, alcoholics, and smokers (for a review, see Rohsenow, Childress,

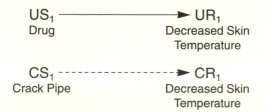

$$US_1 \longrightarrow UR_1$$
Drug   Decreased Skin Temperature

$$CS_1 \dashrightarrow CR_1$$
Crack Pipe   Decreased Skin Temperature

FIGURE 14.2   Classical Conditioning Paradigm

Monti, Niaura, & Abrams, 1991). However, this finding does not clarify how classically conditioned stimuli might induce drug self-administration and drug abuse. In fact, one might speculate that if conditioned stimuli alone can produce the conditioned response, drug self-administration might decrease. However, clinical observation suggests that the conditioned responses prompt drug seeking. It is possible that conditioned physiological responses elicited by classically conditioned stimuli function much like response-independent drug administrations. As mentioned, these noncontingent drug administrations can reinstate previously extinguished responding, possibly by serving as discriminative stimuli that set the occasion for drug self-administration and drug-seeking behavior.

A clinical implication of this model is that by eliminating the conditioned responses to drug-related stimuli, it may be possible to reduce or eliminate drug use. Childress and her colleagues (Childress et al., 1986a, 1988; Rohsenow et al., 1991) have explored this implication, using a procedure in which participants are repeatedly exposed to the conditioned cocaine-related stimuli in the laboratory. Since the drug is never administered in the laboratory, the association between the US and the CS is eliminated, which should extinguish the conditioned response. Data from these studies show a reduction in all ratings over extinction sessions, but after as many as 15 sessions, conditioned responses sometimes still occurred. This is particularly true of the physiological responses; measures such as skin temperature tend to be more persistent. Furthermore, Childress et al. (1988) have noted additional limitations of this treatment. For example, a wide variety of conditioned stimuli may be present, some of which are difficult to simulate in the laboratory. Some data suggest that extinction to the cues used in the laboratory does not generalize well to cues in the natural environment (Childress et al., 1986a). Also, a single pairing of the conditioned and unconditioned stimuli can reinstate the conditioned responses to full strength. Participants who receive the classical extinction procedure show better treatment retention and more cocaine-free urines than control patients receiving like amounts of therapy or counseling; however, Childress et al. concluded that the benefits from classical extinction are modest. Applications of classical extinction to other addictions have produced similar conclusions (e.g., Brandon, Zelman, & Baker, 1987).

Although the classical extinction procedure has limitations as a drug-abuse treatment, the research from which it evolved has played an important role in furthering our understanding of antecedent control of drug abuse. Future research might take advantage of conditioned responses to drug-related cues rather than eliminating them. If recovering drug abusers can be trained to recognize the physiological cues of the conditioned response and use them to set the occasion for drug-avoidance responses, classically conditioned responses to drug-related cues could become an asset.

Operantly Conditioned Antecedents

Triggers was when I had money, and triggers was when I was in an argument. . . . Triggers was when I seen people do it. Triggers was when I talked about it and started thinking about it. Lots of times too it was when I'd walk past the drug dealers. Every time I see [my boyfriend] I kept thinking about the times we used to get high. Then I used to get that urge because . . . that's another trigger for me . . . is being around him. [From E. G.]

In addition to eliciting functions, cocaine-related stimuli probably have discriminative functions. In the presence of some drug-related stimuli, drug seeking is reinforced, and in the absence of those stimuli, it is extinguished. Many researchers confine their analysis of drug-related stimuli to a classical conditioning model because of the direct relationship between drug administration and the physiological drug effects. That is, the administration of the drug (US) elicits the physiological effects (UR) without any operant response requirement on the part of the participant. However, classical and operant conditioning are not as separate as once believed (e.g., Bouton & Swartzentruber, 1991; Rescorla, 1987). Although there may not be an operant component required in the relationship between the drug and the drug effect, there are clear operant components to the drug seeking and self-administration that lead to the presentation of the US (i.e., the drug). Therefore, it is likely that drug-related stimuli not only elicit conditioned drug effects, but also operantly occasion drug seeking and self-administration.

Stimulus control of drug self-administration by environmental stimuli has been suggested on the basis of a variety of nonhuman studies (for a review, see Young & Herling, 1986, pp. 34–42). For example, the likelihood of reinstating drug self-administration after a period of extinction is increased by introducing stimuli that were present when drug self-administration was established (Thompson & Ostlund, 1965). Conversely, stimuli that occurred only in the absence of drug reinforcement can suppress drug self-administration (Young, Thompson, Jensen, & Muchow, 1979). Little operant research in humans has addressed the discriminative functions of drug-related stimuli, but research in relapse prevention has extensively examined this issue.

Relapse-prevention training generally assumes an operant perspective (e.g., Marlatt, 1985; McAuliffe, Albert, Cordill-London, & Garraghy, 1991), which predicts the likelihood of relapse under conditions of exposure to conditioned discriminative stimuli (McAuliffe et al., 1991). This principle has resulted in one of the most important strategies of relapse prevention: identifying and avoiding "high-risk situations" (Daley, 1987; Marlatt & Gordon, 1980; McAuliffe & Chein, 1986). Drug administration is also viewed as the terminal behavior in a behavior chain. For example, a woman who is trying to stop using cocaine sits alone at home in the afternoon watching television. Often, a friend drops by to watch with her. After the program, the friend usually goes to buy some cocaine and persuades the woman to come along. When the woman sees the supplier, she cannot resist buying a little cocaine. This is the beginning of a cocaine binge. In this example, the first discriminative stimulus in the behavior chain (the television program), although seemingly innocuous, can be considered a high-risk situation for this woman.

Many relapse-prevention studies identify high-risk situations. Among smokers, negative affect (e.g., anxiety, anger, frustration, depression) and interpersonal or work-related stress (Carmody, 1990; Shiffman, 1982) are high-risk situations. The presence of other smokers (Carmody, 1990; Cummings, Gordon, & Marlatt, 1980; Shiffman, 1982), smoking paraphernalia (Carmody, 1990; Cummings et al., 1980; Shiffman, 1982), and consumption of food or drink (Shiffman, 1982) are other often-cited antecedents. Alcohol consumption, in particular, was cited as an antecedent for nearly one-fifth of Shiffman's (1982) respondents. These results are consistent with laboratory studies suggesting that alcohol consumption promotes smoking, perhaps through pharmacological interactions (Griffiths, Bigelow, & Liebson, 1976; Mello, Mendelson, Sellers, & Kuehnle, 1980).

Relapse situations for alcoholics are similar to those of smokers, with negative affect and socialization reported frequently (Cummings et al., 1980; Marlatt & Gordon, 1980). Allen, Faden, and Rawlings (1992) found feeling bad about life, feelings of loss, taste or smell of alcohol, boredom, and frustration were the five situations most cited by alcoholic participants. Data suggest that among individuals who relapse, unpleasant affect is among the most dangerous situations.

Research examining relapses in abusing opiate, cocaine, and other substances has identified situations similar to those found for alcoholics and smokers. Interpersonal stress and social pressure again figure prominently (Tucker, Vuchinich, & Gladsjo, 1991; Wallace, 1992). Allen et al. (1992) found that participants who were treated for abuse of both alcohol and another drug most frequently cited the same five situations as the alcoholic participants. An additional situation that was quite prominent for the dual-substance users was being in the place where they had used the substance before. Other high-risk situations include substance availability, people and places associated with use, and use of another drug (Iguchi & Stitzer, 1991; Tucker et al., 1991; Wallace, 1992).

We conducted a study to determine which situations in the natural environment tended to have a discriminative function for cocaine use (Kirby, Lamb, Iguchi, Husband, & Platt, 1995). Although direct observation of the behaviors of interest would have been ideal, it was impractical. We therefore relied on self-reports, interviewing 265 cocaine users at four outpatient methadone-maintenance programs in the Philadelphia area. The interview had a semi-structured format and provided participants with a list of drug-related stimuli, activities, and emotions. They were asked to identify all the items that were likely to lead them to use cocaine. After they had gone through the list, we asked them to look at the items they had identified and choose a "high-impact situation," that is, the situation that was most likely to lead to use even if it did not occur very often.

The five occasions participants most commonly identified were having the drug present (86% of participants), being offered the drug (85%), having money available (83%), feeling bored (74%), and having nothing to do (72%). Having the drug present, having money available, and being bored were also among the five most frequently identified high-impact situations, suggesting that these tend to be particularly difficult situations for many cocaine users. Although these situations were the most commonly identified, the importance of remaining sensitive to the variety of stimuli that were identified as setting occasions was clear. Virtually all of the situations we listed were identified by some participants as setting occasions, and the participants suggested four additional ones we had not listed. If we had listed more situations, it is likely that more would have been identified. On the average, each participant identified about 15 items as stimuli that set the occasion for cocaine use, with some naming as many as 30. Also, all but four of the situations listed were chosen by at least one participant as a high-impact situation.

These data emphasize the importance of conducting an individual analysis in cocaine treatment, since the stimuli that are most problematic for a given individual can cover a wide range of situations. The results also showed that of the nine different emotions we listed, participants most frequently endorsed boredom and least frequently endorsed fatigue as a setting occasion. The remaining emotions listed were endorsed by over half the participants, but there was little difference between emotions. The list included negative affects that are widely cited as high-risk situations, but happiness—a positive affect—was equally endorsed.

Our data replicated the findings of previous studies, in that situations associated with socialization (i.e., being offered the drug, seeing others using, seeing the person they used with, or hearing others talk about drugs), stress, and boredom all were frequently cited as setting the occasion for cocaine use. Unlike researchers of previous studies, we emphasized the prevalence of drug-related stimuli and identification of these stimuli, and we questioned focusing on distinctions among emotional conditions, a frequent practice in relapse-prevention research (e.g., Shiffman, 1982). Also, we emphasized the importance of individual analysis of the setting occasions.

The importance of individual analysis was clearly demonstrated in a study examining situational factors in smoking (Hatsukami, Morgan, Pickens, & Champagne, 1990). Using a portable electronic smoking device and participants' self-reports, this study showed that smoking behavior varied as a function of the situational factors in the environment. There was considerable variability in the distribution of cigarettes smoked across situational categories, and smoking topography could vary dramatically from situation to situation. These differences became clear, however, only through a within-subject analysis. Some relapse-prevention researchers have been aware of individual variability and the need to tailor interventions, but most research in this area has depended on traditional experimental designs that average across subjects. It seems likely that behavior analysis, with its unique focus on the individual and its rich history of research in stimulus control, has much to offer to the analysis of antecedents to drug abuse.

Strategies for Dealing with Discriminative Stimuli for Drug Abuse

Generally, a behavior analysis might suggest several strategies for disrupting an established relationship between a discriminative stimulus and a response. The most obvious one, eliminating reinforcement for the behavior altogether, is not possible when applied to most drug abuse, so other strategies are needed. Eliminating or avoiding the discriminative stimulus is a possibility. Alternatively, we might arrange reinforcement of a new response in the presence of the discriminative stimulus. Or we could introduce new stimuli and reinforce competing repertoires in their presence.

In addition to investigating the natural setting occasions for cocaine use, the study we described previously (Kirby et al., 1995) also examined the strategies individuals used when facing high-risk situations. In addition to the list of situations, participants were shown a list of strategies. Some strategies were for dealing with high-risk situations they were already in, for example, leaving the situation. Others were general actions that they might take to help them quit, such as entering a treatment program. Other strategies involved helping them avoid situations, such as looking for a job so that they would have less time available to use. Finally, we asked about life events that were not explicitly planned as strategies to assist them in stopping drug use but that had nonetheless helped them to achieve abstinence.

We found that avoiding high-risk people and places was the strategy most frequently identified. Leaving the situation was the next most common, whereas entering treatment, getting counseling, giving money to someone else to manage, and making new friends were all identified by about half of the participants. Generally, there were a surprising number and variety of strategies that participants said they had employed. On the average, they identified about seven or eight strategies. However, once again, there was wide variability among individuals. Some participants identified as many as 17 strategies, whereas others could identify few or none at all.

One implication of these results is that treatment should begin with a baseline assessment of alternative response strategies and use strategies that patients already report. It is likely that some strategies will need to be refined and improved, but there is little advantage in assuming that patients are starting from a zero baseline. Another implication is that many patients will need to be taught new strategies for supporting abstinence, since some identified only a few strategies. Although avoiding people and places was the strategy most frequently cited, this is often impossible to achieve; many cocaine-dependent individuals live in heavily drug-infested neighborhoods where drug-related stimuli surround them. Even patients who can successfully avoid drug-infested neighborhoods are likely to have difficulty avoiding all discriminative stimuli for drug use, since stimulus control can generalize to otherwise innocuous stimuli, and innocuous stimuli may enter into the initial links of a behavior chain. Therefore, in addition to using and improving on the strategies people bring to treatment, it is important to establish a variety of strategies, including new ways to respond when faced with unavoidable discriminative stimuli, and to introduce new, competing repertoires. Most behaviorally based cocaine treatment programs train patients to recognize stimuli that occur early in the behavior chain and to develop alternative responses to discriminative stimuli for cocaine use. By teaching new responses to emit in the presence of stimuli discriminative for drug use, not only is a new operant relation established, but the existing respondent relation undergoes extinction in the natural environment.

> *If I see a trigger now, I don't get the feeling too much. . . . It come in my mind . . . "Wow! I used to use that." . . . It's the same old [triggers] but I got used to not really letting it get too far.* [From E. G.]

Recent research suggests that developing new competing repertoires with associated new, naturally occurring reinforcers is an important component in a comprehensive behavioral treatment program for drug addiction. Although this strategy also has been stressed by researchers in relapse prevention (e.g., McAuliffe et al., 1991), it may be that a complete behavior analysis provides the strongest basis for arranging appropriate contingencies and developing competing repertoires. Some of the most successful interventions in addiction have been conducted by well-trained behavior analysts employing a comprehensive behavioral intervention known as community reinforcement (Azrin, 1976; Higgins, Delaney, Budney, Bickel, Hughes, Foerg, & Fenwick, 1991; Hunt & Azrin, 1973), in which the antecedents and consequences of drug abuse are explicitly analyzed and the development of competing repertoires is emphasized.

Conclusion

Strategies addressing stimulus control have been incorporated into drug-abuse treatments, but stimulus control as a behavioral process in drug abuse has not received much explicit scientific attention. Much more research is needed before we will have a basic understanding of the processes involved and the necessary tools for systematically applying that knowledge to the treatment of substance abuse. In a review of the relationship of stimulus control to the treatment of substance abuse, Bickel and Kelly (1986) concluded that a behavior analysis of substance abuse will be incomplete if researchers continue to ignore stimulus-control processes. We echo that conclusion and suggest that substantial increases in our understanding of these processes could most readily be advanced by a small community of behavior analysts with a thorough understanding of the operant analysis of stimulus control.

References

Allen, J. P., Faden, V., & Rawlings, R. (1992). *Addictive Behaviors, 17,* 359–366.

Azrin, N. H. (1976). Improvements in the community-reinforcement approach to alcoholism. *Behavior Research and Therapy, 14,* 339–348.

Bickel, W. K., & Kelly, T. H. (1986). The relationship of stimulus control to the treatment of substance abuse. In B. A. Ray (Ed.), *Learning factors in substance abuse* (National

Institute of Drug Abuse [NIDA] Monograph No. 84, pp. 122–140). Washington, DC: U.S. Government Printing Office.

Bickel, W. K., Preston, K. L., Bigelow, G. E., & Liebson, I. A. (1986). Three-way drug discrimination in post-addict volunteers. Hydromorphone, pentazocine and saline. In L. S. Harris (Ed.), *Problems of drug dependence* (National Institute of Drug Abuse [NIDA] Monograph No. 67, pp. 177–183). Washington, DC: U.S. Government Printing Office.

Bigelow, G. E., Griffiths, R. R., & Liebson, I. A. (1977). Pharmacological influences upon ethanol self-administration. In M. M. Gross (Ed.), *Alcohol intoxication and withdrawal* (Vol. IIIB, pp. 523–538). New York: Plenum Press.

Bouton, M. E., & Swartzentruber, D. (1991). Sources of relapse after extinction in Pavlovian and instrumental learning. *Clinical Psychology Review, 11,* 123–140.

Brandon, T. H., Zelman, D. C., & Baker, T. B. (1987). Effects of maintenance sessions on smoking relapse: Delaying the inevitable? *Journal of Consulting and Clinical Psychology, 55,* 780–782.

Carmody, T. P. (1990). Preventing relapse in the treatment of nicotine addiction: Current issues and future directions. *Journal of Psychoactive Drugs, 22,* 211–238.

Chait, L. D., Uhlenhuth, E. H., & Johanson, C. E. (1986). The discriminative stimulus and subjective effects of d-amphetamine, phenmetrazine and fenfluramine in humans. *Psychopharmacology* (Berlin), *89,* 301–306.

Childress, A. R., McLellan, A. T., Ehrman, R., & O'Brien, C. P. (1988). Classically conditioned responses in opioid and cocaine dependence: A role in relapse? In B. A. Ray (Ed.), *Learning factors in substance abuse* (National Institute of Drug Abuse [NIDA] Research Monograph No. 84, pp. 25–43). Washington, DC: U.S. Government Printing Office.

Childress, A. R., McLellan, A. T., & O'Brien, C. P. (1986a). Abstinent opiate abusers exhibit conditioned craving, conditioned withdrawal and reductions in both through extinction. *British Journal of Addiction, 81,* 655–660.

Childress, A. R., McLellan, A. T., & O'Brien, C. P. (1986b). Conditioned responses in a methadone population. *Journal of Substance Abuse Treatment, 3,* 173–179.

Cummings, C., Gordon, J. R., & Marlatt, G. A. (1980). Relapse: Prevention and prediction. In W. R. Miller (Ed.), *The Addictive Behaviors.* New York: Pergamon Press.

Daley, D. C. (1987). Relapse prevention with substance abusers: Clinical issues and myths. *Social Work, 32,* 138–142.

Davis, W. M., & Smith, S. G. (1976). Role of conditioned reinforcers in the initiation, maintenance and extinction of drug-seeking behavior. *Pavlovian Journal of Biological Science, 11,* 222–236.

de Wit, H., & Stewart, J. (1981). Reinstatement of cocaine-reinforced responding in the rat. *Psychopharmacology, 75,* 134–143.

de Wit, H., & Stewart, J. (1983). Drug reinstatement of heroin reinforced responding in the rat. *Psychopharmacology, 79,* 29–31.

Glennon, R. A., Järbe, T., & Frankenheim, J. (1991). *Drug discrimination: Applications to drug abuse research.* (National Institute of Drug Abuse [NIDA] Monograph No. 116). Washington, DC: U.S. Government Printing Office.

Griffiths, R. R., Bigelow, G. E., & Liebson, I. (1976). Facilitation of human tobacco self-administration by ethanol: A behavioral analysis. *Journal of the Experimental Analysis of Behavior, 25,* 279–292.

Hatsukami, D. K., Morgan, S. F., Pickens, R. W., & Champagne, S. E. (1990). Situational factors in smoking. *Addictive Behaviors, 15,* 1–12.

Higgins, S. T., Delaney, D. D., Budney, A. J., Bickel, W. K., Hughes, J. R., Foerg, F., & Fenwick, J. W. (1991). A behavioral approach to achieving initial cocaine abstinence. *American Journal of Psychiatry, 148,* 1218–1224.

Hunt, G. M., & Azrin, N. H. (1973). A community-reinforcement approach to alcoholism. *Behavior Research and Therapy, 11,* 91–104.

Iguchi, M. Y., & Stitzer, M. L. (1991). Predictors of opiate drug abuse during a 90-day methadone detoxification. *American Journal of Drug and Alcohol Abuse, 17,* 279–294.

Karoly, A. J., Winger, G., Ikomi, F., & Woods, J. H. (1978). The reinforcing property of ethanol in the rhesus monkey: II. Some variables related to maintenance of intravenous ethanol-reinforced responding. *Psychopharmacology, 58,* 19–25.

Kirby, K. C., Lamb, R. J., Iguchi, M. Y., Husband, S., & Platt, J. J. (1995). Situations occasioning cocaine use and cocaine abstinence strategies. *Addiction, 90,* 1241–1252.

Marlatt, G. A. (1985) Relapse prevention: Theoretical rationale and overview of the model. In G. A. Marlatt & J. R. Gordon (Eds.), *Relapse prevention: Maintenance strategies in the treatment of addictive behaviors* (pp. 3–70). New York: Guilford Press.

Marlatt, G. A., & Gordon, J. R. (1980). Determinants of relapse: Implications for the maintenance of behavior change. In P. Davidson & S. M. Davidson (Eds.), *Behavioral medicine: Changing health lifestyles* (pp. 1410–1452). New York: Brunner/Mazel.

McAuliffe, W. E., Albert, J., Cordill-London, G., & Garraghy, T. K. (1991). Contributions to a social conditioning model of cocaine recovery. *International Journal of the Addictions, 25,* 1141–1177.

McAuliffe, W. E., & Chein, J. M. N. (1986). Recovery training and self help: A relapse-prevention program for treated heroin addicts. *Journal of Substance Abuse Treatment, 3,* 9–20.

Mello, N. K., Mendelson, J. H., Sellers, M. L., & Kuehnle, J. C. (1980). Effect of alcohol and marijuana on tobacco smoking. *Clinical Pharmacology and Therapeutics, 27,* 202–209.

Pear, J. J., & Eldridge, G. D. (1984). The operant-respondent distinction: Future directions. *Journal of the Experimental Analysis of Behavior, 42,* 453–467.

Preston, K. L., Bigelow, G. E., Bickel, W. K., & Liebson, I. A. (1987). Three-choice drug discrimination in opioid-dependent humans: Effects of naloxone after acute morphine exposure. *Journal of Pharmacology and Experimental Therapeutics, 243,* 1002–1009.

Rescorla, R. A. (1987). A Pavlovian analysis of goal-directed behavior. *American Psychologist, 42,* 119–129.

Rohsenow, D. J., Childress, A. R., Monti, P. M., Niaura, R. S., & Abrams, D. B. (1991). Cue reactivity in addictive behaviors: Theoretical and treatment implications. *The International Journal of the Addictions, 25,* 957–993.

Shiffman, S. (1982). Relapse following smoking cessation: A situational analysis. *Journal of Consulting and Clinical Psychology, 50,* 71–86.

Siegel, S. (1983). Classical conditioning, drug tolerance, and drug dependence. In R. G. Smart, F. B. Glaser, & Y. Israel (Eds.), *Research advances in alcohol and drug problems* (Vol. 7, pp. 207–246). New York: Plenum Press.

Stewart, J., de Wit, H., & Eikelboom, R. (1984). The role of unconditioned and conditioned drug effects in self-administration of opiates and stimulants. *Psychological Review, 91,* 251–268.

Stitzer, M. L., Bigelow, G. E., & McCaul, M. E. (1983). Behavioral approaches to drug abuse. In M. Hersen & L. Eisler (Eds.), *Progress in behavior modification* (Vol. 14, pp. 49–124). New York: Academic Press.

Thompson, T., & Ostlund, W. (1965). Susceptibility to readdiction as a function of the addiction and withdrawal environments. *Journal of Comprehensive Physiological Psychology, 3,* 388–392.

Tucker, J. A., Vuchinich, R. E., & Gladsjo, J. A. (1991). Environmental influences on relapse in substance use disorders. *International Journal of the Addictions, 25,* 1017–1050.

Wallace, B. C. (1992). Treating crack cocaine dependence: The critical role of relapse prevention. *Journal of Psychoactive Drugs, 24,* 213–222.

Wikler, A. (1980). *Opioid dependence: Mechanisms and treatment*. New York: Plenum Press.
Young, A. M., & Herling, S. (1986). Drugs as reinforcers: Studies in laboratory animals. In
S. R. Goldberg & I. P. Stolerman (Eds.), *Behavioral analysis of drug dependence* (pp.
9–86). New York: Academic Press.
Young, A. M., Thompson, T., Jensen, M. A., & Muchow, L. R. (1979). Effects of response
contingent clock stimuli on behavior maintained by intravenous codeine in the rhesus
monkey. *Pharmacology, Biochemistry, & Behavior, 11*, 43–49.

15

Stimulus Control Processes in Drug Taking: Implications for Treatment

Warren K. Bickel and Thomas H. Kelly

When drug use surpasses other important behaviors, a stimulus-control interpretation suggests an increase in the range of stimuli that set the occasion for drug-taking. In this chapter, we describe stimulus-control processes that might operate in drug dependence. We briefly review the role of stimulus control in drug self-administration and describe some ways that stimulus control may be used to treat drug dependence.

Stimulus Control of Drug Self-Administration

Environmental stimuli previously correlated with drug taking engender current drug seeking. Those stimuli can be *interoceptive*, such as the feelings caused by drugs when ingested, or *exteroceptive*, such as events or objects correlated with drug delivery. Both can set the occasion for drug self-administration (Bickel et al., 1987).

Interoceptive Stimuli

Drugs, once taken, can reinforce behavior and set the occasion for further behavior. For example, a drug discrimination can be trained by exclusively reinforcing a response class in the presence of the interoceptive effects of a drug and reinforcing a different response class following injections of saline or some other drug. That attaches the new behavior to the presence of the interoceptive drug cue (Bickel, Bigelow, Preston, & Liebson, 1989; Bickel, Oliveto, Kamein, Higgins, & Hughes, 1993; Chait, Uhlenhuth, & Johanson, 1986; see Kamein, Bickel, Hughes, Higgins, & Smith, 1993, for a review).

A germane problem is the ability of interoceptive drug stimuli to reinstate previously extinguished drug-seeking behavior. For example, de Wit and Stewart (1981) trained rats to respond for intravenous cocaine. Extinction conditions were introduced so that responding no longer produced cocaine. When responding had decreased to low levels, non-response-contingent cocaine injections restored responding even when the extinction conditions remained in effect. A range of drugs pharmacologically similar to the drug previously self-administered can engender reinstatement (Carrol & Comer, 1996; for other reviews, see de Wit, 1996; Young & Herling, 1986).

This reinstatement effect has also been demonstrated in studies of alcohol self-administration in humans. Bigelow, Griffiths, and Liebson (1977) suppressed the alcohol consumption of alcoholics living in a research ward by time-out or response-cost procedures. But the administration of a single response-independent dose of alcohol reinstated their consumption. Similar results have been obtained by Funderbunk and Allen (1977).

Reinstatement may be related to relapse. Once relapse has occurred, the interoceptive stimulus properties of the drug may lead to continued drug taking. Reinstatement is not unique to drug stimuli; it has been observed with a variety of reinforcers. Research needs to address whether the reinstatement effect persists throughout the duration of action of the initiating dose, or whether it is restricted to onset or offset of drug action; additionally, researchers need to understand the complicating factors of drug tolerance and physical dependence.

Exteroceptive Stimuli

Various exteroceptive stimuli can evoke drug self-administration. Some of these effects are seen most clearly in human behavior (e.g., modeling, rule-governed behavior, and stimulus equivalence); they are largely conditioned drug effects (Wikler, 1965) resulting from the pairing of pharmacological drug or withdrawal effects and exteroceptive stimuli. As a result of this pairing, the environmental stimuli come to elicit withdrawal or agonistic responses associated with drug craving. For example, if a light is paired with injections of nalorphine (an opioid antagonist) in morphine-dependent monkeys, the presentation of this light will elicit certain signs of the morphine-abstinence syndrome and thus evoke large increases in the rates of morphine self-administration (Goldberg & Schuster, 1967; Goldberg & Schuster, 1970; Goldberg, Woods, & Schuster, 1969). This line of study has been examined extensively and productively with animals and humans (O'Brien, Ehrman, & Ternes, 1986).

When stimuli paired with drug consumption function simultaneously as conditioned reinforcers and discriminative stimuli, they control extensive chains of drug-seeking behavior. There have been many demonstrations of the reinforcing efficacy of stimuli paired with drug consumption (Goldberg, Kelleher, & Goldberg, 1981; Goldberg, Spealman, & Kelleher, 1979; Kelleher & Goldberg, 1977). One example of the role of conditioned stimuli setting the occasion for human self-administration of drugs can be found in the role of social context in using alcohol and marijuana (e.g., Doty & de Wit, 1995; Kelly, Foltin, Emurian, & Fishman, 1994; Kelly, Foltin, Mayr, & Fishman, 1994).

Modeling can affect drug self-administration. Garlington and Dericco (1977) studied three college students who were moderate drinkers in a naturalistic bar environment with confederates who, under one condition, consumed alcohol at a high rate, and under another condition, consumed alcohol at a low rate. The participants matched the consumption of their confederates. The stimulus control of a model on alcohol consumption has been demonstrated with alcoholics (Caudill & Lipscomb, 1980) and heavy drinkers (Caudill & Marlatt, 1975) under laboratory conditions, and with free-ranging normal drinkers in a public tavern (Reid, 1978). Similar results were obtained in a study with cigarette smokers (Lichtenstein, 1977). One interesting aspect of this study was that the topography of smoking (smoking behavior) was not influenced by the model, only the initiation of a cigarette. These studies indicate that a model can be a controlling stimulus for human self-administration of drugs.

Rule-governed behavior (Skinner, 1969) has been shown to be insensitive to reinforcement. However, rule-governed behavior is itself an operant class that can be reinforced, extinguished, or brought under stimulus control (Galizio, 1979). Rules may alter the topography of drug self-administration, the reinforcing efficacy of a drug, or even behavioral responses typically emitted in complex chains of drug-seeking behavior.

Frederikson and Simon (1978) examined how instructions could modify the topography of cigarette smoking. Participants were instructed to decrease the number of puffs and puff duration. The effects of these instructions were first documented in a laboratory setting; then a contract was drawn to generalize this change to other settings. The topography did change in these other settings, and these changes were maintained at a 6-month follow-up session. The clinical significance of these findings was validated by documenting a decrease in expired carbon dioxide levels, reliably indicating decreased exposure to cigarette smoke.

Instruction can also alter the reinforcing efficacy of drugs. Hughes, Pickens, Spring, and Keenan (1985) found that cigarette smokers who were required to stop smoking with the aid of nicotine gum were strongly influenced by verbal instructions about what to expect from the two gums that were offered, one of which contained nicotine, and the other a placebo. When told the two gums might be any combination—both nicotine, both placebo, or one of each—participants preferred the nicotine gum. When told both gums contained nicotine but one had fewer side effects, participants showed no preference for nicotine. When told one gum had nicotine and the other a placebo with worse side effects than nicotine, participants showed no preference for nicotine. Clearly, instructions can control whether a drug acts as a reinforcer. Bickel, Higgins, and Stitzer (1986) also suggested that providing instructions to patients on methadone-maintenance therapy about the size of an increase in dose would enhance its reinforcing efficacy, compared to the same increase without confirming instruction.

A conditional discrimination relevant to drug self-administration is seen in a study by Stretch, Gerber, and Wood (1971). They reinstated amphetamine self-administration and paired a noise with its availability. Self-administration was then extinguished by the withdrawal of amphetamine. Then, a presession injection of amphetamine reinstated responding but only when the noise was present. The success of reinstatement now was conditional on the presence of the noise. Clearly, many stimuli may be involved in these complex interactions. In the treatment of substance abuse, complexity may be the rule, and it may indicate why treatment is so difficult.

The concept of stimulus equivalence addresses the transfer of stimulus control to other stimuli that do not share topographical features (Sidman & Tailby, 1982). For example, it provides a powerful account of naming, that is, the equivalence between the written word for, the spoken word for, the picture of, and the actual presence of something (Sidman, 1990). The importance of this phenomenon is that only a few of the relations need to be trained for the others to emerge. Therefore, stimulus equivalence may indicate how stimuli never directly paired with drug taking nonetheless set the occasion for it.

Bickel and DeGrandpre examined equivalence with a sample of cigarette smokers. Three plungers were used as tasks. Plunger pulling resulted in two puffs on a cigarette, $1.00, or $0.05, depending on which of the three plungers was used. Visual stimuli (i.e., A1, A2, A3) were then correlated with each of the plungers. Once stimulus control by these stimuli was established, these stimuli were used in a matching-to-sample format that related them to three other stimuli (i.e., B1, B2, B3). These B stimuli were then used in a matching-to-sample task, and a relation was trained that related them to three other stimuli (i.e., C1, C2, C3). The B and C stimuli were then presented together with the plungers to see what response they would occasion. Four of the five participants showed 100 percent "correct" responding. That is, the B and C stimuli, never paired directly with drug taking but instead paired only with stimuli that had been paired with drug taking, now evoked drug self-administration. A fifth participant showed 100 percent "correct" responding for the C stimulus and 67 percent for the B stimulus. Similar results occurred for the money responding.

Stimuli proximal to drug taking, therefore, can acquire stimulus control of it. The stimulus-equivalence research begins to suggest how stimulus control of drug taking can be broadened and extended to stimuli distal to drug taking, perhaps leading to the syndrome of drug dependence (DeGrandpre & Bickel, 1993). Along with the prior finding that the interoceptive effects of drugs can participate in stimulus-equivalence relations with exteroceptive stimuli, this finding suggests that this process has great promise for issues of drug dependence (DeGrandpre, Bickel, & Higgins, 1992). However, this conclusion must be tentative; to our knowledge, this is the only study examining stimulus equivalence and drug taking.

Stimulus Control and the Reduction of Drug Self-Administration

If discriminative stimuli can influence drug self-administration, there is reason to believe that stimulus control can be employed for therapeutic purposes. Three distinct tactics can be seen: (a) changing the function of stimuli already controlling drug self-administration, (b) removing stimuli now in control, and (c) providing stimuli that will compete with the stimuli now in control (Schroeder, Bickel, & Richmond, 1986).

Punishment procedures typically decrease drug self-administration. If self-administration is punished in the presence of stimuli that previously set the occasion for drug taking, those stimuli should come to evoke behavior other than self-administration. Similar interpretations could be made for reinforcement or extinction.

The long-term success of this tactic is doubtful. For example, Wilson, Leaf, and Nathan (1975) examined the effects of shock punishment on alcohol self-administration by chronic alcoholics living in a research ward. The shock effectively suppressed alcohol consumption, but drinking later returned to baseline levels. Similar studies suggest there is a difference between reducing a stimulus-response relation in frequency and changing the relation. Ray (1969) showed that training a new response to a stimulus with a previously established discriminative function decreases the frequency of the previously controlled response without necessarily altering any properties of the original stimulus-control relationship. Under new circumstances, therefore, the original behavior previously controlled by the stimulus may emerge. Stoddard and Sidman (1971) showed, however, that stimulus control *can* be abolished. Generally, the necessary conditions are not yet well understood. Until they are, a diminished frequency of behavior will be impossible to evaluate; it may or may not prove durable. Indeed, numerous procedures reduce drug taking, and most of them produce only temporary changes. Apparently, the procedures effective in decreasing drug consumption typically do not abolish previous stimulus control.

If the stimuli controlling drug self-administration are specific or few, removing them from the substance abuser's environment might work (e.g., stop the substance abuser from associating with a particular group of drug-using individuals). However, if the controlling stimuli are numerous and widely distributed, removal might not be practical. Unfortunately, the latter case is more typical for humans.

The effects of removing the organism from the drug-controlling environment were examined by Thompson and Ostlund (1965). They established morphine self-administration in rats. After responding was stable, the rats were withdrawn from morphine. Thirty days later, they were reexposed to morphine in either the same or a different environment. Rats reexposed in the same environment were readdicted faster than rats reexposed in a novel environment. This finding is consistent with clinical outcomes. Cushman (1974) reported that addicts who were detoxified and then returned to the environment in which the addiction occurred showed a readdiction rate of 90 percent, whereas other studies found that only a small percentage of Vietnam veterans who began their addiction in Vietnam continued excessive drug use on returning to the United States (O'Brien, Nace, Mintz, Meyer, & Ream, 1980; Robins, Davis, & Goodwin, 1974). These studies indicate that drug-associated environments may be an important determinant of drug relapse.

Another tactic is to evoke behavior incompatible with drug seeking. For humans, rules might prove useful, if in fact rule-governed behavior is temporarily insensitive to reinforcement contingencies. But Hayes and his colleagues (Hayes, Brownstein, Haas, & Greenway, 1986; Hayes, Brownstein, Zettle, Rosenfarb, & Korn, 1986; Zettle & Hayes, 1982) argue that rule-induced insensitivity to one set of contingencies results from additional contingencies brought into play by instructional control: Insensitivity "is not a reduction in contingency control but rather an effect of competing contingencies, such as the social consequences for rule following" (Hayes, Brownstein, Zettle, et al., 1986, p. 238). Rule-governed behavior can be considered the introduction of competing stimuli and associated contingencies.

Still, verbal rules have altered drug-maintained behavior: Rules can alter the topography of drug self-administration and modify the reinforcing efficacy of drugs of abuse. Rules are most likely an important part of most traditional therapies for substance abuse (Skinner, 1953). What must be determined are the functional properties of rules, the conditions under which they will be followed, as well as whether there are different functional categories of rules (e.g., Zettle & Hayes, 1982).

Conclusion

We have reviewed the ways in which stimulus-control processes are intimately involved in drug taking and thus ought to play a significant role in the treatment of substance abuse. Unfortunately, stimulus control is a behavioral process that has not received a great deal of scientific attention in relation to either the basic processes involved or the application of that knowledge to the socially important problems of substance abuse. More research on each of these levels is needed. In particular, a basic understanding of rule-governed behavior, modeling, and stimulus equivalence is needed for better application of these processes to therapeutic ends. If we extend our analyses to address these issues and to explore how they can be employed in treatment, greater progress may be made toward reducing the societal problem of drug abuse.

Acknowledgments

Preparation of this manuscript was supported by National Institute on Drug Abuse Grants RO1 DA06526, RO1 DA06969, and RO1 DA06205.

References

Bickel, W. K., Bigelow, G. E., Preston, K. L., & Liebson, I. A. (1989). Opioid drug discrimination in humans: Stability, specificity, and relation to self reported drug effect. *Journal of Pharmacology and Experimental Therapeutics, 251,* 1053–1062.

Bickel, W. K., Higgins, S. T., & Stitzer, M. L. (1986). Choice of blind methadone dose increases by methadone maintenance patients. *Drug Alcohol Dependence, 18,* 165–171.

Bickel, W. K., Mathis, D., Emmett-Oglesby, M., Harris, C., Lal, H., Gauvin, D. V., Young, A. M., Wiess, S., Schindler, C., & Williams, B. A. (1987). Stimulus control: Continuity or discontinuity? Views from the study of interoceptive and exteroceptive stimuli. *Psychological Record, 37,* 153–198.

Bickel, W. K., Oliveto, A. H., Kamein, J. B., Higgins, S. T., & Hughes, J. R. (1993). A novel response procedure enhances the sensitivity and selectivity of a triazolam discrimination in humans. *Journal of Pharmacology and Experimental Therapeutics, 264,* 360–367.

Bigelow, G. E., Griffiths, R. R., & Liebson, I. A. (1977). Pharmacological influences upon ethanol self-administration. In M. M. Gross (Ed.), *Alcohol intoxication and withdrawal* (Vol. 111B, pp. 523–538). New York: Plenum Press.

Carroll, M. E., & Comer, S. D. (1996). Animal models of relapse. *Experimental and Clinical Psychopharmacology, 4,* 11–18.

Caudill, B. D., & Lipscomb, T. R. (1980). Modeling influences on alcoholics' rates of alcohol consumption. *Journal of Applied Behavioral Analysis, 13,* 355–365.

Caudill, B. D., & Marlatt, G. A. (1975). Modeling influences in social drinking: An experimental analogue. *Journal of Consulting and Clinical Psychology, 43,* 405–415.

Chait, L. D., Uhlenhuth, E. H., and Johanson, C. E. (1986). The discriminative stimulus and subjective effects of d-amphetamine, phenmetrazine and fenfluramine in humans. *Psychopharmacology* (Berlin), *89,* 301–306.

Cushman, P. (1974). Detoxification of rehabilitated methadone patients: Frequency and predictors of long term success. *American Journal of Alcohol Abuse, 1,* 393–408.

DeGrandpre, R. J., & Bickel, W. K. (1993). Stimulus control and drug dependence. *Psychological Record, 43,* 651–666.

DeGrandpre, R. J., Bickel, W. K., & Higgins, S. T. (1992). Emergent equivalence relations between interoceptive (drug) stimuli and exteroceptive (visual) stimuli. *Journal of the Experimental Analysis of Behavior, 58,* 9–18.

de Wit, H. (1996). Priming effects with drugs and other reinforcers. *Experimental and Clinical Psychopharmacology, 4,* 5–10.

de Wit, H., & Stewart, J. (1981). Reinstatement of cocaine-reinforced responding in the rat. *Psychopharmacology* (Berlin), *75,* 134–143.

Doty, P., & de Wit, H. (1995). Effect of setting on the reinforcing and subjective effects of ethanol in social drinkers. *Psychopharmacology, 118,* 19–27.

Frederikson, L. W., & Simon, S. J. (1978). Modifying how people smoke: Instructional control and generalization. *Journal of Applied Behavioral Analysis, 11,* 431–432.

Funderbunk, F. R., & Allen, R. P. (1977). Alcoholics' disposition to drink. *Journal of Studies on Alcohol, 38,* 410–425.

Galizio, M. (1979). Contingency-shaped and rule-governed behavior: Instructional control of human loss avoidance. *Journal of the Experimental Analysis of Behavior, 31,* 53–70.

Garlington, W. K., & Dericco, D. A. (1977). The effect of modeling on drinking rate. *Journal of Applied Behavioral Analysis, 10,* 207–211.

Goldberg, S. R., Kelleher, R. T., & Goldberg, D. M. (1981). Fixed-ration responding under second-order schedules of food presentation or cocaine injection. *Journal of Pharmacology and Experimental Therapeutics, 218,* 271–281.

Goldberg, S. R., & Schuster, C. R. (1967). Conditioned suppression by a stimulus associated with nalorphine in morphine-dependent monkeys. *Journal of Experimental Analysis of Behavior, 10,* 232–241.

Goldberg, S. R., & Schuster, C. R. (1970). Conditioned nalorphine-induced abstinence changes: Persistence in post morphine dependent monkeys. *Journal of Experimental Analysis of Behavior, 14,* 33–46.

Goldberg, S. R., Spealman, R. D., & Kelleher, R. T. (1979). Enhancement of drug-seeking by environmental stimuli associated with cocaine or morphine injections. *Neuropharmacology, 18,* 1015–1017.

Goldberg, S. R., Woods, J. H., & Schuster, C. R. (1969). Morphine: Conditioned increases in self-administration in rhesus monkeys. *Science, 166,* 1306–1307.

Hayes, S. C., Brownstein, A. J., Haas, J. R., & Greenway, D. E. (1986). Instructions, multiple schedules, and extinction: Distinguishing rule-governed from schedule-controlled behavior. *Journal of Experimental Analysis of Behavior, 46,* 137–147.

Hayes, S. C., Brownstein, A. J., Zettle, R. D., Rosenfarb, I., & Korn, Z. (1986). Rule-governed behavior and sensitivity to changing consequences of responding. *Journal of Experimental Analysis of Behavior, 45,* 237–256.

Hughes, J. R., Pickens, R. W., Spring, W., & Keenan, R. M. (1985). Instructions control whether nicotine will serve as a reinforcer. *Journal of Pharmacology and Experimental Therapeutics, 235,* 106–112.

Hurse, S. R. (1977). The conditioned reinforcement of repeated acquisition. *Journal of Experimental Analysis of Behavior, 27,* 315–327.

Kamein, J. B., Bickel, W. K., Hughes, J. R., Higgins, S. T., & Smith, B. (1993). Drug discrimination by humans compared with nonhumans: Current status and future directions. *Psychopharmacology, 111,* 259–270.

Katz, J. L., & Valentino, R. J. (1986). Pharmacological and behavioral factors in opioid dependence in animals. In S. R. Goldberg & I. P. Stolerman (Eds.), *Behavioral analysis of drug dependence* (pp. 287–327). New York: Academic Press.

Kelleher, R. T., & Goldberg, S. R. (1977). Fixed-interval responding under second-order schedules of food presentation or cocaine injection. *Journal of Experimental Analysis of Behavior, 28,* 221–231.

Kelly, T. H., Foltin, R. W., Emurian, C. S., & Fishman, M. W. (1994). Effects of Delta^9–THC on marijuana smoking, dose choice, and verbal report of drug liking. *Journal of the Experimental Analysis of Behavior, 61,* 203–211.

Kelly, T. H., Foltin, R. W., Mayr, M. T., & Fishman, M. W. (1994). Effects of Delta^9–tetrahydrocannainol and social context on marijuana self-administration by humans. *Pharmacology, Biochemistry & Behavior, 49,* 763–768.

Levine, D. G. (1974). Needle freaks: Compulsive self-injections by drug-users. *American Journal of Psychiatry, 131,* 297–300.

Lichtenstein, E. (1977). Social learning, smoking, and substance abuse. In N. A. Krasnegor (Ed.), *Behavioral analysis and treatment of substance abuse.* (National Institute on Drug Abuse Research Monograph No. 25, pp. 193–200. DHEW Publication No. ADM 79-839). Washington, DC: U.S. Government Printing Office.

Ludwig, A. M., Wikler, A., & Stark, L. H. (1974). The first drink: Psychobiological aspects of craving. *Archives of General Psychiatry, 30,* 539–547.

Meyer, R. E., & Mirin, S. M. (1979). *The heroin stimulus: Implications for a theory of addiction.* New York: Plenum Press.

O'Brien, C. P., Ehrman, R. N., & Ternes, J. W. (1986). Classical conditioning in human opioid dependence. In S. R. Goldberg & I. P. Stolerman (Eds.), *Behavioral analysis of drug dependence* (pp. 329–356). New York: Academic Press.

O'Brien, C. P., Nace, E., Mintz, J., Meyer, A., & Ream, N. (1980). Follow-up of the Vietnam veteran: Part 1. Relapse to drug use after Vietnam service. *Drug and Alcohol Dependence, 5,* 333–340.

Preston, K. L., Bigelow, G. E., Bickel, W. K., & Liebson, I. A. (in press). Three-choice drug discrimination in opioid-dependent humans: Effects of naloxone after acute morphine exposure. *Journal of Pharmacology and Experimental Therapeutics.*

Ray, B. A. (1969). Selective attention: The effects of combining stimuli which control incompatible behavior. *Journal of Experimental Analysis of Behavior, 12,* 539–550.

Reid, J. B. (1978). The study of drinking in natural settings. In G. A. Marlatt & P. E. Nathan (Eds.), *Behavioral approaches to alcoholism.* New Brunswick, NJ: Rutgers University Center for Alcohol Studies.

Robins, L. N., Davis, D. H., & Goodwin, D. W. (1974). Drug use by U.S. Army enlisted men in Vietnam: A followup upon their return home. *American Journal of Epidemiology, 99,* 235–249.

Schroeder, S. R., Bickel, W. K., & Richmond, G. (1986). Primary and secondary prevention of self-injurious behavior. In K. D. Gadows (Ed.), *Advances in learning and behavioral disabilities* (Vol. 5, pp. 63–85). Greenwich, CT: JAI Press.

Sidman, M. (1990). Equivalence relations: Where do they come from? In D. E. Blackman & H. Lejeune (Eds.), *Behavior analysis in theory and practise.* Hove, England: Erlbaum.

Sidman, M., & Tailby, W. (1982). Conditional discrimination vs. matching to sample: An expansion of testing paradigm. *Journal of the Experimental Analysis of Behavior, 7,* 5–22.

Skinner, B. F. (1953). *Science and human behavior.* New York: Free Press.

Skinner, B. F. (1969). *Contingencies of reinforcement: A theoretical analysis.* Englewood Cliffs, NJ: Prentice-Hall.

Stoddard, L. T., & Sidman, M. (1971). The removal and the restoration of stimulus control. *Journal of Experimental Analysis of Behavior, 16,* 143–154.

Stretch, R., Gerber, G. J., & Wood, S. M. (1971). Factors affecting behavior maintained by response-contingent intravenous infusions of amphetamine by squirrel monkeys. *Canadian Journal of Physiology and Pharmacology, 49,* 581–589.

Thompson, T., & Ostlund, W., Jr. (1965). Susceptibility to readdiction as a function of the addiction and withdrawal environments. *Journal of Comparative Physiology and Psychology, 3,* 388–392.

Wikler, A. (1965). Conditioning factors in opiate addiction and relapse. In D. I. Wiher & G. G. Kassenbaum (Ed.), *Narcotics* (pp. 85–100). New York: McGraw-Hill.

Wilson, G. T., Leaf, R. C., & Nathan, P. E. (1975). The aversive control of excessive alcohol consumption by chronic alcoholics in the laboratory setting. *Journal of Applied Behavioral Analysis, 8,* 13–26.

Young, A. M., & Herling, S. (1986). Drugs as reinforcers: Studies in laboratory animals. In S. R. Goldberg & I. P. Stolerman (Eds.), *Behavioral analysis of drug dependence* (pp. 9–68). New York: Academic Press.

Zettle, R. D., & Hayes, S. C. (1982). Rule-governed behavior: A potential theoretical framework for cognitive behavior therapy. In P. C. Kendall (Ed.), *Advances in cognitive-behavioral research* (Vol. 1, pp. 73–118). New York: Academic Press.

16

Caffeine as a Model Drug of Abuse for the Development of Sensitive Behavioral Measures

Kenneth Silverman

The widespread abuse of cocaine is a serious public health problem; it has stimulated laboratory searches for new behavioral and pharmacological treatments (Meyer, 1992). Those experiments evaluate the effectiveness of potential treatments in diminishing cocaine's discriminative-stimulus and reinforcing effects.

A recent evaluation of desipramine provides a useful example. Desipramine is an antidepressant drug that may be a pharmacological adjunct for the treatment of cocaine abuse. One experiment evaluated the effect of desipramine on cocaine self-administration by 10 adult male volunteers with histories of cocaine use (Fischman, Foltin, Nestadt, & Pearlson, 1990). In daily 3-hour laboratory sessions, participants were repeatedly allowed to choose between intravenous injections of either cocaine or saline. The choices were studied under two conditions: In one condition, the participants received daily doses of desipramine; in the other condition, they did not receive desipramine. The question was whether daily dosing with desipramine would decrease the participants' self-administration of cocaine.

This experiment allowed some of the toxic effects that are inevitably produced by cocaine; those effects created serious impediments to the research. First, the doses of cocaine studied (8, 16, and 32 mg per injection) produced increases in heart rate and blood pressure. Those elevations in heart rate and blood pressure required the experimenters to withhold some of the scheduled cocaine doses to protect the participants' health. In addition, desipramine alone increased both heart rate and blood pressure, and in combination with cocaine produced increases well above the levels produced by cocaine alone. As a result, a larger number of scheduled cocaine injections were withheld when participants were receiving daily doses of desipramine than when they were not, which made for incomplete data.

Second, those effects and their associated medical risks (Bunn & Giannini, 1992) meant that this experiment, and other similar studies, had to be conducted under extremely close medical supervision by specially trained nurses and a physician. The cost was high; few research centers are capable of conducting such research.

Another point: Identifying effective treatments for cocaine abuse, particularly pharmacological treatments, is difficult and will probably require a large number of experiments. The results of the desipramine experiment were disappointing; the procedure did not reduce cocaine self-administration. The majority of well-controlled studies evaluating pharmacotherapies for cocaine abuse (Hollister, Krajewski, Rustin, & Gillespie, 1992; Meyer, 1992) have been similarly disappointing. Despite the growing number of laboratory evaluations and clinical trials examining other measures and other treatment drugs, no effective pharmacotherapy for cocaine abuse has been identified. If these recent investigations are any indication, many more pharmacological agents will be tested in the human laboratory before an effective treatment agent is identified. If many compounds are to be tested, there will be a need for efficient and economical methods for evaluating potential pharmacotherapies in the laboratory. The current methods will require a large number of very expensive investigations.

Safer Methods of Investigation

The laboratory search for treatments for cocaine abuse might advance faster if a safer method of studying cocaine in humans could be developed—one that would not pose serious risk to participants and require extensive medical support. An obvious solution might be to reduce the doses of cocaine employed; however, doses that reliably produce the behavioral effects of interest also reliably produce cardiovascular effects that can place participants at medical risk. In the desipramine evaluation described previously, even one injection of the lowest cocaine dose administered, 8 mg, seriously increased both heart rate and blood pressure and had only inconsistent behavioral effects according to self-reports of mood. The cardiovascular effects of a single injection of 8 mg of cocaine appeared to be equally or more robust than the behavioral effects produced by the same cocaine dose, suggesting that 8 mg of cocaine may be a threshold dose for producing behavioral effects. (Higher cocaine doses reliably altered self-reports of mood.) Other studies have observed cardiovascular effects at all doses that produce behavioral effects (Fischman et al., 1976; Higgins et al., in press; Preston, Sullivan, Strain, & Bigelow, 1992). Another approach is needed.

The Development of Sensitive Behavioral Procedures

Perhaps the behavioral measures used to study cocaine effects in humans are not sensitive enough to detect subtle behavioral effects that might be produced by very low doses of cocaine. If so, cocaine research could be advanced by developing more sensitive behavioral measures; that would allow the investigation of lower, safer doses. Sensitive behavioral measures that may be useful in studying drugs of abuse *are* currently under development in research into the discriminative-stimulus, reinforcing, and withdrawal effects of caffeine. Caffeine is the most widely used behaviorally active drug in the world (Gilbert, 1984). At dietary doses, caffeine poses little if any medical risk to healthy people (Rall, 1990). Significantly, caffeine produces many of the effects that define drugs of abuse (Holtzman, 1990): It can serve as a discriminative stimulus (Griffiths et al., 1990; Silverman & Griffiths, 1992). Under some circumstances, it can be a positive reinforcer (Griffiths, Bigelow, & Liebson, 1989; Griffiths & Woodson, 1988b; Hughes et al., 1991). Repeated exposure to caffeine produces tolerance to its cardiovascular (Robertson, Wade, Workman, & Woosley, 1981) and behavioral (Evans & Griffiths, 1992) effects. Finally, chronic caffeine administration can produce physical dependence, as evidenced by a withdrawal syndrome that emerges when daily caffeine consumption is abruptly terminated (Griffiths & Woodson, 1988a; Silverman, Evans, Strain, & Griffiths, 1992).

Although caffeine can have all of these effects, its effects are often subtle and difficult to demonstrate experimentally. As a result, more sensitive procedures have been developed to capture caffeine's effects. Nowhere is the sensitivity of this emerging methodology better illustrated than in the search for the lowest caffeine doses that affect human behavior.

Although caffeine is consumed regularly in coffee, tea, soft drinks, and chocolate, there has been little evidence that the amount of caffeine found in individual portions of these sources can affect human behavior. A typical 148-mL (6-oz.) cup of roasted and ground brewed coffee, for example, contains about 100 mg caffeine; the same amount of tea contains 48 mg caffeine; a 355-mL (12-oz.) can of regular cola soft drink contains 36 mg; and a 30-g (1-oz.) chocolate bar contains 20 mg caffeine (Barone & Roberts, 1984). Most investigations have failed to find behavioral effects of caffeine at doses below 200–300 mg (Dews, 1984; Gilbert, 1976; James, 1991), doses far exceeding the amounts found in individual portions of common caffeine sources. The difficulty of detecting behavioral effects of caffeine has led observers to conclude that "a coherent account of the salient selective effects of caffeine on behavior cannot be given (as is possible with other compounds like amphetamine)" (Dews, 1984, p. 99), that "the behavioral effects of caffeine at levels causing selective changes are modest and even subtle" (Dews, 1984, p. 100), and that caffeine "bestows little if any benefit on psychomotor and cognitive performance" (James, 1991, p. 271).

Only rarely have doses below 100 mg altered self-reports of mood or performance. An impressive pair of studies found that caffeine enhanced auditory vigilance and reaction time at doses as low as 32 mg (Lieberman, Wurtman, Emde, & Coviella, 1987) and affected self-reports of mood at doses as low as 64 mg (Lieberman, Wurtman, Emde, Roberts, & Coviella, 1987). In the first of this pair of studies, four doses of caffeine and a placebo were administered in capsules, in counterbalanced order and under double-blind conditions, to each of 20 participants. After each administration, participants completed a battery of performance tasks and completed questionnaires about how they felt. Caffeine affected performance on two of the eight tasks administered, an auditory-vigilance task and a four-choice visual-reaction task. In the auditory-vigilance task, a tone was presented every 2 seconds for 1 hour, and participants were required to press a key when a "short" duration tone was presented. Only 40 tones were short. On each of 500 trials of the reaction-time task, a visual stimulus was presented in one of four locations on a screen, and participants had to press one of four keys to indicate the location of the stimulus on each trial. All doses of caffeine, even 32 mg, significantly affected both the average number of short tones the participants correctly detected on the auditory-vigilance task and the average latency on the reaction-time task. In other studies, caffeine had similar effects on the performance of a similar auditory-vigilance task at doses as low as 64 mg (Lieberman, Wurtman, Emde, & Coviella, 1987) and 75 mg (Clubley, Bye, Henson, Peck, & Riddington, 1979). In some of these experiments, low doses of caffeine affected self-reports of mood (e.g., "alert"). As little caffeine as 64 mg (Lieberman, Wurtman, Emde, & Coviella, 1987) and 75 mg (Clubley et al., 1979) affected self-reports of mood.

Although these effects are impressive and demonstrate the behavioral activity of caffeine at relatively low dietary doses, some of the effects have eluded efforts at replication, even by the same investigators in the same laboratory. For example, Clubley et al. (1979) found that 75, 150, and 300 mg of caffeine affected auditory vigilance. However, in a second experiment, 100 mg failed to alter performance on the auditory-vigilance task. Similarly, Lieberman, Wurtman, Emde, Roberts, and Coviella (1987) found that 64 mg altered self-reports of mood, whereas under very similar circumstances, 32, 64, 128, and 256 mg caffeine did not (Lieberman, Wurtman, Emde, & Coviella, 1987).

The known limits of human behavioral sensitivity to caffeine have recently been extended, using operant stimulus-discrimination and fading procedures. In general, these procedures involve establishing a discrimination between the presence and absence of a particular stimulus and then progressively decreasing the strength of that stimulus until it fails to control responding. Previously, stimulus-fading procedures have been effective in estimating the limits of organisms' sensitivities to various auditory and visual stimuli (Blough & Blough, 1977) and, on rare occasions, to drugs (Colpaert, Niemegeers, & Janssen, 1980; Overton, 1979; Zenick & Goldsmith, 1981). Variations of these procedures have also been employed to teach young children and developmentally delayed persons difficult discriminations (Schilmoeller & Etzel, 1977; Sidman & Stoddard, 1966).

Stimulus-fading procedures have been employed in two studies to assess the limits of human behavioral sensitivity to caffeine (Griffiths et al., 1990; Silverman & Griffiths, 1992). In one of those studies (Griffiths et al., 1990), 7 caffeine-abstinent participants were taught a caffeine (178 mg or 100 mg) versus placebo discrimination and then exposed to progressively lower caffeine doses, until each participant failed to discriminate. All acquired the initial discrimination. Three participants discriminated 56 mg of caffeine, 3 discriminated 18 mg, and 1 subject maintained the discrimination at 10 mg. This drug-discrimination procedure revealed behavioral effects of dietary doses of caffeine previously thought to be behaviorally and physiologically inactive, thereby extending the known limits of human sensitivity to caffeine.

It may have been significant that behavior pharmacologists served as both the investigators and the participants in that study. Informed of the drugs under study and of their likely effects and knowledgeable about the pharmacokinetic and pharmacodynamic effects of caffeine, these participants brought unique sophistication to the experiment, which may have enhanced their ability to acquire and maintain the low-dose caffeine discriminations. The extent to which those extraordinary effects were due to the discrimination procedure or to the nature of the participants is still unclear.

A second study employed similar discrimination procedures to determine whether stimulus-fading procedures could produce comparable low-dose effects in normal, minimally instructed volunteers, uninformed of the specific drugs under study or of their likely effects (Silverman & Griffiths, 1992). In that study, caffeine-abstinent adult volunteers participated in one discrimination-training session each weekday. During each session, each participant ingested a capsule containing 178 mg of caffeine or placebo. The participants were told that throughout the study, they would receive one of two compounds found in coffee, tea, chocolate, and soft drinks, but they were not told the names of the compounds. Instead, the two compounds were identified by letter codes (e.g., Drug O and Drug G) that were unique for each participant. The compounds were administered under double-blind conditions and in usually identical capsules. The order of caffeine and placebo was randomized across days. Fifteen, 30, and 45 minutes after each capsule ingestion, participants guessed the capsule's letter code. They were paid $10 if their 45-minute guess was correct.

After the original discrimination was established (75% correct over 20 sessions), 9 of the participants who acquired the 178-mg caffeine versus placebo discrimination had their caffeine dose progressively decreased until their discrimination accuracy fell below 75 percent correct in 20 sessions. Each participant was exposed to each dose for 20 sessions. If the discrimination accuracy for the final (45-minute) guess was at or above 75 percent correct, the caffeine dose was decreased to the next lower dose. If the discrimination accuracy for a dose condition was below 75 percent correct, the caffeine dose was increased to 178 mg to recover the initial discrimination.

Figure 16.1 shows the discrimination accuracy during the last 20 sessions for each of the dose conditions studied in each participant. One person discriminated as low as 18 mg caffeine (S27); another discriminated as low as 32 mg (S19); two discriminated 56 mg (S1 and S8); four discriminated 100 mg (S9, S16, S18, and S24); and one discriminated only 178 mg (S15).

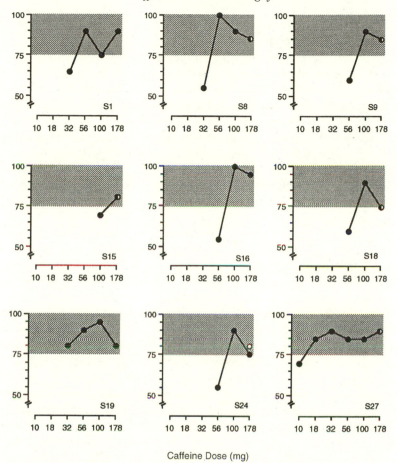

Caffeine Dose (mg)

FIGURE 16.1   Caffeine Versus Placebo Discrimination Accuracy as a Function of Dose in 9 Participants in the Decreasing Dose Phase. Data are based on the final guesses of the last 20 sessions of each condition. Points overlapping the shaded areas indicate significant discrimination performance (binomial probability distribution, $p < .05$). Doses were studied in decreasing order with 178 mg as the first (filled point) and last (open point) dose condition; overlapping data points in the 178-mg dose condition are half-filled points. Three participants were terminated from the study prematurely (S19 in the 18-mg condition and S1 and S16 in the final, 178-mg condition).

Using stimulus-discrimination and fading procedures, these studies demonstrated the behavioral activity of caffeine doses lower than those previously shown to affect human behavior. Dietary doses of caffeine equal to or less than the amounts found in individual portions of coffee, tea, and soft drinks produced significant discrimination in one or more participants; a subgroup of participants discriminated as little as 18 or 10 mg of caffeine, which is less than the amount of caffeine found in some chocolate bars.

A study conducted by Evans and Griffiths (1991) suggested that discrimination training alone is not sufficient to achieve the low-dose caffeine effects described above. They taught five adult volunteers a 200- or 300-mg caffeine versus placebo discrimination and then presented in random order test doses of caffeine between 50 and 600 mg. These participants only infrequently identified 50 mg as caffeine and thereby failed to show clear behavioral activity of caffeine below 100 mg.

Stimulus-fading procedures have recently been used to explore the limits of human sensitivity to theobromine (Mumford et al., 1992), a methylxanthine structurally similar to caffeine and found in chocolate. A typical 1.45-oz. milk chocolate bar contains 90 mg theobromine; a comparable sized dark chocolate bar contains 185 mg. Dietary doses of theobromine have long been considered behaviorally inactive in humans (Rall, 1990; Stavric, 1988). However, stimulus-fading procedures similar to the ones previously described produced discriminative control by theobromine at doses as low as 100 mg, a dose within the range of doses provided by individual servings of normal dietary sources.

Clearly, the discrimination and stimulus-fading procedures are usually sensitive in revealing subtle behavioral effects of drugs, suggesting that they may be used to reveal the behavioral activity of cocaine doses previously considered inactive. The procedures may well make available for investigation in humans a new and safer range of cocaine doses. In discrimination procedures, the lower doses could be used, for example, to screen potential pharmacological treatments for cocaine abuse, to determine whether the agents under investigation block or diminish cocaine's discriminative-stimulus effects. Clearly, investigations at very low cocaine doses would provide only preliminary information about potential treatments. Treatments found effective at blocking or diminishing the discriminative-stimulus effects of low cocaine doses would have to be evaluated using higher cocaine doses that more closely approximated the cocaine doses typically abused. Nevertheless, the use of the low-dose method could reduce the number of treatments that would have to be evaluated at the higher, more toxic cocaine doses.

Conclusion

The subtle effects of caffeine represent a challenge and an opportunity to develop, under conditions that represent little risk to participants, sensitive behavioral procedures that can be used to investigate the discriminative-stimulus, reinforcing, and withdrawal effects of more toxic drugs of abuse. Caffeine's reinforcing (Griffiths & Woodson, 1988b) and withdrawal (Griffiths & Woodson, 1988a) effects can be subtle as well, and researchers are currently attempting to clarify the conditions under which caffeine serves as a reinforcer (Griffiths et al., 1989; Hughes et al., 1991), as well as the conditions under which it produces physical dependence

(Hughes et al., 1991; Silverman et al., 1992). As in the case of drug discrimination, this research could result in the development of more sensitive procedures to study the reinforcing and withdrawal effects of other drugs of abuse.

References

Barone, J. J., & Roberts, H. (1984). Human consumption of caffeine. In P. B. Dews (Ed.), *Caffeine: Perspectives from recent research* (pp. 59–73). Berlin: Springer-Verlag.

Blough, D., & Blough, P. (1977). Animal psychophysics. In W. K. Honig & J. E. R. Staddon (Eds.), *Handbook of operant behavior* (pp. 514–539). Englewood Cliffs, NJ: Prentice-Hall.

Bunn, W. H., and Giannini, A. J. (1992). Cardiovascular complications of cocaine abuse. *American Family Physician, 46,* 769–773.

Clubley, M., Bye, C. E., Henson, T. A., Peck, A. W., & Riddington, C. J. (1979). Effects of caffeine and cyclizine alone and in combination on human performance: Subjective effects and EEG activity. *British Journal of Clinical Pharmacology, 7,* 157–163.

Colpaert, F. C., Niemegeers, C. J. E., & Janssen, P. A. J. (1980). Factors regulating drug cue sensitivity: Limits of discriminability and the role of a progressively decreasing training dose in fentanyl-saline discrimination. *Journal of Pharmacology and Experimental Therapeutics, 212,* 474–480.

Dews, P. B. (1984) Behavioral effects of caffeine. In P. B. Dews (Ed.), *Caffeine: Perspectives from recent research* (pp. 86–103). Berlin: Springer-Verlag.

Evans, S. M., & Griffiths, R. R. (1991). Dose-related caffeine discrimination in normal volunteers: Individual differences in subjective effects and cues. *Behavioural Pharmacology, 1,* 345–356.

Evans, S. M., & Griffiths, R. R. (1992). Caffeine tolerance and choice in humans. *Psychopharmacology, 108,* 51–59.

Fischman, M. W., Foltin, R. W., Nestadt, G., & Pearlson, G. D. (1990). Effects of desipramine maintenance on cocaine self-administration by humans. *The Journal of Pharmacology and Experimental Therapeutics, 253,* 760–770.

Fischman, M. W., Schuster, C. R., Resnekov, L., Shick, J. F. E., Krasnegor, N. A., Fennel, W., & Freedman, D. X. (1976). Cardiovascular and subjective effects of intravenous cocaine administration in humans. *Archives of General Psychiatry, 33,* 983–989.

Gilbert, R. M. (1976). Caffeine as a drug of abuse. In R. J. Gibbins, Y. Israel, H. Kalant, R. E. Popham, W. Schmidt, & R. G. Smart (Eds.), *Research advances in alcohol and drug problems* (Vol. 3). New York: Wiley.

Gilbert, R. M. (1984). Caffeine consumption. In G. A. Spiller (Ed.), *The methylxanthine beverages and foods: Chemistry, consumption, and health effects* (pp. 185–213). New York: Alan R. Liss.

Griffiths, R. R., Bigelow, G. E., & Liebson, I. A. (1989). Reinforcing effects of caffeine in coffee and capsules. *Journal of the Experimental Analysis of Behavior, 52,* 127–140.

Griffiths, R. R., Evans, S. M., Heishman, S. J., Preston, K. L., Sannerud, C. A., Wolf, B., & Woodson, P. P. (1990). Low-dose caffeine discrimination in humans. *Journal of Pharmacology and Experimental Therapeutics, 252,* 970–978.

Griffiths, R. R., & Woodson, P. P. (1988a). Caffeine physical dependence: A review of human and laboratory animal studies. *Psychopharmacology, 94,* 437–451.

Griffiths, R. R., & Woodson, P. P. (1988b). Reinforcing properties of caffeine: Studies in humans and laboratory animals. *Pharmacology, Biochemistry, and Behavior, ii,* 419–427.

Higgins, S. T., Rush, C. R., Bickel, W. K., Hughes, J. R., Lynn, M., & Capeless, M. A. (in press). Acute behavioral and cardiac effects of cocaine and alcohol combinations in humans. *Psychopharmacology.*

Hollister, L. E., Krajewski, K., Rustin, T., & Gillespie, H. (1992). Drug for cocaine dependence: Not easy. *Archives of General Psychiatry, 49,* 905.

Holtzman, S. G. (1990). Caffeine as a model drug of abuse. *Trends in Pharmacological Sciences, v,* 355–356.

Hughes, J. R., Higgins, S. T., Bickel, W. K., Hunt, W. K., Fenwick, J. W., Gulliver, S. B., & Mireault, G. C. (1991). Caffeine self-administration: Withdrawal and adverse effects among coffee drinkers. *Archives of General Psychiatry, 48,* 611–617.

James, J. E. (1991). *Caffeine and Health.* London: Academic Press.

Lieberman, H. R., Wurtman, R. J., Emde, G. G., & Coviella, I. L. G. (1987). The effects of caffeine and aspirin on mood and performance. *Journal of Clinical Psychopharmacology, 1,* 315–320.

Lieberman, H. R., Wurtman, R. J., Emde, G. G., Roberts, C., & Coviella, I. L. G. (1987). The effects of low doses of caffeine on human performance and mood. *Psychopharmacology, 92,* 308–312.

Meyer, R. E. (1992). New pharmacotherapies for cocaine dependence . . . revisited. *Archives of General Psychiatry, 49,* 900–904.

Mumford, G. K., Evans, S. M., Kaminski, B. J., Preston, K. L., Sannerud, C. A., Silverman, K., & Griffiths, R. R. (1992, November). *Discriminative stimulus effects of theobromine and caffeine in humans.* Presented at the annual meeting of the Society for the Stimulus Properties of Drugs, Anaheim, CA.

Overton, D. A. (1979). Drug discrimination training with progressively lowered doses. *Science, 205,* 720–721.

Preston, K. L., Sullivan, J. T., Strain, E. C., & Bigelow, G. E. (1992). Effects of cocaine alone and in combination with bromocriptine in human cocaine abusers. *Journal of Pharmacology and Experimental Therapeutics, 262,* 279–291.

Rall, T. W. (1990). Drugs used in the treatment of asthma. In T. W. Rall, A. S. Nies, & P. Taylor (Eds.), *Goodman and Gilman's the pharmacological basis of therapeutics* (8th ed., pp. 618–635). New York: Pergamon Press.

Robertson, D., Wade, D., Workman, R., & Woosley, R. L. (1981). Tolerance to the humoral and hemodynamic effects of caffeine in man. *Journal of Clinical Investigations, 67,* 1111–1117.

Schilmoeller, K. J., & Etzel, B. C. (1977). An experimental analysis of criterion-related and noncriterion-related cues in "errorless" stimulus control procedures. In B. C. Etzel, J. M. LeBlanc, & D. M. Baer (Eds.), *New developments in behavioral research* (pp. 317–347). Hillsdale, NJ: Erlbaum.

Sidman, M., & Stoddard, L. T. (1966). Programming perception and learning for retarded children. In N. R. Ellis (Ed.), *International review of research in mental retardation* (Vol. 2). New York: Academic Press.

Silverman, K., Evans, S. M., Strain, E. C., & Griffiths, R. R. (1992). Withdrawal syndrome after double-blind cessation of caffeine consumption. *New England Journal of Medicine, 327,* 1109–1114.

Silverman, K., & Griffiths, R. R. (1992). Low-dose caffeine discrimination and self-reported mood effects in normal volunteers. *Journal of the Experimental Analysis of Behavior, 57,* 91–107.

Stavric, B. (1988). Methylxanthines: Toxicity to humans: 3. Theobromine, paraxanthine, and the combined effects of methylxanthines. *Food Chemistry and Toxicity, 26,* 725–733.

Zenick, H., & Goldsmith, M. (1981). Drug discrimination learning in lead-exposed rats. *Science, 212,* 569–571.

17

The Study of Stimulus Control in Autism

Laura Schreibman

For typical children, the normal developmental sequence begins with reliance on near receptors (tactile, gustatory) and proceeds to reliance on distal receptors (vision, audition). However, early literature suggested that some children with autism remain more responsive to near-receptor stimulation than distal-receptor stimulation. This theory of sensory dominance (e.g., Schopler, 1966) was subjected to empirical investigation by experiments within the discrimination paradigm. Autistic, retarded, and normal children were taught to press a lever in the presence of a complex stimulus composed of visual, auditory, and tactile components. After discriminated responding was established, the control exerted by the individual components was assessed by interspersing presentations of the individual components amongst presentations of the complex stimulus. According to the theory of deviant sensory hierarchy, one would predict responding by the children with autism would be controlled mainly by the tactile cue and less by the auditory or visual cue and that normal children's responding would show the opposite trend. In fact, children with autism did not show a hierarchy of stimulus control but a restricted one: Their responses tended to come under the control of a single component. Some of them responded primarily to the visual cue and some primarily to the auditory cue. In contrast, the normal controls typically responded equally to all three of the components. Mentally retarded children responded between the autistic and normal groups. If presented with each previously nonfunctional single cue and reinforced for correct responding, however, the autistic children did respond to them. Their problem was not one of responding to a cue, therefore, but rather of responding to the cue in the *context* of other cues, a phenomenon termed "stimulus overselectivity" (Lovaas, Schreibman, Koegel, & Rehm, 1971).

What are the controlling parameters of overselectivity? Perhaps children with autism are "overloaded" by three cues. The experiment described was duplicated but with only two cues (auditory and visual). The overselective pattern was again apparent (Lovaas & Schreibman, 1972). Perhaps the phenomenon was restricted to discriminations in which the compound was composed of cross-modality stimuli. Koegel and Wilhelm (1973) used a similar discrimination paradigm employing multiple visual cues (pictures on cards) and again found overselective responding by children with autism in comparison to normal controls. Similarly, Reynolds, Newsom, and Lovaas (1974) used a successive-discrimination paradigm to test autistic children and normal controls for overselectivity within the auditory modality and found that the overselective response pattern was apparent even when the multiple cues fell within the same modality.

Overselectivity is real outside the laboratory, as some examples will illustrate. One child known to the author had no difficulty recognizing his father until the father removed his (own) glasses. When the father was not wearing glasses, the child responded to him as just another object in the environment. A mother reported that her son became extremely upset whenever she wore a new dress. A little girl worked with a therapist 6 days a week for an entire summer. At the end of the summer, the therapist changed her hairstyle, only to discover that now the child did not recognize her at all.

Informally observed patterns of behavior need to be established experimentally. Could the frequently reported failure of children with autism to establish sustained social recognition result from overselective responding? In a study to address this possibility, Schreibman and Lovaas (1973) taught normal and autistic children to discriminate between male and female dolls (Ken and Barbie dolls). Each doll was appropriately attired. When the discrimination was established, control by the various components was assessed, to see which could control the children's responses, by switching one aspect of the dolls at a time. For example, the skirt was put on the male doll and the trousers on the female doll, and the child was asked to point to the boy (girl) doll. If the child pointed to the wrong doll, the skirt or trousers were controlling the responding. The same was done with each of the clothing components and with the dolls' heads. With normal children, the dolls' heads controlled identification of boy versus girl doll. With children with autism, some idiosyncratic and objectively unreliable cue (e.g., socks, jacket) controlled that response.

Clearly, autistic children may identify an individual by an objectively irrelevant stimulus component. If an autistic child responds to a new person on the basis of a shirt, the child will not recognize the person in a different shirt.

It appears that this attentional pattern can help clarify the syndrome of autism. Rincover and Koegel (1975) presented data suggesting that overselectivity might be a basis for autistic children's renowned difficulties with generalization. They found that when these children learn a new behavior, their responses may be controlled originally by an irrelevant cue (e.g., a therapist's hand movement) to the exclusion of the intended, appropriate one (e.g., "Touch your nose"). Varni, Lovaas, Koegel, and Everett (1979) presented data suggesting that overselectivity impedes observational learning. Autistic children observed a model respond to a teacher's instruction. After several trials, the child was placed in the model's seat and presented with the same instruction. Their responses indicated they had learned only a portion of the modeled response. Schreibman, Kohlenberg, and

Britten (1986) noted that autistic children who are echolalic (i.e., repeat all or part of a verbal stimulus) may produce speech that is well articulated and accurate in terms of prosodic features such as pitch, inflection, and rate, but often do not use the echoic speech in context, indicating a lack of comprehension. Conversely, mute children who learn speech through training often exhibit speech that is monotonic and poorly articulated. Speculating that the echolalic children might be overselective in responding to intonation and mute children overselective in responding to content, a discrimination was taught in which both content (phonetic) and intonation of verbal stimuli were redundant and relevant cues. Single-cue assessments indicated that, in general, the echolalic children learned the discrimination on the basis of intonation, and the mute children learned it on the basis of content.

Koegel and Rincover (1976) provided data suggesting that overselective responding by autistic children may underlie the often reported failure of these children to benefit from prompt stimuli. In an analog study, these investigators sought to teach children with autism and normal children difficult auditory discriminations (tones) by presenting pretrained color prompts simultaneously with tones (e.g., red color with high tone, green color with low tone) and then fading out the color prompts. The color prompts enhanced acquisition of the auditory discriminations in the normal children but interfered with the discriminations in the children with autism. The children with autism persisted in their responding to the color cues; control was not transferred to the auditory stimuli. However, the children with autism did acquire the auditory discriminations when the colors were not used as prompts.

Overselectivity appears not to be peculiar to autism. It is more likely a function of mental age (e.g., Schover & Newsom, 1976; Wilhelm & Lovaas, 1976). The results reported previously were consistent with the literature showing a positive correlation between the number of cues controlling responding in a visual discrimination task and mental age in normal children and children with retardation (e.g., Eimas, 1969; Fisher & Zeaman, 1973). The fact that the overly restrictive stimulus control was frequently encountered in the autistic population is not surprising, since many of these children have low mental ages.

Still, overrestrictive stimulus control is indeed implicated in a number of the severe behavioral deficits associated with the population of autistic children. The challenge is how to use that information to develop more effective and efficient teaching procedures for them.

Rincover and Koegel (1975) showed that the teaching problem typically was not being able to fade the prompt completely. In that case, the children remain hopelessly dependent on the prompt. Indeed, in one experiment, the teacher prompted responding by pointing to the correct stimulus. To test when the children became independent of this prompt, the teacher sometimes kept her hands in her lap. On those occasions, several children stood up, reached over, and pointed to her hands.

A prompting procedure that does not require response to simultaneous stimuli (i.e., training events and prompts) should be effective in avoiding overselectivity. Schreibman (1975) taught children a discrimination that was based on the relevant cue in a difficult visual discrimination. All other cues were redundant. For example, one discrimination involved stick figures that were identical except that one arm was raised in one figure, and both arms were down in the other. The head, legs, and body were redundant in both stimuli. The child was taught to respond to the arm orientation, using an exaggerated version of it versus a blank card. Then, the S- relevant stimulus component (i.e., an inverted "V") was faded in at an exaggerated level. When the child was correctly responding to the exaggerated versions of the relevant stimuli, the stimuli were gradually reduced in size until they reached the size in the criterion discrimination. At this point, the redundant aspects of the discrimination (i.e., head, body, legs) were faded in. Using this procedure, the child at no time was required to respond to simultaneous multiple cues, since the relevant (criterion-related) cue was present throughout the training. This prompt was "within-stimulus"; it was contained within the relevant aspect of the discrimination, rather than "extra-stimulus," that is, presented as an additional cue to guide responding. Within-stimulus prompting taught the children difficult discriminations they did not learn either without a prompt or with an extra-stimulus (pointing) prompt. The efficacy of within-stimulus prompting was ascertained with visual discriminations, as described previously, and with auditory discriminations. These results were replicated, and the importance of prompting along the criterion-related ("distinctive feature") cue was demonstrated (Rincover, 1978).

Research in stimulus fading and stimulus shaping has been widely studied and refined (Etzel & LeBlanc, 1979). That research shows that within-stimulus prompting is not a readily helpful procedure in teaching children with autism. It can be difficult to implement by teachers who may not have the time, inclination, or skill to make the required materials. It may be time-consuming. Most limiting of all, it cannot be used to teach all types of discriminations (e.g., cross-modality transfers). An entirely different approach is needed.

Instead of designing a teaching procedure that allowed the children to learn even though they were responding in an overselective manner (e.g., within-stimulus prompting), it would be better to eliminate the overselectivity and allow the children to learn from extra-stimulus prompts. This would "normalize" the children's response and allow them to learn from the type of teaching procedures already used in schools.

The possibility of reducing or eliminating overselectivity was suggested by the fact that in prior overselectivity research it was apparent that the phenomenon was variable: Some conditions reduced it. Schover and Newsom (1976) demonstrated that overtraining discriminations reduced overselectivity. Subsequently, Schreibman, Koegel, and Craig (1977) showed that although simple overtraining per se did not reduce overselectivity, prolonged testing with unreinforced probe trials interspersed among reinforced training trials eliminated overselective responding in many children. In addition, prior clinical demonstrations with the children had shown that they eventually learned to use extra-stimulus prompts (e.g., Risley & Wolf, 1967). Clearly, the problem was amenable to modification.

Can children with autism be taught to respond correctly to simultaneous multiple cues? Koegel and Schreibman (1977) taught conditional discriminations directly. Autistic children had difficulty learning these discriminations and did so in a manner different from normal controls, but they *did* learn. In addition, one child in this investigation, who was taught a series of nine successive conditional discriminations, then learned new discriminations on the basis of multiple cues. It appeared the child learned a set to respond to all of the multiple cues and applied this set to new discriminations. These results were particularly exciting; they suggested not only that overselectivity could be remediated (at least for some of the children), but also that a pattern of responding to simultaneous multiple cues might then be applied to new situations. If overselectivity was responsible for the typical failure of extra-stimulus prompting procedures, and if overselectivity could be eliminated, children who no longer responded in an overselective manner might then demonstrate transfer from extra-stimulus prompts. Schreibman, Charlop, and Koegel (1982) showed this was indeed the case. In a multiple-baseline design across subjects, four children with autism failed to learn difficult visual discriminations without prompts, even with pointing; after exposure to successive visual conditional discriminations, they could learn with the extra-stimulus prompts that previously had been ineffective.

Burke and Koegel (1982) showed that teaching autistic children to respond to simultaneous multiple cues resulted in increased social responsiveness and increased responsivity to incidental environmental cues (i.e., cues to which main attention might not be focused, such as the comments of another person that are not directed at the child).

In the past few years, Schreibman and Koegel have increased the breadth of stimulus control, as if doing so could be "pivotal" in the treatment of autistic children. After finding that one limitation to the effectiveness of their parent-training program was nongeneralization of treatment effects (e.g., Schreibman, 1988), they taught the pivotal behaviors of motivation and responsivity to multiple cues. Perhaps the difficulties these children had in generalizing new skills were due to a lack of motivation and a failure to respond to the requisite number and types of stimuli in the environment. These are pivotal if changing them would lead to concomitant changes in many other behaviors. Consider here only the work on increasing the children's responsiveness to simultaneous multiple cues.

Koegel, Schreibman, Good, Cerniglia, Murphy, and Koegel (1989) developed a training manual that describes in detail how to teach these children using procedures that should increase their motivation and teach them to respond to multiple cues. The approach uses successive conditional-discrimination training to establish a set to respond to multiple cues and does so with naturalistic stimuli.

The parent or therapist is taught, for example, to ask the child to "get your red sweater" rather than "get your sweater." To be correct, the child must respond to multiple cues, in this case color and object. Since the child is likely to have sweaters of different colors and more than one red article of clothing, the child is essentially being confronted with a conditional discrimination. The treatment provider uses such conditional discrimination tasks throughout the ongoing language-training program.

This training should reduce or remediate overselective responding and autistic symptoms. Data analyzed to date support these expectations. To illustrate, the Assessment of Children's Language Comprehension (ACLC), a gauge of the child's receptive language comprehension, measures the extent to which the child responds to one, two, three, and four elements of a verbal stimulus. An example of one element would be "Point to dog" when presented with a picture array of four animals. An example of three elements would be "Point to big girl jumping" in a picture array consisting of a big girl jumping, a small girl jumping, a big girl sitting, and so on. These presentations steadily increase conditional-discrimination difficulty. Compared to children taught through successive target behaviors, children taught these pivotal skills show substantial improvement on the ACLC, suggesting improved responsivity to multiple cues. These results are most encouraging and may signal further beneficial effects of normalizing responsiveness in these children, if the approach is intensified.

A continued research focus on stimulus control in autism will surely lead to even more exciting findings and improved treatment of these children. The field has come far in 25 years of research.

Acknowledgments

Some of the research reported in this paper was supported and preparation of this manuscript was facilitated by U.S.P.H.S. Research Grants MH 39434, MH 28231, and 28210 from the National Institute of Mental Health.

References

Burke, J. C., & Koegel, R. L. (1982, May). *The relationship between stimulus overselectivity and autistic children's social responsiveness and incidental learning.* Paper presented at the annual convention of the Association for Behavior Analysis, Milwaukee, WI.

Eimas, P. (1969). Multiple-cue discrimination learning in children. *Psychological Record, 19,* 417–424.

Etzel, B. C., & LeBlanc, J. M. (1979). The simplest treatment alternative: The law of parsimony applied to choosing appropriate instructional control and errorless-learning procedures for the difficult-to-teach child. *Journal of Autism and Developmental Disorders, 4,* 361–382.

Fisher, M. A., & Zeaman, D. (1973). An attention-retention theory of retardate discrimination learning. In N. R. Ellis (Ed.), *International review of research in mental retardation* (Vol. 6). New York: Academic Press.

Koegel, R. L., & Rincover, A. (1976). Some detrimental effects of using extra stimuli to guide responding in autistic and normal children. *Journal of Abnormal Child Psychology, 4,* 59–71.

Koegel, R. L., & Schreibman, L. (1977). Teaching autistic children to respond to simultaneous multiple cues. *Journal of Experimental Child Psychology, 24,* 299–311.

Koegel, R. L., Schreibman, L., Good, A. B., Cerniglia, L., Murphy, C., & Koegel, L. K. (1989). *How to teach pivotal behaviors to autistic children.* University of California, Santa Barbara.

Koegel, R. L., & Wilhelm, H. (1973). Selective responding to the components of multiple visual cues by autistic children. *Journal of Experimental Child Psychology, 15,* 442–453.

Lovaas, O. I., & Schreibman, L. (1972). Stimulus overselectivity of autistic children in a two stimulus situation. *Behaviour Research and Therapy, 9,* 305–310.

Lovaas, O. I., Schreibman, L., Koegel, R. L., & Rehm, R. (1971). Selective responding by autistic children to multiple sensory input. *Journal of Abnormal Psychology, 77,* 211–222.

Reynolds, B. S., Newsom, C. D., & Lovaas, O. I. (1974). Auditory overselectivity in autistic children. *Journal of Abnormal Child Psychology, 2,* 253–263.

Rincover, A. (1978). Variables affecting stimulus fading and discriminative responding in psychotic children. *Journal of Abnormal Psychology, 87,* 541–553.

Rincover, A., & Koegel, R. L. (1975). Setting generality and stimulus control in autistic children. *Journal of Applied Behavior Analysis, 8,* 235–246.

Risley, T. R., & Wolf, M. M. (1967). Establishing functional speech in echolalic children. *Behaviour Research and Therapy, 5,* 73–88.

Schopler, E. (1966). Visual versus tactile receptor preference in normal and schizophrenic children. *Journal of Abnormal Psychology, 71,* 108–114.

Schover, L. R., & Newsom, C. D. (1976). Overselectivity, developmental level, and overtraining in autistic and normal children. *Journal of Abnormal Child Psychology, 4,* 289–298.

Schreibman, L. (1975). Effects of within-stimulus and extra-stimulus prompting on discrimination learning in autistic children. *Journal of Applied Behavior Analysis, 8,* 91–112.

Schreibman, L. (1988). Parent training as a means of facilitating generalization in autistic children. In R. H. Horner, G. Dunlap, & R. L. Koegel (Eds.), *Generalization and maintenance: Lifestyle changes in applied settings.* New York: Pergamon Press.

Schreibman, L., Charlop, M. H., & Koegel, R. L. (1982). Teaching autistic children to use extra-stimulus prompts. *Journal of Experimental Child Psychology, 33,* 475–491.

Schreibman, L., Koegel, R. L., & Craig, M. S. (1977). Reducing stimulus overselectivity in autistic children. *Journal of Abnormal Child Psychology, 5,* 425–436.

Schreibman, L., Kohlenberg, B. S., & Britten, K. R. (1986). Differential responding to content and intonation components of a complex auditory stimulus by nonverbal and echolalic autistic children. *Analysis and Intervention in Developmental Disabilities, 6,* 109–125.

Schreibman, L., & Lovaas, O. I. (1973). Overselective response to social stimuli by autistic children. *Journal of Abnormal Child Psychology, 1,* 152–168.

Varni, J. W., Lovaas, O. I., Koegel, R. L., & Everett, N. L. (1979). An analysis of observational learning in autistic and normal children. *Journal of Abnormal Child Psychology, 7,* 31–43.

Wilhelm, H., & Lovaas, O. I. (1976). Stimulus overselectivity: A common feature in autism and mental retardation. *American Journal of Mental Deficiency, 81,* 227–241.

18

Overselectivity in the Naming of Suddenly and Gradually Constructed Faces

Angela M. M. Duarte and Donald M. Baer

Stimulus overselectivity refers to partial stimulus control: the control of responses by one or a few components of the stimulus complex programmed as discriminative for reinforcement (Lovaas, Koegel, & Schreibman, 1979).

Bickel, Stella, and Etzel (1984) suggested that overselectivity might be assessed by first establishing a discrimination between two or more complex stimuli; once discrimination is achieved (90% correct responses to the S+ complex), the elements of the stimulus complex are presented singly, to reveal which of the elements control responding. If only one or a small number show control, that is labeled *overselectivity*.

Unusually persistent, generalized overselectivity is sometimes seen as clinically significant. It is considered especially characteristic of people with autism and perhaps fundamental to their condition (see Chapter 17, this volume), which leads to the suggestion that we make some analysis of the conditions that create overselectivity in the behavior of normal people. A functional understanding of it, apart from its presumed clinical significance, may yield a better perspective. This chapter reports on a study that investigated some conditions that might create extreme and durable overselectivity in high-functioning adults—university students.

The present study investigates overselectivity through a procedure designed to emphasize specific attributes (hair) of stimulus complexes (faces). The stimulus complexes were eight two-dimensional computer-generated drawings of human faces, each with a different, distinctive name to be learned by the participant. In succeeding cycles, new names were to be learned for the same faces. The participant's task was to learn each face's name. In the initial trials, however, only the hair of the face-to-be was present; it was established as the initial stimulus control over the name of the face-to-be. Subsequent trials added the remainder of the face's features, allowing but not requiring the possible extension of that stimulus control to other aspects of the faces. The subsequent test of discrimination removed the initially programmed source of stimulus control, the hair, to assess whether any other stimulus controls within the face were operative, despite the fact that they had not been required for correct discrimination up to that point. Further analysis investigated whether such stimulus controls might be affected by the sudden or gradual construction of the stimuli: Some faces were added to their hair as an immediately complete version (sudden construction); others were added gradually to their hair, one attribute at a time (gradual construction).

Method

Participants

The participants were 12 college students, 8 men and 4 women. For 8 of them, English was a second language. They were recruited essentially through their friendships to the senior author, and they agreed to participate in what was described as probably a five-session study of individual differences in visual discrimination. They were asked to serve without monetary or course-credit compensation. They represented a wide range of majors and ranged in age from 18 to 27.

Setting

All participants were seen individually in a 3- × 5-meter university research room allowing observation through a one-way mirror. The experimenter and the participant sat on adjacent sides of a small table so that the experimenter could easily show the participant the successive pages of a loose-leaf notebook.

Stimuli

The basic stimuli were eight different computer-generated male faces, selected from the roughly quarter-million that the MacIntosh Mac-A-Mug program can generate; these faces are shown in Figure 18.1. Each face was printed in black and white on a 4- × 6-inch piece of white paper, mounted in the center of an 8.5- × 11-inch page of black construction paper. The preliminary stimuli of the study were the pictures of only the hair of each of the faces in Figure 18.1, entirely divorced from all facial features, as shown in Figure 18.2. Participants saw these eight pictures (and all subsequent pictures) one at a time, each on a separate page in the loose-leaf notebook. For each participant, half of these hair pictures would later suddenly acquire the full face associated with them in Figure 18.1; the other half of these hair pictures would acquire their faces in a gradual manner over trials, as illustrated in Figure 18.3, gaining first a chin, then a mouth, then a nose, then eyebrows, and then eyes.

The final probe was the presentation for naming of the same eight faces without their hair, as shown in Figure 18.4.

Procedure

In the first session of the study, all participants were shown the pictures of hair illustrated in Figure 18.2 and asked to memorize their names (see Session 1,

212

FIGURE 18.1   Display of the Eight Full Faces According to Sudden or Gradual
Construction

FIGURE 18.2   Initially Programmed Stimulus Controls

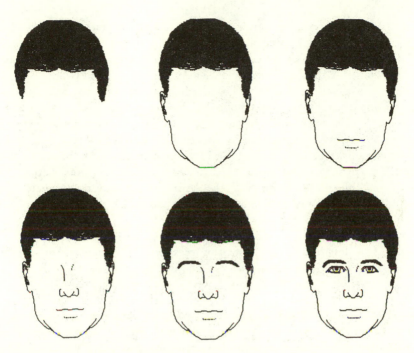

FIGURE 18.3   Sample of the Sequence of the Gradual Presentation of Faces (Hair, Hair-Chin, Hair-Chin-Mouth, Hair-Chin-Mouth-Nose, Hair-Chin-Mouth-Nose-Eyebrows, and Hair-Chin-Mouth-Nose-Eyebrows-Eyes).

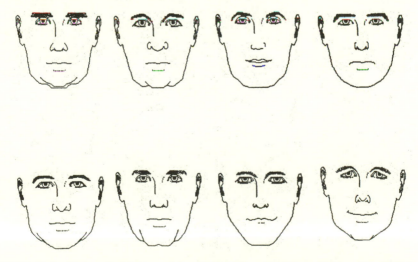

FIGURE 18.4   Probes: Suddenly and Gradually Constructed Faces Without Their Hair

Table 18.1). The experimenter presented one picture of hair at a time, saying, "This is [Name]. Say [Name]," until all eight had been shown. The experimenter then began a second cycle of eight trials within that session, repeating these hair-picture presentations in a different order, and saying each time, "Who is this?" Correct namings were acknowledged with, "That's right"; incorrect namings were answered with, "This is [Name]." Repetitions of two eight-face cycles, one always in a different order from the other, continued until the participant had named each picture of hair correctly in two consecutive cycles (and thus in two different orders).

Subsequently, the faces chosen for Sudden Construction were added to their hair pictures in one trial, and naming and feedback continued in pairs of cycles, one always in a different order from the other, as before. At the same time, the faces chosen for Gradual Construction began to form under their hair pictures, one element at a time. Each successive element was added only after the participant had correctly named all faces in their current state and in two different orders.

Table 18.1 describes the assignment of faces for six participants. For six other participants, the assignments of Faces 1 and 2 were exchanged with Faces 3 and 4, and the assignments of Faces 5 and 6 were exchanged with Faces 7 and 8.

After a participant had correctly named each of the eight faces in two consecutive cycles (one in a different order from the other), four repetitions of an eight-face probe were administered. This probe consisted of displaying each face in four eight-face cycles differing in order; but each face was shown without its hair (Figure 18.4). As before, the participant was asked to name each face, but no feedback was supplied by the experimenter about the correctness of the name. The almost invariable complaints, expressions of surprise, and questions in participants' first encounters with the probe were answered by the request, "Just do your best."

TABLE 18.1   Names Assigned to Faces 1–8 in Study of Overselectivity

| Session | Face Construction | | | |
	Sudden		Gradual	
1	Jim-1	Bill-2	Mike-3	Glen-4
	Dave-5	Andy-6	Eric-7	Paul-8
2	Greg-1	Mark-2	Don-3	Alan-4
	Joe-5	Peter-6	Bryan-7	Larry-8
3	Frank-3	John-4	Bob-1	Sam-2
	Tony-7	Steve-8	Rick-5	Dennis-6
4	Tom-1	Gary-2	Phil-3	Chris-4
	Jack-5	Sean-6	Kevin-7	George-8
5	Harry-3	Fred-4	Kurt-1	Chuck-2
	Jay-7	Ken-8	Scott-5	Lee-6

Results

The fundamental question was whether the test, presenting faces without the hair that had been the initial stimulus controls for their names and were the only stimulus controls required for correctness, would reveal any stimulus control by the remainder of the face. A subsidiary question was whether Sudden and Gradual conditions of face construction would differentially affect accurate naming during the probe. Figure 18.5 displays the 12 participants' average number of correctly named probes (of 16 possible—4 repetitions of 4 faces) across successive sessions, graphed to compare the effects of the prior Sudden (4 faces) or Gradual (4 faces) Construction of the faces. This figure shows that on the first probe, the absence of hair, the initial and only required stimulus control, greatly reduced the probability of correct naming but not to chance levels. On the average, the participants named about 4 or 5 of the 16 face trials in each construction condition correctly in that first probe. Figure 18.6 shows each participant's responses separately; it

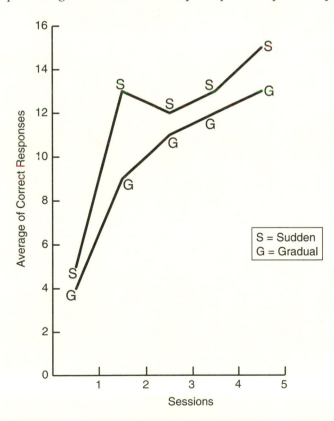

FIGURE 18.5   Average Number of Correctly Named Probes Across All Participants (Five Sessions)

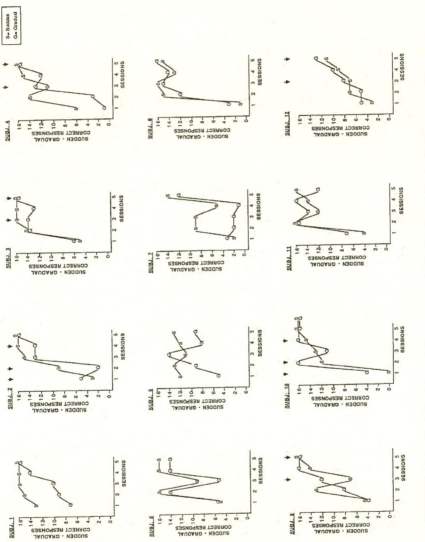

FIGURE 18.6 Each Participant's Responses to the Suddenly and Gradually Constructed Faces

reveals that S2, S4, S7, S8, and S10 showed naming levels close to the chance expectation (2 of 16) in one or both of the construction conditions; the other participants showed appreciably better response than that.

Figures 18.5 and 18.6 show that accurate naming usually increased steadily with repeated sessions of new names to memorize, with the largest gain made during the second session (now that the probes were no longer surprising to the participants and the nature of their real task was clear). These figures also show that, to a small extent, correct naming occurred most often when the faces had been constructed suddenly. The participants are graphed in Figure 18.6 roughly in order of the clarity of these effects.

An analysis of variance revealed a significant main effect of sessions in both the Sudden and Gradual conditions (Sudden: $F = 18.2$, $p = .00001$, $df = 4, 55$; Gradual: $F = 11.9$, $p = .00001$, $df = 4, 55$).

Discussion

These results clearly show that when a single stimulus is programmed as the only possible initial stimulus control, the subsequent addition of more potential stimulus controls can produce quite variable amounts of overselectivity. These 12 college adults showed on average a great deal of overselectivity in their first probes. Yet one participant (S1) showed little overselectivity, whereas five other participants (Ss 2, 4, 7, 8, and 10) showed a great deal. This overselectivity clearly was a result of establishing one face attribute as the only possible initial stimulus control; yet even after the participants saw in the first probe that this single attribute would not prove reliable, they continued to show overselectivity, overcoming it only over a series of successive sessions. That independence was gained, on the average, a little more quickly with Sudden Construction of faces than with Gradual, but this difference did not achieve statistical significance.

These results may be special to faces. It has been suggested that different forms of stimulus control operate in the recognition of faces than in the recognition of other objects. For example, Davidoff and Donnelly (1990) showed that scrambled drawings of chairs are easier to recognize as such than scrambled drawings of faces. It has also been shown that newly learned faces are less likely to be recognized when shown upside down (Yin, 1969) or slightly modified than are similar transformations of scenes (Standing, Conezio, & Haber, 1970).

Perhaps faces are special because of the features or portions of the faces that are most likely to function as stimulus controls. McKelvie (1976), studying the roles of eyes and mouth, found that most of his 115 college student participants recognized fewer faces when the eyes were masked than when the mouth was masked. In addition, Ellis, Shepherd, and Davies (1975) found that when reconstructing pictures of faces (reduced to jigsaw puzzles), participants typically used a top-to-bottom approach, perhaps suggesting that the upper parts are more important.

Similar conclusions were drawn by Goldstein and Mackenberg (1966) and Davies, Ellis, and Shepherd (1977), each with somewhat different procedures.

It might be argued, however, that the results of the present study could have allowed the Sudden-Construction faces to be less sensitive to overselectivity, because Sudden Construction allowed the participants repeated exposure to the upper portion of the face (viz., eyes and eyebrows), whereas Gradual Construction introduced the features from bottom to top, allowing less exposure of the eyes before probing.

References

Bickel, W. K., Stella, M. E., & Etzel, B. C. (1984). A reevaluation of stimulus overselectivity: Restricted stimulus control of stimulus control hierarchies. *Journal of Autism and Developmental Disabilities, 14,* 137–157.

Davidoff, J., & Donnely, N. (1990). Object superiority: A comparison of complete and part probes. *Acta Psychologica, 73,* 225–243.

Davies, G., Ellis, H., & Shepherd, J. (1977). Cue saliency in faces as assessed by the Photo-fit technique. *Perception, 6,* 263–269.

Ellis, H., Shepherd, J., & Davies, G. (1975). An investigation of the use of the Photo-fit technique for recalling faces. *British Journal of Psychology, 66,* 29–37.

Etzel, B. C., Bickel, W. K., Stella, M. E., & LeBlanc, J. M. (1982). The assessment of problem-solving skills of atypical children. *Analysis and Intervention in Developmental Disabilities, 1,* 187–206.

Etzel, B. C., McCartney, L. L. A., & LeBlanc, J. M. (1986, May). *An update on errorless stimulus control technology.* Paper presented at the 12th annual meeting of the Association for Behavior Analysis, Milwaukee, WI.

Goldstein, A. G., & Mackenberg, E. J. (1966). Recognition of human faces from isolated facial features: A developmental study. *Psychonomic Science, 6,* 149–150.

Hochberg, J., & Galper, R. E. (1967). Recognition of faces: I. An exploratory study. *Psychonomic Science, 9,* 619–620.

Lovaas, O. I., Koegel, R. L., & Schreibman, L. (1979). Stimulus overselectivity in autism: A review of research. *Psychological Bulletin, 86,* 1236–1245.

McKelvie, S. J. (1976). The roles of eyes and mouth in the memory of a face. *American Journal of Psychology, 89,* 311–323.

Standing, L. G., Conezio, J., & Haber, R. N. (1970). Perception and memory for pictures: Single-trial learning of 2560 visual stimuli. *Psychonomic Science, 19,* 73–74.

Yin, R. K. (1969). Looking at upside-down faces. *Journal of Experimental Psychology, 81,* 141–145.

19

The Environmental Antecedents of Spontaneous Social Behavior

Kathleen Zanolli

Be careful what you say,
Children will listen.
Be careful where you go,
Children will follow.

Into the Woods,
Stephen Sondheim

One of the goals of developmentally appropriate early education is to allow children to practice spontaneous play and social skills. Behavior that is initiated by the child, rather than directed by the teacher, is highly valued in developmental education, because it is believed that young children will learn more when they initiate the learning process themselves (National Association for the Education of Young Children, 1986). Although this is a statement more of policy than of fact, it illustrates the value our culture places on child-initiated behavior. However, we should be cautious in assuming that child-initiated, or "spontaneous," behavior originates in the child and is independent of the environment. As the song says, "Be careful." Children may be influenced by events in ways we cannot easily predict.

Developmental education is often contrasted with behavior-analytic teaching, which is characterized by frequent prompts (instructions, modeling, physical guidance), programmed learning materials, and reinforcement of clearly defined correct responses (cf. Lovaas, 1977). Such behavioral techniques, it has been argued, do not encourage children to behave spontaneously. Behavior analysis itself is sometimes seen as excluding spontaneity, because behavior analysts look for the causes of behavior in the environment, not in the child. Contrary to this assumption, *spontaneity* has been defined in the behavior-analytic literature as the occurrence of a behavior in the absence of verbal prompts or modeling from others (Charlop, Schreibman, & Thibodeau, 1985). In this chapter, we present an example of how antecedent events can affect spontaneous social behavior.

We looked at the problem of teaching autistic children to initiate social interactions with their peers. Although most 3- and 4-year-old children have no problem initiating interactions without adult help, children with autism usually do not initiate affection or verbal communication such as requests unless an adult or peer prompts them to do it (Lord & Hopkins, 1986; Odom & Strain, 1986). A social behavior that is prompted by teachers or peers cannot be spontaneous. This leaves many autistic children in the position of always responding to others and never initiating or controlling their social world.

An intervention designed to increase the social initiations of autistic children must address four issues if it is to be successful in a classroom. First, it must result in the autistic child making spontaneous initiations as well as responding to others. Second, initiations must be successful; that is, they must elicit responses from typically developing peers (Strain & Fox, 1981). Third, the child should use a variety of behaviors to initiate social interactions; children without this flexibility are at a disadvantage in most situations (Dodge, Pettit, McClaskey, & Brown, 1986). Finally, the intervention cannot be so time consuming that it takes teacher attention away from other children in the classroom (Odom & Strain, 1986).

Priming is one intervention strategy that has recently been shown to increase autistic preschoolers' spontaneous, successful, varied initiations to peers without demanding teacher involvement during school activities (Zanolli, Daggett, & Adams, in press). There are three defining aspects of priming: (a) Priming is conducted prior to a school activity, using the materials of that activity; (b) the priming session is low in demands, containing tasks the child can easily complete; and (c) the priming session is rich in potential sources of reinforcement (Wilde, Koegel, & Koegel, 1992). The priming intervention for social initiations can be done in the regular classroom, and it is conducted immediately prior to a regular play activity. When priming, the teacher prompts the autistic child to direct social behaviors to peers. The peer responds to the autistic child's initiation by talking and, when appropriate, giving the child access to something tangible (a sticker or a toy). Priming sessions are immediately followed by the regular play activity, in which the autistic child receives no prompts from teachers or peers. One strength of the priming procedure is that it is easy to do. It allows the teacher to conduct the activity as usual, without spending extra time on the autistic child's social skills during the activity.

My colleagues and I used this priming procedure in a preschool classroom with two boys who had autism and severe developmental delays, and it worked well. The boys initiated socially to their peers after almost every priming session; their initiations were unprompted and varied; and the peers responded to them consistently. The situation was not trouble-free, however. There were many days when one of the boys either did not initiate at all or initiated infrequently. On days when there were few initiations, teachers would say that the boy was "in a bad mood" or that he needed extra medication.

It seemed to us there were other possible explanations for the inconsistency in the boys' behavior, explanations that, unlike "mood," would help us improve their social life. One possible explanation, suggested by prior research, was related to how rapidly the teacher conducted the priming session. Rapid prompting generally results in a greater proportion of correct responses during discrete-trial teaching than does slow prompting for both autistic (Koegel, Dunlap, & Dyer, 1980) and typically developing children (Carnine, 1976). Rapid priming increases the rate of initiations during the priming session, which could, in turn, affect the rate of initiations in the subsequent activity (cf. Rowe & Malone, 1981). We decided to test this possible explanation in a brief experiment.

Method

Participants

Jeff (age 5 years, 2 months) had been diagnosed with autism before age 2 by a neurologist using criteria of the *Diagnostic and Statistical Manual* (DSM-II-R). His adaptive-behavior score on the Vineland Adaptive Behavior Scale was 51; his level of functioning in social, communication, daily living, and motor skills was low. Jeff was in intensive home-based behavior therapy for 3 years prior to the study. His home program at the time of the study included identifying objects verbally and by pointing; functional language (requests, personal information, and greetings); and play skills.

Bob (age 4 years, 8 months) was diagnosed with autism at age 2 by a psychiatrist using DSM-III-R criteria. Bob's adaptive behavior score on the Vineland Scale was 52. Like Jeff, Bob was involved in home-based behavior therapy for 2 years prior to the study; he was learning to identify objects verbally and make requests at the time of the study.

Setting

The study took place in a university preschool classroom during free play. There were six activity areas in the classroom: large motor, dramatic play, fine motor, language, numbers, art, and a water table. Materials were kept constant during activities in which study sessions were conducted. For Bob, the activities were coloring and playing with cars. For Jeff, the activity was coloring.

Peers

For Jeff, two girls (ages 4 and 6) and two boys (age 4) were trained to respond to initiations. For Bob, four girls (age range 4–6) and two boys (ages 4 and 5) were trained. Peers were selected from among the typically developing children enrolled in the preschool program. A child was invited to be a peer in the study if parent permission was given and if the child frequently expressed an interest in playing with Jeff or Bob. Peers were trained before participating in Jeff and Bob's priming intervention in the classroom. By the time the study began, the peers were independently responding to 80 percent or more of Jeff and Bob's initiations during play activities.

Measures

Behavior definitions are listed in Table 19.1. Participant, peer, and teacher behaviors were recorded on data sheets that had session time in minutes and seconds written down the side and columns corresponding to each behavior category across the top. When a behavior occurred, the observer looked at the stopwatch,

TABLE 19.1   Behavior Definitions

	Teacher or Peer Behavior
Prompt	The teacher asked, told, or showed the peer or participant (how) to do or say something. Prompts were scored with a "P" in the same column as the peer or participant behavior that was prompted.
Deliver tangible	The peer or teacher (recipient of initiation) handed the participant one of the following items: small piece of food, car, balloon, crayon, or preferred cup (at the water table).
Approval/respond	The peer (recipient of the initiation) said any of the following to the participant: high five, way to go, good job, nice talking, hi, that's good.
	Participant Behavior[a]
Smile	The participant smiled while looking at the peer's face.
Look	The participant looked at the peer's face for 2 seconds or until the peer delivered a consequence (excluded looking while performing any other initiation behavior).
"Look at me"	The participant said, "Look at me," or "look," while looking at the peer's face by the end of the phrase.
Say peer's name	The participant said the peer's name while looking at the peer's face.
"Give me that"	The participant said, "Give me," or "Give me that," while looking at the peer's face or at an object held by the peer.
Touch peer	The participant touched the peer (excluded hitting or pinching).
Other verbal	The participant said any English words while looking at the peer's face or an object held by the peer (excluded nonword vocalizations and naming the tangible consequence).

[a]All participant behaviors were scored as spontaneous initiations only if there was no teacher prompt or peer behavior within the preceding 5 seconds.

then made a check on the data sheet next to the time of occurrence and in the column corresponding to the behavior. In this way, the time of occurrence, frequency, and sequence of behaviors were recorded as accurately as possible.

Observers were undergraduate and graduate students working for course credit. Observers were trained, using a quiz on all behavior categories and practice observations of children other than the participants. Observers were considered qualified to record data independently once they achieved the criterion of 80 percent agreement with an experienced observer on all behaviors.

The measure of reliability was percentage of interobserver agreement. An agreement was scored if an observer marked the same behavior within 3 seconds of the other observer and in the same sequence as the other observer; all other marks on the data sheet were counted as disagreements. Interobserver agreement was calculated as Agreements/(Agreements + Disagreements) × 100.

Interobserver agreement was checked for 33 percent of sessions for Bob and 38 percent of sessions for Jeff. Agreement was over 85 percent for every behavior. The results are shown in Table 19.2.

Procedures

Play Activity Sessions.   All sessions were conducted in the classroom during the regular free-play period. When the participant went to the activity in which the session was conducted, the teacher asked one trained peer to join in the activity with the participant. Peers were invited in a predetermined order. Five or six other children were usually in the same activity area; the teacher was responsible for supervising all of them.

During the play activity sessions, the teacher told the participant to play and remained in the area, working with other children as needed. The participant remained in the activity for 5 minutes. No prompts or consequences for initiations

TABLE 19.2   Interobserver Agreement (in percentages)

Behavior	Bob		Jeff	
	Overall	*Range*	*Overall*	*Range*
Prompt	100	—	99	92–100
Deliver tangible	97	91–100	91	85–100
Approval/respond	92	78–100	89	71–100
Smile	100	—	88	75–100
Look	98	75–100	90	71–100
"Look at me"	100	—	N/A	—
Say peer's name	N/A	—	98	66–100
"Give me that"	100	—	88	70–100
Touch peer	95	66–100	97	66–100
Other verbal	100	—	86	66–100

were delivered by the teacher to the participant or peers during play activity sessions. Each time the participant directed a spontaneous initiation to the peer, the peer delivered consequences to the participant. All spontaneous initiations, including behaviors that were not prompted during the priming sessions, received consequences.

Priming Sessions.   Priming sessions were conducted immediately prior to play activity sessions. For Jeff, there were five initiation behaviors that were prompted during priming sessions: Smile at the peer, look at the peer for 2 seconds, touch the peer's hand, say the peer's name, and say "give me that" to the peer. For Bob, the initiation behaviors were smile, look, touch, say "give me that," and say "look at me." The teacher prompted the initiation behaviors in a prearranged random order, with each behavior appearing twice in the order, for a total of 10 trials per priming session.

On each trial during the priming session, the teacher gave a verbal instruction and modeled the behavior to the participant. For example, the teacher would say, "Jeff, smile at Lucy," while smiling and pointing at the peer. If Jeff did not respond, the teacher repeated the prompt once before moving on to the next item. If Jeff performed the initiation behavior but directed the behavior to the teacher instead of the peer, the teacher pointed to the peer and said, "Jeff, smile at Lucy." Each time the participant responded correctly, the peer delivered the consequences in the same way as in the play activity sessions.

Immediately after each priming session, a play activity session was conducted in the same activity and with the same peer who took part in the priming. There were three priming conditions used in the study:

1. Uncontrolled priming rate. The teacher was told to prompt the initiation behaviors as she had been doing in Jeff and Bob's ongoing classroom programs, at a rate that seemed "natural" or comfortable. The actual rates of prompts in this condition were once every 20–30 seconds for Jeff and once every 20–45 seconds for Bob.

2. Rapid priming. In rapid priming sessions, the participant was prompted a minimum of once every 15 seconds during the session.

3. Slow priming. In this condition, the participant was prompted once every 45–60 seconds.

Design

The independent variable was the rate of priming (rapid or slow). The dependent variable was the rate of spontaneous initiations to the peer during the play activity sessions. For Bob, the first baseline consisted of sessions in which the rate of priming was uncontrolled, which was consistent with Bob's classroom program at the time of the study. Baseline was followed by a multielement comparison between rapid and slow priming in the car activity. This was followed by a baseline consisting of play activity sessions only, with no priming, in a new activity, coloring. This baseline was followed by another multielement comparison, which was then followed by rapid priming only. Sessions in this phase were conducted in any activity the participant chose first.

For Jeff, the design was the same, except there was no replication across activities and no baseline without priming. This was at the request of his parents, who felt that removing priming would jeopardize Jeff's social life in the classroom. Since the objective of the study was to compare rapid and slow priming, rather than to establish the effects of priming itself, this modification did not pose a significant design problem.

Results

Priming Sessions

Both Jeff and Bob responded correctly to 90 percent or more of the prompts during all priming sessions. The overall percentage of correct responses was 96 percent in rapid priming and 98 percent in slow priming for Jeff, and 94 percent in rapid priming and 91 percent in slow priming for Bob.

Play Activity Sessions

Spontaneous Initiation Rate. Figure 19.1 shows the total rate per minute of Jeff and Bob's spontaneous initiations to the peer during the play activity sessions. During the first baseline, in which the rate of priming was uncontrolled, spontaneous initiations occurred in every session for Jeff and in two out of three sessions for Bob.

During the multi-element comparison of rapid and slow priming in the cars activity, Bob consistently had a higher rate of initiations after rapid priming. During the next baseline, in which no priming was done in the coloring activity, initiations occurred on only 3 out of 6 days. The second comparison between rapid and slow priming showed similar results to the first, except that the rate of initiations in both conditions was somewhat lower, and initiations after slow priming equaled or exceeded those after rapid priming on 2 days in the beginning of the phase. By the end of the phase, the rate of initiations was rising in the rapid priming condition and falling in the slow priming condition.

In the follow-up phase, in which rapid priming was conducted in the activity the participant chose first, the rate of initiations was slightly higher than in the initial baseline (uncontrolled priming rate), and it was ascending by the end of the phase.

Jeff's performance was similar to Bob's. In the first comparison between rapid and slow priming conditions, Jeff's rate of initiations was consistently higher in the rapid priming condition. The rate of initiations after slow priming decreased

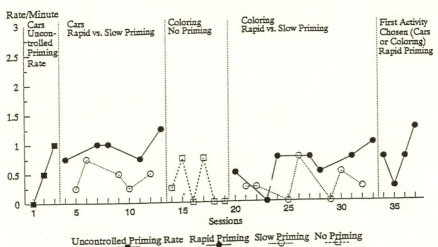

**Spontaneous Initiations to Peers During Play
Activities: Bob**

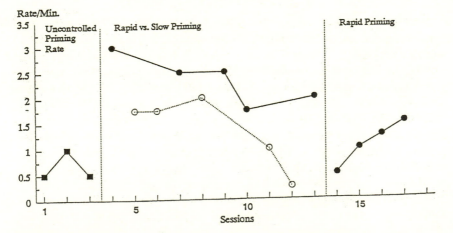

**Spontaneous Initiations to a Peer During a
Play Activity (Coloring): Jeff**

FIGURE 19.1   Spontaneous Initiations to Peers During Play Activities

substantially in the last two sessions of the phase; there was a smaller decrease in the rate of initiations after rapid priming. During the rapid priming only phase, Jeff's initiations occurred in all four sessions and steadily increased throughout the phase.

Variety of Initiations. Jeff and Bob used a variety of behaviors to initiate, including verbal behaviors that were not prompted during the priming session.

Discussion

In this study, my colleagues and I examined the effects of rapid priming on Jeff and Bob's spontaneous initiations to peers in play activities. We found that rapid priming resulted in higher rates of initiations during the subsequent activity than did slow priming. Rapid prompting generally results in a greater proportion of correct responses during discrete-trial teaching of new material than does slow prompting. This effect of rapid prompting is usually explained by saying that children have fewer opportunities to engage in self-stimulation or other competing behaviors. However, in our study, the percentage of correct responses to prompts during priming sessions was very high in both rapid- and slow-priming conditions, so this explanation is not adequate. It may be that faster prompting is associated with faster reinforcement (when continuous or ratio schedules are used, as in our study) and with higher initial response rates. Both of these factors have been shown to influence subsequent response rates in basic research with animals (cf. Malone & Rowe, 1981; Nevin, Mandell, & Atak, 1983).

Our study did not completely explain why rapid priming caused Jeff and Bob to perform more spontaneous social behavior. However, it did clearly show that rapid priming was an effective environmental antecedent. As it turned out, the variation in Jeff and Bob's behavior that their teachers had assumed was due to "mood" was more likely caused by variations in how the teachers were doing the procedure. Once they understood this, the teachers were able to provide rapid priming every day and greatly increased Jeff and Bob's consistency, frequency, and variety of spontaneous initiations to their peers.

This study illustrated a curious thing about "spontaneous" social behavior: It is more closely related to the environment than most of us suspect. We showed that even subtle variations in antecedent events can have powerful and unexpected effects on a child's social world. Be careful what you say: Children will listen.

References

Carnine, D. W. (1976). Effects of two teacher-presentation rates on off-task behavior, answering correctly, and participation. *Journal of Applied Behavior Analysis, 9*, 199–206.

Charlop, M. H., Schreibman, L., & Thibodeau, M. G. (1985). Increasing spontaneous verbal responding in autistic children using a time delay procedure. *Journal of Applied Behavior Analysis, 18*, 155–166.

Dodge, K., Pettit, G., McClaskey, C., & Brown, M. (1986). Social competence in children. *Monographs of the Society for Research in Child Development, 51*(2).

Koegel, R. L., Dunlap, G., & Dyer, K. (1980). Intertrial interval duration and learning in autistic children. *Journal of Applied Behavior Analysis, 13*, 91–99.

Lord, C., & Hopkins, J. (1986). The social behavior of autistic children with younger and same-age nonhandicapped peers. *Journal of Autism and Developmental Disorders, 16*, 249–262.

Lovaas, O. I. (1977). *The autistic child: Language development through behavior modification.* New York: Irvington.

National Association for the Education of Young Children (1986). NAEYC position statement on *developmentally appropriate practice* in early childhood programs serving children from birth to age 8. *Young Children, 41*(6), 3–19.

Nevin, J. A., Mandell, C., & Atak, J. R. (1983). The analysis of behavioral momentum. *Journal of the Experimental Analysis of Behavior, 39*, 49–59.

Odom, S. L., & Strain, P. S. (1986). A comparison of peer-initiation and teacher antecedent interventions for promoting reciprocal social interactions of autistic preschoolers. *Journal of Applied Behavior Analysis, 19*, 59–71.

Rowe, D. W., & Malone, J. C. (1981). Multiple-schedule interactions and discrimination. *Animal Learning & Behavior, 9*, 115–126.

Strain, P. S., & Fox, J. J. (1981). Peer social initiations and the modification of social withdrawal: A review and future perspective. *Journal of Pediatric Psychiatry, 6*, 417–433.

Wilde, L. D., Koegel, L. K., & Koegel, R. L. (1992). *Increasing success in school through priming: A training manual.* Graduate School of Education, University of California, Santa Barbara.

Zanolli, K., Daggett, J., & Adams, S. (in press). Teaching autistic children to initiate to peers using priming. *Journal of Autism and Developmental Disorders.*

Part Four

Constructing the Whole Environment

Stimulus control most often takes a delimited view of the control of behavior by its antecedents. That is habit, not necessity. As stated earlier, the proper applied view of stimulus control is that a behavior should be evoked by every problem it could solve and that a useful behavior should never be under the control of so few stimuli that their absence from some problem's environment leaves us incapable of using a solution our teachers thought we knew. This properly applied view urges us to design whole environments so that the stimulus controls for everything our students and clients should do in those environments are present.

The design of environments as efficient wholes is obviously a large job. Nevertheless, it has been done, perhaps most often in other disciplines concerned primarily with safety, efficiency, and comfort. Business has made much use of the concept of an efficient environment. The design of places where behavior is crucial and intense—airplane cockpits, driver's seats, keyboards, intensive-care wards, and the like—has seen much pragmatic effort. It is past time to insert the concepts of behavioral science, especially stimulus control, in such efforts and to extend the result to environments most useful to the greatest number of us.

We need to design home environments that, as a whole, support families in being families. We need to design specialized versions of those environments that, as a whole, support elderly persons well enough to let them stay in their homes if they wish, living as near to independently as possible, rather than be moved to nursing-care institutions. But we also need to design nursing-home environments that, as a whole, support clients in being as well, happy, and independent as possible, while supporting staff in doing gentle and friendly client caretaking. We need to design teaching environments that support students in learning, teachers in teaching, and friendship between the two.

Some of that has been investigated. Paula Davis and Anthony Cuvo review this literature relevant to retardation and find a number of environmental restructurings aimed at client independence from constant supervision. They also note that the success of that restructuring depends on two things: First, clients must be taught, and taught well, how to use the new environment; second, because we still sometimes fail in our teaching and in our environmental redesigns, staff must be trained to compensate for those failures as they become apparent, because it will take us time to redesign once again or improve our teaching.

John Lutzker, considering the problem of child abuse, reminds us that some family troubles are better described as problems of lifestyle rather than of the absence of a particular skill or the failure of a particular stimulus control. Striking a child may seem an outrageous but nonetheless limited response class; striking a child in a context of poverty, substance abuse, neglect, frequent parent absence, and family disintegration will not seem that simple. Remediation must target many skills and their supportive contingencies at once. Lutzker guesses that just as the unfortunate natural contingencies that support lifestyle are based on subtle consequences, remediations of that lifestyle will work best if they rely mainly on equally subtle consequences. The consequences that control life are often subtle, he suggests; therefore, remediations of those events should be similarly subtle, but stimulus controls should always be clear, obvious, and salient.

Yosikazu DeRoos and Elsie Pinkston take a similarly whole-environment approach to the day-care techniques that ought to be used with the elderly. The nature of day care is that staff behavior is most of the functional environment; therefore, staff training is the essence of environmental design. That training, they argue, should use the standard three-term contingency of behavior management and change (antecedent-response-consequence) to teach staff to use the same three-term contingency to maintain desirable client behaviors.

Elsie Pinkston makes the same kind of point in designing supportive environments for the elderly at home as well as in day care or institutions. Her preference is to find ways to allow the elderly to remain in their homes as long as they wish, but her principles of environmental design are the same in all three settings. She finds a special use for contingency contracting in establishing the right pattern of stimulus controls and reinforcement contingencies among caretakers.

20

Environmental Approaches to Mental Retardation

Paula K. Davis and Anthony J. Cuvo

Although various definitions exist, the term *mental retardation* generally refers to substantial limitations in intellectual development that result in problems with the performance of the activities of daily living. People who are mentally retarded may experience these problems in school, in social situations, and in their homes and communities. For example, children and adolescents who are mentally retarded may have difficulty with the academic skills their classmates are learning, may lack the social and play skills to interact appropriately with their classmates, and may not have the self-care skills needed to take care of themselves (e.g., tooth brushing, bathing, dressing). In addition to deficits in self-care skills, adults may experience problems in the activities of daily living such as making purchases, paying bills, and budgeting money; meal planning, grocery shopping, and cooking; doing laundry; obtaining and maintaining employment; developing and maintaining friendships; and using leisure time. Although it is widely reported that 3 percent of the population of the United States is mentally retarded, most professionals agree that the prevalence is probably less than 1 percent (Beirne-Smith, Patton, & Ittenbach, 1994). The American Association on Mental Retardation (AAMR) defines mental retardation as

> substantial limitations in present functioning. . . . characterized by significantly sub-average intellectual functioning, existing concurrently with related limitations in two or more of the following applicable adaptive skill areas: communication, self-care, home living, social skills, community use, self-direction, health and safety, functional academics, leisure and work. Mental retardation manifests before age 18. (1992, p. 1)

Although this definition of mental retardation maintains the critical components of this group's earlier definition of mental retardation (Grossman, 1983), one significant change is that it replaces previous severity levels of retardation (i.e., mild, moderate, severe, profound) with a description of the amount of support needed by the individual in the various adaptive skill areas. Four support levels are specified, including intermittent (less support), limited, extensive, and pervasive.

One of the assumptions of the 1992 AAMR definition is that people with mental retardation can make improvements in life functioning with appropriate environmental supports. By providing appropriate supports, which may take a variety of forms, people with mental retardation can become more skilled, experience greater independence, and ultimately enjoy a greater quality of life. The assumptions of the 1992 AAMR definition support the ideas that the environment plays a substantial role in mental retardation and that mental retardation is not a permanent or static condition. Instead, mental retardation reflects someone's performance at a point in time; it can be improved with the appropriate modifications in the environment.

Until the 1960s, people with mental retardation often were placed in large public residential facilities. Beginning in the late 1950s, a normalization principle began to guide services to people with mental retardation. Normalization is defined as "making available to the mentally retarded patterns and conditions of everyday life which are as close as possible to the norms and patterns of the mainstream of society" (Nirje, 1969, p. 181). That principle increased emphasis on community-based services to people with mental retardation. As a result, the deinstitutionalization movement was begun; people with mental retardation were moved out of large public residential facilities into smaller community-based settings such as group homes, foster care, supervised apartments, semi-independent living, and independent living (Beirne-Smith et al., 1994).

A variety of environmental supports are necessary to enable people with mental retardation to live successfully in community alternatives. This chapter examines three strategies for providing environmental supports to adults with mental retardation. The focus is on adults because by adulthood people are expected to be self-supporting and living independently.

Three environmental approaches may assist people who are mentally retarded to live as independently as possible. These include (a) providing effective instruction so that people with mental retardation can learn the skills required to be more independent, (b) restructuring the environment or the task so that people with mental retardation will find it easier to engage in the desired performance, and (c) providing personal supports so that people who do not acquire the skills and who do not respond to the restructured environment may still experience their desired lifestyle. The three approaches are not mutually exclusive. People with mental retardation may benefit from the application of all three simultaneously.

Systematic Instruction

One environmental approach used to improve the level of independence experienced by adults with mental retardation is systematic instruction. The literature has shown that instructional programs have been successful in teaching community living, vocational, social, academic, leisure, and other skills to people with mental retardation (Cuvo & Davis, 1983). The programs typically combine (a) instructional prompts, (b) reinforcement of consequences for performance, and (c) strategies for the transfer of stimulus control for gradually and systematically eliminating the prompts and reinforcers so that learners are performing in response to naturally occurring cues and consequences. Each of these components of instructional programs is described in the chapter, and examples using community living skills are provided.

Instructional Prompts

People with mental retardation often have difficulty responding to the cues in the natural environment that tell people without disabilities how to perform. For example, they may not be able to recognize the difference between the "men's room" and the "women's room" in public facilities, or the difference between tomato soup and chicken noodle soup on the cabinet shelf. Other people with mental retardation may be able to make those discriminations but not able to perform all the steps involved in completing tasks such as using the rest room independently or heating the can of soup. Still others may have difficulty with both the recognition and the performance parts of the task. Individuals with limited skills may benefit from instruction provided by a variety of trainer-delivered prompts, which are cues that provide the learner with additional information about how to respond. Four of the most commonly used prompts are verbal instruction, gestures, modeling, and physical prompts. Each of these has advantages and disadvantages that should be considered when deciding which one to use (Cuvo & Davis, 1983).

Verbal Instruction

Verbal instructions are part of virtually every community-living training program. They may be provided as a question or as a verbal description of the behavior to be performed, and they may be implemented along a continuum from less to more explicit response specification. Providing the least information about how to respond are nonspecific verbal prompts, such as asking questions about the response that should be emitted. For example, if a young man who is learning to use a clothes dryer fails to press the "on" button to activate the machine after closing the dryer door, he could be asked the general question, "What's next?" or the specific question, "What do you do after you close the dryer door?" Such questions may evoke the appropriate behavior.

A more explicit verbal prompt is a succinct statement specifying the response to be performed. For example, to teach laundry skills, a verbal prompt could be a brief statement such as, "Measure the soap." On the other hand, a verbal prompt could be more descriptive and include the specific actions to be performed, for example, "Pour the soap into the cup until the soap reaches the top line on the cup."

Verbal instructions are among the least intrusive and most efficient types of prompts (Cuvo & Davis, 1983; Sulzer-Azaroff & Mayer, 1991). They generally require little trainer effort, are easy to fade out, and do not require additional materials or expense. Additionally, they may be less stigmatizing than other types of prompts, because they are used frequently by a variety of people (e.g., teachers, coaches, work supervisors, parents) in various settings. When using verbal instructions, care must be taken to use words the learner understands. Sometimes telling someone what to do or how to do it does not provide enough information. In those cases, the verbal instruction could be delivered along with another prompt that provides more direction.

Gestures

Pointing by a trainer may prompt learner responses. For example, when teaching someone to write the date on a check, the trainer may point to the place on the check where the date should be written, saying, "Write the date here." Similarly, the trainer can use a pointing prompt to teach the specific position at which to set a kitchen timer or stove dials, or the level to which liquids should be poured in a saucepan or measuring cup.

Gestural prompts are easy to use, do not require close proximity to the learner, and are employed by the general public. Their primary disadvantage is that they may not provide specific enough information about how to perform tasks. For that reason, gestures are often accompanied by verbal instructions as illustrated in the check-writing example.

Modeling

The trainer may demonstrate to the learner what to do. The learner then imitates what the trainer did and is reinforced by the trainer. Modeling also is typically accompanied by verbal instructions. Using the example of setting a kitchen timer, the trainer may demonstrate how to set the timer and simultaneously describe what is being done: "Turn the arrow to 30 minutes." The trainer would then turn the timer back to its original position, ask the learner to set the timer, and reinforce correct performance. Similarly, a trainer might show and tell a learner the appropriate way to stir soup and then reinforce the learner for correct imitation. Modeling may be more effective than verbal cues because it is a direct demonstration of the response to be performed. A disadvantage is that it may be more time consuming and less efficient than merely providing verbal prompts.

Physical Prompts

The most intensive level of prompting used in the community-living-skills literature is physical guidance, by which the learner is physically assisted through the response. This type of prompting has been used most often with people with severe and profound mental retardation. The typical format has been to provide physical prompting and verbal instruction together. Physical prompts usually have been used when learners have not responded to the less intrusive prompts described previously. Physical prompts can be seen as on a continuum that ranges from full prompting to light touches that prompt responding. For example, a trainer using full physical guidance to teach someone to turn the dial of a washing machine would place his or her hand on the learner's hand and guide the learner's hand through the response of turning the dial to the correct position. In contrast, less physical guidance can be used: The trainer can rest his or her hand lightly on the learner's hand and provide more guidance only if the learner does not respond.

An advantage of physical guidance is the high probability that learners will perform the response when this prompt is provided. Less intensive prompts, such as verbal instruction or modeling, may be less successful. One disadvantage is that physical prompts provide little opportunity for the learner to emit the behavior without the direct assistance of the trainer (Sulzer-Azaroff & Mayer, 1991). Other disadvantages are that the trainer and learner must be in close physical proximity (Cuvo & Davis, 1983) and that it is not the type of instruction typically used by the general public.

Consequences

For instructional prompts to become effective cues, it is necessary that the response emitted by the learner be followed by positive reinforcement. Positive reinforcement is a consequence, delivered immediately after the desired response, that increases the probability that the behavior will occur again in the future. A wide variety of consequences have been used to reinforce community-living skills, but verbal and social consequences predominate (Cuvo & Davis, 1983). Participants typically are told that their performance is correct, and they may be praised as well. Other reinforcers that have been used include pennies exchangeable for food or activity reinforcers, graphic feedback, self-recording, self-evaluation, and tokens. Edibles, such as M&Ms, apple slices, and candy bars, also have been provided contingent on correct performance. Edibles are used primarily with children and persons with the most severe impairments in intellectual functioning.

As the learner becomes more skilled, the reinforcement used during instruction should be gradually reduced, if possible, until the learner is receiving the type and amount of reinforcer that naturally occurs when the skill is performed. For example, the natural reinforcer for cooking is eating the food one cooks. In situations in which the natural reinforcer is not powerful enough to maintain the behavior, it may be necessary to provide additional reinforcers. It may be possible, however, to reduce the amount of artificial reinforcement provided. When people need additional reinforcement, it may be possible to teach them to provide the reinforcers to themselves so that they are less dependent on a trainer.

Transfer of Stimulus Control

If learners perform a correct response only when prompted, their responses are under the control of the trainer-delivered prompts. Because the ultimate goal of training is usually to elicit behavior in response to naturally occurring stimuli, eliminating the trainer-delivered prompts becomes a crucial issue in training community-living skills (Cuvo & Davis, 1983). Several strategies can be used to transfer stimulus control from the trainer-delivered prompts to the natural stimulus. Three frequently used strategies are least-to-most prompts, most-to-least prompts, and prompt-delay.

The frequently cited "system of least prompts" orders instructional prompts from lesser to greater intensity. Initially, the learner is allowed to perform with no help. When the learner makes an error or does not respond, a prompt is delivered to occasion the response. Verbal instruction typically is tried first. If the learner does not respond correctly to the verbal instruction, a gesture or model is delivered next. If the gesture or model is not sufficient to prompt the correct response, the learner is given physical guidance.

On subsequent trials, learners again are given the opportunity to perform without assistance. Instructional prompts may be faded in once again, as required. Each new trial of a response provides an opportunity for the learner to respond to the natural discriminative stimuli. A review of the literature shows that this prompt-fading procedure has been used to teach a variety of community-living responses, such as pedestrian, fire-escape, cleaning, bus-riding, and cooking skills (e.g., Cuvo & Davis, 1983).

The reverse sequence of prompts also can be employed; in this case, learners receive assistance before they respond. The prompt hierarchy could begin with a highly controlling prompt (e.g., physical guidance) and fade to less intrusive prompts to transfer stimulus control to natural stimuli. Using this system, the probability of errors is reduced.

Prompt-delay, also termed time-delay, has been used to transfer stimulus control in community-living research. Instead of fading the type of assistance provided, the trainer transfers stimulus control by increasing the time between the presentation of the natural environmental cue and the trainer prompt. The initial step in this procedure is for the trainer to select one prompt that is likely to be effective with the learner. For the first few training trials, that prompt is delivered in the presence of the natural discriminative stimulus before the learner responds, thereby ensuring a correct performance of the response. After the first few trials, transfer of stimulus control is attempted by programming either a constant or an increasing delay between presentation of the natural discriminative stimulus and the trainer's prompt (Snell & Gast, 1981). Prompt-delay procedures have been used to teach people with mental retardation to make a bed, read community sight words, follow recipes, and the like (Cuvo & Davis, 1983).

A study to teach vending-machine use to students with mental retardation illustrates the prompt-delay procedure (Browder, Snell, & Wildonger, 1988). The trainer combined a gestural cue with verbal instructions to prompt responding at each step of the task. For example, to teach the response of inserting coins, the trainer pointed to the coin slot and told students to insert the coins. On the first two trials, the combined verbal and gestural prompt was delivered as soon as the students completed the previous step. On the next two trials, the trainer waited 2 seconds before delivering the prompt. On the following two trials, she waited 4 seconds to prompt the students. On all subsequent trials, the trainer waited 6 seconds before delivering the prompt. If at any point the student made an error before or after the prompt, the teacher returned to a 0-second delay and then repeated the delay-increasing schedule. Using this procedure, students began to respond appropriately before delivery of the prompt, and stimulus control was transferred successfully from the trainer-delivered prompt to the naturally occurring discriminative stimulus in the environment.

Environmental and Task Modifications

Sometimes people with mental retardation have a difficult time learning a task, even when systematic instruction such as described previously is provided. The difficulties often result from problems with academic portions of tasks requiring reading, mathematics, and writing responses. As a result, learners may be indefinitely dependent on someone to assist them in completing the portions of the tasks they cannot do. In those cases, the trainer should examine the environment, the materials, and the task itself to determine whether any of these can be modified to make the tasks easier to perform. Many examples of modifications (sometimes called permanent prompts) exist in the community-living-skills literature (Cuvo & Davis, 1983).

Modifications are an important part of any program to teach skills to people with mental retardation, because the modifications may permit increased independence in the activities of daily life. Additionally, modifications are used on a regular basis by those without disabilities. One of the first steps to determine an appropriate modification, therefore, might be to look at the modifications people without disabilities use, for example, calculators to develop a grocery list within a budget, to shop for the groceries, to balance a checkbook, and to budget monthly bills. Likewise, people without disabilities use digital watches to tell time, shoes with Velcro instead of laces, grocery lists to help them remember what to buy in the store, cookbooks to remind themselves how to prepare meal items, and microwave ovens and prepackaged meals to eliminate many cooking skills. They also program their telephones to dial emergency and frequently used numbers. These modifications also can be used by people with retardation.

Some people, however, may need additional, specialized modifications as well. One of the most frequently used specialized modifications is a visual cue, often in the form of pictures. For example, picture recipes have been used by people with mental retardation and limited reading skills to cook simple meal items (Johnson & Cuvo, 1981). Pictures of food items rather than written grocery lists have been used when grocery shopping (Aeschleman & Schladenhauffen, 1984). Pictures also have been used to prompt learners to perform housekeeping tasks such as dusting and folding laundry (Wacker, Berg, Berrie, & Swatta, 1985), to manage work and break time (Sowers, Rusch, Connis, & Cummings, 1980), and to perform grooming tasks (Thinesen & Bryan, 1981).

Nonpictorial forms of visual cues can assist people to perform difficult tasks. For those who have basic reading skills, written rather than pictorial prompts can be used. For example, adults with mild disabilities used written lists of the steps needed to clean appliances and do laundry (Cuvo, Davis, O'Reilly, Mooney, & Crowley, 1992). A combination of written, picture, and color cues was used by a young woman who was severely handicapped to assist in riding a public bus (Coon, Vogelsberg, & Williams, 1981). She used pocket-sized bus-route cards that contained the bus-route name and intended bus stop, and picture cues that permitted her to choose the route card for a specific destination. To increase her attention to the relevant aspects of the stimuli during training, color and size cues on the bus-route name cards were highlighted and then faded. Tape-recorded instructions have been used as permanent prompts to assist people with mental retardation to prepare a sandwich and cup of soup, operate a washing machine, and complete a vocational assembly task (Alberto, Sharpton, Briggs, & Stright, 1986). Finally, boards with preprinted questions and spaces for written cashier responses have been used to place orders at a fast-food restaurant (van den Pol et al., 1981).

In addition to the permanent prompts, which require tangible changes in the environment, special techniques can be developed that help a person complete a task. For example, people having difficulty learning to count change in the traditional fashion can use a special finger-counting procedure (Lowe & Cuvo, 1976). In another money-management example, people can be taught to carry single dollar bills and always pay one dollar more than the dollar amount requested (van den Pol et al., 1981) so that they need not learn to count change. In an example concerning cooking skills, a woman who was profoundly mentally retarded was taught three simple cooking skills by a combination of systematic instruction including permanent prompts (e.g., color-coded dials and burners) and task modifications (Schleien, Ash, Kiernan, & Wehman, 1981). For example, to simplify the task of boiling an egg, the woman was taught to place the egg into an empty saucepan and then fill the saucepan with water. Following this order decreased the likelihood of spills and burns.

These examples illustrate the fact that people with mental retardation may be able to complete community-living tasks even when they do not have the skills usually identified as prerequisites. Care should be taken in the selection and use of the modifications (Cuvo & Davis, 1983); they should not be programmed indiscriminately, especially in a socially stigmatizing manner. Furthermore, learners should be given the opportunity, at first, to learn a skill they might be able to acquire without the modification. Additionally, a decision must be made about the length of time the modification will be used. In some cases, the modifications remain in place permanently; in other cases, it may be possible to implement a systematic transfer of stimulus control in much the same way that instructional prompts are gradually eliminated, so that the person performs without the modification.

Personal Supports

In the typical approach to independent living, people who do not acquire the skills needed to live without assistance are required to live in restrictive settings, sometimes in large institutions. In those settings they receive the services they need to survive and instruction in the skills needed to live independently. As they gain these skills, they may be permitted to move to less restrictive settings, such as group homes or supervised apartments, until they finally master the skills needed to live independently; then they can live alone if they choose. In this continuum model, people who do not master specified skills are not permitted to move to a less restrictive setting, even if they would like to.

"Supported living" has emerged as an alternative approach to the continuum model of residential services (Bellamy & Horner, 1987). It is defined as people "living where and with whom they want, for as long as they want, with the ongoing support needed to sustain that choice" (Fredericks, cited in Bellamy & Horner, 1987, p. 506). In the supported-living paradigm, a variety of personal supports are provided to assist people with mental retardation achieve their chosen lifestyles. These supports are individually determined and may vary with time as the person's preferences and needs change.

Supported living is a comprehensive approach to the problems experienced by people with mental retardation. Unlike the continuum approach to community living, there are no skill prerequisites to attaining the chosen lifestyle. The focus is on determining a person's desired lifestyle and establishing the environmental supports necessary to attain that lifestyle. The supports may include instruction and modifications, as described previously, to assist a person in independent task performance; however, accessing a chosen lifestyle is not contingent on achieving independence. Instead, the focus is on personal supports, a variety of which may be necessary at any given time. The 1992 AAMR definition of mental retardation lists seven general functions that supports may serve: befriending, financial planning, employee assistance, behavioral support, in-home living assistance, community access and use, and health assistance (AAMR, 1992). As mentioned previously, the degree of support required may range from intermittent to pervasive and may change over time for different functions.

All the personal supports that might be provided cannot be listed because they vary according to individual needs and can be as unique as the individuals who need them; however, some common examples follow. First, differing amounts of assistance may be needed to perform the activities of daily living such as bathing, cooking, budgeting, and shopping. A person with mental retardation also may require assistance to communicate with human service agencies (e.g., public assis-

tance, vocational rehabilitation, legal and advocacy services) and community resources (e.g., physician, bank, shopping mall, library). Instruction may or may not
be part of this support. These supports may be needed only occasionally or may
be required 24 hours per day. For example, one person may need assistance only
one time per month in paying bills and establishing a budget. In contrast, another
person might need someone to cook the evening meal every day and assist with
the budget weekly. In still another situation, a person might need 24-hour supervision and guidance in virtually all aspects of daily life.

Other supports that may be beneficial to people with mental retardation who
choose to live in the community include assistance in developing social skills,
making friends, and using leisure time; in maintaining and obtaining employment; and in developing intimate relationships that may include marriage and a
family. People with mental retardation also may need assistance to manage their
physical and mental health needs. Another support often needed is transportation, especially for people who live in an area with limited or no public transportation. Because the support needs of people with mental retardation can be
extensive and require the services of a variety of agencies, case coordination may
be necessary. Case coordinators do not provide needed supports; rather, they assist the person in accessing the supports.

Depending on individual needs, people with mental retardation may receive a
variety of services and a number of supports simultaneously; these may include
instruction, environmental and task modifications, and the various supports described in this section. These supports may be provided formally or informally
(Beirne-Smith et al., 1994). Formal supports are performed by a paid staff member working for a human service agency. Informal supports usually are provided
by volunteers, neighbors, friends, family members, or coworkers.

The specific supports should be individualized and modified as necessary to
meet the changing needs and preferences of the person receiving the support. Because the major purpose of supports is to increase the community integration of
people with mental retardation, natural, informal supports should be used as
much as possible (AAMR, 1992). Finally, persons with mental retardation should
be monitored on an ongoing basis to determine current support needs.

Conclusion

As this discussion illustrates, an environmental approach to mental retardation
focuses on three methods that are not mutually exclusive. The most holistic approach would probably include a combination of all three: systematic instruction,
environmental and task modification, and personal supports. The following vi-
gnette illustrates how a combination of supports may assist people with mental
retardation to achieve their chosen lifestyles.

Jody, a 30-year-old woman who is mentally retarded, lives in an apartment
in the community and works at a restaurant within walking distance of her

apartment. Jody walks to work most days, but when the weather is bad a coworker usually offers Jody a ride. Jody receives three visits per week from a paid staff member, who provides her with instruction in cooking and doing laundry. On the days the staff member does not come, Jody fixes sandwiches or prepares simple meals in the microwave. Jody's sister visits weekly to take her grocery shopping. Jody keeps track of items she needs, using a picture grocery-shopping list. Jody and her sister also go to the movies or the mall at least once per week. Jody's mother calls Jody every few days, just to talk. She also assists Jody with her budget.

A neighbor usually stops by several times a week for a cup of coffee, to play cards, or to watch TV with Jody. Almost every evening Jody talks to friends on the phone. She uses a programmed phone with pictures of her friends on the call buttons. Through this combination of instruction, environmental modifications, and personal supports, Jody lives and works in the community and participates in daily life including an active social life.

References

Aeschleman, S. R., & Schladenhauffen, J. (1984). Acquisition, generalization, and maintenance of grocery shopping skills by severely mentally retarded adolescents. *Applied Research in Mental Retardation, 5,* 245–258.

Alberto, P. A., Sharpton, W. R., Briggs, A., & Stright, M. H. (1986). Facilitating task acquisition through the use of a self-operated auditory prompting system. *Journal of the Association for the Severely Handicapped, 11,* 85–91.

American Association on Mental Retardation. (1992). *Mental retardation: Definition, classification, and systems of supports* (9th ed.). Washington, DC: Author.

Beirne-Smith, M., Patton, J. R., & Ittenbach, R. (1994). *Mental retardation* (4th ed.). Columbus, OH: Charles E. Merrill.

Bellamy, G. T., & Horner, R. H. (1987). Beyond high school: Residential and employment options after graduation. In M. E. Snell (Ed.), *Systematic instruction of persons with severe handicaps* (3rd ed., pp. 491–510). Columbus, OH: Merrill.

Browder, D. M., Snell, M. E., & Wildonger, B. A. (1988). Simulation and community-based instruction of vending machines with time delay. *Education and Training in Mental Retardation, 23,* 175–185.

Coon, M. E., Vogelsberg, R. T., & Williams, W. (1981). Effects of classroom public transportation instruction on generalization to the natural environment. *Journal of the Association for the Severely Handicapped, 6,* 23–29.

Cuvo, A. J., & Davis, P. K. (1983). Behavior therapy and community living skills. In M. Hersen, R. M. Eisler, & P. M. Miller (Eds.), *Progress in behavior modification* (Vol. 14, pp. 125–172). New York: Academic Press.

Cuvo, A. J., Davis, P. K., O'Reilly, M. F., Mooney, B. M., & Crowley, R. (1992). Promoting stimulus control with textual prompts and performance feedback for persons with mild disabilities. *Journal of Applied Behavior Analysis, 25,* 477–489.

Grossman, H. J. (Ed.). (1983). *Classification in mental retardation.* Washington, DC: American Association on Mental Retardation.

Johnson, B. F., & Cuvo, A. J. (1981). Teaching mentally retarded adults to cook. *Behavior Modification, 5,* 187–202.

Lowe, M., & Cuvo, A. J. (1976). Teaching coin summation to the mentally retarded. *Journal of Applied Behavior Analysis, 9,* 483–489.

Nirje, B. (1969). The normalization principle and its human management implications. In R. B. Kugel & W. Wolfensberger (Eds.), *Changing patterns in residential services for the mentally retarded* (pp. 179–195). Washington, DC: President's Committee on Mental Retardation.

Schleien, S. J., Ash, T., Kiernan, J., & Wehman, P. (1981). Developing independent cooking skills in a profoundly retarded woman. *Journal of the Association for the Severely Handicapped, 6,* 23–29.

Snell, M. E., & Gast, D. L. (1981). Applying the time delay procedure to the instruction of the severely handicapped. *Journal of the Association for the Severely Handicapped, 6,* 3–14.

Sowers, J., Rusch, F. R., Connis, R., & Cummings, L. (1980). Teaching mentally retarded adults to time manage in a vocational setting. *Journal of Applied Behavior Analysis, 13,* 119–128.

Sulzer-Azaroff, B., & Mayer, G. R. (1991). *Behavior analysis for lasting change.* Fort Worth, TX: Holt, Rinehart & Winston.

Thinesen, P. J., & Bryan, A. J. (1981). The use of sequential pictorial cues in the initiation and maintenance of grooming behaviors with mentally retarded adults. *Mental Retardation, 19,* 247–250.

van den Pol, R. A., Iwata, B. A., Ivancic, M. T., Page, T. J., Neef, N. A., & Whitley, F. P. (1981). Teaching the handicapped to eat in public places: Acquisition, generalization and maintenance of restaurant skills. *Journal of Applied Behavior Analysis, 14,* 61–69.

Wacker, D. P., Berg, W. K., Berrie, P., & Swatta, P. (1985). Generalization and maintenance of complex skills by severely handicapped adolescents following picture prompt training. *Journal of Applied Behavior Analysis, 18,* 329–336.

21

Ecobehavioral Approaches in Child Abuse and Developmental Disabilities Mirroring Life

John R. Lutzker

This chapter discusses the critical relevance of the social-significance aspect of behavioral psychology to antecedent behavioral control.

Clinical Goals

In the seminal issue of the *Journal of Applied Behavior Analysis*, Baer, Wolf, and Risley (1968) defined *applied* as work that is of social significance. It seems that this definition could also refer to clinical goals; that is, the goal of any treatment program should be one of social significance. Targets for behavior change should produce change that is good for the individual and his or her social ecology, and that change should be durable over time.

To achieve these goals, it has been suggested that treatment strategies need to be developed that produce natural maintaining contingencies from the environment (Stokes & Baer, 1977). The very behaviors that are taught need to be practical for the individual and society, or there are not likely to be natural maintaining contingencies. It is here that antecedent behavioral control plays such a major role. Most of everyday life is governed by antecedent events far more than by artificially arranged consequences for behaviors. It seems only logical, therefore, that to produce lasting behavior change, we must apply procedures that are easy to use and that set the occasion for adaptive behavior, thus preventing challenging behaviors. Such strategies allow us to worry less about the occurrence of challenging behaviors and what consequences to arrange for them.

Three Ecobehavioral Models

In the ecobehavioral models described here for child abuse and neglect (Lutzker, 1984) and developmental disabilities (Lutzker, Campbell, Harrold, & Huynen, 1992), the assumption has been made that the problems faced by the families involved are multifaceted and need multifaceted treatment. To rearrange these families' social ecologies in a productive manner, we must develop treatment strategies that are practical and likely to produce durable change.

Project 12-Ways is an ecobehavioral model for the treatment and prevention of child abuse and neglect. The services provided by Project 12-Ways have included parent-child training, stress reduction, basic skill training for children, home safety, home cleanliness, and a host of strategies aimed at preventing abuse by single mothers. Several examples of antecedent control procedures have been reported in research conducted on Project 12-Ways. Also described have been several clinical treatment strategies using antecedent control procedures.

The clearest example of antecedent control procedures used by Project 12-Ways counselors is the teaching of nutritious meal planning and shopping skills to a mother with mental retardation, whose daughter had been removed from the home because of the mother's inability to plan and shop for nutritious meals (Sarber, Halasz, Messmer, Bickett, & Lutzker, 1983). Confounding the difficulties in this small family was the fact that the mother was illiterate.

Match-to-sample procedures were used by Project 12-Ways counselors to teach the mother to plan nutritious meals. She placed photos of foods (clipped from magazines), representing the four basic food groups, on a large planning board. At the bottom of the board were four index cards of differing colors. Each represented one food group. The photos of foods were placed on cards that matched the food group: Meats were placed on red cards, fruits and vegetables were placed on green cards, dairy product photos were placed on white cards, and grains and other carbohydrates were placed on blue cards. The board contained three horizontal and four vertical rows of small envelopes. The horizontal rows represented breakfast, lunch, and dinner. The vertical rows corresponded with the color-coded cards at the bottom of the board to represent the food groups. To plan nutritious meals, the mother matched the color of the card at the bottom of the row and placed it in the envelope corresponding with the meal that she was planning. She constructed seven of these boards to plan a week's worth of meals.

To help the mother shop for what she had planned, match-to-sample procedures were used again. For each photo that had been placed in the envelopes on the planning boards, the mother found another matching photo from the collection her counselors had provided. She then placed the matching photo in a plastic page of a two-ring binder, which came to serve as a shopping list to take to the grocery store. Match-to-sample was used a third time when the mother went to the store with her list. As she pushed her grocery cart through the store, she matched pictures from her "list" with actual store products.

The effect of meal planning was demonstrated in a pretest-posttest design. The effects of teaching correct shopping were assessed one food group at a time. Additionally, generalization was seen: The mother had been trained in a small grocery store. After training, a new supermarket was built within walking distance of her home, and she transferred 100 percent of her newly learned shopping skills to the new, larger store. After some parent training and demonstration of maintenance of the mother's new meal-planning and shopping skills, the daughter was returned to the home.

Another example of the use of antecedent control procedures involved teaching single mothers to provide stimulation activities for their babies (Lutzker, Lutzker, Braunling-McMorrow, & Eddleman, 1987). Large bright cards were used to prompt the mothers to engage independently in the stimulation activities. Some generalization across settings and activities was seen.

An antecedent in the form of an audiotape–slide presentation was quite successful in reducing hazards in the homes of children whose parents had been referred to authorities for child abuse or neglect (Barone, Greene, & Lutzker, 1986). The program set the occasion for the parents to make inaccessible various hazards such as poisons, fire and electrical problems, and items on which a child could suffocate or choke.

Another example of antecedent control involved Brian, a 6-year-old boy referred to Project Ecosystems by a pediatric neurologist because of seizures that were not controlled by medication (Kiesel, Lutzker, & Campbell, 1989). This project involves teaching parents skills that can prevent the foster placement of their children with developmental disabilities. It had been noted by Brian's teachers and mother that most of his seizures were preceded by hyperventilation. A functional analysis conducted in the home and at school confirmed this; it also showed that hyperventilation was preceded by demand situations or any transitions or changes. The goal of the treatment, therefore, was to change the antecedent events related to the chain of demand-hyperventilation-seizure.

To have Brian respond other than with hyperventilation to a demand situation or to change, the Project Ecosystems counselor provided him with behavioral relaxation training (BRT; Schilling & Poppen, 1983). This involved teaching postures that resemble the postures of individuals who have been taught to relax by imagery-oriented techniques such as progressive relaxation.

Teaching these skills to Brian involved modeling and social reinforcement. After he mastered the skills, he was taught to respond to the cue "open mouth." This cue was used by the counselor, the parents, and the teacher to remind Brian to relax. A multiple baseline design across settings, school, and home showed that the BRT reduced his hyperventilation: Not only was hyperventilation reduced to nearly zero, but so were the consequent seizures. Antecedent control procedures were effective in nearly eliminating a serious medical problem of a child with developmental disabilities.

Models, which involve a form of antecedent, were used to teach adult-child interaction skills to staff working for Project 12-Ways (Lutzker, Megson, Webb, & Dachman, 1985; McGimsey, Greene, & Lutzker, 1995). After a variety of professionals validated the skills that are important for adults to display when working with young children, teachers were filmed using these skills in a preschool classroom. Staff from Project 12-Ways were then filmed in their interactions with individual children. The entire training involved showing the staff the tapes of the teachers and pointing out to staff members any behaviors they lacked that were displayed by the model teachers. This modeling produced subsequent criterion performance by the staff members when they were reassessed in their interactions with different children.

Modeling has also been used to teach single parents health-related skills in caring for their young infants (Delgado & Lutzker, 1988). After 13 skills were validated by family-practice physicians as necessary in the care of infants, these skills were taught to the single parents using modeling and role-playing techniques. Not only did the parents master the skills, such as taking a temperature or distinguishing between two kinds of coughs, but they showed generalization of these skills when their children were actually ill, as reported by their physicians.

Almost all the parents who receive services from these projects (Lutzker & Doctor, 1994–1995) now receive planned-activities training (PAT). The focus of PAT is to establish antecedent control in preventing challenging behaviors. Project SafeCare teaches PAT, home safety, and infant health care skills to parents who have been involved in the justice system or are at high risk for child abuse and neglect. The emphasis of PAT is on antecedents, specifically on incidental teaching and the planning of activities or engagement as preventive strategies.

Incidental teaching (Hart & Risley, 1975) involves incorporating teaching moments into ordinary activities. For example, if a mother who has learned PAT takes her child to the grocery store, she will have multiple opportunities to use incidental teaching. As they push the shopping cart through the store, the mother might say, "We need cereal. Can you find the cereal in the yellow box?" After finding the yellow boxes of cereal, the mother might then ask, "Do you notice that there are big and little boxes of Cheerios? Pull out a big one." In this case the mother has at once engaged the child in the activity (shopping) and used a teaching moment productively.

Planning for this shopping activity would involve the mother's advising the child when they would go shopping, stating the rules of shopping (keep hands on the cart, never stray from mother), and reminding the child that following the rules leads to a treat, such as being able to buy a candy bar or a video. Prior to the shopping trip, the mother would have reviewed the PAT strategies, decided on the rules for shopping, and made a written or mental list of the incidental-teaching opportunities she might use during shopping.

Huynen, Lutzker, Touchette, and Campbell (in press) examined the generalized effects of PAT across settings and time. Four mothers and their children received PAT in their homes. Before and after training, generalization data were collected in a variety of settings, such as places in the home other than where training occurred and in many community settings such as video stores, the library, a dentist's office, a grocery store, and a shopping mall. All parents and children showed considerable improvement over baseline in these settings. Mothers clearly generalized the skills they learned in their homes, and child compliance and appropriate behavior were near maximum levels. The mothers reported considerable satisfaction with PAT and said that they were using it with their other children. Follow-up data collected 6 months after training showed strong maintenance of these gains.

PAT has proved to be an effective treatment tool for families with children with conduct disorder (Sanders & Dadds, 1982) and developmental disabilities. It has also been useful in training staff in a residential setting with patients suffering from chronic schizophrenia (Gershater, Lutzker, & Kuehnel, in press) and in a post-acute-care setting for traumatic brain injury (Lutzker, 1993). PAT is commonly seen in good teaching and parenting, and it is more natural than contingency-management training.

Prompting, goal setting, and simple reinforcement were used by Bigelow, Huynen, and Lutzker (1993) to teach fire-escape skills to an adolescent with developmental disabilities who lived in a group home. Prior to training, the young woman would not respond to warnings to leave the home during fire drills. The licensing personnel threatened to remove her from the home unless she could demonstrate an ability to respond appropriately to a fire drill. Using a changing-criterion design, she was gradually taught to leave the home in response to a verbal cue. Training began by placing the youngster very near the door and gently physically prompting her to leave in response to the cue. Each session, she was moved slightly further from the door, until eventually she went outside in response to the cue from anywhere in the home.

Campbell and Lutzker (1993) described teaching communication skills to a child who displayed highly disruptive, lengthy tantrums and self-injurious behavior. Once he and his parents learned these communication skills, the challenging behaviors were virtually eliminated without any direct treatment. Communication-skill training was used after a functional assessment suggested the tantrums and self-injury were a function of inability to communicate needs. Again, an antecedent (language) was used in the treatment of challenging behavior.

Conclusion

Antecedent events govern everyone's everyday behavior. It seems only logical that the most effective treatments that can be offered to families involved with the serious problem of child abuse and neglect or who have children with developmental disabilities would most resemble everyday life. For is not life salient antecedents and subtle consequences? If it is, should not treatment be similar?

References

Baer, D. M., Wolf, M. M., & Risley, T. R. (1968). Some current dimensions of applied behavior analysis. *Journal of Applied Behavior Analysis, 1,* 91–98.

Barone, V. J., Greene, B. F., and Lutzker, J. R. (1986). Home safety with families being treated for child abuse and neglect. *Behavior Modification, 10,* 93–114.

Bigelow, K. M., Huynen, K. B., & Lutzker, J. R. (1993). Using a changing criterion design to teach fire escape to a child with developmental disabilities. *Journal of Developmental and Physical Disabilities, 5,* 121–128.

Campbell, R. V., & Lutzker, J. R. (1993). Using functional equivalence training to reduce severe challenging behavior: A case study. *Journal of Developmental and Physical Disabilities, 5,* 203–215.

Delgado, L. E., & Lutzker, J. R. (1988). Training young parents to identify and report their children's illnesses. *Journal of Applied Behavior Analysis, 21,* 311–319.

Gershater, R. M., Lutzker, J. R., & Kuehnel, T. G. (in press). Activity scheduling to increase staff-patient interactions. *The Clinical Supervisor.*

Harrold, M., Lutzker, J. R., Campbell, R. V., & Huynen, K. B. (1992). Project Ecosystems: An ecobehavioral approach to families with children with developmental disabilities. *Journal of Developmental and Physical Disabilities, 4,* 1–14.

Hart, B. M., & Risley, T. R. (1975). Incidental teaching of language in the preschool. *Journal of Applied Behavior Analysis, 8,* 411–420.

Huynen, K. B., Lutzker, J. R., Touchette, P. E., & Campbell, R. V. (in press). Mothers of children with developmental disabilities: Community generalization and follow-up. *Behavior Modification.*

Kiesel, K. B., Lutzker, J. R., & Campbell, R. V. (1989). Behavioral relaxation training to reduce hyperventilation and seizures in a profoundly retarded epileptic child. *Journal of the Multihandicapped Person, 2,* 179–190.

Lutzker, J. R. (1984). Project 12-Ways: Treating child abuse and neglect from an ecobehavioral perspective. In R. F. Dangel & R. A. Polster (Eds.), *Parent training: Foundations of research and practice* (pp. 260–291). New York: Guilford Press.

Lutzker, J. R. (1993, February 18–20). *Engagement: Another name for stimulus control. Treating families, head injury, development disabilities.* Invited address at the 12th annual conference of the Northern California Association for Behavior Analysis, Oakland, CA.

Lutzker, J. R., Campbell, R. V., Harrold, M., & Huynen, K. (1992). Project Ecosystems: An ecobehavioral approach to families with children with developmental disabilities. *Journal of Developmental and Physical Disabilities, 4,* 1–14.

Lutzker, J. R., & Doctor, R. M. (1994–1995, Fall-Winter). Project SafeCare: Health, safety and bonding with child abusive and high-risk mothers and their children. *Cal-ABA Newsletter,* 4–5.

Lutzker, J. R., Megson, D. A., Webb, M. E., & Dachman, R. S. (1985). Validation and training adult-child interaction skills to professionals and to parents indicted for child abuse and neglect. *Journal of Child and Adolescent Psychotherapy, 2,* 91–104.

Lutzker, S. Z., Lutzker, J. R., Braunling-McMorrow, D., & Eddleman, J. (1987). Prompting to increase mother-baby stimulation with single mothers. *Journal of Child and Adolescent Psychotherapy, 4,* 3–12.

McGimsey, J. M., Greene, B. F., & Lutzker, J. R. (1995). Competence in aspects of behavioral treatment and consultation: Implications for service delivery and graduate training. *Journal of Applied Behavior Analysis, 28,* 301–315.

Sanders, M. R., & Dadds, M. R. (1982). The effects of planned activities and child management training: An analysis of setting generality. *Behavior Therapy, 13,* 1–11.

Sarber, R. E., Halasz, M. M., Messmer, M. C., Bickett, A. D., & Lutzker, J. R. (1983). Teaching menu planning and grocery shopping skills to a mentally retarded mother. *Mental Retardation, 21,* 101–106.

Schilling, D. J., & Poppen, R. (1983). Behavioral relaxation training and assessment. *Journal of Behavior Therapy and Experimental Psychiatry, 14,* 99–107.

Stokes, T., & Baer, D. M. (1977). An implicit technology of generalization. *Journal of Applied Behavior Analysis, 10,* 349–367.

Training Adult-Day-Care Staff

Yosikazu S. DeRoos and Elsie M. Pinkston

In this study of adult day care, direct-service staff were taught to be more effective caregivers. Specifically, they were taught four behavioral skills sufficient to make them effective caregivers: behavioral task analysis, contracting, cueing, and reinforcement. The first three of these skills were stimulus-control procedures.

Community-based adult-day-care centers are an alternative to institutional care, an alternative that can preserve self-maintenance and family-centered life (Bogner, 1978). By 1990, there were more than 3,000 of them in the United States (National Institute on Adult Day Care, personal communication, November 12, 1993). Unfortunately, according to Rathbone-McCuan and Weiler (1978), some centers foster dependency rather than independence. Weissert (1975) also found that some centers excluded those with behavioral difficulties in toileting or talking: behaviors that respond to environmental intervention. These facts underscore the need for staff training that addresses behavioral deficits and excesses and enhances independent functioning.

Because most agency administrators prefer a training program that minimally disrupts agency routine, we designed a behavioral training program to (a) incorporate training into the normal activities of staffs and agencies and (b) teach adult-day-care staff skills sufficient for behavior management. This chapter evaluates the new abilities of the program-trained adult-day-care staff to support their clients' behavior.

The usual training of institutional staff uses verbal, visual, or written techniques, such as lectures, discussions, reading materials, and slides (Hersen & Bellack, 1978). These methods are informative and useful for increasing caregivers' knowledge about general behavioral principles. However, they generally do not teach the skills but *about* the skills and procedures (Cuff, 1977; Delameter, Conners, & Wells, 1984; Gardner, 1972; Schinke & Wong, 1977). They have little or no effect in developing the skills (Bernstein, 1982; Delameter et al., 1984). They are most useful when combined with other methods (Kazdin, 1994; McMahon, Forehand, & Griest, 1981).

Effective methods include use of clear cues and instructions (Pinkston & Herbert-Jackson, 1975); modeling and rehearsing the desired behavior (Gladstone & Spencer, 1977; Pinkston, Levitt, Green, Linsk, & Rzepnicki, 1982); feedback to trainees about their performance (Bernstein, 1982; Parsonson, Baer, & Baer, 1974); reinforcement to increase the desired behavior (Delameter et al., 1984); and various combinations of these methods (Dancer et al., 1978; Jones & Eimers, 1975; Koegel, Russo, & Rincover, 1977). These procedures are effective not only for staff training, but also for the clients (Gajar, Schloss, Schloss, & Thompson, 1984; Hoyer, 1973; Schulman, Suran, Stevens, & Kupst, 1979; Turner, Hersen, & Bellack, 1978).

Research on staff and parent training shows that modeling, instructions, feedback, and cueing are effective. They provide information about specific skills, how and when to perform them, their results, and what should happen next (Pinkston et al., 1982). In short, pairing information about skill with its performance is effective staff training. If the information is also reinforcing, the training procedure should be even more effective.

Method

Participants and Setting

Data were gathered on 13 caregivers at four adult-day-care centers. They consisted of 1 African-American and 12 Caucasian females. Their ages ranged from 21 to 51, and their education ranged from a high school diploma to a master's degree. Some were registered nurses, licensed practical nurses, social workers, recreational therapists, or physical therapists; others had no formal professional training. Initially, all direct-care staff at the four centers took part in training. Eleven caregivers completed the training; a 12th resigned from her position during training; and a 13th withdrew from training to take on the departed staff member's workload. Twelve had been required by their supervisor or agency director to participate in the training. The thirteenth participant, the staff member who withdrew from training, was an agency director who had volunteered to participate.

All four day-care centers were in the greater Chicago area. The largest of them had four caregivers, and the smallest had two.

Research Design

We used a pretest-posttest single-group design with data gathered before and after 10 training sessions. Data were collected on the adult-day-care staff using four behavioral observation scales focusing on task analysis, cueing, contracting, and reinforcement. After pretest data were collected, the adult-day-care staff took part in orientation and training. At the end of the 10 training sessions, posttest data were gathered. Behavior-analytic methods were used for data analysis.

Instruments Used

The behavioral observation scales (adapted from Budd & Fabry, 1984) consisted of four item sets, one each to record data on task analysis, cueing, behavioral contracting, and reinforcement (see Table 22.1). The data for these scales were collected through direct observation of the staff members' behaviors or evaluation of their written products. One of two trainers observed staff performance or written products. Interrater reliability, assessed between the two trainers, ranged from 89 to 100 percent.

Observation and data collection concerning these four skills occurred immediately before and immediately after 10 sessions of training. Each caregiver taking part in training was observed performing each of the four skills.

For pre- and posttest data collection, the trainer asked each staff member to perform the four skills, one at a time. The observer recorded staff performance on

TABLE 22.1   The Four Behavioral Skills

Behavioral Contracting
1. Gets client's attention
2. Identifies for client the activity or task to be performed
3. Specifies subtasks to be completed by client
4. Specifies subtasks to be completed by staff
5. Specifies when the activity or task is to occur
6. Specifies where the activity or task is to occur
7. Specifies who will participate in the activity or task
8. Specifies the consequences contingent on completing the task
9. Specifies when the consequences will be delivered
10. Completes a written contract

Cueing
1. Gets client's attention
2. Gives clear instruction
3. Repeats instruction if necessary
4. Offers physical guidance if necessary

Reinforcement
1. Identifies behavior to be reinforced
2. Contingently delivers direct reinforcement
3. Contingently delivers indirect reinforcement

Task Analysis
1. Selects a client with a behavior to be increased
2. Describes the behavior to be increased
3. Lists steps the client will need to perform to accomplish the behavior
4. Lists materials the client may need to carry out the behavior
5. Lists staff instructions in steps or cues to the client regarding the behavior to be increased
6. Describes circumstances under which the client is most likely to succeed in accomplishing the behavior

an observation form. Each staff member was given 8–10 minutes to perform each of the skills.

Data analysis consisted of the assessment of staff performance according to the criteria defining the four behavioral skills, as listed in Table 22.1. Each step in a skill was scored as 1 if it was completed correctly and as 0 if otherwise. Correct steps were divided by the number of steps required for that skill to yield an overall percentage of success for the training program.

Training Project

The training program consisted of 15 sessions, the first 10 for training and the last 5 for single-case evaluations of training. This report focuses on the 10 training sessions. The training focused on staff and client skills rather than on problems; therefore, it used reinforcement without punishment. That focus avoided the perspective of many adult-day-care centers, nursing homes, and similar institutions: the quasimedical focus on client problems and deficits (Barker, 1987). To improve the quality of clients' lives requires more than reducing or eliminating problems. Increasing opportunities for responses that lead to positive experiences is better than only addressing problems. Because many clients' problems cannot be ameliorated medically, we used a social-support model focused on existing strengths, and we developed or redeveloped and maintained prosocial behaviors.

Staff members were trained as a group during at least part of each training session. Most sessions included both group and individual training. Most sessions began with a review of material from the previous session and presentation of new material. Including the group and individual work, training sessions for each caregiver took from 15 to 30 minutes per session. Some sessions required staff members to complete homework. Each session focused on one topic and built the skills taught in previous sessions. Training centered on teaching the four behavioral procedures: task analysis, contracting, cueing, and reinforcement. Training took place during working hours and in the areas where activities normally took place. Skills transfer to the work setting, always an issue in training, was obviated by conducting the training in the environment in which the caregivers worked and with clients with whom they routinely worked; the desired stimulus controls were established *directly*, not by generalization.

The four skills were defined as follows: *Cueing* refers to symbols, signs, or simple instructions to start or stop an action (Bernstein, 1982). A *task analysis* specifies the cues required for a client to perform a complex behavior, or a set of related behaviors, to complete some task; it also specifies the relationship between the cues and the behaviors. A *behavioral contract* is an agreement between the caregiver and the client defining the contingencies between the performance of some behaviors and the reinforcers that will result (Pinkston et al., 1982). It makes explicit and negotiable the behavioral expectations of both client and caregiver. A *reinforcer* is any event occurring after a behavior that increases the likelihood the behavior will recur.

We conducted training at a time designated by most staff as convenient for them. When a caregiver missed a session, we rescheduled her session. We scheduled some sessions during times when staff were assigned to work with clients; this gave caregivers the opportunity to use their skills with clients during regular work activities.

Each training session consisted of the following:

1. A group review and discussion of the previous session's material
2. Group instruction by the trainer about the skill or task of the week, followed by discussion
3. Observation by the trainer of each staff member applying the skill or carrying out the task with a client or client group
4. The trainer cueing and giving feedback and positive reinforcement (a) as caregivers completed the activity or task, (b) after the staff member completed the exercise, and (c) during the review at the next training session

Results

Data from the behavioral observation scales, shown in Table 22.2 and Figure 22.1, revealed varying degrees of success. On the pretest for task analysis, a mean of 45 percent of the steps were performed correctly; at posttest the percentage rose to over 81 percent. The combined percentage rose from a mean of 46 percent at pretest to 80 percent at posttest. For behavioral contracting, a mean of 31 percent of the steps were completed correctly at pretest, and that rose to 71 percent at posttest. Cueing was performed correctly 75 percent of the time at pretest and 95 percent at posttest. For reinforcement, a mean of 32 percent of the steps were completed correctly at pretest, compared to 73 percent at posttest. When summarized, the results from the four scales show considerable improvement from pretest to posttest.

Depending on the particular skill, 9, 10, or 11 persons produced both pretest and posttest scores, making 42 paired scores. Of these 42 paired scores, 32 were higher and 2 were lower at posttest, and 8 showed no change. Of the last 8, 4 showed full success at both pretest and posttest.

These results, in which 23 of 41 posttest scores were at 80 percent or above, with an overall success rate of 80.2 percent at posttest, clearly indicate both a substantial positive change from pretest to posttest and an overall level of success for those who took part in the training. The training program is clearly useful.

TABLE 22.2 Behavioral Observation Scale Pretest, Posttest, and Difference Scores: Percentage of Successful Steps

Caregiver	Behavioral contracting			Cueing			Reinforcement			Task analysis		
	Pre	Post	Diff	Pre	Post	Diff	Pre	Post	Diff	Pre	Post	Diff
1A	70	70	0	54	75	21	33	67	34	67	80	13
1B	10	40	30	100	100	0	11	11	0	50	83	33
1C	0	100	100	100	100	0	11	78	67	17	83	66
1D	80	80	0	83	100	17	56	100	44	40	83	43
2A	67	70	3	25	100	75	67	78	11	50	83	33
2B	0	70	70	75	100	25	44	78	34	20	83	63
3A		100		67	100	33	56	78	22	60	83	23
3B	0	82	82	100	100	0	22	67	45	50	67	17
3C		82		100	100	0	0	89	89	100	83	-17
4A	25			38			0			83		
4B	40			50			11			0		
4C	0	40	40	75	100	25	33	78	45	17	83	66
4D	50	50	0	100	75	-25	67	78	11	33	83	50
Mean	31.1	71.3	40.2	74.4	95.4	21.0	31.6	72.9	41.3	45.2	81.3	36.1
Mdn	25.0	80.0	55.0	75.2	99.9	24.7	32.8	77.9	45.1	49.7	82.9	33.2

Note: For pretest, *N* = 13 except for behavioral contracting, in which *N* = 11. For posttest, *N* = 11. Score percentages may range from 0%, indicating none of the behaviors in a given task were completed correctly, to 100%, indicating all behaviors were completed correctly.

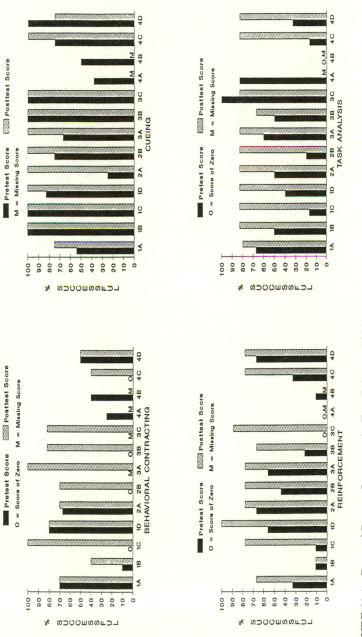

FIGURE 22.1   Pre- and Posttest Scores on the Four Behavioral Skills

Discussion

The training program taught adult-day-care staff skills sufficient to bring about positive behavior change in their clients. Although many training programs have done that, this one demonstrated that caregiver training can be conducted during working hours in the adult-day-care setting. That aspect should have considerable appeal to directors who cannot remove staff for long periods of time. Because this program is done in the work setting, staff can resolve work-related problems while they take part in the training.

The differences in staff success between pretest and posttest lead us to recommend modifying the training program to include repeated trials of skills until each staff member achieves a minimum of 80 percent success in that skill. Although a higher rate would be desirable, the time required to achieve it might make the program too long.

Future research might focus on how to teach the four behavioral skills more rapidly and completely. The program can be refined to minimize the time needed for training and improve training effectiveness. Development and evaluation of maintenance procedures would be useful. Behavior theory predicts that the effective application of the skills would help to maintain their use, although other factors may affect whether that occurs. One way to maintain their use is to have periodic refresher sessions that reteach and reinforce the skills, which would also allow the trainers to monitor the maintenance of the skills. The same evaluation tools used in this study would be useful to determine changes in skills over time.

Acknowledgments

We thank the Retirement Research Foundation for their funding of the research reported in this chapter and the Andrus Foundation for funding the research from which we developed an earlier version of these procedures.

References

Barker, R. L. (1987). *The social work dictionary*. Silver Springs, MD: National Association of Social Workers.

Bernstein, G. S. (1982). Training behavior change agents: A conceptual review. *Behavior Therapy, 13*, 1–23.

Bogner, B. J. (1978, November). *Social model day care: Funding programming and evaluation*. Paper presented at the 31st annual scientific meeting of the Gerontological Society, Dallas, TX.

Budd, K. S., & Fabry, P. (1984). Behavioral assessment in applied parent training: Use of a structural observational system. In R. F. Dangel & R. A. Polster (Eds.), *Parent training: Foundations of research and practice*. New York: Guilford Press.

Cuff, G. N. (1977). A strategy for evaluating a short course on behavior modification. *Mental Retardation, 2*, 48.

Dancer, D. D., Braukmann, L. J., Schumaker, J. B., Kirigin, K. A., Willner, A. G., & Wolf, M. M. (1978). The training and validation of behavior observation and description skills. *Behavior Modification, 2*, 113–134.

Delameter, A. M., Conners, C. K., & Wells, K. C. (1984). A comparison of staff training procedures: Behavioral application in the child psychiatric inpatient setting. *Behavior Modification, 8,* 39–58.

Gajar, A., Schloss, P. J., Schloss, C. N., & Thompson, C. K. (1984). Effects of feedback and self-monitoring on head trauma youths' conversation skills. *Journal of Applied Behavior Analysis, 17,* 353–358.

Gardner, J. A. (1972). Teaching behavior modification to nonprofessionals. *Journal of Applied Behavior Analysis, 5,* 517–521.

Gladstone, B. W., & Spencer, C. J. (1977). The effects of modelling on the contingent praise of mental retardation counsellors. *Journal of Applied Behavior Analysis, 10,* 75–84.

Hersen, M., & Bellack, A. S. (1978). Staff training and consultation. In M. Hersen & A. S. Bellack (Eds.), *Behavior therapy in a psychiatric setting.* Baltimore: William & Wilkens.

Hoyer, W. J. (1973). Application of operant techniques to the modification of elderly behavior. *Gerontologist, 13,* 18–22.

Jones, F. H., & Eimers, R. C. (1975). Role playing to train elementary teachers to use a classroom management "skill package." *Journal of Applied Behavior Analysis, 8,* 421–433.

Koegel, R. L., Russo, D. C., & Rincover, A. (1977). Assessing and training teachers in the generalized use of behavior modification with autistic children. *Journal of Applied Behavior Analysis, 10,* 197–205.

McMahon, R. J., Forehand, R., & Griest, D. L. (1981). Effects of knowledge on social learning principles on enhancing treatment outcome and generalization in a parent training program. *Journal of Consulting and Clinical Psychology, 49,* 526–532.

Parsonson, B. S., Baer, A. M., & Baer, D. M. (1974). The application of generalized correct social contingencies: An evaluation of a training program. *Journal of Applied Behavior Analysis, 7,* 427–437.

Pinkston, E. M., & Herbert-Jackson, E. W. (1975). Modification of irrelevant and bizarre verbal behavior using mother as therapist. *Social Service Review, 49,* 46–63.

Pinkston, E. M., Levitt, J. L., Green, G. R., Linsk, N. L., & Rzepnicki, T. L. (1982). *Effective social work practice.* San Francisco: Jossey-Bass.

Rathbone-McCuan, E., & Weiler, P. G. (1978). *Adult day care.* New York: Springer.

Schinke, S. P., & Wong, S. E. (1977). Evaluation of staff training in group homes for retarded persons. *American Journal of Mental Deficiency, 82,* 130–136.

Schulman, J. L., Suran, B. G., Stevens, T. M., & Kupst, M. J. (1979). Instructions, feedback, and reinforcement in reducing activity levels in the classroom. *Journal of Applied Behavior Analysis, 12,* 441–447.

Turner, S. M., Hersen, M., & Bellack, A. S. (1978). Social skills training to teach prosocial behaviors in an organically impaired and retarded patient. *Journal of Behaviour Therapy and Experimental Psychiatry, 9,* 253–258.

Weissert, W. G. (1975, September). *A final report: Adult day care in the United States.* Washington, DC: National Center for Health Service Research.

A Supportive Environment for Old Age

Elsie M. Pinkston

Problems of Aging

In the United States, the family is the primary unit for the delivery of development and nurturance (Atchley, 1972). Most people are born into a family, and most people live their lives and die in a family. It is our most basic social institution, and it recently has become a political unit in proposed solutions to the problems of aging. This chapter examines the problems of caring for the elderly and describes the development of a prosthetic environment to support solutions to those problems.

Neugarten (1990) declared that "long life is a major achievement of the 20th century in all developed countries of the world" (p. 28). How we age is a topic that interests most of us; we observe it in our parents and their parents, and finally we see and feel it in ourselves. Noting great diversity in the aging experience, Neugarten coined the terms *young-old* and *old-old* to denote social and health characteristics: Young-old individuals are the vigorous and competent; old-old individuals are "those who suffer major physical, mental, or social losses, and who require a range of supportive and restorative health and social services" (p. 33).

The stubborn view that aging is a disease has led to the coining of the term *oldest-old,* overturning Neugarten's focus on diversity and returning to an age-based criterion, in this case 85+ years. Yet preliminary descriptions of the oldest-old suggest that "the older people get the more heterogeneous they become" (Neugarten, 1990); therefore, these terms are not particularly helpful to us. The positive news is that about 80 percent of people over 65 fall into the young-old group; only about 20 percent are in the old-old category; and only about 1 percent are by age in the oldest-old group (although the projection for the year 2030 is 3 percent).

An American myth is that we do not care for our elderly. Despite research findings to the contrary, this myth continues. It is true that most elderly people are not cared for by their families, but that is because they tend to care for themselves and lead vigorous or at least independent lives.

Most people do care for their elderly family members when it is necessary. Research indicates that women, despite their changing work patterns, expect to continue that care (Doty, 1986; Washington & Pinkston, 1986). Only 1 percent of the elderly between the ages of 65 and 74 are in nursing homes. (Men may take heart because two-thirds of those are women.) From ages 74 to 84, only 6 percent of men and women are in nursing homes, but beyond age 85, 22 percent are.

In middle age, we begin to lose the connection we had with the young community through our children. Between ages 65 and 75, we lose our work roles and associations, and we move to smaller living spaces or struggle with increased maintenance costs. Between the ages of 75 and 79, we lose the ability to drive; we rely on others for transportation and need more supportive housing. Finally, we need many more supportive services. Important environmental losses are associated with old age, with few positive compensations. Approximately one-third of elderly persons report that their life is better than they expected, and about 10 percent say it is worse (Harris, 1975). However, for nearly one-third of the elderly, health eventually becomes a problem. This problem can be addressed at home, in the community, or by institutional care.

Problems associated with old age are too frequently thought of as physiological. Too much of that view distracts attention from what are actually failing environmental structures and breakdowns of general support systems. Additionally, the problems of the elderly are frequently described as involving daily living activities, social behavior, indirect self-destructive behavior, low rates of physical activity, verbal and physical antisocial behavior, and incontinence (Pinkston & Linsk, 1984a, 1984b; Pinkston, Linsk, & Young, 1988). These problems may not result from age itself but from an ineffective learning history, the current absence of opportunities to respond, or the absence of support. If so, the problem is not some form of psychopathology. We can enhance general mental health by increasing people's ability to obtain their reinforcers and avoid negative consequences (Pinkston & Linsk, 1984b).

This type of enhancement may be possible for caregivers as well as those who receive their care (Pinkston & Linsk, 1984b). Caregiving is likely to reduce the caregiver's usual reinforcers and, more important, increase their aversive conditions. The literature on caregiver stress suggests a third factor: The caregiver may have difficulty achieving both accustomed performances and the additional duties associated with caregiving. All three mechanisms can reduce productive responding (Pinkston et al., 1989). Caregiving too often demands more and more work while one watches the deterioration of a beloved person, with increasingly reduced opportunities for both interpersonal and material gratification. Stress and emotional problems are the usual costs of caregiving, but they are not the problem; they are the result of the problem. The problem is an unsupportive environment. The solution to the problem requires a focus on contexts and must build on existing environmental resources.

Initially, most behavior research on aging was directed toward mentally impaired nursing home residents (for reviews, see Burgio & Burgio, 1986; Carstensen, 1988). Nursing homes invite the extension of procedures developed for other institutional populations. However, even the most impaired people can be helped to the extent that organicity will allow. "Excess disability" (Kahn, 1965) is often a result of contextual variables. It has been found that altering only social- and physical-environment variables can improve the behavior of elders (Hoyer, 1973; Linsk, Howe, & Pinkston, 1975; MacDonald, 1978; McClannahan, 1973).

Behavioral Approaches to Assistance

Treatment procedures for mental health problems in this population are particularly important to long-term care providers, families, practitioners, and gerontologists. With limited resources, increased awareness of the limits of long-term care arrangements, and an increasing population of older persons with behavioral difficulties, the development of mental health interventions is essential. Specific programs are needed to help caregivers deal with problematic behavior patterns such as incontinence and to integrate technologies into professional-practice procedures (Linsk, Hanrahan, & Pinkston, 1991). Initial studies have developed and tested short-term intervention models that are helpful in improving specific behavior problems such as repetitive and bizarre behaviors, poor self-maintenance, and withdrawal from social activities. These problems provoke unnecessary institutional placement (Simos, 1973; Tobin & Lieberman, 1976; York & Calsyn, 1977). Instead, we need to teach the technology that can improve these problems and to design better caregiving environments both in the community and in nursing homes.

A Home-Based Intervention

My colleagues and I have developed effective operant procedures to be used with seriously impaired elderly living at home (Green, Linsk, & Pinkston, 1986; Linsk, Pinkston, & Green, 1982; Pinkston & Linsk, 1984a, 1884b). We have found that family caregivers of the elderly can implement behavioral methods; that stimulus control and reinforcement are particularly useful; that behavioral family interventions reduce excesses and deficits of the impaired elderly; that caregivers improve their skills, as institutional staff have in previous research; and that single-case methods help to plan and implement interventions as well as evaluate results.

Our 66 clients all had a caregiver who let us apply the behavior family-training research. Our clients were at least 60 years old, had physical or psychological problems, showed "excess disability" (Kahn, 1965), behaved badly, and used very little of the available community resources. Besides being able to participate in the efforts to change behavior, the caregivers had time for the program, were motivated (adversely affected by the client's behavior), had access to the client's important consequences, had adequate skills or the ability to learn skills, and were in good mental and physical health.

The elderly support program (ESP) was implemented in seven steps: (a) referral; (b) assessment; (c) definition of excesses and deficits and recording of baseline data; (d) education of support persons; (e) development of intervention plan using contracting, modeling, cueing, and reinforcement; (f) development of a plan for maintenance of intervention effects; and (g) follow-up. (For a detailed description of the program, see Pinkston & Linsk, 1984b.)

Research Design.   Single-case designs (Baer, Wolf, & Risley, 1968) were used to evaluate the effects of intervention by comparing baseline observations with intervention observations. Clinical multiple-baseline designs (Pinkston, Levitt, Green, Linsk, & Rzepnicki, 1982)—multiple-baseline and AB (baseline, treatment)—were used most frequently if the behavior problems under study were not life threatening. These designs showed caregivers the power of their interventions. Pre- and posttests determined the mental status and other demographic characteristics of the clients and their caregivers.

We used direct observations by clients, families, and research staff. The primary observers were usually family members; reliability observations were made by staff members other than the practitioner. These observations were recorded using time-sampling (Baer et al., 1968) and on checklists.

Results.   Our 66 clients had serious impairments: Their mental status scores averaged 54 on a scale ranging from 0 to 100. On scales ranging from 1 to 6, in which 6 represents the most impaired, their physical health rated a mean of 5.57, and their mental health averaged 4.12. The mean for their activities of daily living was 4.77, for social resources was 3.00, and for economic resources was 2.36 (Pfeiffer, 1976).

The average age of the clients was 73; the male-to-female ratio was 45:55; and 66 percent were white and 34 percent black. The clients' marital status was 58 percent married, 36 percent widowed, and the rest divorced or single. Their mean income was $13,020, with 56 percent of them living in their own homes.

The mean age of the caregivers was 64; 75 percent of them were female. Their relationships to the clients were as follows: 45 percent spouse, 28 percent child, and the rest spread evenly among siblings, friends, or other relatives.

In keeping with the behavioral clinical approach, 86 percent of the interventions were aimed at increasing desirable behaviors. Improvements in behavior occurred in 76 percent of the cases; they were sometimes small, but they were valued by these caregivers.

Failures to improve were associated with poor health of the caregiver, a nonreversible physical condition of the client, and in a few cases, refusal by the caregiver to record data and implement the program. Caregivers reported a greater degree of personal competence following training; they said they felt more able to cope with their problems. However, they did not show a significant decrease in scores on the Zarit Burden Scale (Zarit, Reever, & Bachman-Peterson, 1980).

These procedures fulfilled the promise shown in earlier research with depressed and demented elderly clients at home; the study added to the literature concerning research conducted in nursing homes with a similarly impaired population of elderly people. It is apparent that caregivers can be taught to use behavioral procedures including contracting, cueing (verbal and physical), modeling, and differential reinforcement, and thereby can provide a more prosthetic environment for maintaining elderly people at home.

Nursing Home Interventions

Taking good care of nursing home residents is largely a matter of behavior: the staff's and the residents' behavior. From the residents' point of view, the most important part of a nursing home environment is the behavior of the staff. Behavioral science has developed useful procedures that can add an important structure to that environment. These procedures are useful in staff training, and they prevent or remediate the excessive disability many residents develop in response to the distinctive emotional and environmental dimensions of a nursing home (Brody, Kleban, Lawton, & Silverman, 1971; Kahn, 1965). When disabilities suddenly exceed the biologically determined ones, some simple alterations of the environment and of the current social patterns can help significantly. Pioneering examples have been provided by Baltes and Barton (1977), Hoyer (1973), McClannahan and Risley (1974), Linsk et al. (1975), and MacDonald (1978).

Subsequently, experimentally controlled studies added many more procedures to improve the behavior and quality of life of mentally and physically impaired elderly people. The single-case designs of these studies offered staff and practitioners immediately applicable procedures and a clear demonstration of exactly how well they had worked to improve behaviors of the individuals and groups. This evaluation is accomplished by comparing resident behaviors between baseline and intervention to assess improvement and to discover the power of the variables responsible for it.

The methods of behavioral gerontology have been used in institutions to treat a wide range of problems (Hussian, 1981). These issues include self-care (Baltes & Zerbe, 1976; Mishara, Robertson, & Kastenbaum, 1974), incontinence (Atthowe, 1972), adherence to medical regimens (Dapcich-Miura & Hovell, 1979), walking (MacDonald & Butler, 1974), and improved participation in social activities (Hoyer, Kafer, Simpson, & Hoyer, 1974; McClannahan & Risley, 1974). Behavioral approaches are just beginning to be used in community settings (Wheeler & Knight, 1981; Zarit, 1980).

A behavioral view of the mental and physical impairments in the elderly leads to the development of prosthetic environments for them (Pinkston & Linsk, 1984a). Behavioral procedures involve an interaction among specific deficiencies or disabilities; program opportunities for reinforcement; and the availability, clarity, and salience of the stimuli or cues that signal those opportunities. We should understand the developing deficiencies and disabilities in terms of what valuable reinforcers are being lost because skills that used to achieve them are lost and what cues to the opportunity for achieving them are losing salience or relevance; at that point, we can look for other, more salient cues to signal new opportunities. The new ways and their cues make up the therapeutic, prosthetic environment, represented by the staff. Behavioral gerontology emphasizes staff when it analyzes the living environments of the elderly and redesigns them (Hussian, 1981; Hussian & Davis, 1985; McClannahan & Risley, 1974).

Investigations typically include assessment, analysis, treatment, evaluation of treatment outcome, and proof that the change was attributable to the intervention. Taken as a whole, these investigations constitute a substantial procedure bank. Some of these procedures decrease negative behaviors, but most teach newly useful skills or recover recently lost ones. Others create a dependably stimulating environment.

The most relevant self-care goals are usually the activities of daily living, including eating, dressing, cleanliness, elimination, walking, and exercise. The procedures found useful in developing or recovering independent eating, for example, include staff cueing, modeling, feedback, redirection, and positive reinforcement, especially social reinforcement (Baltes & Zerbe, 1976; Blackman, Gehle, & Pinkston, 1979; Quattrochi-Tubin & Jason, 1980). All these procedures are relatively simple; they assume the practitioner has the resources to couple them with tray preparations, cut-up meat, open milk cartons, and the like. Carried out correctly, these procedures result in more independent eating with minimal help from others, as well as a more normal dining environment.

Incontinence is an example of great importance in most settings and consequently was targeted early in the development of behavioral gerontology. A variety of reasonably effective procedures have been developed (Pinkston, Howe, & Blackman, 1987). These procedures involved prompts that opportunities to void existed. Interest continues today; Burgio and his colleagues conducted a long-range study of intervention procedures (Burgio, Engel, Hawkins, McCormick, Scheve, & Jones, 1990) and of staff training in the application of those procedures (Burgio et al., 1990). Similarly, Schnelle and his colleagues have used prompted voiding successfully with large numbers of residents (Schnelle, 1990; Schnelle, Traughber, Sowell, & Newman, 1989). These independent studies have presented convincing evidence of the effectiveness of behavioral techniques.

Many similar examples with other behavioral targets use prompting, assistance, goal setting, and praise to recover a significant amount of independence for the elderly resident, rather than resort to an apparently safer but more restrictive environment. (For reviews, see Burgio & Burgio, 1986; Carstensen, 1988.)

Many behavioral gerontologists, like behaviorists working in other areas of mental health or disability, see the recovery, maintenance, extension, expansion, and development of positive activities as both remedial and preventive of many pathological behavior patterns, patterns such as systematic self-stimulation, self-injury, aggression, destruction, tantrums, and passivity. So much of undesirable behavior develops as the resident's most efficient way to recover social contact; it occurs in an environment that no longer matches the needs of the residents. Even inactivity often represents a response to the present environment, and it is particularly self-destructive in its closing of opportunities for stimulation and a better quality of life.

It is essential to *program* activities for the elderly—not only exercise activities (Perkins, Rapp, Carlson, & Wallace, 1986), but also compliance with a nearly inevitable medical regimen of medications. McClannahan and Risley (1974) compared a number of procedures to motivate such activities and found the combination of staff reinforcement with its salient discriminative cues particularly effective for structured social activities. They found that program materials could be made into sufficiently salient cues for activities, thus decreasing staff costs. Following that strategy, Blackman, Howe, and Pinkston (1976) rearranged part of a nursing home environment to accomplish the same goal: Using a naturalistic arrangement, they changed the time for early-morning coffee, tea, and juice and moved the activity from the dining room to the solarium to reinforce the residents' social proximity. That change made the new time and place both the cue and the reinforcement for groupings of residents that were quite different from the usual stations—awaiting breakfast isolated just outside the door of their private rooms. They became a group with the potential for conversation over a pre-breakfast drink. Like so many of the interventions described here, this one required no special materials or equipment, only a rearrangement of the existing environment. Similarly, Stock and Milan (1993) used prompts, feedback, and praise to improve dietary choices, mostly to get clients to choose healthier desserts.

Just as the environment can be rearranged, so can staff work patterns; again, relatively small rearrangements can produce exceptional changes in resident participation. For example, teaching staff to ask more systematic questions increased the frequency of impaired elderly residents' participation and talking in a social group (Linsk et al., 1975). As a result, the group leader no longer did most of the talking; her role changed from lecturer to participant.

Although the best targets of behavior management are the residents' positive skills, negative behaviors can be so aversive they demand treatment first. Behaviors like repetitive screaming (Cariaga, Burgio, Flynn, & Martin, 1991), self-injury (Mishara, Robertson, & Kastenbaum, 1974), and the repetitive stereotypes typical of tardive dyskinesia have been reduced by simply reinforcing desirable behaviors incompatible with them (Albanese & Gardner, 1977; Jackson, 1980). The remediation of screaming still attracts more and more refined experimental analysis; we may soon have procedures not only to reinforce attractive incompatible alternatives, but also to change staff behavior to reduce the cues for screaming and make more salient the cues for its desirable behavior.

The enhancement of memory and orientation and the reduction of confusion in the elderly have been targeted as well for behavior reprogramming (Eisdorfer, Cohen, & Preston, 1978). Bourgeois (1990) brought that focus to recovering and developing the memory aids necessary for effective conversation, especially for residents with Alzheimer's disease. These techniques are effective; they increase residents' responsiveness, make them more coherent, and allow lengthier effective social disclosure.

All of these examples are illustrative of a much larger literature. At present, that literature continues to grow, although slowly; its newest studies represent unusually careful and analytic solutions to the major problems that still trouble nursing home staffs and residents and the residents' families. This literature makes clear that these procedures can be made to work effectively and efficiently.

References

Albanese, H., & Gardner, K. (1977). Biofeedback treatment of tardive dyskinesia: Two case reports. *American Journal of Psychiatry, 134,* 1149–1150.

Atchley, R. C. (1972). *The social forces in later life: An introduction to social gerontology.* Belmont, CA: Wadsworth Press.

Atthowe, J. (1972). Controlling nocturnal enuresis in severely disabled and chronic patients. *Behavior Therapy, 3,* 232–239.

Baer, D. M., Wolf, M. M., & Risley, T. R. (1968). Some current dimensions of applied behavior analysis. *Journal of Applied Behavior Analysis, 1,* 9–97.

Baer, D. M., Wolf, M. M., & Risley, T. R. (1987). Some still-current dimensions of applied behavior analysis. *Journal of Applied Behavior Analysis, 20,* 313–327.

Baltes, M. M., & Barton, E. M. (1977). New approaches toward aging: A case for the operant model. *Educational Gerontology, 2,* 383–405.

Baltes, M. M., & Zerbe, M. B. (1976). Independent training in nursing home residents. *The Gerontologist, 16,* 428–432.

Blackman, D. K., Gehle, C., & Pinkston, E. M. (1979). Modifying eating habits of the institutionalized elderly. *Social Work Research and Abstracts, 15,* 18–24.

Blackman, D. K., Howe, M., & Pinkston, E. M. (1976). Increasing participation in social interaction of the institutionalized elderly. *The Gerontologist, 16,* 69–76.

Bourgeois, M. S. (1990). Enhancing conversation skills in patients with Alzheimer's disease using a prosthetic memory aid. *Journal of Applied Behavior Analysis, 23,* 29–42.

Brody, E. M., Kleban, M. H., Lawton, M. P., & Silverman, H. A. (1971). Excess disability of mentally impaired aged: Impact of individualized treatment. *The Gerontologist, 1,* 124–133.

Burgio, L. D., & Burgio, K. L. (1986). Behavioral gerontology: Applications of behavioral methods to the problem of older adults. *Journal of Applied Behavior Analysis, 19,* 321–328.

Burgio, L. D., Burgio, K. L., Engel, B. T., & Tice, L. M. (1986). Increasing distance and independence of ambulation in elderly nursing home residents. *Journal of Applied Behavior Analysis, 19,* 357–366.

Burgio, L. D., Engel, B. T., Hawkins, A., McCormick, K., Scheve, A., & Jones, L. T. (1990). A staff management system for maintaining improvements in continence with elderly nursing home residents. *Journal of Applied Behavior Analysis, 19,* 111–118.

Burgio, L. D., Whitman, T. L., & Reid, D. H. (1983). A participative management approach for improving direct-care staff performance in an institutional setting. *Journal of Applied Behavior Analysis, 16*, 37–53.

Cariaga, J., Burgio, L. F., Flynn, W., & Martin, D. (1991). A controlled study of disruptive vocalizations among geriatric residents in nursing homes. *Journal of the American Geriatric Society, 39*, 501–507.

Carstensen, L. L. (1988). The emerging field of behavioral gerontology. *Behavior Therapy, 19*, 259–281.

Dapcich-Miura, E., & Hovell, M. (1979). Contingency management of adherence to a complex medical regimen in an elderly heart patient. *Behavior Therapy, 10*, 193–201.

Doty, P. (1986). Family care of the elderly: The role of public policy. *The Milbank Quarterly, 64*, 34–69.

Eisdorfer, C., Cohen, D., & Preston, C. (1978, December). Paper presented at the National Institute of Health Conference on Behavioral Aspects of Senile Dementia, Washington, DC.

Geiger, O. G., & Johnson, L. A. (1974). Positive education for elderly persons: Correct eating through reinforcement. *Gerontologist, 14*, 432–436.

Green, G. R., Linsk, N. L., & Pinkston, E. M. (1986). Modification of verbal behavior of the mentally impaired elderly by their spouses. *Journal of Applied Behavior Analysis, 4*, 329–336.

Harris, L. (1975). *The myth and reality of aging in America.* Washington, DC: The National Council on Aging.

Hoyer, W. J. (1973). Application of operant techniques for the modification of elderly behavior. *The Gerontologist, 13*, 18–22.

Hoyer, W. J., Kafer, R. A., Simpson, S. S., & Hoyer, F. W. (1974). A reinstatement of verbal behavior in elderly patients using operant procedures. *The Gerontologist, 14*, 149–152.

Hussian, R. A. (1981). *Geriatric psychology: A behavioral perspective.* New York: Van Nostrand Reinhold.

Hussian, R. A., & Davis, R. A. (1985). *Responsive care: Behavioral intervention with elderly persons.* Champaign, IL: Research Press.

Jackson, G. M. (1980, February). *The behavior treatment of orafacial tardive dyskinesia.* Paper presented at the first Conference on Behavior Gerontology, Nova University, Miami, FL.

Kahn, R. (1965). Comments. In *Proceedings of the York House Institute on mentally impaired aged.* Philadelphia: Philadelphia Geriatric Center.

Kahn, R. S., Goldfarb, A. I., Pollock, M., & Peck, R. (1960). Brief objective measures for the determination of mental status in the aged. *American Journal of Psychiatry, 117*, 326–328.

Linsk, N. L., Hanrahan, P., & Pinkston, E. M. (1991). Teaching elderly people and their families to use community services. In P. A. Wisocki (Ed.), *Handbook of clinical behavior therapy for the elderly client* (pp. 479–504). New York: Plenum Press.

Linsk, N. L., Howe, M. W., & Pinkston, E. M. (1975). Behavioral group work in a home for the aged. *Social Work, 20*, 454–463.

Linsk, N. L., Pinkston, E. M., & Green, G. R. (1982). Home-based behavioral social work with the impaired elderly. In E. M. Pinkston, J. L. Levitt, G. R. Green, N. L. Linsk, & T. L. Rzepnicki (Eds.), *Effective social work practice: Advanced techniques for behavioral intervention with individuals, families, and institutional staff* (pp. 220–232). San Francisco: Jossey-Bass.

MacDonald, M. L. (1978). Environmental programming for the socially isolated aging. *The Gerontologist, 18,* 350–354.

MacDonald, M. L., & Butler, A. K. (1974). Reversal of helplessness: Producing walking behavior in nursing home wheelchair residents using behavior modification procedures. *Journal of Gerontology, 29,* 97–101.

McClannahan, L. E. (1973). Therapeutic and prosthetic living environments for nursing home residents. *The Gerontologist, 13,* 424–429.

McClannahan, L. E., & Risley, T. R. (1974). Designs of living environments for nursing home residents: Recruiting attendance in activities. *The Gerontologist, 14,* 236–240.

Mishara, B. L., Robertson, B., & Kastenbaum, R. (1974). Self-injurious behavior in the elderly. *The Gerontologist, 14,* 273–280.

Neugarten, B. (1990). Social and psychological characteristics of older persons. In C. K. Cassel, D. E. Riesenberg, L. B. Sorenson, & J. R. Walsh (Eds.), *Geriatric medicine* (2nd ed., pp. 28–37). New York: Springer-Verlag.

Perkins, K. A., Rapp, S. R., Carlson, C. R., & Wallace, M. D. (1986). A behavioral intervention to increase exercise among nursing home residents. *The Gerontologist, 26,* 479–481.

Pfeiffer, E. (1976). *Multidimensional functional assessment: The OARS methodology.* Duke University Center for the Study of Aging and Human Development, Chapel Hill, NC.

Pinkston, E. M., Howe, E. M., & Blackman, D. K. (1987). Medical social work management of urinary incontinence in the elderly: A behavioral approach. *Journal of Social Service Research, 10,* 179–194.

Pinkston, E. M., Levitt, J. L., Green, G. R., Linsk, N. L., & Rzepnicki, T. L. (1982). *Effective social work practice: Advanced techniques for behavioral intervention with individuals, families, and institutional staff.* San Francisco: Jossey-Bass.

Pinkston, E. M., & Linsk, N. L. (1984a). Behavioral family intervention with the impaired elderly. *The Gerontologist, 24,* 576–583.

Pinkston, E. M., & Linsk, N. L. (1984b). *Care of the elderly: A family approach.* New York: Pergamon Press.

Pinkston, E. M., Linsk, N. L., & Young, R. N. (1988). Home-based behavioral family treatment of the impaired elderly. *Behavior therapy, 19,* 331–344.

Quattrochi-Tubin, S., & Jason, L. A. (1980). Enhancing social interactions and activity among the elderly through stimulus control. *Journal of Applied Behavior Analysis, 13,* 150–163.

Schnelle, J. F. (1990). Treatment of urinary incontinence in nursing home patients by prompted voiding. *Journal of the American Geriatric Society, 38,* 356–360.

Schnelle, J. F., Traughber, B., Sowell, V. A., & Newman, D. R. (1989). Prompted voiding treatment of urinary incontinence in nursing home patients: A behavioral management approach for nursing home staff. *Journal of the American Geriatric Society, 37,* 1051–1057.

Sidman, M. (1960). *Tactics of scientific research.* New York: Basic Books.

Simos, B. (1973). Adult children and their aged parents. *Social Work, 18,* 78–85.

Stock, L., & Milan, M. A. (1993). Improving dietary practices of elderly individuals: The power of prompting, feedback, and social reinforcement. *Journal of Applied Behavior Analysis, 26,* 379–387.

Tobin, S. S., & Lieberman, M. A. (1976). *Last home for the aged: Critical implications of institutionalization.* San Francisco: Jossey-Bass.

Washington, E. M., & Pinkston, E. M. (1986). Positive consequences of helping for informal caregivers: A conceptual model for research. In E. M. Pinkston, P. Hanrahan, &

E. M. Washington (Eds.), *Proceedings of the Charlotte Towle Symposium on Behavioral Gerontology*. Chicago: The Charlotte Towle Foundation.

Wheeler, E. G., & Knight, B. (1981). Morrie: A case study. *The Gerontologist, 21,* 323–328.

York, S., & Calsyn, R. J. (1977). Family involvement in nursing homes. *The Gerontologist, 17,* 500–505.

Zarit, S. H. (1980). *Aging and mental disorders: Psychological approaches to assessment and treatment.* New York: Free Press.

Zarit, S. H., Reever, K., & Bachman-Peterson, S. (1980). The burden interview. *The Gerontologist, 20,* 649–656.

Part Five
Make Your Own Environment!

A basic theme in the design of whole environments is the maximization of independence for the people who live or work in those environments. One meaning of independence is freedom from instructions, prompts, and demands; another is the ability to do what we will when we want. Targeting independence seems the fitting conclusion for a book emphasizing environmental mechanisms in applied behavior management. We can conceptualize independence as a behavior-environment arrangement we can confer on our students and clients. We can also conceptualize it as a behavior-environment arrangement we can confer on ourselves.

When are you most independent? When you have all the skills necessary to solve all the problems that confront you. But having learned the skills is not the same as having them available. Skills, like all behavior, inevitably come under the close control of stimulus and contextual events; if the stimulus controls for one of your skills are missing from an environment, you do not have that skill in that environment. You should construct at least your most frequently used environments so they contain the stimulus controls for the skills you will need there.

A special case arises when you want an environment to evoke only a special class of problem solutions, studying, for example. You should construct that environment to contain every stimulus control for study, which means everything study ever requires and nothing else. If study requires the assignment, paper and pencil for notes, a dictionary, a good light, a comfortable seat, a work surface of the right height, and silence, then all that should be easily available in that environment—but nothing else. If all that is available, study likely will be evoked and supported; if nothing else is available, for example a TV screen, nothing else competitive with study will be evoked and supported. You will be studious there. You can always leave, but when you return, there will be little else to do there but study.

Lynn McClannahan and Patricia Krantz report their designing of an environment for clients with autism, one that maximizes the client's freedom from the constant supervision previously thought necessary for their daily activities. Their new environment is no larger than a book of photographs; the photographs simply illustrate the client's successive activities, so that the client may page through the book and be reminded by every page of what else can and should be done. The book is small, but it transforms the client's group home from a place where people constantly follow the client about, giving instructions or prompts, into a place where the client does all the same things without supervision.

The logical extension of that technique was to teach clients to find their own photographs or pictures of new activities they would like to add to their daily activities and place those new pictures in their photo schedule books. A parallel skill would be knowing they can take old pictures out of their schedule book. The combination would indeed approximate the usual meaning of self-control, especially if the reasons and lack of reasons for each activity are salient.

Tanya Eckert and Diane Browder similarly have designed school curricula to include elements of self-control by the students; they do this largely by relying on techniques such as incidental teaching and activity-based instruction as well as stimulus-control procedures to make teaching more and more a student-controlled event.

A current topic of much interest is the development of therapies for schizophrenia combining medications and behavioral training. Irene Grote considers these combination therapies and argues that their most crucial components probably include the self-medication and self-control techniques they sometimes incorporate. The success of medication finally depends on whether clients can follow their prescribed medication schedule and can recognize the symptoms that called for additional or resumed medication. Similarly, the point of their medication is to let them function in the real-world settings of home and employment, and much of that is a matter of social skills, which also need self-control techniques to be extended appropriately to new situations not encompassed in their therapeutic training.

In short, the success of any program is that all the correct stimulus controls operate, and none of the incorrect ones, in every needed setting and at every necessary time. Establishing that range of correct stimulus controls is prohibitively laborious if the therapist must do it; on the other hand, it seems possible to achieve if we can teach clients the self-control skills to do it themselves.

Perhaps the most important future direction of stimulus control is provided by its ability to convey self-control. Exemplifying that idea seems the correct topic for the final section of this book.

24

In Search of Solutions to Prompt Dependence: Teaching Children with Autism to Use Photographic Activity Schedules

Lynn E. McClannahan and Patricia J. Krantz

The progress of children with autism is often impeded by overdependence on prompts delivered by other people. Children who have learned to dress, play with toys, complete household chores, or greet other people often fail to display these responses unless teachers or parents prompt them to do so. Although verbal prompts may be carefully faded from instructions to single words, to initial sounds, and finally, to expectant looks, and although these cues may be progressively delayed, transfer of stimulus control from prompts to task-related stimuli frequently fails to occur.

It is possible that discrete-trial training and other forms of teacher-directed instruction foster prompt dependence. For example, in a discrete-trial paradigm, the teacher gives an instruction or asks a question, and the learner attempts (or does not attempt) to follow the instruction, receives (or does not receive) a reward, and waits for the teacher to initiate the next trial. Typically, intertrial latencies are determined at least in part by child performance: Behavior other than quiet waiting delays the next trial and the next reinforcement opportunity. Therefore, both passive waiting and adult instructions may become discriminative for reinforcement. Early in intervention, however, discrete-trial training is often necessary to diminish incompatible responses and shape critical skills such as sitting quietly, looking at relevant materials, and pointing when requested to do so (Etzel & LeBlanc, 1979), as well as to establish vocal and motor imitation.

Children's dependence on adults' prompts may promote an undesirable set of contingencies; children may be rewarded for prompted performances, and adults may be rewarded by children's compliance. Under these circumstances, prompts are likely to accelerate, and there are fewer opportunities for transitions from prompted to unprompted responding. Some years ago, we attempted to address this problem by establishing gradually decreasing criteria for the number of verbal prompts that intervention agents might deliver in specified time periods. This strategy did not achieve the desired outcome, because prompt fading was associated with increases in children's stereotypic and disruptive responses.

If children with autism could respond to stimuli in the physical environment without prompts from other people, their daily activities would more closely approximate those of their nondisabled peers. In addition, parents would be spared the virtually continuous supervision that is often perceived as highly stressful and isolating.

Research on Pictorial Stimuli

Between 1979 and 1985, a number of investigators (e.g., Connis, 1979; Frank, Wacker, Berg, & McMahon, 1985; Martin, Rusch, James, Decker, & Trtol, 1982; Sowers, Rusch, Connis, & Cummings, 1980; Thinesen & Bryan, 1981; Wacker & Berg, 1983, 1984; Wacker, Berg, Berrie, & Swatta, 1985) reported using pictorial cues (line drawings, pictures, or photographs) to help children, adolescents, and adults with mild-to-severe retardation engage in self-care, home-living activities, and vocational tasks. These studies used packages of prompting procedures. Typically, some combination of instruction, modeling, verbal and physical correction, behavioral rehearsal, and contingent praise and snacks was used to teach participants to engage in a depicted task, turn to the next picture, complete that pictured activity, and so on.

A first investigation of the use of pictorial stimuli with children with autism (Knapp, McClannahan, & Krantz, 1986) used a multiple-baseline design across three children, ages 6, 10, and 14, who were taught to follow a five-component photographic activity schedule that included jigsaw puzzles, parquetry design blocks and boards, an audiotape player and exercise tape, dot-to-dot worksheets, and handwriting worksheets. Photographs of these materials were mounted on cardboard and prominently displayed in consecutive order. Preinvestigation assessment documented that, when instructed to do so, the children could complete all target activities without further assistance and could correctly label each activity represented in the photographs.

Teaching procedures initially included verbal prompts, modeling, behavioral rehearsal, behavior-specific praise, and contingent delivery of tangible rewards, but as children learned to follow their pictorial schedules, verbal prompts were replaced by gestural prompts, and the teacher's presence was gradually faded, so that by the end of the training condition, she was no longer present. The youngsters met criterion in the training setting (a school dining room) in 5–15 sessions, but probes conducted in a different setting (a classroom) at a different time of day showed that schedule-following skills did not transfer until the trainer provided verbal prompts in that setting. Although two of the participants responded to a single instruction to generalize and subsequently displayed high levels of engagement while completing depicted tasks without prompts, the third remained dependent on the trainer's directions throughout the study.

This unwanted but familiar outcome led to a reassessment of teaching procedures. Because the goal was enabling children to remain engaged in appropriate activities in the absence of adult instruction, verbal prompts were limited to single, beginning instructions, such as "go and play" or "find something to do," and teachers subsequently used only manual guidance to teach children to point to a picture, obtain necessary materials, complete a depicted activity, put materials away, return to the photographic schedule, turn a page, and repeat this series.

In addition, a sequence of most-to-least prompts was selected because it was comparatively errorless. Teachers were trained to guide children manually through activities and to prevent errors, long interresponse times, and stereotypies. Gestural prompts were prohibited, and manual prompts were delivered from behind the children, so that stimuli associated with adult supervision would not intervene and interrupt response chains. As children developed proficiency in following picture schedules, prompts shifted from graduated guidance, to spatial fading, to shadowing, and ultimately the teacher's presence was faded from the room or activity area.

Consequent events were also scrutinized, and rewards for following pictorial activity schedules were embedded in schedules; preferred stimuli (e.g., snacks, TV, play activities) became depicted activities. In addition, for very young children and children with severe disabilities who were learning to follow their first pictorial schedules, edibles were contingently delivered from behind; teachers continued to "stay out of the way" (i.e., not intervene between children and their pictures and activities).

The efficacy of these procedures was documented in a multiple-baseline design across four boys with autism who resided in a community-based group home (MacDuff, Krantz, & McClannahan, 1993). Photographic activity schedules that depicted six after-school activities were taught with graduated guidance. The pictorial stimuli generated sustained engagement in an hour-long sequence of home-living activities in the absence of adults' instructions; in addition, engagement and schedule-following skills were maintained over a significant period of time and generalized to a different sequence of photographs and to different photographs of new activities.

Subsequent to this investigation, the boys' photographic schedules were gradually extended, eventually encompassing all of their waking hours from their arrival home from school until bedtime. Although they appropriately engaged in and completed depicted activities, independently changed tasks, and moved across different group-home settings, they were, for the most part, silent participants in family living, in spite of the fact that all had acquired some expressive language skills. Interaction tasks—greeting others, requesting assistance with homework assignments, asking for adult attention (e.g., tickling, wrestling), and requesting preferred snacks—were added to their picture schedules and gradually acquired stimulus control.

Concomitantly, data from the clinic suggested the usefulness of including photographic activity schedules in home programs. Photographs are readily transported to a variety of settings, and they can easily be programmed for use in training settings and children's own homes (Stokes & Baer, 1977). Therefore, an investigation was designed to assess the effects of intensive, short-term, in-home assistance to teach the parents of three boys with autism to use graduated guidance to help their children follow photographic schedules that began after school and concluded after dinner. In addition to leisure, self-care, homework, and housekeeping tasks, the schedules depicted social interactions (Krantz, MacDuff, & McClannahan, 1993). A multiple-baseline design across participants showed that when parents taught their children to follow picture schedules, there were marked increases in engagement and social initiations and decreases in disruptive behavior; these behavior changes were maintained for as long as 10 months.

Photographs as "Natural" Stimuli

Two of the four group-home youths who learned to follow pictorial schedules (MacDuff et al., 1993) later followed written activity schedules (Krantz & Mc-Clannahan, 1993). When sight-word reading skills were first acquired, however, words such as *bike* did not evoke bike riding, although a photograph of a bike typically resulted in a correct response. Therefore, superimposition and stimulus fading (Etzel, LeBlanc, Schilmoeller, & Stella, 1981) were used to shift stimulus control from pictures to words; specifically, sight words were superimposed on familiar photographs and were faded in as photographs were faded out. As youngsters' reading skills continued to develop, written schedules were lengthened and elaborated, so that they increasingly resembled "to do" lists or appointment books: stimuli that many would acknowledge as naturalistic.

Other "picture readers" have not yet learned to respond to textual stimuli, and they continue to use photographic schedules that enable them to complete socially relevant tasks, change activities, and engage in social interaction—all in the absence of prompts from other people. Their pictorial stimuli seem to be as naturalistic as glasses for people with visual impairment or wheelchairs for people with paraplegia.

Fading Pictorial Stimuli

When photographs are used to evoke complex response chains, it is often necessary to begin with a series of pictures that cue successive, discrete responses. For example, the task of feeding the dog might be sequenced into pictures of the dog's food bowl, a can of dog food, a utensil, a can opener and a partially opened can, the bowl filled with food, the bowl placed in a location where the dog is typically fed, and the dog eating. After children master the responses cued by these photographs, however, it is often possible to fade picture sequences from beginning to end so that feeding the dog is eventually evoked by the last photograph: the dog eating. Similarly, response chains such as table setting or making a school lunch may initially be represented by many separate photographs but ultimately come under the control of single pictures (e.g., a table that is set or a prepared lunch).

Photographic Stimuli and Choice-Making Skills

The procedures that are effective in teaching youngsters with severe developmental disabilities to respond to pictorial stimuli are also useful in teaching them to make choices. Initially, a child is taught that, on encountering a blank page in the schedule book, she or he should select one of two pictures, mount the chosen photo in the book (Velcro is helpful here), and then engage in the depicted activity. As these skills are acquired, the field of photographs is gradually expanded. Many young people have learned to respond to blank pages in their schedules by making selections from a file box that contains many photographs (e.g., having a snack, taking a rest, looking at magazines, going outdoors, playing the piano).

When the aforementioned skills are mastered, a next programming step involves displaying a variety of photographs on a tabletop or bulletin board and teaching the children, youths, or adults to select and sequence several pictures (i.e., to create a part of their own schedule). Subsequently, the number of photographs is gradually increased so that eventually the clients are specifying the order and content of their own daily schedule and making choices from a large pool of pictures. Many youths with autism have learned to structure their own daily schedules from after school until bedtime. They frequently vary their routines, sometimes completing all work assignments before engaging in leisure activities, sometimes playing first and working later, and sometimes intermixing home-living responsibilities and recreational pursuits.

Pictorial Cues and Time Management

When a child or youth is first taught to follow a photographic activity schedule, activities are selected not only with regard to age appropriateness and current skill levels, but also with attention to the ease of determining when a target activity is completed. For example, a puzzle is finished when the last piece is in place; play with beads concludes when all the beads are strung; and snack is over when the food has been consumed. But many activities do not have clear endings; looking at books, playing with wheeled toys, and listening to music are examples of activities of indeterminate duration. Many people who have acquired the skills prerequisite to schedule following have not yet learned to tell time.

Sowers et al. (1980) addressed this problem by teaching three adults with mental retardation to match pictures of clock faces to real clocks, enabling the trainees to go to and from lunch and coffee breaks at relevant times; however, the sustained vigilance required by this matching task is difficult for some young children with autism, as well as for older persons with severe developmental disabilities.

Alternatively, it is possible to use photographic cues to enable people to set digital timers for designated periods and to put materials away and move to their next activities when timers signal. Initially, several photographs depict the series of (usually color-coded) buttons that must be pressed; later, the relevant responses may be evoked by a single picture. (This strategy has also been useful in teaching people with autism to use microwave ovens and oven timers). It is worthy of note that some children and adults who master the use of digital or kitchen timers later begin to adjust the durations of their own activities; such responses might be taken as indicators of preference.

Photographic activity schedules are also useful vehicles for helping people to schedule temporally remote events and to engage in activities that do not occur on daily bases. For example, a picture of a calendar may evoke checking the calendar for activities, responding to photographs on the calendar (e.g., responding to a picture of a trash can by taking containers to the curb or to a picture of a telephone by calling a friend or relative), and "crossing off" that day so that the next day's date will be readily identifiable.

Clients Prompting Intervention Agents

For many years, there has been broad agreement on the importance of activity schedules as a key feature of human service programs (Favell, Favell, Riddle, & Risley, 1984). Activity schedules identify planned activities, specify when and where they will occur, and note which clients and staff members will participate. Typically, however, activity schedules are managed by intervention agents who prompt clients to go to designated areas at specific times and to engage in previously selected activities with previously identified others. In the interest of efficient intervention, "many service providers exercise a great deal of control over the lives of clients with developmental disabilities" (Bannerman, Sheldon, Sherman, & Harchik, 1990, p. 79); typically, much of this control is exerted through instructions that promote or exacerbate dependence on verbal prompts.

Teaching people with autism to use photographic activity schedules creates another alternative, one in which clients prompt their helpers. A child who has learned to select and use pictorial cues may choose a photograph of the staff member whose help will be enlisted as well as a photograph of a target activity (e.g., a piggyback ride, a walk, a hug). Youngsters may also use photographic cues to initiate instruction: Pictures of relevant materials may evoke requests such as the following:

"Will you teach me *same* and *different?*"
"It's time for reading."
"Could you check my work?"

Those who have not yet acquired expressive language may achieve similar outcomes by presenting photographs or materials to caregivers.

Conclusion

Children, youths, and adults with autism who are nonreaders and who have very small expressive-language repertoires have learned to use photographic cues that enable them to remain engaged in appropriate and relevant activities, to change tasks without prompts from others, and to enter and leave a variety of home, school, and group-home settings independently. Learning to follow photographic activity schedules is associated with decreases in the disruptive behavior of people with lengthy histories of stereotypies, tantrums, aggression, and self-injury. Furthermore, pictorial stimuli can evoke social interactions with staff members, peers, siblings, and parents, and brief, home-based assistance has enabled parents to teach their own children to follow picture schedules at home.

It has been suggested that intervention programs should be responsible for helping individuals perform daily routines that are enjoyable and functional and that these routines should be similar to the usual activities of nondisabled persons (Saunders & Spradlin, 1991). Picture schedules are instrumental in achieving these goals: They facilitate engagement in social-interaction, self-care, academic, home-living, and leisure activities with minimal prompts from others, and they present opportunities to teach choice making and time-management skills that ultimately enable people to construct their own daily routines.

When pictures acquire stimulus control and people with autism are no longer dependent on verbal prompts from staff members, the role of the intervention agent changes. Staff members can circulate among clients, respond to their requests, prompt briefly when necessary, praise good performance, take advantage of opportunities for incidental teaching, make observations that are useful in determining when to add new photographs or fade existing pictorial cues, and interact with clients in ways that more closely approximate typical social exchanges.

References

Bannerman, D. J., Sheldon, J. B., Sherman, J. A., & Harchik, A. E. (1990). Balancing the right to habilitation with the right to personal liberties: The rights of people with developmental disabilities to eat too many doughnuts and take a nap. *Journal of Applied Behavior Analysis, 23,* 79–89.

Connis, R. T. (1979). The effects of sequential pictorial cues, self-recording, and praise on the job task sequencing of retarded adults. *Journal of Applied Behavior Analysis, 12,* 353–362.

Etzel, B. C., & LeBlanc, J. M. (1979). The simplest treatment alternative: The law of parsimony applied to choosing appropriate instructional control and errorless-learning procedures for the difficult-to-teach child. *Journal of Autism and Developmental Disorders, 9,* 361–382.

Etzel, B. C., LeBlanc, J. M., Schilmoeller, K. J., & Stella, M. E. (1981). Stimulus control procedures in the education of young children. In S. W. Bijou and R. Ruiz (Eds.), *Behavior modification contributions to education.* Hillsdale, NJ: Erlbaum.

Favell, J. E., Favell, J. E., Riddle, J. I., & Risley, T. R. (1984). Promoting change in mental retardation facilities: Getting services from the paper to the people. In W. P. Christian,

G. T. Hannah, & T. J. Glahn (Eds.), *Programming effective human services: Strategies for institutional change and client transition.* New York: Plenum Press.

Frank, A. R., Wacker, D. P., Berg, W. K., & McMahon, C. M. (1985). Teaching selected microcomputer skills to retarded students via picture prompts. *Journal of Applied Behavior Analysis, 18,* 179–185.

Knapp, L., McClannahan, L. E., & Krantz, P. J. (1986). *Using photographic activity schedules to program generalization of autistic children's academic and leisure skills.* Unpublished manuscript.

Krantz, P. J., MacDuff, M. T., & McClannahan, L. E. (1993). Programming participation in family activities for children with autism: Parents' use of photographic activity schedules. *Journal of Applied Behavior Analysis, 26,* 137–138.

Krantz, P. J., & McClannahan, L. E. (1993). Teaching children with autism to initiate to peers: Effects of a script-fading procedure. *Journal of Applied Behavior Analysis, 26,* 121–132.

MacDuff, G. S., Krantz, P. J., & McClannahan, L. E. (1993). Teaching children with autism to use photographic activity schedules: Maintenance and generalization of complex response chains. *Journal of Applied Behavior Analysis, 26,* 89–97.

Martin, J., Rusch, F., James, V., Decker, P., & Trtol, K. (1982). The use of picture cues to establish self-control in the preparation of complex meals by mentally retarded adults. *Applied Research in Mental Retardation, 3,* 105–119.

Saunders, R. R., & Spradlin, J. E. (1991). A supported routines approach to active treatment for enhancing independence, competence, and self-worth. *Behavioral Residential Treatment, 6,* 11–37.

Sowers, J., Rusch, F., Connis, R., & Cummings, L. (1980). Teaching mentally retarded adults to time-manage in a vocational setting. *Journal of Applied Behavior Analysis, 13,* 119–128.

Stokes, T. F., & Baer, D. M. (1977). An implicit technology of generalization. *Journal of Applied Behavior Analysis, 10,* 349–367.

Thinesen, P., & Bryan, A. (1981). The use of sequential picture cues in the initiation and maintenance of grooming behaviors with mentally retarded adults. *Mental Retardation, 19,* 246–250.

Wacker, D. P., & Berg, W. K. (1983). Effects of picture prompts on the acquisition of complex vocational tasks by mentally retarded adolescents. *Journal of Applied Behavior Analysis, 16,* 417–433.

Wacker, D. P., & Berg, W. K. (1984). Training adolescents with severe handicaps to set up job tasks independently using picture prompts. *Analysis and Intervention in Developmental Disabilities, 4,* 353–365.

Wacker, D. P., Berg, W. K., Berrie, P., & Swatta, P. (1985). Generalization and maintenance of complex skills by severely handicapped adolescents following picture prompt training. *Journal of Applied Behavior Analysis, 18,* 329–336.

Stimulus Manipulations: Enhancing Materials for Self-Directed Learning

Tanya L. Eckert and Diane M. Browder

One problem commonly faced by special education and early childhood teachers is to teach autonomy, independence, and decision making. Although self-direction is an important social skill, the learning paradigm employed in classroom settings contradicts self-determinism (Schloss, Alper, & Jayne, 1993). That is, children learn to depend on teachers to initiate activities, make choices, and exercise control over their learning environment. For children with disabilities, this dependence may be especially difficult to overcome as they move into adult living.

A number of instructional procedures exist that help to develop self-determinism (see Brown & Cohen, 1996, for a review). These strategies alter educational objectives to allow students to exert control over their environment. Examples of these strategies include teaching within the context of daily routines, incidental teaching, and activity-based instruction. In addition to these procedures, opportunities for self-determinism can be facilitated by a number of stimulus-control procedures, such as stimulus shaping and stimulus fading. Both stimulus shaping and stimulus fading are antecedent, errorless learning procedures in which the learner directs the learning process. These two teaching procedures allow the learner to take a more active role in learning without the teacher providing verbal or physical prompts. Unfortunately, the terms *stimulus shaping* and *stimulus fading* have been used inconsistently in the literature (McIlvane & Dube, 1992), perhaps because there are a number of variations of each procedure. However, this inconsistency and confusion of terminology create a difficult challenge in translating research into practice.

The purpose of this chapter is to define and describe the concept of stimulus manipulation, including both stimulus shaping and stimulus fading, for practitioners and researchers who are interested in developing self-directed learning. A classification system based on the term *stimulus manipulation* is suggested for the various manipulations that can be made to stimuli, and several well-documented stimulus manipulations are presented.

Definitions of Stimulus Shaping and Stimulus Fading

The origins of the concepts of stimulus shaping and stimulus fading can be traced to Terrace's (1963) basic research with pigeons. By introducing distracting stimuli and altering the stimuli through successive, errorless trials, he taught pigeons to peck in the presence of the criterion stimulus (S+) but not peck in the presence of the distracting stimulus (S-). On the basis of Terrace's work, Sidman and Stoddard (1966) taught children with developmental disabilities a circle-ellipse discrimination through a stimulus-shaping procedure and found the discrimination could be learned with almost no errors.

After reviewing the work of Terrace (1963) and Sidman and Stoddard (1966), Etzel and LeBlanc (1979) differentiated stimulus shaping from stimulus fading. Stimulus fading was defined as a stimulus-control procedure in which "the overall configuration or topography of the stimulus is not changed" (p. 369). Stimulus shaping was defined as a stimulus-control procedure in which the initial stimulus (S+) varies from the "final or criterion level stimulus because its topography is to be gradually altered to form the criterion stimulus" (p. 369). For example, in stimulus fading the S+ initially might be increased in size to cue the correct response. Over teaching trials, the size of the S+ would be gradually reduced to the same size as the S-. By contrast, in Etzel and LeBlanc's definition of stimulus shaping, the original S+ would be topographically altered. For example, the work "LOOK" might be presented initially as two eyes, "@ @." Over teaching trials, the letters "L" and "K" would be added (L@ @K) and then the pupils would be gradually withdrawn, leaving the two letter O's. In Etzel and LeBlanc's definitions and illustrations, the S- remains unaltered.

Cooper, Heron, and Heward (1987) adopted a similar definition in their textbook on applied behavior analysis. They defined *stimulus fading* as "highlighting a physical dimension (e.g., color, size, position) of a stimulus to increase the likelihood of a correct response" (p. 317). In addition to increasing the size of the S+ to cue the correct response, therefore, the teacher might choose to color-code the S+ or give it a more salient position.

Ault, Wolery, Doyle, and Gast (1989) used definitions similar to those of Etzel and LeBlanc (1979) and Cooper et al. (1987), but the relevance of the dimension of the stimulus manipulation differed. Ault and colleagues defined *stimulus shaping* as occurring when the "stimulus is presented in a form in which a student can respond correctly. Relevant dimensions of the stimulus are then gradually changed until a student responds correctly to the target stimulus" (p. 349). By contrast, Ault and colleagues defined *stimulus fading* as presenting the stimulus "in a form in which a student can respond correctly by enhancing an irrelevant dimension of the stimulus. The stimulus is gradually changed until a student responds correctly to the target stimulus" (p. 349). Although the term *relevance* is introduced, the type of stimulus manipulation is the same as that offered in Etzel and LeBlanc's (1979) definition. Color, position, and size of the S+ are irrelevant to discriminations of letters or numbers, for example. Changes in these irrelevant dimensions would constitute stimulus fading. By contrast, changing the letter or number's configuration (i.e., its relevant dimension) to cue correct responding (e.g., making an "S" look like a snake) would be stimulus shaping.

Terminology and Classification

Given the complexities of stimulus-control technology and the numerous possible variations of the S+ and S-, it is not surprising to find inconsistent terminology. Table 25.1 presents a sample of studies that used S+ and S- manipulations. As the table illustrates, several terms have been used to describe similar procedures; however, in some instances, the same term is used to describe differing procedures. For example, McGee, Krantz, and McClannahan (1986) used the term *stimulus fading* to refer to manipulations in the number of S- stimuli presented. By contrast, Dorry and Zeaman (1975) and Rincover (1978) used the term *fading* to refer to a procedure in which a cue is added to the S+ (e.g., picture or highlighting), with the cue gradually withdrawn across training trials.

TABLE 25.1   Examples of Inconsistent Terminology Used for S+ or S- Manipulations

Terminology	*Citation*
Stimulus shaping	Mosk and Bucher (1984)
Stimulus fading	McGee, Krantz, and McClannahan (1986)
Extra-stimulus prompting	Wolfe and Cuvo (1978)
Within-stimulus prompting	Wolfe and Cuvo (1978)
Graduated stimulus-change methods	Richmond and Bell (1986)
Fading on relevant dimensions	Zawlocki and Walls (1983)
Errorless discrimination	Walsh and Lamberts (1979)
Picture fading	Walsh and Lamberts (1979)
Within-stimulus fading	Schreibman and Charlop (1981)
Prompt fading	Rincover (1978); Hoogeven, Smeets, and Lancioni (1989)
Distinctive-nondistinctive feature fading	Rincover (1978)
Within- and extra-stimulus fading	Rincover (1978)
Task demonstration model	Karsh, Repp, and Lenz (1990); Repp, Karsh, and Lenz (1990)
Fading	Dorry and Zeaman (1973, 1975)
Fade picture out	Dorry (1976)
Fade word out	Dorry (1976)
Double fade	Dorry (1976)

Proposed Terminology

The need exists for a broad terminology that refers to all combinations of S+ and S- manipulations used to achieve stimulus control; we also need a method to describe the variations within this technology. McIlvane and Dube (1992) offered the term *stimulus-control shaping* to refer to the creation of new controlling environment-behavior relations. However, the definition is sufficiently broad to make the term a synonym for any prompt procedure. It may include not only stimulus manipulation but also time delay and response prompting (e.g., physical guidance of the target response).

In contrast, we propose that the term *stimulus manipulation* be used to refer to stimulus-shaping or stimulus-fading procedures. The term *stimulus manipulation* more precisely makes reference to changes in the S+ or S- and can be considered a subset of the strategies called "stimulus-control shaping." The definition for the more specific subset of procedures termed *stimulus manipulation* could be changing the target discriminative stimulus (S+) or its distractors (S-) to facilitate errorless responding during the acquisition of a discrimination.

This definition clearly includes procedures that have been termed *stimulus shaping* or *stimulus fading*. A distinction that can help clarify whether or not to include delayed cues in the definition of stimulus manipulation is the differentiation of within-stimulus and extra-stimulus cues (Repp, Karsh, & Lenz, 1990), or what are sometimes referred to as *stimulus prompts* and *response prompts* (Snell & Zirpoli, 1987). Within-stimulus cues manipulate the S+ or S-. By contrast, extra-stimulus cues facilitate responding to the S+, for example by modeling or guiding the response. Considering this distinction between within-stimulus and extra-stimulus cues, the term *stimulus manipulation* is best reserved for procedures that use within-stimulus cues with S+ or S- manipulations and not those that use extra-stimulus cues with no S+ or S- manipulation. Therefore, the term *stimulus manipulation* would be applicable to all of the procedures listed in Table 25.1 and would subsume both the terms *stimulus shaping* and *stimulus fading*.

Classification of Stimulus Manipulation

On the basis of the proposed definition of stimulus manipulation, the variations of stimulus manipulation need to be further classified to facilitate an understanding of what manipulations are possible and effective. A method to classify procedures for which the terms *stimulus shaping* and *stimulus fading* have been used or S+ or S- manipulations have been described is shown in Figure 25.1.

S+ or S- Manipulation.   The first level of classification concerns whether the manipulation occurs for the S+, the S-, or both. A review of the applied literature suggests that typically either the S+ or S- has been manipulated. For example, the Edmark Reading Program was developed based on fading-in the S- so that it be-

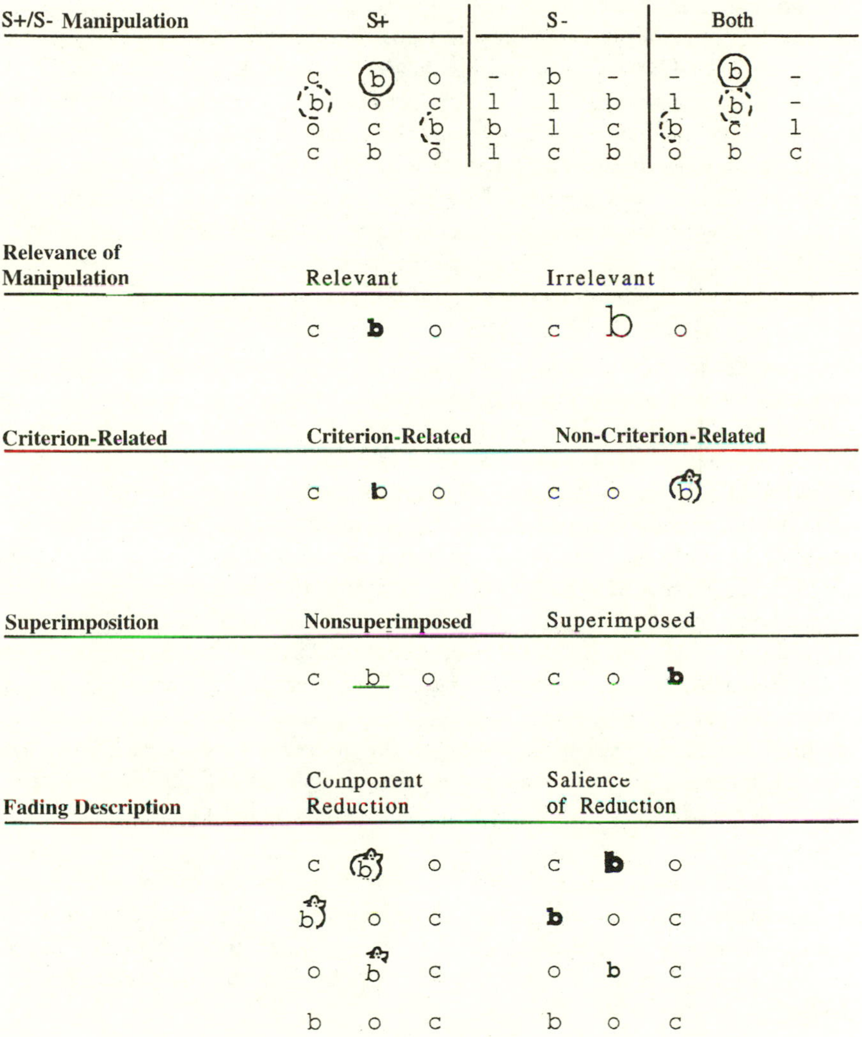
S+/S- Manipulation
S+
S-
Both
Relevance of Manipulation
Relevant
Irrelevant
Criterion-Related
Criterion-Related
Non-Criterion-Related
Superimposition
Nonsuperimposed
Superimposed
Fading Description
Component Reduction
Salience of Reduction

FIGURE 25.1 Teaching Options for Stimulus Manipulation

comes more similar to the S+. This has been an effective strategy for teaching reading to children with developmental disabilities (Vandever & Stubbs, 1977).

Relevance of Manipulation. The second level of classification focuses on whether the manipulation is for a relevant or irrelevant dimension of the discrimination (Ault et al., 1989). This can be clarified by defining the relevant dimension. In teaching discrimination of letters, words, or numbers, the relevant dimension is the configuration of the symbol or symbols. Examples of irrelevant dimensions include highlighting, color coding, and position cues for the correct response. The research of Dorry (1976) and Hoogeveen, Smeets, and Lancioni (1989) illustrates the classification of relevant and irrelevant dimensions. Both studies incorporated picture cues with fading to teach reading to individuals with developmental disabilities. However, Dorry chose pictures of the word concept (e.g., a picture of a dog for the word "dog"), whereas Hoogeveen et al. chose pictures to focus on the configuration of the letter (e.g., a martini glass for the letter "Y," a face for the letter "O"). Dorry's pictures used an irrelevant dimension, and Hoogeveen et al.'s pictures used a relevant dimension.

Criterion-Related Manipulation.   The third level of classification is whether the manipulation is criterion-related or non-criterion-related. For example, the criterion for the discrimination between the letters "J" and "S" is the top half of the letter. The letter "J" has a crossbar, whereas the letter "S" has a curve. A criterion-related manipulation would focus on the crossbar (e.g., highlighting the crossbar). A noncriterion manipulation might simply highlight the entire letter or focus on the common stimuli of the bottom curve. Research conducted by Dorry (1976) and Hoogeveen et al. (1989) also illustrates the classification of criterion-related and non-criterion-related cues. Dorry's picture cue of a dog was not criterion-related; that is, the picture cue was not related to the final discrimination of the individual letter shapes. By contrast, Hoogeveen et al.'s martini glass used both a relevant dimension (e.g., manipulation of shape) and a criterion-related cue that focused the learner's attention on the unique features of each letter. For example, by adding olives to the martini glass of the letter "Y," the learner's attention was focused on the open lines and stem that resembled a martini glass.

Superimposition Manipulation.   The fourth level of classification is whether the manipulation is superimposed or not superimposed. If the manipulation is not superimposed, the cue is in proximity to the S+ (e.g., an arrow above the correct answer). By contrast, for a superimposed manipulation, the cue is embedded in the S+.

Fading Technique.   Finally, procedures may be classified according to the manner in which the stimulus manipulation occurs. The S+ cues may be faded out, either by eliminating components over trials or by reducing the salience of the cues; for example, the picture becomes progressively fainter as shown in Figure 25.2.

Teaching Options for Stimulus Manipulation

On the basis of the most commonly used manipulations found in the literature, several options emerge as strategies for instructing children with disabilities to

Option 1.	Fade in S-			Comments
	–	car	–	S+ is the "car." "Cat" is a highly similar distractor that is faded in progressively.
	car	c	box	
	ca	box	car	
	car	box	cat	

Option 2.	Manipulate S+: Relevant, Criterion-Related Dimension		Comments
	P	B̲	S+ is "B." The relevance is the shape of the letters. Criterion is the number of loops.
	B̲	P	
	P	B	

Option 3.	Manipulate S+: Irrelevant Dimension, Criterion-Related Cue			Comments
	SALLY	GARY	GREG	"Greg" is S+. Size is the irrelevant dimension. Letter shape is the criterion for the discrimination.
	GARY	GREG	SALLY	
	GARY	GREG	SALLY	

Option 4.	Manipulate S+: Irrelevant Dimension, Non-Criterion-Related Cue		Comments
	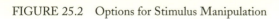 CAR	CAT	The cue can be superimposed on the word as shown here. S+ is the car; S- is the word "cat."
	CAR	CAT	
	CAT	CAR	
	CAR	CAT	

FIGURE 25.2   Options for Stimulus Manipulation

learn visual discriminations of numbers, letters, and words. These strategies encourage children to learn from the materials themselves rather than depending on teacher cues; they are shown in Figure 25.2.

Option 1: Fade-in S-

The first option illustrated is to fade in the S- while holding the S+ constant. Research studies illustrating this stimulus manipulation have included teaching sight words (Lalli & Browder, 1993; McGee et al., 1986) and self-care tasks (Mosk & Bucher, 1986).

Option 2: Manipulate S+ (Relevant, Criterion-Related Dimension)

A second option shown in Figure 25.2 involves manipulating a relevant dimension of the S+ using a criterion-related cue. To use this approach, practitioners need first to clarify the relevant shape and then to decide how to accentuate the part of the shape that distinguishes it from distractors. This "letter or word accentuation" approach may work especially well in teaching discrimination between easily confused letters (e.g., "b" and "d"). For example, some teachers used the word "bed" to teach this distinction by making the word look like a bed and noting that the headboard is the letter "b" and the footboard is the letter "d." When students encounter other words, they can presumably discriminate whether the letter is a headboard (the letter "b") or a footboard ("d"). Any accentuation of letters may be faded using either component reduction, as illustrated by Hoogeveen et al. (1989), or making the accentuation less salient (e.g., fainter).

Option 3: Manipulate S+ (Irrelevant Dimension, Criterion-Related Cue)

A third option is to manipulate an irrelevant dimension of the S+, for example by color coding or increasing the size of the correct answer. This method of "cueing the correct answer" may work especially well when the discrimination is too complex to make a relevant-dimension manipulation or when the discrimination is embedded in tasks of daily living. An example of this manipulation can be found in Lalli and Browder's (1993) work that used color highlighting in sight-word instruction. The example given in Figure 25.2 demonstrates a way to teach children to recognize their names by using size to cue the correct response.

Option 4: Manipulate S+ (Irrelevant Dimension, Non-Criterion-Related Cue

The fourth option involves using a non-criterion-related cue (e.g., a picture). Non-criterion-related cues might be useful in teaching incidental information such as word comprehension. In the example in Figure 25.2, the picture of the car might enhance comprehension of the word.

Stimulus Manipulation and Self-Determinism

The stimulus-manipulation procedures described provide cues for learning within the materials themselves and encourage self-directed learning. The research literature on stimulus manipulation is confusing because of inconsistencies in terminology. The classification and techniques described here can be used to guide the development of self-directed learning materials.

The use of stimulus manipulation is especially appropriate for students with developmental disabilities, who may need enhanced methods to learn reading and other academic skills and who also may need to acquire skills of self-direction. Although the benefits of stimulus manipulation in teaching academic skills such as sight-word reading are clear in research (e.g., Lalli & Browder, 1993; McGee et al., 1986), the social benefits are less well known. Future research is needed to determine the impact of stimulus manipulation on self-direction. This research may be especially relevant to students with disabilities in inclusive classrooms.

Acknowledgments

We express our gratitude to David Gast, F. Charles Mace, and Mark Wolery for their helpful feedback during the preparation of this manuscript.

References

Ault, M. J., Wolery, M., Doyle, P. M., & Gast, D. L. (1989). Review of comparative studies in the instructing of students with moderate and severe handicaps. *Exceptional Children, 55,* 346–356.

Brown, F., & Cohen, S. (1996). Self-determinism and young children. *Journal of The Association for Persons with Severe Handicaps, 21,* 22–30.

Cooper, J. O., Heron, T. E., & Heward, W. L. (1987). *Applied Behavior Analysis.* Columbus OH: Charles E. Merrill.

Deitz, S. M., & Malone, L. W. (1989). On terms: Stimulus control terminology. *Behavior Analyst, 8,* 259–264.

Dorry, G. W. (1976). Attentional model for the effectiveness of fading in training reading-vocabulary with retarded persons. *American Journal of Mental Deficiency, 81,* 271–279.

Dorry, G. W., & Zeaman, D. (1973). The use of fading techniques in paired associate teaching of reading-vocabulary with retardates. *Mental Retardation, 11,* 3–6.

Dorry, G. W., & Zeaman, D. (1975). Teaching simple reading vocabulary to retarded children: Effectiveness of fading and non-fading procedures. *American Journal of Mental Deficiency, 79,* 711–716.

Etzel, B., & LeBlanc, J. (1979). The simplest treatment alternative: The law of parsimony applied to choosing appropriate instructional control and errorless-learning procedures for the difficult to teach child. *Journal of Autism and Developmental Disabilities, 9,* 361–382.

Hoogeveen, F. R., Smeets, P. M., & Lancioni, G. E. (1989). Teaching moderately mentally retarded children basic reading skills. *Research in Developmental Disabilities, 10,* 1–18.

Karsh, K. G., Repp, A. C., & Lenz, M. W. (1990). A comparison of the task demonstration model and the standard prompting hierarchy in teaching word identification to persons with moderate retardation. *Research in Developmental Disabilities, 11,* 395–410.

Lalli, J. S., & Browder, D. M. (1993). Comparison of sight word training with validation of the most practical procedure in teaching reading for daily living. *Research in Developmental Disabilities, 14,* 107–127.

McGee, G. G., Krantz, P. J., & McClannahan, L. E. (1986). An extension of incidental teaching procedures to reading instruction for autistic children. *Journal of Applied Behavior Analysis, 19,* 147–157.

McIlvane, W. J., & Dube, W. V. (1992). Stimulus control shaping and stimulus control topographies. *The Behavior Analyst, 15,* 89–94.

Mosk, M. D., & Bucher, B. (1984). Prompting and stimulus shaping procedures for teaching visual-motor skills to retarded children. *Journal of Applied Behavior Analysis, 17,* 23–34.

Repp, A. C., Karsh, K. G., & Lenz, M. W. (1990). Discrimination training for persons with developmental disabilities: A comparison of the task demonstration model and the standard prompting hierarchy. *Journal of Applied Behavior Analysis, 23,* 43–52.

Richmond, G., & Bell, J. (1986). Comparison of trial-and-error and graduated stimulus change procedures across tasks. *Analysis and Intervention in Developmental Disabilities, 6,* 127–136.

Rincover, A. (1978). Variables affecting stimulus fading and discriminative responding in psychotic children. *Journal of Abnormal Psychology, 87,* 541–553.

Schloss, P. J., Alper, S., & Jayne, D. (1993). Self-determinism for persons with disabilities: Choice, risk, and dignity. *Exceptional Children, 60,* 215–225.

Schreibman, L., & Charlop, M. H. (1981). S+ versus S- fading in prompting procedures with autistic children. *Journal of Experimental Child Psychology, 31,* 508–520.

Sidman, M., & Stoddard, L. T. (1966). Programming perception and learning for retarded children. In N. R. Ellis (Ed.), *International review of research in mental retardation* (Vol. 2, pp. 151–208). New York: Academic Press.

Sidman, M., & Stoddard, L. T. (1987). The effectiveness of fading in programming a simultaneous form discrimination for retarded children. *Journal of the Experimental Analysis of Behavior, 10,* 3–15.

Snell, M. E., & Zirpoli, T. J. (1987). Intervention strategies. In M. E. Snell (Ed.), *Systematic instruction of persons with severe handicaps.* Columbus, OH: Charles E. Merrill.

Terrace, H. S. (1963). Discrimination learning with and without "errors." *Journal of the Experimental Analysis of Behavior, 6,* 1–27.

Vandever, T. J., & Stubbs, J. C. (1977). Reading retention and transfer in TMR students. *American Journal of Mental Deficiency, 79,* 210–213.

Walsh, B. F., & Lamberts, F. (1979). Errorless discrimination and picture fading as techniques for teaching sight words to TMR students. *American Journal of Mental Deficiency, 5,* 473–479.

Wolfe, V. F., & Cuvo, A. J. (1978). Effects of within-stimulus and extra-stimulus prompting on letter discrimination by mentally retarded persons. *American Journal of Mental Deficiency, 83,* 297–303.

Zawlocki, R. J., & Walls, R. T. (1983). Fading on the S+, the S-, both or neither. *American Journal of Mental Deficiency, 87,* 462–464.

26

The Emergence of Combination Therapies Intensifies the Need for Generalization Technologies

Irene Grote

Certain risk-benefit ratios should control our search for the new-hope therapy that is even newer than yesterday's new-hope therapy. The current case in point seems to be the combination of drug therapy and behavior therapy. Their current combinations feature cognitive behavior therapy and applied behavior analysis, both of which recommend self-management of medication. Ironically, self-management could transcend and survive both the medications with which it is initially paired and the pharmacological problem-solving conceptualizations that see problems only as brain functions and structures. On the assumption that drugs can facilitate training but do not teach skills, self-management should be examined for its ongoing relevance, availability, and potential for generalized increments in the life skills of people whose central treatment is medication. This chapter sketches four contexts qualifying a *technology* of generalization: (a) the conceptual role of "emergence" in an applied technology of generalization, (b) current combinations of therapies, (c) the role of self-control as a component of therapy and as a product of generalization, and (d) generalization concepts in behavior therapy and cognitive therapy.

"Emergence" in an Applied Technology of Generalization

To define *emerge*, *The American Heritage Dictionary* (1978) uses terms such as "rise up," "come forth . . . as if from immersion," "come into sight," "become evident or obvious," "issue, as from obscurity or an unfortunate condition," and "come into existence." This reliance on connotation and metaphor reveals an indeterminate concept: Emergence has no consistent mechanism, form, specific agent, substantive composition, timing, or end point; it signifies only change from less of something to more of something. When things change systematically from less to more, Western thought has always asked about causation (cf. Aristotle's "prime mover," Aristotle, 1947; Reese, 1984).

Emergence is a term used frequently in evolutionary biology, developmental psychology, and embryology (e.g., Dobzhansky, 1962/1978; Lovejoy, 1927/1962). These disciplines describe, and sometimes try to explain, phylogeny (evolution), ontogeny (individual development), and their interaction. Much of phylogeny and ontogeny appears to be relatively complex but to be growing systematically from relative simplicity. *Emergence* only denotes such change. Explaining what emerges requires well-understood mechanisms that make simple material and forms into complex material and forms. *Emergence* only invites explanation, especially for scientists trained in the analysis of cause. For them, *emergence* can be used to label clear, systematic movement, to denote its systematic nature, and to prescribe the analysis of its causation as the next problem.

A parallel can be seen in behavior analysis, when terms like *adduction* are used to mark a systematic but apparently inexplicable change (a "quantum leap") in student ability (Andronis, 1983, cited in Johnson & Layng, 1992, pp. 1487–1488). Johnson and Layng label as *adduction* untaught, rapid increments in students' problem solving evoked by suddenly more difficult academic problems. They argue that teaching establishes a variety of student problem-solving skills; later, when new, suddenly more difficult academic problems are encountered, untaught "recombinations" of these skills may emerge, and the consistently successful recombinations are selected from that variety. Johnson and Layng (1992) do not explain emergence; but they do cite a measurable, experimentable variable as strongly influential: fluency. *Fluency* refers to high-rate, short-latency, almost-always-correct responses to the components of a problem. Johnson and Layng argue that making more complex combinations of those components is more likely when the relevant component responses are fluent than when the same probability of correct responses is achieved only by long-latency, low-rate responses.

That proposition is testable. If appropriate tests confirm it across an impressive variety of students, problems to be solved, and problem-solving skills to be recombined, this idea of emergence becomes steadily more familiar and manageable, although no more understandable: The question of *why* fluency improves problem solving remains unanswered. Fluency is not a primitive term in behavior theory; therefore, when research shows it to be crucial to some outcome, the fact does not explain itself. But *adduction* only labels the role of fluency; therefore, it does not explain, either. It merely reports that students confronted with suddenly more difficult problems are more likely to recombine previously taught problem-solving skills into effective solutions, if those skills are fluent. We understand why that is true only when we can replace *fluency* with a behaviorally primitive, and hence explanatory, term.

This case is like many in the development of a technology of generalization. At present, that technology is at least a collection of procedures that create many adductions: untaught but recognizably correct extensions of the effects of previous teaching; that previous teaching often was done as it was on the premise that doing it that way ought to yield those untaught changes. The meaning of *ought* might be that we know a well-understood generalization mechanism for that kind of teaching. Or it might mean only that when we have taught this way in the past, we have more often produced the desired generalizations, without knowing why. It is possible to collect a generalization technology without knowing why it works (cf. Stokes & Baer, 1977). But it is more satisfying, and probably more effective, when it is explained.

The literature of behavior analysis contains attempts to explain generalization. Most such attempts center on determining what stimuli were given control over the trained response during training; the premise is that whenever and wherever those stimuli recur, so will the response (cf. Horner, Dunlap, & Koegel, 1988, for a review). A variant of this approach is strikingly similar to renaming "emergence" as "self-direction." That approach argues that generalized problem solving results from a self-behavior, often in the form of a self-instruction, acting as a stimulus control that can be brought by the student to every nontraining time and setting to evoke the correct response then and there.

In evaluating a self-control explanation, the first crucial question is whether the self-behavior is observable and experimentable or only inferred. The second crucial question is whether the self-behavior, if observable and experimentable, is also explanatory of the resultant generalization. Is it best interpreted simply as the importation of stimulus control? Does that importation require a stimulus control of its own? And a reinforcer?

Evolutionary biologists may well be forced to use the term *emergence* only to denote systematic change; they often cannot subject their topic of study to experimental analysis. But behavior analysts often can. Therefore, behavior analysts can be asked to produce not only a generalization technology based on the observation that it often works, but also a generalization technology based on an understanding of why and how it works.

To the extent that we still value parsimony as a hallmark of the most satisfying scientific explanations, we should coin new descriptors for phenomena only when existing terms or principles cannot name and account for the phenomena. There is a special danger in labeling the currently inexplicable with analogous terms from other sciences. Analogous labels lead too easily to assuming analogous mechanisms as well, an argument often present in debates about using science analogies (e.g., Laudan, 1981). If this is so, many terms may be only descriptive, rather than explanatory, and hence more dangerous than useful, because they may be taken for explanation. Terms like *exaptation* and *evolutionary psychology* (Gould, 1991, p. 60), or *adduction* as a special case of *exaptation* (Johnson & Layng, 1992), label events as "emerging" within individuals, cultures, or phyla, but they do not explain those events or make them manageable. Therefore, they do not improve our ability to offer teaching, therapy, or training or to get the results of those processes generalized in a truly analytic way (cf. Beach, 1955, and Fruton, 1992, for a similar argument). Until these terms reveal empirical events accessible to experimental analysis, they remain analogies, metaphors, and models. That is not a criticism: Analogies, metaphors, and models are often useful. The point is always to understand that they are not explanations or analyses and that their best function is to invite explanatory analysis. *Emergence,* thus qualified, prompts us to examine the emergence of combination therapies.

The Combination of Therapies

Today, psychotherapy increasingly combines pharmaco- and nonpharmacotherapies. It is important to examine the rationales for that combination. In doing so, three large problems arise, which are best considered within some important case in point. For this chapter, that case is schizophrenia.

The first problem is to decide on all the behavior changes that we wish for individuals with schizophrenia: the behavior changes that would best alleviate the most problematic symptoms (Cancro, 1982). The second problem arises from the demonstration that some drugs cause striking changes in many of those behaviors (Klerman, 1984) but often with some undesired side effects (Gerlach & Casey, 1988). Those two events set the occasion for choosing the drug that best accomplishes those behavior changes (Skelton, Pepe, & Pineo, 1995). The third problem, that no drug will accomplish all those changes (Baldessarini & Frankenburg, 1991), prompts asking what additional techniques will best impart those missing client skills (Liberman, Kopelowicz, & Young, 1994; Wong et al., 1993).

A therapy that combines medication and other techniques suggests a fourth problem: Should these components be selected so that each simply does its own job optimally, independently of the others, or should they be selected on the basis of how well they interact in accomplishing the total job? The answer to this question is a cost-benefit analysis. This analysis in turn hinges on measurement of the benefits and, therefore, on the choice of outcome measures. The generalizations from the clinical setting to the relevant life settings of whatever therapeutic changes are targeted seem good outcome measures. If we see the eventual independence of clients as an important outcome, then without such generalization, therapy is not useful. Techniques for generalizing treatment effects—for making them independent of the therapist—exist in considerable degree (cf. Baer, 1982b; Gambrill, 1981; Horner et al., 1988; Stokes & Baer, 1977). Measuring practitioners' diverse uses of these techniques, and of their outcomes, lets us evaluate any therapy.

Various rationales are cited for combining schizophrenia therapies in a way that best solves those problems. One group argues that a high stress level must be reduced (Feinstein, Kettering, & Harrow, 1990); a second believes that seriously flawed information processing must be corrected (Alford & Correia, 1994); a third that inadvertent reinforcement of schizophrenic behaviors must be corrected (Liberman et al., 1994); a fourth that social skills crucial to social integration are absent and must be taught (Baldessarini & Frankenburg, 1991); a fifth that medication must become self-medication (Corrigan, Wallace, Schade, &

Green, 1994); and a sixth that any treatment must achieve the client's independence (Torrey, 1974). In considering each of these six rationales, it should be remembered that cure and cause are often independent issues (cf. Horst, 1990).

The six rationales may lead to use of different combinations of therapies. Those differences may change with the nature of the problem at hand: Schizophrenia, for instance, arguably may dictate a different set of choices than depression (Elmer-Dewitt, 1992; Paykel, 1989). The numerous current variants of behavioral and cognitive therapies complicate the problem of choosing among them (Baer, 1982a; Grawe, Bernauer, & Donati, 1990). Even so, it seems clear that—as long as client independence is valued—treatment will combine pharmaceutical therapy with behavioral techniques that aim at generalized effects (Baer, 1984; Wong et al., 1993), especially through self-control.

Choosing pharmacological agents is as complex as choosing behavioral programs. Currently, clozapine may be used when other neuropharmaceuticals fail for clients whose condition is labeled refractory (cf. Brenner et al., 1990). Although the side effects of clozapine are serious and expensive to monitor (Claghorn et al., 1987) and a substantial subpopulation is not helped by this drug (Gilbert, Harris, McAdams, & Jeste, 1995), its effects may be dramatic (Wallis & Willwerth, 1992), which intensifies the need for concomitant behavioral programming. Indeed, Baldessarini and Frankenburg (1991) concluded their review of the effects of clozapine by acknowledging that such dramatic improvement, especially after prolonged baselines of failure with other drugs, obligates clinicians to offer additional social and clinical rehabilitation to those benefited by this new drug.

Future drugs, like current ones, will differ in their effects; however, stress management, information processing, self-medication, and social skills will continue to be targets for training and eventual independence. For such clients, life in the real world requires these skills, and drugs alone do not produce them.

In summary, the need for combination therapies is a logical one, derived from two sets of facts. First, some of the outcomes desired for individuals with schizophrenia can be accomplished by drugs and others by behavioral programs. Second, according to a small number of studies, behavioral effects are accomplished better when the right drugs are used, and drug effects are accomplished better when the right behavioral programming is used. It bears repeating that some members of the behavioral classes usually labeled as self-management or self-control should be essential goals for almost any combination of therapies.

Self-Control: Component of Therapy and Product of Generalization

A long-standing value in education and therapy is that behavior changes accomplished should endure after the intervention stops, as if the intervention created or refined a self-regulatory skill that maintained those changes. This section compares and contrasts the roles of *self-control* and *self-management* in achieving that goal. Self-control and self-management are best conceptualized as skills that can be analyzed in terms of the instructions, models, and contingencies that establish, refine, and maintain them. First, however, one must ask who performs each of these skills.

Self-management can be seen as a chain including the following five links: (a) The clinician-teacher (C-T) identifies client-student problems to be solved; (b) the C-T pinpoints the client-student behaviors that, if changed, should solve that problem; (c) the C-T contrives contingencies to change those behaviors; (d) anticipating leaving the client-student soon, the C-T teaches the client-student to self-monitor, self-evaluate, or self-instruct these performances to maintain them before their long-term consequences are achieved; and (e) the C-T records and graphs the whole process, letting the client-student record (and perhaps graph) only the self-monitoring, self-evaluating, or self-instructing. The process is seen as a "self-process" mainly because of steps d and e.

After reviewing the procedures said to define self-regulation, Baer (1982a, 1982b, 1984) noted that many of these procedures gave the client or student control of only a small portion of the chain: only self-monitoring, self-evaluation, or self-instruction in one or two steps near the end of the chain. These techniques often proved useful for short-term management (e.g., Malott, 1986), but alone they seem insufficient for the independent management of long-term contingencies. Long-term independence would mean that clients or students (a) chose the target skills; (b) chose, designed, and implemented strategies and tactics to develop, manage, generalize, and maintain them; and (c) as Malott advised (1986), chose and implemented ongoing short-term techniques such as self-monitoring, self-evaluation, and self-reinforcement to produce symbolic maintaining consequences for the ongoing performances until the long-term consequences were achieved.

Malott and Baer both argued that many target skills are distant in time from the natural consequences that should maintain them; these target skills need a chain of subsidiary self-control skills to maintain them (which in turn would need their own maintenance, part of which might be supplied by the long-term natural consequences). When all or most of the tasks of that chain are accomplished by the client or student, the result can fairly be called *self-control*, usually seen as attractive or desirable. When the C-T imposes most of the chain, giving the client or student only the self-techniques to bridge current performance and long-term consequences, the result might better be called *self-management*, often seen as undesirably dependent.

In the logic of discrimination training, durable self-control depends on the durability of the stimulus control. The technology of programming durable stimulus control has not yet been developed. Perhaps well-analyzed anecdotal reports of self-help strategies can contribute to that development. Two noteworthy anecdotes of self-management are provided by Mann (related by Baer, 1984) and by Wirshing, Eckman, Liberman, and Marder (1991). In Mann's case, the client was placed under successful weight-loss contingencies, but when he moved away, he began to regain weight. He then recruited and taught a friend to impose on him those same contingencies, and he resumed his weight loss. In the case related by Wirshing et al., a schizophrenic outpatient, skilled at self-monitoring his symptoms and medication, taught those skills to his roommate, whose similar behavior was deteriorating. This client solved his roommate's long-term problem and thereby one of his own, because the roommate's deterioration was probably aversive. Perhaps this is an instance of meta-self-control.

The potential shift from self-management to self-control, implicit in Table 26.1, requires work in refining generalization techniques. The argument that self-*control* skills are essential for transfer of therapeutic gains requires analysis of the functional relations between the events that produce and maintain these skills.

TABLE 26.1   Parallels of Self-Management and Self-Control

Self-Management: *Clinicians or Teachers . . .*	*Self-Control:* *Individuals Themselves . . .*
1. Identify problems and pinpoint behaviors to be changed	1. Construct a checklist of high-probability problem areas (as a working document for continuous updating based on documented analyses)
2. Designate behaviors to be changed	2. Identify rapidly a need for change and consult high-probability checklist
3. Arrange contrived contingencies (left without support when the clinician or teacher leaves)	3. Pinpoint behaviors to be changed
4. Teach self-monitoring, self-evaluation, or self-instruction to produce direct results in form of SDs for long-term but inefficient contingencies	4. Find natural or temporarily contrived contingencies to acquire and maintain behavior changes
5. Record and represent graphically the whole process, except for the individual's recording of self-evaluating or self-instructing (marker stimuli)	5. Reset their environment to have the new contingencies produce directly or mediate through marker stimuli the desired behavior changes (in chained rather than tandem schedules)
	6. Record and represent graphically and continuously their self-controlling actions
	7. Analyze continuously, and revise when necessary, every link in the whole chain of relations between events and behavior for its potential for producing generalization
	8. Update checklist with documented analysis and append with strategies and tactics for use in other areas

Clearly, the argument assumes that the key process is generalization (or transfer) and that self-control processes may be specially suited for such generalization. That control of behavior changes should shift from C-T to client or student is an obvious, frequent, but still contextual value.

Generalization Concepts in Behavior Therapy and Cognitive Therapy

In a little-noticed translation of a 1966 Russian text, Landa (1974) distinguished between learning "content" and learning "how to learn." The former is the familiar memorization of facts, usually under the stimulus control of teachers' queries and test questions; the latter is the memorization of algorithms that can be applied to the mastery of any topic and thus represents a generalized way of learning anything, without an external instructor-interrogator or test. Landa's examples are meant to illustrate the possibility that algorithmic learning is the most effective form of generalization. Whether that is true or not, algorithmic learning (i.e., rule-driven generalization) offers an interesting contrast to procedures for case-by-case learning and generalization, because it forces some crucial procedural choices concerning the technologies that target generalized learning.

Traditionally, treatment effects do not self-propel from therapeutic to nontherapeutic settings. Therapists need to program transfer of therapeutic gains to natural environments (cf. Baer, Wolf, & Risley, 1988). Whitman (1990) argued that self-regulation is central to the durable transfer of learning, and Brenner et al. (1990) stated that definable degrees of independent functioning *are* therapeutic gains.

Research has yielded a variety of therapist-arrangeable contingencies that produce or enhance generalization and a set of theoretical considerations for the design of more of them. Meichenbaum (1976) offered procedures and arguments to guide current practice and conceptualization for cognitive therapists. Horner et al. (1988) edited a recent collection of procedures and arguments to guide current practice and conceptualization for behavior-analytic therapists. Apparently, most cognitive psychologists expect participants to induce the rules of generalization, and most behavior analysts expect to teach the participants those rules. The most likely parallel between cognitive behavior therapy and behavior-analytic therapy appears to emerge from those conceptualizations in which therapeutic gains depend on client-managed instead of therapist-managed contingencies.

Baer (1982b) elaborated the review by Stokes and Baer (1977) into a set of methods (and "nonmethods") to assist technologists in programming generalization. Baer's distinction between methods and nonmethods hinged on the presence or absence of "direct" experimenter-arranged contingencies to support the behavior change desired as a generalization. Absence of those "direct" contingencies made a technique class a generalization method (p. 203). This distinction recalls Landa's algorithmic learning and generalization, contrasted with procedures for case-by-case learning and generalization. This distinction may also reveal the place in such chains for a concept of self-instruction. Self-instruction could be of remarkable value in generalization; however, self-instructed skills are not automatically generalized skills, and self-instruction is not automatically a generalized ability to generalize.

Theoretically, self-instruction is subject to stimulus control; whatever its benefits may be, they too are subject to the nature of that stimulus control, or what we can make that nature to be. At this point, the evidence of self-control testifies to the clinical significance of whatever procedure produced it. In summary, well-designed outcome measures of *generalized* client skills should be part of the cost-benefit studies that inform a tax-paying public whether technology-based combination therapies have emerged.

Acknowledgments

I thank Professor Donald M. Baer for his generous feedback on earlier versions of this chapter. My appreciation also extends to Professors Don G. Bushell, Stephen C. Fowler, Eli K. Michaelis, Stephen S. Schroeder, and Montrose M. Wolf for their helpful comments; particular thanks go to Professor Sigrid S. Glenn for her extensive feedback on an earlier version of part of this chapter.

References

Alford, B. A., & Correia, C. J. (1994). Cognitive therapy of schizophrenia: Theory and empirical status. *Behavior Therapy, 25,* 17–33.

Aristotle. (1947). Physics. In R. McKeon (Ed.), *Introduction to Aristotle* (pp. 116–138; R. P. Hardie & R. K. Gaye, Trans.). New York: Random House.

Baer, D. M. (1982a). Applied behavior analysis. In G. T. Wilson & C. M. Franks (Eds.), *Contemporary behavior therapy* (pp. 277–309). New York: Guilford Press.

Baer, D. M. (1982b). The role of current pragmatics in the future analysis of generalization technology. In R. B. Stuart (Ed.), *Adherence, compliance, and generalization in behavioral medicine* (pp. 192–212). New York: Brunner/Mazel.

Baer, D. M. (1984). Does research on self-control need more control? *Analysis and Intervention in Developmental Disabilities, 4,* 211–218.

Baer, D. M., Wolf, M. M., & Risley, T. R. (1988). Some still-current dimensions of applied behavior analysis. *Journal of Applied Behavior Analysis, 20,* 313–327.

Baldessarini, R. J., & Frankenburg, F. R. (1991). Clozapine: A novel antipsychotic agent. *New England Journal of Medicine, 324,* 746–757.

Beach, F. A. (1955). The descent of instinct. *The Psychological Review, 62,* 401–410.

Brenner, H. D., Dencker, S. J., Goldstein, M. J., Hubbard, J. W., Keegan, D. L., Kruger, G., Kulhanek, F., Liberman, R. P., Malm, U., & Midha, K. K. (1990). Defining treatment refractoriness in schizophrenia. *Schizophrenia Bulletin, 16,* 551–561.

Cancro, R. (1982). Schizophrenic and paranoid disorders. In D. Oken & M. Lakovics (Eds.), *A clinical manual of psychiatry* (pp. 53–66). New York: Elsevier.

Claghorn, J., Honigfeld, G., Abuzzahab, F. S., Wang, R., Steinbook, R., Tuason, V., & Klerman, G. (1987). The risks and benefits of clozapine versus chlorpromazine. *Journal of Clinical Psychopharmacology, 7,* 377–384.

Corrigan, P. W., Wallace, C. J., Schade, M. L., & Green, M. F. (1994). Learning medication self-management skills in schizophrenia: Relationships with cognitive deficits and psychiatric symptoms. *Behavior Therapy, 25*, 5–15.

Dobzhansky, T. (1978). *Mankind evolving: The evolution of the human species.* New Haven: Yale University Press. (Original work published 1962)

Elmer-Dewitt, P. (1992, July 6). Depression: The growing role of drug therapies. *Time*, pp. 57–60.

Feinstein, S. C., Kettering, R., & Harrow, M. (1990). Adjustment reactions: The psychotic syndrome. In J. D. Noshpitz & R. D. Coddington (Eds.), *Stressors and the adjustment disorders* (pp. 559–568). New York: Wiley.

Fruton, J. S. (1992). *A skeptical biochemist.* Cambridge: Harvard University Press.

Gambrill, E. D. (1981). *Behavior modification: Handbook of assessment, intervention, and evaluation.* San Francisco: Jossey-Bass.

Gerlach, J., & Casey, D. E. (1988). Tardive dyskinesia. *Acta Psychiatrica Scandinavica, 77,* 369–378.

Gilbert, P. L., Harris, M. J., McAdams, L. A., & Jeste, D. V. (1995). Neuroleptic withdrawal in schizophrenic patients. *Archives of General Psychiatry, 52,* 173–188.

Gould, S. J. (1991). Exaptation: A crucial tool for an evolutionary psychology. *Journal of Social Issues, 47*(3), 43–65.

Grawe, K., Bernauer, F., & Donati, R. (1990). Psychotherapien im Vergleich: Haben wirklich alle einen Preis verdient? [Comparison of psychotherapies: Are all really praiseworthy?]. *Psychotherapie, Medizinische Psychologie, 40,* 102–114.

Horner, R. H., Dunlap, G., & Koegel, R. L. (Eds.). (1988). *Generalization and maintenance: Life-style changes in applied settings.* Baltimore: Brookes.

Horst, W. D. (1990). New horizons in the psychopharmacology of anxiety and affective disorders. *Psychiatric Annals, 20,* 436–439.

Johnson, K. R., & Layng, T. V. J. (1992). Breaking the structuralist barrier: Literacy and numeracy with fluency. *American Psychologist, 47,* 1475–1490.

Klerman, G. L. (1984). Ideology and science in the individual psychotherapy of schizophrenia. *Schizophrenia Bulletin, 10,* 608–612.

Landa, L. N. (1974). *Algorithmization in learning and instruction* (V. Bennett, Trans.). Englewood Cliffs, NJ: Educational Technology Publications. (Original work published 1966)

Laudan, L. (1981). *Science and hypothesis: Historical essays on scientific methodology.* Boston: Reidel.

Liberman, R. P., Kopelowicz, A., & Young, A. S. (1994). Biobehavioral treatment and rehabilitation of schizophrenia. *Behavior Therapy, 25,* 89–107.

Lovejoy, A. O. (1962). The meanings of "emergence" and its modes. In P. P. Wiener (Ed.), *Readings in philosophy of science: Introduction to the foundations and cultural aspects of the sciences* (pp. 585–596). New York: Scribner. (Original work published 1927)

Malott, R. W. (1986). Self-management, rule-governed behavior, and everyday life. In H. W. Reese & L. J. Parrott (Eds.), *Behavior science: Philosophical, methodological, and empirical advances.* Hillsdale, NJ: Erlbaum.

Meichenbaum, D. (1976). Toward a cognitive theory of self-control. In G. E. Schwartz & D. Shapiro (Eds.), *Consciousness and self-regulation: Advances in research* (Vol. 1, pp. 223–260). New York: Plenum Press.

Morris, W. (1978). *The American Heritage Dictionary of the English Language.* Boston: Houghton Mifflin.

Paykel, E. S. (1989). Treatment of depression: The relevance of research for clinical practice. *British Journal of Psychiatry, 155,* 754–763.

Reese, H. W. (1984, May). Historical and philosophical analysis of causality. In H. W. Reese (Chair), *Philosophical foundations and current views of causality in radical behavior-*

ism. Symposium conducted at the meeting of the Association for Behavior Analysis, Columbus, OH.

Skelton, J. A., Pepe, M. M., & Pineo, T. S. (1995). How much better is clozapine? A meta-analytic review and critical appraisal. *Experimental & Clinical Psychopharmacology, 3,* 270–279.

Stokes, T. F., & Baer, D. M. (1977). An implicit technology of generalization. *Journal of Applied Behavior Analysis, 10,* 349–367.

Torrey, E. F. (1974). *The death of psychiatry.* New York: Penguin Books.

Wallis, C., & Willwerth, J. (1992, July 6). Awakenings: Schizophrenia, a new drug brings patients back to life. *Time,* pp. 52–57.

Whitman, T. L. (1990). Self-regulation and mental retardation. *American Journal on Mental Retardation, 94,* 347–362.

Wirshing, W. C., Eckman, T., Liberman, R. P., & Marder, S. R. (1991). Management of risk of relapse through skills training of chronic schizophrenics. In C. A. Tammings & S. C. Schulz (Eds.), *Advances in neuropsychiatry and psychopharmacology: Vol. 1. Schizophrenia research* (pp. 255–267). New York: Raven Press.

Wong, S. E., Martinez-Díaz, J. A., Massel, H. K., Edelstein, B. A., Wiegand, W., Bowen, L., & Liberman, R. P. (1993). Conversational skills training with schizophrenic inpatients: A study of generalization across settings and conversants. *Behavior Therapy, 24,* 285–304.

About the Book and Editors

Analysis of the way the environment influences behavior is essential to our understanding of human development. This volume collects original, never-published work that describes how people conceptualize, think, and behave. *Environment and Behavior* presents empirical studies that test theoretical assumptions and illustrate how to integrate environmental awareness into professional practice and design.

The ability to categorize—to think in larger and more inclusive classifications and, at the same time, in smaller and more exclusive subdivisions—is a hallmark of conceptual development. It is the kind of development that makes humans distinctly rational, symbolic, and logical. This book presents a new way of viewing the conceptual development of normal and developmentally disabled children and the conceptual reorganization of adults. Individual conceptual ability is demonstrated across an impressive range of issues: private events, language development and function, child abuse, sexual abuse, drug abuse, autism, aging, professional practice, and environmental and cultural design. Additional commentary for each section is provided by the editors.

Those working or studying in the areas of psychology, education, human development, social work, and disability will find this book to be a current and thorough introduction to the subject. Professionals and researchers also will find much of interest in this collection.

Donald M. Baer is Roy A. Roberts Distinguished Professor of Human Development and Family Life at the University of Kansas. **Elsie M. Pinkston** is professor of social service administration and director of the Center for Social Work Practice Research, School of Social Service Administration, at the University of Chicago.

Index